Welcoming New Americans?

Welcoming New Americans?

Local Governments and
Immigrant Incorporation

ABIGAIL FISHER WILLIAMSON

THE UNIVERSITY OF CHICAGO PRESS   CHICAGO AND LONDON

The University of Chicago Press, Chicago 60637
The University of Chicago Press, Ltd., London
© 2018 by The University of Chicago
Published 2018
Printed in the United States of America

27 26 25 24 23 22 21 20 19 18   1 2 3 4 5

ISBN-13: 978-0-226-57251-2 (cloth)
ISBN-13: 978-0-226-57265-9 (paper)
ISBN-13: 978-0-226-57279-6 (e-book)
DOI: https://doi.org/10.7208/chicago/[9780226572796].001.0001

Library of Congress Cataloging-in-Publication Data:

Names: Williamson, Abigail Fisher, author.
Title: Welcoming new Americans? : local governments and immigrant incorporation /
    Abigail Fisher Williamson.
Description: Chicago ; London : The University of Chicago Press, 2018. | Includes
    bibliographical references and index.
Identifiers: LCCN 2018000464 | ISBN 9780226572512 (cloth : alk. paper) |
    ISBN 9780226572659 (pbk. : alk. paper) | ISBN 9780226572796 (e-book)
Subjects: LCSH: Immigrants—Government policy—United States. | United States—
    Emigration and immigration—Government policy. | Urban policy—United States. |
    Municipal government—United States.
Classification: LCC JV6483 .W54 2018 | DDC 325.73—dc23
LC record available at https://lccn.loc.gov/2018000464

♾ This paper meets the requirements of ANSI/NISO Z39.48-1992 (Permanence of Paper).

FOR ADAM GRANVILLE FISHER

Contents

Acknowledgments

This book argues that despite challenging fiscal environments and the turbulent political rhetoric surrounding immigration, local government officials in cities across the United States tend to welcome rather than oppose the presence of immigrants. I was a beneficiary of this welcome when I arrived as a stranger to conduct research in several small US cities. Hundreds of people took time out of their busy lives to speak with me. Since I promised not to reveal the identities of those I interviewed, I cannot thank them by name. Nonetheless, I am grateful to those who accepted unsolicited phone calls and e-mails and invited me to luncheons, meetings, or coffee klatches or welcomed me into their homes. I am particularly grateful to those who made lists of others to interview, contacted colleagues on my behalf, or allowed me to use their names in reaching out to acquaintances. Several organizations and individuals helped me reach informants, including David Brewster, Marvin Druker, Luis Fraga, Meredith Jones, Margaret Levi, Sylvia Puente, Betty Robinson, Adele Simmons, Steven S. Smith, Jean Teahan, and the Grand Victoria Foundation. In addition, I appreciate the more than five hundred officials who took the time to complete my survey. The unstinting willingness of all of these individuals made my job inestimably easier and truly enjoyable.

I am also grateful for funding from several sources. This book was made possible in part by financial assistance from the Ruth Landes Memorial Fund, a program of the Reed Foundation. At earlier stages of the project I received assistance from Harvard's Ash Center for Democratic Governance and Innovation, Center for American Political Studies, Hauser Center for Nonprofit Organizations, and Taubman Center for State and Local Government. The Maine Community Foundation and the Libra Foundation's Fitzgerald Gubernatorial Fund for Maine supported research in Lewiston. The ZEIT-Stiftung Bucerius Scholarship in Migration Studies offered both financial support and the valuable opportunity for feedback from young and established migration scholars.

I owe special thanks to Robert D. Putnam, Archon Fung, Jennifer Hochschild, and Mary Waters, who nurtured this project in its earliest stages. All of them provide tremendous models of using rigorous scholarship to further the public good. Their generous mentorship and insights strengthened this work. I owe a particularly large debt to Bob, who introduced me to the fertile theoretical ground of new immigrant destinations, let me make the project my own, and worked with my committee to identify resources that allowed me to complete the project with year-old twins.

In addition to support from these excellent mentors, I have been fortunate to present elements of this project at several conferences and receive feedback from a generous community of scholars, including Tony Affigne, Richard Alba, Ryan Allen, Gustavo Cano, Porsha Cropper, Els de Graauw, Katherine Fennelly, Michael Jones-Correa, Rey Koslowski, Jonathan Laurence, Peggy Levitt, Rahsaan Maxwell, John Mollenkopf, Karthick Ramakrishnan, Audrey Singer, Rogers Smith, Justin Steil, Jessica Trounstine, Steve Vertovec, Stephen Wasby, Michael Werz, and Cara Wong. Harvard's Migration and Immigrant Incorporation Seminar deserves special recognition as a congenial environment where I presented this research several times. I likewise owe special thanks to Debbie Schildkraut, who generously read and commented on the entire manuscript as part of a book workshop. My graduate school friends and collaborators provided insight and camaraderie, including Hamutal Bernstein, Anna Boucher, Ina Ganguli, Justin Grimmer, Daniel Hopkins, Helen Marrow, and Van Tran.

At Trinity College, I am lucky to have found a supportive administration, generous colleagues, and engaging students. I am grateful to the Faculty Research Committee for financial support, as well as to Dean Melanie Stein and Kristin Magendantz for helping me to attract funding that allowed additional time for writing. My colleagues provide both intellectual stimulation and thoughtful advice about academic life, including Ned Cabot, Benjamin Carbonetti, Sonia Cardenas, Andrew Flibbert, Isaac Kamola, Thomas Regan-Lefebvre, Reo Matsuzaki, Lida Maxwell, and Rachel Moskowitz. Special thanks to Rachael Barlow, Stefanie Chambers, Diana Evans, Adrienne Fulco, and Serena Laws, who assisted with my survey or commented on various chapters, and particularly to Kevin McMahon, Anthony Messina, and Nichole Szembrot, who read the entire manuscript as part of a book workshop sponsored by Trinity's Institute for Interdisciplinary Studies. Javier Arroyo, Phil Duffy, Curt Leonard, David Tatem, Rob Walsh, and Mary Beth White provided valuable technological or administrative support.

Trinity has also generously funded several undergraduate research assistants, who have made essential contributions to this project, including Tasmiah Ahmad, Nour Chamseddine, Magdalena Filippone, Kaitlyn Sprague, Raekwon Wheeler, and especially Bettina Cecelia Gonzalez and Brooke Williams. My doctoral student at Harvard, Shanna Weitz, likewise provided vital assistance. For translation assistance, I am grateful to Bridges Language, Training, and Staffing in Elgin and to Alba Enterprises in Yakima, as well as to María Chávez. Deb Altman provided rapid, precise transcriptions.

At the University of Chicago Press, I am indebted to my editor, Chuck Myers, for his insightful questions and comments. Alice Bennett provided meticulous copyediting. Two thoughtful anonymous reviewers likewise improved the manuscript with their suggestions. A portion of chapter 8 appeared as "Mechanisms of Declining Intra-ethnic Trust in New Immigrant Destinations" in the *Journal of Ethnic and Migration Studies* 41 (11): 1725–45.

Several friends have provided crucial support or respite in the course of this project, including Lauren and Tony Barnes, Jill Marshall, Kathy and Pete Mumma, Kerri and Tony Raissian, and Janée and Matt Woods Weber. I am also incredibly grateful for wonderful neighbors, including Sonal Jain and Dilip Nair, Yukiyo Iida and Pete Sanborn, Ragini Potluri and Chandra Kankanala, Golda Ginsburg, and Paul Herrnson. By some stroke of luck, my neighbor Paul happens to be an accomplished scholar in my field, and he has become a valued mentor and collaborator.

My family, who have to deal with me when I am under deadline, deserve my greatest thanks. My late grandparents, Joan Brewer and Barney Williamson, became authors late in life and have inspired me in this and many other ways. I am thankful for my grandmother, Taeko Williamson, who continues to brighten my days with e-mails of encouragement. My mother-in-law, Patricia Fisher, deserves special thanks for enabling several weekend writing retreats while she and my husband cared for our children. My late father-in-law, Charles Fisher, read an early version of the manuscript and buoyed my confidence with his enthusiasm.

My siblings, Sarah and Tom Williamson, and their partners, Bree Allen and Claribell Gomez, make me laugh and forget work every so often. I will never be able to adequately thank my parents, Peggy and Chris Williamson, for all they have done to support me. They are honestly parenting geniuses.

My amazing daughters, who give me an added incentive to write efficiently, have long been waiting for the book that would have their names in it. Here it is, Anya and Lyla, with all of my love. Finally, I dedicate this book to my husband, Adam, who came into my life just at this project's inception and has supported me every step of the way.

CHAPTER ONE

Introduction

In 2005 the Chicago suburb of Elgin, Illinois, advertised its embrace of a growing immigrant population with billboards tagging it "Diver-City." A few years later a politically conservative mayor in Yakima, Washington—a pastor at a local evangelical church—responded to a growing Latino population by appointing the city's first Hispanic council member to a vacancy. Meanwhile the city council in Lewiston, Maine, began funding a Somali Independence Day festival alongside its traditional Franco-American heritage celebration. And Wausau, Wisconsin, hired a full-time diversity affairs director charged with supporting Hmong refugees. Why would local officials undertake these at times costly and potentially unpopular efforts to serve immigrants? Moreover, do these efforts actually help immigrants to integrate? Do they encourage established residents to accept the newcomers?

Cities today, more so than any other level of American government, are at the forefront of efforts to welcome immigrants. As a result, places labeled sanctuary cities are key villains for President Donald Trump and other advocates of more restrictive immigration policies. Trump's first immigration executive order sought to revoke federal funding to sanctuary jurisdictions, a catchall term for places that limit participation in federal immigration enforcement. Rather than acquiescing to these demands, some sanctuary cities successfully challenged the order in court (Valencia 2017; Yee 2017). While sanctuary cities have become a focus of debate, cities are also speaking out in favor of immigration in other ways. Following the terrorist attacks in San Bernardino and in Paris, when thirty-one state governors said they would oppose further Syrian refugee resettlement, more than half of the nation's fifty largest cities issued statements in support of refugee resettlement, and only four issued statements in opposition (Capps 2015). Many leaders in these cities raised their voices again when President Trump issued restrictions on travel from six predominantly Muslim countries (Temple 2017). Beyond speaking out, cities are taking action. At least twenty-seven cities nationwide now have designated mayor's offices to support immigrant affairs (Pastor, Ortiz, and de Graauw 2015).

Support for immigrants from large, usually politically liberal cities is not necessarily all that surprising. But as the examples from Elgin, Yakima, Lewiston, and Wausau attest, efforts to assist immigrants are not limited to large cities. When twenty-six large cities defended Syrian refugee resettlement, so did at least fifty-four smaller cities and towns, including Swisher, Iowa (population 900) (Capps 2015). Although they rarely become sanctuary cities or establish formal offices to support immigrants, small to midsize cities and towns across the United States implement a range of informal practices that tend to support rather than oppose immigrants. This book describes accommodating practices toward immigrants in small to midsize towns and cities nationwide, identifies when and where these responses are likely to arise, and illustrates that municipal efforts to welcome immigrants have both benefits and pitfalls for immigrant incorporation. Understanding local responses to immigrants is crucial as the foreign-born disperse to ever more towns and cities, as municipalities find themselves playing a central role in responding to the newcomers, and as these responses at times fail to advance immigrants' prospects or improve the public's attitudes toward their presence.

All together, immigrants and their children constitute a quarter of the US population (Current Population Survey 2013). Historically, immigrants clustered in traditional gateways like New York and Los Angeles. Indeed, a quarter of America's foreign-born population continues to reside in the state of California alone. Since the 1990s, however, immigrant populations have grown more quickly in suburbs and rural areas than in cities, as well as most quickly in the nontraditional regions of the Southeast and Midwest. This dispersion has led to a proliferation of new immigrant destinations nationwide (Singer 2004; Marrow 2005; Waters and Jiménez 2005). By 2014, more than eight thousand locales across the country had populations that were at least 5 percent foreign-born. Of the 805 places exceeding 50,000 residents, more than two-thirds were at least 10 percent foreign-born, and more than a third were at least 20 percent foreign-born (American Community Survey 2010–14).

Responses to immigrants in these towns and cities deserve our attention because they have the potential to substantially shape immigrant incorporation, a concept that encompasses both how newcomers adapt and whether established residents accept them. The mix of institutions central to incorporation has changed since the height of immigration in the early twentieth century (DeSipio 2001; Gerstle and Mollenkopf 2001; Anderson and Cohen 2005; Jones-Correa 2005; Wong 2006). Traditional civic organizations, including unions, are in decline (Putnam 2000; Skocpol 2003). Parties target consistent voters rather than mobilizing new voters (Rosenstone and Hansen 1993; Schier 2000). With other institutions waning in influence, municipal aid to immigrants offers a potentially crucial mechanism for incorporation. As immigration scholars John Mollenkopf and Manuel Pastor (2016, 4) put it, the relative warmth of a town's welcome to immigrants "can help determine whether a first location is a stepping stone or a sinkhole."

As towns and cities nationwide become home to significant immigrant populations, they find themselves grappling with how to respond to ethnically, culturally, and linguistically distinct groups. Because responding to immigrants can be challenging, costly, and unpopular, it is easy to imagine why local governments would seek to restrict growing immigrant populations. Local governments in new destinations have limited experience in responding to immigrants (Gozdziak and Martin 2005; Waters and Jiménez 2005; Zúñiga and Hernández-León 2005; Massey 2008; Marrow 2011). The federal government provides little direct guidance on how to incorporate immigrants, but it requires municipalities to provide the foreign-born with certain services—sometimes regardless of immigrant legal status. Over the past twenty years, the federal government has devolved additional decisions about immigration enforcement to localities (Varsanyi 2010a; Varsanyi et al. 2012; Gulasekaram and Ramakrishnan 2015). Although immigration may provide long-term economic benefits for localities (Lewis and Peri 2015), responding to immigrants can present short-term fiscal costs (Smith and Edmontson 1997; US Congressional Budget Office 2007).

In part as a result, elected leaders see that cracking down on immigration is popular among some segments of the electorate. Critics of immigration have popularized the notion that something about today's immigrants will prevent their incorporation (Huntington 2004). Immigrants today differ from historical waves of newcomers in that nearly half are Hispanic and a quarter are Asian (American Community Survey

2010–14). Owing in part to contemporary immigration policies that limit immigration from the Western Hemisphere and strengthen enforcement along the southern US border (Massey, Durand and Malone 2002), today's immigrants include 11.3 million unauthorized residents, approximately 28 percent of the foreign-born (Krogstad and Passel 2015).

An increasingly polarized Congress has not passed comprehensive reforms to address the status of unauthorized immigrants for more than thirty years. In response, some states have pursued restrictive policies against immigrants, most notably Arizona's controversial 2010 law (SB 1070). In the 2016 presidential election, Donald Trump made unauthorized immigration the centerpiece of his campaign, winning the presidency in part because of his enthusiasm for building a border wall, deporting unauthorized immigrants, and excluding Muslim refugees (Klinkner 2017; Sides 2017).

In this context of potential local costs, voters' demands for restriction, and a federal stalemate preventing comprehensive reform, it is not surprising that some cities have opposed immigrant settlement. At the restrictive extreme, in 2006 Hazleton, Pennsylvania, passed an "Illegal Immigration Relief Act" to "abate the nuisance of illegal immigration." According to the city council, the presence of unauthorized immigrants contributed to rising crime, failing schools, substandard health care, and diminished quality of life (Hazleton Ordinance 2006–18 [City Council of Hazleton, Pennsylvania 2006]). Yet we also see highly accommodating responses, not only in major gateways like New York and Los Angeles, but also beyond them. At the accommodating extreme, in 2007 New Haven, Connecticut, voted to develop an "Elm City Resident Card," a locally recognized form of identification to aid unauthorized immigrants. Mayor John DiStefano justified the need for the municipal ID card, describing unauthorized residents as "having children who are U.S. citizens, . . . mak[ing] up a critical component of our work force, and . . . shar[ing] the basic values of America" (DiStefano 2007). Highly restrictive and highly accommodating policies, like those in Hazleton and in New Haven, are newsworthy and have captured the bulk of both media and scholarly attention to municipal responses.

Focusing on the extremes of local response, however, obscures the more prevalent practices emerging in communities nationwide and leads us to emphasize variation in response rather than recognizing the broader trend toward municipal accommodation. Beyond the largest cities, very few local governments have implemented formal policies aimed at serving or excluding immigrants. Instead, local governments nationwide are adopting informal practices, many of which accommodate or even celebrate immigrants, with important implications for the future of immigrant incorporation.

This book contributes to our understanding of local government responses and immigrant incorporation in three central ways. First, by coupling investigation of four new immigrant destinations with a national survey of local government officials, I move beyond a focus on cities at the extremes of local response to examine incorporation processes more comprehensively. Second, while some scholars have examined local responses, few have considered how these responses shape immigrant political incorporation and even fewer have investigated how municipal responses shape public receptivity to immigrants. Third, the book introduces a theory to explain why local governments respond as they do—largely choosing to accommodate immigrants rather than exclude them—which also explains why these responses do not consistently achieve their incorporation aims.

Specifically, municipal responses to immigrants depend on how local officials perceive immigrants, whether as clients or outsiders, contributors or dependents, a protected class or "illegal aliens." A powerful combination of federal policies that frame immigrants as clients coupled with local understandings of immigrants as economic contributors has directed municipal responses toward accommodation. Of course, local officials do face countervailing pressures for restrictive action, particularly amid devolution of federal immigration enforcement and the increasingly polarized national debate over immigration. Even where restrictive responses arise, scrutiny from federal regulators, national advocacy organizations, and the media often brings federal civil rights regulations to bear in a way that frames immigrants as worthy of protection from discrimination, thereby reining in restriction and perpetuating the general trajectory toward accommodation.

To those who support immigration, municipal officials' distinct legal and economic incentives to accommodate immigrants may seem like good news. But the distinctiveness of these incentives can also be bad news for supporters of immigrants. Local officials often accommodate in ways that facilitate cooperative relations between immigrant elites and local elites but do not necessarily assist immigrants more broadly. Moreover, since the public does not always share local officials' incentives, some forms of municipal accommodation can spur backlash against immigrants and the officials who support them. Resentment toward immigrants and supportive officials provides an opening for anti-immigration political entrepreneurs like President Trump to attract supporters. Therefore, cities that support immigrants must attend carefully to both immigrants' advancement and their societal acceptance, in order to achieve incorporation. Before elaborating on this theory and the study's research design, I will describe federal requirements for how local governments respond to immigrants, the resultant mix of municipal responses, and existing findings about how these responses shape immigrant incorporation.

Federal Regulation of Local Government Responses to Immigration

Wherever immigrants settle in the United States, they end up within several nested jurisdictions at the federal, state, and local levels. From a historical perspective, municipal responses to immigrants are nothing new. During the nineteenth century, gateway port cities used inspection and quarantine laws to control the flow of immigrants (Rodriguez 2008; Gulasekaram and Ramakrishnan 2015). By the late nineteenth century, the federal government began to assert control over immigration policy. Today few dispute the federal government's authority over the nation's borders. Once immigrants have entered the United States, however, the question arises, Who bears responsibility for managing their incorporation?

Although direct federal guidance on local government's role in relation to immigrants is limited, a few laws and Supreme Court rulings place clear obligations on municipalities to provide certain services to immigrants with respect to education, health care, and language access. Public schools are required to serve immigrant students, including providing programs for English-language learners (ELLs), regardless of their immigration status (*Lau v. Nichols* 1974; *Plyler v. Doe* 1982). Federal regulations also require that local health providers accepting federal funds provide emergency care to those who cannot pay, including immigrants of any legal status (Emergency Medical Treatment and Active Labor Act, 1986).

In areas with significant language-minority populations, recipients of federal funds typically must translate documents and provide interpreters. Title VI of the 1964 Civil Rights Act prohibits federal fund recipients from discriminating based on race, ancestry, national origin, or ethnicity, a stipulation that has been interpreted to require language access, since language is so closely tied to nationality (*Lau v. Nichols* 1974). A Clinton-era executive order requires that federal agencies devise plans to ensure that non-English speakers can "meaningfully access" services for which they are eligible (Executive Order 13166, 2000). The Voting Rights Act further requires that localities with large language-minority populations provide bilingual voting materials (Schmidt 2000). Local governments that do not comply with these rules may face legal or administrative action.[1] In combination, federal educational, health care, and civil rights regulations constrain local governments to serve immigrants in key ways.

On the other hand, over the past twenty years, federal policies have increasingly involved local police in immigration enforcement. Two reforms passed in 1996 gave state and local law enforcement the right to enforce immigration law in some circumstances. The Anti-terrorism and Effective Death Penalty Act extended the authority to arrest previously deported immigrant felons to subnational officers. The Illegal Immigration and Immigrant Responsibility Act (IIAIRA) introduced the notion of deputizing state and local police to enforce immigration law through the 287(g) provision, which President Trump has revived with his first immigration executive order.

Although 287(g) is a voluntary program, local police face more direct requirements to participate in enforcement through Secure Communities, a George W. Bush–era program, expanded but then rescinded by Obama, and now reinstated by Trump. Under Secure Communities, when local law enforcement books suspects and runs their fingerprints through FBI databases, the FBI shares information with Immigration and Customs Enforcement (ICE). When ICE identifies unauthorized immigrants, it can issue a detainer, asking that the local agency hold suspects for two days beyond when they ordinarily would be released so that ICE can take enforcement action.

With annual rates of deportation ballooning under Bush and Obama and threatening to increase further under Trump, local police find that by complying with ICE detainers they are perceived as immigration enforcement agents, undermining the trust some departments aim to build with all residents of their communities (Varsanyi et al. 2017).[2] Localities cannot opt out of Secure Communities, but some resist complying with detainers. By 2014, thirty-three cities, 263 counties, and two states (California and Connecticut) had declared their intention not to honor ICE detainers (Catholic Legal Immigration Network [CLINIC] 2014).

Beyond mandated duties related to education, health, language access, and law enforcement, the federal government provides little guidance and limited resources for immigrant incorporation. Although it has marginally increased its efforts at promoting naturalization, for the most part US policy takes a laissez-faire approach to incorporation, expecting immigrants and the communities they live in to pick up the slack (Schmidt 2007; Bloemraad and de Graauw 2012). One notable exception is policies on assisting refugees, those immigrants forced to flee their home countries and approved for resettlement by the US State Department. As I will discuss more fully in chapter 4, refugee resettlement programs, managed out of the US Department of Health and Human Services, provide cash assistance to new arrivals, coupled with funding for nonprofit organizations that aid refugees in finding work and otherwise adjusting to life in the United States (Bloemraad 2006). Limited federal funds devoted to immigrants largely target either refugees or migrant worker families, groups that make up only a small fraction of overall immigrant flows (Gelatt and Fix 2007).

In sum, the federal government requires municipalities to serve immigrants in substantial ways and increasingly involves them in immigration enforcement, but it also allows localities considerable latitude in how they implement the day-to-day functions of responding to immigrant residents. Mixed signals and limited guidance allow localities to craft their own responses, though I will argue that on balance federal policies encourage local governments to accommodate immigrants rather than restrict them.

Debates over Municipal Responses

To date, scholarly and journalistic attention to municipal responses to immigrants has concentrated largely on places with formal ordinances (Hopkins 2010; Ramakrishnan and Wong 2010; Walker and Leitner 2011), which are split roughly evenly between accommodation and restriction (Steil and Vasi 2014). Yet of the eight thousand US locales that are now at least 5 percent foreign-born (American Community Survey 2010–14), the best estimates suggest that only a couple hundred (or

2 percent) have passed any immigration-related ordinances (Gulaseka-ram and Ramakrishnan 2015). In reality, many immigrant destinations lack formal policies addressing the foreign-born (Lewis et al. 2013).

Thus, understanding local government responses and how they shape incorporation requires looking beyond the small number of places that have passed formal ordinances to identify the range and tenor of less formal practices in response to immigrants in destinations across the United States. Since responses can vary across actors within a mu-nicipality (Lewis and Ramakrishnan 2007; Jones-Correa 2008; Mar-row 2009), understanding responses requires examining variation both across towns and across different types of officials within towns.

Traditional theories of political incorporation maintain that local of-ficials will respond substantively to immigrants or ethnic minorities only once these groups consolidate electoral power (Dahl 1961; Browning, Marshall and Tabb 1984). Yet as immigrants have dispersed across the United States, local bureaucrats have played a key role in providing ser-vices and acting as advocates (Lewis and Ramakrishnan 2007; Jones-Correa 2008; Marrow 2011). The professional norms of these bureaucrats lead them to serve immigrants even before there is political pressure to do so, cultivating an unanticipated phenomenon of "immigrant bureau-cratic incorporation" (Jones-Correa 2008). Even some elected officials are spearheading efforts to support immigrants, particularly in large cit-ies (Brettell 2008; Odem 2008; Price and Singer 2008; de Graauw 2014; Pastor, Ortiz, and de Graauw 2015).

The idea that these bureaucrats and elected officials would be in-volved in serving immigrants before they have significant electoral in-fluence upends predominant theories of urban politics (Frasure-Yokley 2015). Public choice theories argue that such efforts to serve immigrants would be unlikely because they attract needy newcomers and repel the businesses and wealthy families needed to maintain local prosperity (Tiebout 1956; Peterson 1981). On the other hand, some argue that local governments and community-based organizations (CBOs) develop part-nerships to serve immigrants because all these groups benefit from the collaboration. CBOs gain access to public resources, while public agen-cies "outsource" the costs of gearing up to serve linguistically and cul-turally distinct newcomers. Elected officials gain legitimacy with new populations (and potential future voters) through collaboration with trusted CBOs (Frasure and Jones-Correa 2010).

This theory is valuable, but it does not entirely explain why elected

officials would be more likely to accommodate than restrict when restriction is popular among current voters. Likewise, it does not explain
why local officials undertake efforts to serve immigrants outside part-
nerships with CBOs. More work is necessary to understand the full
range of municipal efforts to accommodate immigrants, as well as to investigate why such efforts are widespread. Even more important, given
the prevalence of these responses, how will municipal accommodation
affect immigrant incorporation?

Debates over Immigrant Incorporation

The 2015 National Academy of Sciences report on immigrant integration defines it as a "two-way process" through which immigrants change
in response to their new homes and society changes in response to immigrants' presence (Waters and Gerstein Pineau 2015).[3] The report syn-
thesizes the best research available to demonstrate that, along virtually
every dimension, as contemporary immigrants live in the United States
longer they become more like Americans. In subsequent generations
their children and grandchildren become still more like Americans. The
picture is not entirely rosy—immigrants' progress toward incorporation
continues to be shaped by racial inequities and in some cases by discrimination. Over time, however, immigrants increase their educational attainment and income while also learning English, all at rates similar to
previous waves of immigrants (Waters and Gerstein Pineau 2015).

This book devotes particular attention to political incorporation, by
which I mean the process through which immigrants come to take part
in politics and have their interests represented, while Americans come
to accept the newcomers' participation and representation. Though some
see political incorporation as a series of benchmarks, including naturalization, registration, voting, and holding elective office, scholars increasingly recognize it as a process rather than a specific end point (Wolbrecht
and Hero 2005; Hochschild et al. 2010). The National Academy of Sciences report offers some reasons for concern about progress toward political incorporation (Water and Gerstein Pineau 2015). Immigrants in the
United States naturalize at lower rates than similarly situated immigrants
in other countries (Bloemraad 2006), and immigrants remain underrepresented in electoral office, even at the local level (de Graauw 2013).

Individual differences among immigrants fail to entirely explain patterns of political incorporation (Ramakrishnan 2005), suggesting a need to look beyond immigrants' characteristics to understand the institutional context that shapes their opportunities (Jones-Correa 2005; Wolbrecht and Hero 2005; Chambers 2017). Many aspects of this local "context of reception" (Portes and Rumbaut 2006) will likely shape incorporation, but I emphasize local government policies because, as immigrants' most accessible experience of the state, they may powerfully shape political incorporation. At this point, however, we remain uncertain how governments' efforts to accommodate immigrants actually shape incorporation. At the national level, Canada's incorporation policies, more active than the United States', bolster immigrant participation (Bloemraad 2006, 4). In Europe, however, cross-national comparisons have found that varying integration policies have limited influence on immigrant incorporation outcomes (Ersanilli and Koopmans 2011; Morales and Pilati 2014).

In the United States, studies of whether restrictive policies will undermine incorporation have produced equally mixed results. Restrictive local contexts may enhance immigrants' fear and reduce their participation as they curtail activities to avoid being the target of enforcement (Jones-Correa and Fennelly 2009; Furuseth and Smith 2010; Menjívar and Abrego 2012). Yet policy threats to immigrants can also promote mobilization, such as increased information-seeking and voting among Latinos following Proposition 187 in California (Pantoja and Segura 2001, 2003a) and mass protests that followed restrictive national immigration proposals in 2005–6 (Benjamin-Alvarado, DeSipio, and Montoya 2009; Branton et al. 2015; Silber Mohamed 2017). At the local government level, political contexts favorable to immigration may dampen participation (Okamoto and Ebert 2010), but civic efforts to welcome immigrants can also foster immigrant engagement (Ebert and Okamoto 2013).

The scholarship on how local government responses shape immigrant political behavior is limited and variable. Scholarship on how municipal responses shape public receptivity to immigrants is almost nonexistent. Drawing on evidence from Hazleton, one study argues that restrictive ordinances amplify public animosity toward immigrants at least in the short term (Flores 2014). To date, scholars have not focused on how accommodating local government responses influence society's acceptance of immigrants.

Explaining Municipal Accommodation of Immigrants

To address gaps in our understanding of municipal responses and immigrant political incorporation, I develop a theory that explains why local government officials tend to support accommodation, as well as why these efforts do not always advance incorporation. Local government officials face distinct legal and economic incentives that encourage them to define immigrants positively and in turn to accommodate them. Because established residents do not necessarily share these definitions of immigrants, accommodation tends to serve local elites, may not mobilize immigrants, and can alienate established residents.

The ways local government officials define, or frame, immigrants are crucial to generating accommodating municipal responses (de Graauw, Gleeson, and Bloemraad 2013; Steil and Vasi 2014; Provine et al. 2016). This finding is consistent with a broad body of literature arguing that people's views on public issues stem in part from elite frames, typically conveyed by leaders or the media (Chong and Druckman 2007). A frame is a "central organizing idea or story line" (Gamson and Modigliani 1987, 143) that "provide[s] a kind of mental recipe for preparing an opinion" (Nelson and Kinder 1996, 1058). On any given political issue there are a variety of "culturally available frames" (Chong and Druckman 2007, 107). For a frame to affect a person's opinions, it should be accessible, in that it exists in memory and can be retrieved (Chong and Druckman 2007), but it also should be resonant in that it corresponds with an individual's experience and values (Peffley and Hurwitz 2007).

An extensive review of research on Americans' attitudes toward immigrants argues that individuals develop their support or opposition to immigration based on symbolic frames rather than in response to self-interest (Hainmueller and Hopkins 2014). That is, people do not tend to oppose immigrants because they see themselves as directly harmed by them. Rather, opposition stems from broader beliefs about immigrants' effects on the nation as a whole. Those who feel that immigrants present "symbolic threats" to American identity or norms, for instance by failing to learn English or assimilate, are particularly likely to resent the foreign-born (Hainmueller and Hopkins 2014).

Since frames are influential in shaping opinion, advocates on competing sides of the immigration debate use language designed to shift opinions in their direction. Immigrants who enter the country without permission to stay are either "undocumented" or "illegal." Regularizing the status of these unauthorized immigrants can be called a "pathway to citizenship" or "amnesty."[4] As these contrasting terms suggest, Americans encounter a variety of symbolic frames surrounding immigration, and their views in response are quite ambivalent. Although a plurality of Americans consistently supports reducing immigration, Americans are more likely to see immigration as generally positive than as negative. Despite widespread concern about immigrant legal status, a majority of Americans supports earned legalization for unauthorized immigrants currently in the United States (Schildkraut 2011).

That said, Donald Trump won the presidency in part through his anti-immigration appeals, which included calling Mexican immigrants "rapists" (Klinkner 2017; Sides 2017).[5] As the current moment and periodic episodes throughout American history demonstrate, hostility toward immigrants in the United States is far from unusual (Higham 1983). Indeed, some argue that the contemporary media perpetuate a dominant "Latino threat narrative" about America's largest immigrant ethnic group (Chavez 2013). This narrative associates Latinos (and increasingly Muslims) with crime, economic dependency, homeland security threats, and the deterioration of American cultural unity. Recent evidence suggests that media discussions of immigration tend toward this negative coverage, even in outlets some see as left-leaning, such as the *New York Times*. When coverage is more negative, Americans express greater hostility toward immigrants (Abrajano and Hajnal 2015). Thus, while Americans' views on immigrants are ambivalent, many of the dominant frames surrounding immigration are negative.

Local officials are likewise exposed to these negative frames in the media and national political rhetoric. Yet their legal and economic incentives foreground frames of immigrants as clients and contributors. With respect to legal incentives, federal policies require local officials to serve immigrants in certain ways. These policies frame immigrants as deserving local clients and encourage additional support for this population. Even when restrictive responses arise, federal civil rights policies frame immigrants as a group worthy of protection and impose costs for violating antidiscriminatory laws and norms. As for economic incentives, local officials have limited options for raising revenue (Tiebout 1956; Peterson 1981) and thus often find themselves allied with business interests

(Stone 1989). Alliances with businesses that value immigrant labor make frames emphasizing immigrant economic contributions more accessible and resonant.

Positive frames of immigrants resonate with local officials not only because of their position, but also because of their relatively elevated socioeconomic standing. Education is consistently associated with more support for immigrants, less because of economic self-interest than because it captures enhanced tolerance and political correctness (Hainmueller and Hopkins 2014).[6] All together, owing to their elevated socioeconomic standing and distinctive incentives, local officials frame immigrants as clients and contributors and accommodate them more than the general public would choose.

Along these lines, Freeman (1995) contends that national immigration policy has an "expansionary bias" since concentrated benefits accrue to elites who are better able to organize in support, while costs are diffused across the broader, unorganized public. During the late twentieth century, the United States experienced an elite ideological convergence in favor of immigration. Business elites favor immigration to support economic interests, while liberal elites shifted from a focus on workers' rights to concerns about civil rights, amid the growth of immigrant ethnic minority populations (Tichenor 2002). Since resulting policies are more expansionary than the general public would support, elites have an incentive to take discussion of immigration off the public agenda (Messina 1983).

These claims may be surprising amid the current polarized politics of immigration, in which the Republican Party has staked out a position firmly in favor of restriction at the national and, to some extent, state levels. Of course, as Freeman (1995) readily admitted, immigration policy is cyclical, and episodes of restriction arise. Still others argue that Freeman's theory either never fit the reality of immigration politics in the United States or no longer does so amid rising anti-immigration populism and increasing political polarization (Jones-Correa and de Graauw 2013; Tichenor 2013; Klinkner and Smith 2016). Undoubtedly, in the current political environment, local officials face countervailing pressures to exclude immigrants. Police are increasingly involved in federal immigration enforcement. Partisan divides over immigration extend to the local level and can pressure Republican local officials to support restrictive policies.

Yet unlike on the federal (and to some degree state) level, partisanship is not entirely determinative of responses. Local elected officials are more insulated from national partisan politics than state elected officials by the variety of Progressive Era reforms that shield municipalities from mass influence, such as nonpartisan ballots, off-cycle elections, and council-manager forms in which the local executive is appointed rather than elected (see Trounstine 2010 for a review). In many smaller cities, an appointed manager sets the agenda and an appointed police chief manages law enforcement. In these places, elected officials are more likely to be influenced by bureaucratic requirements to serve and protect immigrants, setting local government officials apart from their state and federal counterparts.[7]

Relatively insulated from national political debates over immigration, local officials can pursue distinct legal and economic incentives to accommodate. Yet because officials are following their own elite incentives, they tend to accommodate immigrants in ways that contribute to cooperative relations between immigrant and nonimmigrant elites but do not necessarily mobilize immigrants more broadly. Moreover, because the public at large does not necessarily share officials' incentives surrounding immigrants, municipal accommodation can generate resentment toward immigrants and the officials who serve them. Along these lines, Katherine Cramer (2016) has recently described how a sense of "distributive injustice"—the idea that undeserving groups are getting more than their fair share—cultivates a "politics of resentment" that undermines support for government and redistributive policies in general.

In this way, though the trajectory is toward accommodation, local officials who welcome immigrants are at times vulnerable to electoral challenges. The disjuncture in views between local elites and the public creates opportunities for aspiring politicians to exploit the issue of immigration for electoral gain. Scholars ascribe the recent shift of previously Democratic voters to Republican candidates in part to concerns over immigration (Abrajano and Hajnal 2015). Analysts likewise agree that concerns over immigration contributed to Donald Trump's victory (Klinkner 2017; Sides 2017). These findings do not suggest that local officials should turn away from efforts to accommodate immigrants. Rather, officials who want to advance incorporation must reshape accommodation efforts in ways that make frames of immigrants as deserving clients and contributors more accessible and resonant for established residents.

Investigating Municipal Responses

To investigate the range of local government responses to immigrants and their effects on incorporation, I draw on qualitative work that identifies how policies unfold locally, revealing the development of less visible responses to immigrants over time. Having generated hypotheses that explain local response and its outcomes across four case study cities, I then test these hypotheses on a broader sample, employing an original survey of local government officials across 373 small to midsize immigrant destinations nationwide. This research design intentionally moves from inductive, theory-building fieldwork to deductive, theory-testing survey analysis. Such a design is valuable when we know relatively little about the phenomena in question, to ensure that we are asking the right questions and operationalizing concepts in meaningful ways (Morse 2003; Tarrow 2004; Small 2011). Here fieldwork reveals the broader repertoire of municipal responses to immigrants and how they develop over time, looking beyond prominent examples at the extremes. Because findings across different methods and data sources converge, we can have greater confidence in the conclusions (Putnam 1993; Tarrow 2004).

New Immigrant Destination Case Studies

New immigrant destinations are uniquely suited to investigating local responses and incorporation processes, since these communities have developed systems for interacting with immigrants from the ground up (Gozdziak and Martin 2005; Waters and Jiménez 2005; Zúñiga and Hernández-León 2005; Massey 2008; Marrow 2011; Messina and Williamson 2017). The smaller size of many new immigrant destinations compared with traditional gateway cities means that the early moments of interaction between established residents and immigrants are more visible and accessible (Waters and Jiménez 2005). Municipalities of this size receive limited attention from political scientists yet can serve as "microcosms of American society" (Lay 2012, 143).

The four cities examined here—Yakima, Washington; Elgin, Illinois; Wausau, Wisconsin; and Lewiston, Maine—began experiencing contemporary immigration at different times from the late 1970s to 2001, but they share the characteristics of new immigrant destinations in their rapid demographic change and lack of recent experience with serving immigrants. The variation in when immigrants began to arrive allows me to observe local governments' responses over time.

The destinations were selected not because of the nature of their responses to immigrants, but because of their demographic change. I initially selected Lewiston and Yakima because of their rapid ethnic demographic change and the availability of supplementary data on these cities (Social Capital Community Benchmark Survey 2000, 2006). Using census data on demographic change from 1970 to 2000, I then matched these cities with Wausau and Elgin, respectively, based on their similar population sizes and patterns of ethnic change.

The four cities are similar in terms of their small to medium size, ranging from 36,500 to just over 112,000 residents in 2015 (American Community Survey 2011–15). In 1980 each city was home to mostly non-Hispanic whites, which made up between 87 and 99 percent of the local population. Since then each city has experienced relatively rapid ethnic diversification through the in-migration of refugees or Latino immigrants. By 2010, the relevant incoming ethnic group in each city ranged from 9 to 44 percent of the local population (U.S. Census 2010). Figure 1.1 compares the demographic change across the four cities from 1970 to 2015. As it shows, Elgin and Yakima are home to expanding Latino populations, while Lewiston and Wausau are home to Somali and Hmong refugees, respectively.[8,9]

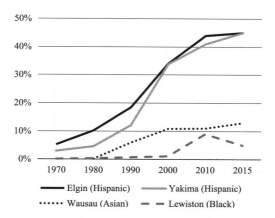

FIGURE 1.1. Ethnic demographic trends in case study cities, 1970–2015. *Sources:* Geolytics (1970–2000 US Census data), US Census 2010, American Community Survey 2011–15.

In Yakima, a city of 93,000 in central Washington State, the Latino population has grown from less than 5 percent in 1980 to constitute 45 percent of residents in 2015 (American Community Survey 2011–15). The city lies in the Yakima Valley, home to the Yakama Nation reservation as well as some of America's most fruitful orchards and hop fields. In 1805, the Lewis and Clark expedition praised the fertile region, thereby attracting the valley's first white settlers. Though Yakima Valley farms have long employed Latino migrants, in 1980 the city of Yakima itself had only a small population of resident Latinos (4.6 percent) (US Census 1980). Former migrant farmworkers began to settle in Yakima after the Immigration Reform and Control Act of 1986 allowed undocumented workers to regularize their status and remain in the United States.

Elgin, a city of 112,000 forty-five minutes due west of Chicago, has also experienced rapid Latino population growth. Economically, Elgin has always been considered a working-class town. In 1867 the Elgin Watch Factory opened and went on to provide the city's major source of employment for much of the next century (Alft 2000). When the factory closed in the late 1960s, it dealt a severe blow to the city's economy. Over the next twenty years, as shopping malls developed beyond the city's core, Elgin lost locally owned businesses and its formerly vibrant downtown. Mexican immigrants were drawn to Elgin beginning in the late 1970s by low-cost housing and proximity to jobs (Alft 2000). By 2015 Latinos made up 45 percent of Elgin's population (American Community Survey 2011–15). In 1994, the city became home to the Grand Victoria Riverboat Casino, which provides substantial funding for municipal infrastructure. Even so, Elgin remains an island of affordable housing in a sea of wealthier Chicago suburbs and is often referred to as the "city in the suburbs."

While Yakima and Elgin are home to growing Latino populations, Lewiston and Wausau are primarily refugee destinations. In Wausau, a city of 39,000 in north-central Wisconsin, churches began to sponsor Hmong refugees in the late 1970s. These refugees had fled Laos after helping US forces during the Vietnam War. By 1990, upward of 70,000 Hmong refugees had been resettled in the United States, particularly in California, Minnesota, and Wisconsin (Hein 1994; Yau 2005).[10] In Wausau the Hmong population grew through additional refugee resettlement as recently as 2005, as well as through "secondary migration," the movement of refugees from their original resettlement sites to other locations they choose. By 2015, Asians made up 13 percent of Wausau's population

(American Community Survey 2011–15). Economically, Wausau appears prosperous but has had its struggles. In the early 1980s, the city lost local ownership of Wausau Insurance, once the employer of 2,000 to 3,000 mostly white-collar workers. Still, the town remains home to generous local philanthropists, including families that made fortunes first in logging or paper and later in workers' compensation insurance.

In Lewiston, a city of 36,500 forty-five minutes north of Portland, Maine, Somalis began arriving in 2001. Like the other cities, Lewiston was largely white before the arrival of recent immigrants, but it also had a prominent immigrant history. Lewiston and its twin city of Auburn grew in two waves as immigrants came to work in shoe and textile mills. Lewiston became home to Irish immigrants in the mid-nineteenth century, and French Canadians began arriving around 1890 (Hodgkin 2001). Franco-American culture remains prominent in Lewiston, with more than a quarter of the population still claiming French Canadian ancestry (American Community Survey 2011–15). In the 1970s, however, Lewiston's mills began to close, leaving thousands unemployed. From 1980 to 2000, the city's population declined by 12 percent. By 2000, 40 percent of downtown residents lived in poverty (US Census 2000).

Although the city showed signs of economic revival in the early years of the twenty-first century, it was by no means a center of economic growth when Somalis began to arrive in early 2001. Somalia's Siad Barre regime dissolved into chaos in 1991, sending over a million Somalis fleeing to neighboring East African nations (Gundel 2003). By 2001, more than 40,000 Somali refugees had been resettled in the United States (Office of Refugee Resettlement 2001). Some Somali elders in places like Atlanta, Georgia, were unhappy with their initial settlement sites and began seeking a new home. At the same time, Catholic Charities, the refugee resettlement contractor in Portland, sought relief from a serious housing crunch and began to direct Somalis toward available housing in Lewiston. Lewiston's early Somali settlers reported their satisfaction with the city to kin elsewhere, and since then more than 5,000 Somalis have made Lewiston their home (Mendoza 2016). By 2006, Somali residents included both Somalis and Somali Bantus, an ethnically and linguistically distinct group enslaved by Somalis beginning in the early 1800s (Kusow 2006). More recently, asylum seekers from a variety of national backgrounds have made the city their home (Seelye 2015).

Since 2003 I have conducted 290 interviews with community leaders and residents from among the immigrant and nonimmigrant populations in the four cities, with no fewer than forty-eight interviews held in a given city. Two-thirds of informants (195 of 290) were community leaders, which I define broadly as individuals who are executives of local organizations or government units, business owners, and others who play key local leadership roles as members of boards or government committees. Of these, 41 were local government bureaucrats from city administration, law enforcement, or the schools, and 29 more were elected officials. In Yakima and Elgin my informants are almost evenly divided between Latinos and non-Latinos. In Wausau, 29 percent of my informants were first- or second-generation immigrants. In Lewiston, where immigration is more recent and fewer immigrants can participate in English-language interviews, my sample consists of 7 Somalis, 2 non-Somali immigrants, and 49 nonimmigrants. In addition to interviews, I observed community events, verified facts using local newspapers and government documents, and conducted ongoing "digital observation" by reading local websites and joining organizations' e-mail lists and social networking groups. (Appendix A details my qualitative methods, including the full interview guide.)

Drawing on interviews and observation, I closely analyzed local responses to immigrants in each city over the twenty-five years from 1990 to 2015. The juxtaposition of the four cities enables me to analyze how various factors influence local government responses and immigrant incorporation outcomes. As previously homogeneous, nontraditional destinations, we might expect these cities would be unlikely to accommodate immigrants. Moreover, to different degrees each of them has experienced economic challenges. Only in Yakima are immigrants central to a dominant local industry's needs. Immigrants to the cities vary in ethnicity and legal status, potentially shaping how local governments and residents respond. The cities also differ in political ideology, with Yakima and Elgin leaning Republican, Lewiston traditionally leaning Democratic, and Wausau in the middle. None of the four cities is in a strongly Republican-leaning state, but Wisconsin is a swing state in national elections—including a surprise upset by Donald Trump in 2016—and Maine and Wisconsin have Republican governors and Republican senators as part of their congressional delegation. The prevalence of accommodation across these cases therefore cannot be easily explained by demography or partisan context. That said, it bears testing whether these patterns are visible beyond the four cities in question.

The Municipal Responses to Immigrants Survey

Thus, from July 2014 to March 2015, I conducted a national survey of local responses to immigrants across a random sample of 503 small to midsize immigrant destinations. I refer to this survey as the Municipal Responses to Immigrants Survey (MRIS). A few previous studies have surveyed local officials about responses to immigrants, but the MRIS is the first national survey of local government responses to immigrants that addresses both appointed and elected local officials.[11]

To identify differences in responses across bureaucrats and politicians, in each town I survey four officials: the mayor, a randomly selected city councilor, the city manager, and the police chief (Ramakrishnan and Lewis 2005).[12] The first half of the survey asks officials about formal and informal responses to immigration. The second half begins by gauging officials' perceptions of local immigrants' "civic presence" (Ramakrishnan and Bloemraad 2008) as well as levels of local interethnic interaction. It then asks officials their views on the role of local government vis-à-vis immigrants in our federal system and concludes with questions on respondents' demographic and ideological characteristics. The survey instruments are the same for the city manager, city councilor, and mayor (which I will refer to as the "city hall respondents"), with slight variations for the police chief (questionnaire in appendix B).[13]

The survey sampling frame is the 4,069 US places that are greater than 5,000 and less than 200,000 in population with a foreign-born population of at least 5 percent (American Community Survey 2008–12).[14] As the bottom row in table 1.1 indicates, 35 percent of the American public lives in these 4,069 immigrant destinations. With the growth of

TABLE 1.1. **Survey sampling frame**

	Number of places	Population (in millions)	Percent total population	Foreign-born (in millions)	Percent total foreign-born
Total places	29,040	309	100	40	100
> 5% foreign-born	8,816	175	57	33	84
Sampling frame	4,069	109	35	19	49

Source: American Community Survey (2008–12).

the foreign-born population in suburban and rural destinations (Marrow 2005; Singer 2008), nearly half (49 percent) of the foreign-born population lives in these places (American Community Survey 2008–12). Although excluding large cities from consideration limits my ability to apply these findings to the nation as a whole, previous analyses have highlighted accommodating policies in many large cities (Pastor, Ortiz, and de Graauw 2015), suggesting that the general pattern introduced here may apply to large cities as well. Nonetheless, findings in this book apply to towns across a wide range of populations, from 5,000 up to 200,000. These cities include more than a third of state capitals as well as the largest cities in eleven states.[15]

From the frame of 4,069 places, I sampled 503 cities and towns, using stratified random sampling based on region and population size to give priority to centers of population. The survey was distributed multimodally, initially by Internet and then by mail (Dillman, Smyth and Christian 2008). I received responses from 598 leaders across 373 towns in forty-six states. I received at least one response from 74 percent of towns surveyed and two or more responses from 33 percent (167 towns). In total, 30 percent of officials surveyed responded, a rate that compares favorably with other recent surveys of organizational executives (Cycyota and Harrison 2006; Baruch and Holtom 2008; Williams 2015; Butler and Dynes 2016). (See appendix C for further details on survey methodology.)

Responding and nonresponding towns are essentially similar, suggesting that responding towns represent the sample as a whole and provide a good picture of small to midsize immigrant destinations across the nation (see table AC3 in appendix C). Importantly, responding cities do not differ from nonresponding cities in partisanship, ruling out the possibility that the sample is ideologically slanted to produce evidence of greater accommodation. Chapter 5 describes the ideological characteristics of individual respondents, demonstrating a similar balance among officials in ideology and partisanship.

In the aggregate, places that responded to the survey effectively represent the characteristics of immigrant destinations of this size while also capturing the vast diversity among immigrant destinations in the United States. Respondent destinations include towns in North Dakota with a foreign-born population of just over 5 percent as well as Florida cities that are as much as 60 percent foreign-born and 76 percent Hispanic. On the other hand, not all immigrant destinations have Hispanic populations. The sample includes Texas towns in which all immigrants are Latino and Michigan cities that are 17 percent foreign-born but less than 2 percent Hispanic. Likewise, the survey represents the diversity of US immigrant destinations in experience with foreign-born residents. More than a third of responding destinations (36 percent) can be considered new destinations in that they were less than 5 percent foreign-born in 1990, exceeded 5 percent by 2012, and experienced more than 100 percent growth in their foreign-born population over this period.[16] In addition to including the full range of the United States' ethnic and racial diversity, responding towns represent strikingly differing socioeconomic and partisan profiles. The vast diversity of small and midsize immigrant destinations allows me to explain how demographic and partisan factors affect local responses as well as how these factors interact with responses to influence outcomes for immigrants and communities as a whole.

Finally, in addition to the case studies and survey, in chapter 6 I draw on an original database that categorizes the current status of responses to immigrants in ninety-four previously restrictive destinations. In combination, these three rich data sources reveal that local government officials face distinct legal and economic incentives to serve immigrants that the broader public does not necessarily share.

Outline of the Book

The first part of the book describes local government responses to immigrants; the second explains when and where certain responses arise; and the third examines the consequences of municipal accommodation for immigrant political incorporation. Building on the book's research design, which develops hypotheses through grounded examination of four case studies then tests them through a national survey, each component begins by introducing findings from the case studies. These findings raise testable hypotheses about municipal responses and how they shape immigrant political incorporation, which I then evaluate using data from the MRIS.

Chapter 2 outlines how responses evolved in Lewiston, Wausau, Elgin, and Yakima from 1990 to 2015. The case studies identify a trend toward accommodation over time as well as revealing the substantive importance of local government inaction in response to immigrants. Drawing on the cases, I introduce a model of local government response, which classifies municipalities in terms of how actively they respond and whether the tenor of response tends toward accommodation or restriction. Chapter 3 then turns to the MRIS, reporting on the prevalence of various accommodating and restrictive practices across towns nationwide. As the case studies predicted, while many towns remain inactive in response to immigrant populations, more than four in five are engaged in efforts to accommodate immigrants, and fewer than one in five has taken any restrictive action.

Since most towns accommodate immigrants, what explains variations in the degree and tenor of response? Chapter 4 investigates the factors that explain inaction, accommodation, and restriction. Local capacity and immigrant visibility influence *whether* local governments take action to respond to immigrants. State and federal policies and national political rhetoric shape officials' framing of immigrants, thereby influencing *how* municipalities respond. Towns where positive framings of immigrants are accessible and resonant—such as places exposed to accommodating state and federal policies—are more likely to accommodate, while towns where negative framings of immigrants are more prevalent—such as places with a greater proportion of Republican voters—are less likely to accommodate and more likely to restrict. Some have argued that ethnic demographic change precipitates restrictive responses (Hopkins 2010; Walker and Leitner 2011), but this chapter demonstrates that factors associated with ethnic threat do not drive municipal responses.

In chapter 5, I turn to explaining what motivates local government officials' responses to immigrants. Local officials' socioeconomic characteristics, coupled with legal and economic incentives associated with their position, foreground understandings of immigrants as clients and contributors. Contrary to findings in earlier studies (Lewis and Ramakrishnan 2007; Jones-Correa 2008; Marrow 2011), both bureaucrats and elected officials have incentives to actively incorporate immigrants. Some officials, however, are less interested in serving immigrants and more interested in enforcement because their official role or political ideology foregrounds negative framings of immigrants. While these findings indicate that some local government officials are susceptible to negative framings, the overall picture suggests that they are relatively supportive of immigrants. Indeed, comparing local officials' views with polling responses from the general public, the officials are distinctly more likely to support immigrants.

Of course, restrictive responses to immigrants do arise, including in three of my four case study cities, as chapter 6 examines. In Lewiston, Wausau, and Elgin, restrictive responses to immigrants generated external scrutiny from federal regulators, national advocacy groups, and the media, which framed immigrants as a protected class under civil rights law. Local officials responded by scaling back restriction and even implementing compensatory accommodation. This pattern is also evident across the ninety-four cities and towns that considered or passed restrictive ordinances in 2006–7. These cities experienced a marked decline in restriction over time, with ordinances remaining in effect in only one-third of towns and scaled back in some way in more than three-quarters. Where external scrutiny was greater, ordinances were less likely to remain in effect, even holding constant other salient factors.

Having established that municipalities tend toward accommodation owing to officials' distinct incentives and understandings of immigrants, in chapters 7 and 8 I turn to the way local accommodation affects immigrant incorporation. Chapter 7 examines how accommodation influences immigrants' inclusion in local politics. In particular, I analyze prevalent local government efforts to hire and appoint immigrant intermediaries, who connect officials and immigrants who are otherwise separated by linguistic and cultural barriers. The MRIS reveals that even beyond new immigrant destinations, local government officials often rely on such individual intermediaries rather than turning to immigrant organizations identified in past literature (Frasure-Yokley 2015; de Graauw 2016). Across the cases and in the survey, local officials act on their own incentives to accommodate immigrants and therefore do so in ways that disproportionately benefit established and immigrant elites rather than immigrants more broadly.

Chapter 8 further illustrates that local officials' distinct motivations to accommodate immigrants do not extend to the public at large. As a result, efforts to accommodate immigrants can result in resentment toward the foreign-born as well as the officials who serve them. Across the four new destinations, long-term residents often perceive efforts to serve immigrants as preferential treatment for undeserving outsiders. Disagreements among established residents over how to respond to immigrants exacerbate divisions between residents and leaders amid socioeconomic inequality. Local officials can promote public acceptance of immigrants by fostering opportunities for meaningful interethnic contact, which make positive perceptions of immigrants more resonant with the public.

Having demonstrated a clear trend toward accommodation, explained how it arose, and detailed its consequences, the conclusion discusses the broader implications of these findings for intergovernmental dynamics and immigrant incorporation. It also takes up the crucial question of whether the trend toward municipal accommodation will continue given President Trump's anti-immigrant rhetoric and changes in federal immigration policy. In sum, by demonstrating the prevalence of municipal accommodation and the uneven distribution of its benefits primarily to local elites, the book encourages scholars and practitioners to examine not only concerns about restrictive responses to immigrants, but also how to accommodate immigrants in ways that will achieve the twofold goals of incorporation: helping immigrants to advance and enabling established residents to accept their presence.

PART I

Local Government Responses to Immigrants

CHAPTER TWO

Municipal Responses across Four New Immigrant Destinations

"D iverCity" read the sign on the back of the city bus in Elgin, Illinois. Elsewhere in the distant Chicago suburb in 2005, one could find billboards enthusiastically announcing "Melting Pot Ahead," in recognition of the city's growing population of Latino immigrants. Before the feature film in local theaters, an advertising reel showed a montage of people of different ethnicities leaning forward as though to embrace. When the Enhancing Elgin committee, a joint effort of the city, the Chamber of Commerce, and other local organizations sought to market the city, they chose to highlight its growing ethnic diversity. Elgin, historically a Republican stronghold that was 87 percent non-Hispanic white until 1980, chose to advertise its welcoming stance toward immigrants through this campaign and a series of other efforts aimed at including Latinos in local public life.

Despite the heated national rhetoric surrounding immigration, Elgin was far from an exception among the four cities examined closely in this book. Lewiston, Maine, and Wausau, Wisconsin—midsize refugee destinations—also devoted considerable resources to serving new immigrant populations, while Yakima, Washington, a Mexican immigrant destination, took some accommodating action but on the whole was relatively inactive. In-depth examination of these cities from 1990 to 2015 allows me to construct a model of municipal response to immigrants. In this chapter I introduce the model of municipal response and explain how the four cities align with the model, demonstrating an overall tendency toward accommodation. In keeping with the book's structure of building from inductive qualitative examination to deductive quantitative testing, chapter 3 then employs a national survey of municipal officials to test the hypothesis that small to midsize US towns are more accommodating than restrictive, finding that this is indeed the case.

The Model of Municipal Response

A comprehensive understanding of how local governments respond to immigrants requires a rubric for measuring local government response. Municipal responses may vary across actors within a town and over time, but it is nonetheless useful to develop a composite measure that allows for comparison across cities. Only with a consistent measure of municipal reception can we analyze which factors predict certain responses, as well as how local government reception is associated with outcomes. Thus this section draws on the four case study cities to present a general model of local government response.

Examining the evolution of municipal response across Lewiston, Wausau, Elgin, and Yakima from 1990 to 2015 identifies three key patterns, reflected in the model presented in figure 2.1. First, the model needs to account for the role of federal requirements in local responses to immigrants. Second, it needs to differentiate responses that go beyond federal requirements with respect to their tenor, whether accommodating or restrictive toward immigrants. Third, the model needs to demonstrate that some towns are largely inactive in response to immigrants, in ways that can make them either more accommodating or more restrictive.

Turning first to the role of federal mandates in shaping local responses, the model of local response takes compliance with federal regulations as a common baseline, since all local governments operate within federal constraints. As figure 2.1 illustrates, the model places municipalities that respond to immigrants by fulfilling federal requirements at the center, which I refer to as the municipal compliance point. At the municipal compliance point, local governments have fulfilled all federal requirements (introduced in chapter 1) but displayed no further

FIGURE 2.1. Categorizing municipal response to immigrants.

independent response to immigrants.[1] Categorizing cities with reference to federal compliance ensures a delineation of the scope of localities' legal constraints, elucidating which practices are merely compliant versus independent efforts to respond to immigrants.

Examining the four case studies shows that these cities were not merely compliant with federal requirements. Rather, in all four cities officials responded to immigrants in ways that went beyond federal requirements, representing independent attempts at accommodation or restriction. Towns are therefore arrayed around the municipal compliance point with respect to their tenor, whether accommodating or restrictive, and their degree, whether active or inactive (Deufel 2006). A response that goes beyond federal requirements and aims to enhance local immigrants' opportunities or presence is classified as accommodating and falls to the right of the municipal compliance point.[2] A response that goes beyond federal mandates and aims to constrict local immigrants' opportunities or presence is classified as restrictive and falls to the left of the municipal compliance point. By enhancing or restricting opportunities, I refer to practices that make it easier or more difficult for immigrants to live in the locality, such as promoting or withholding language access for non-English speakers. By enhancing or restricting presence, I refer to practices that aim to increase or reduce immigrants' local visibility, legitimacy, or actual numbers, such as efforts to include or exclude them from local government committees (Ramakrishnan and Bloemraad 2008).

Further, the four cases show that towns are at times inactive in responding to immigrants in ways that make them substantively more accommodating or restrictive. Therefore, in addition to classifying responses to immigrants by their tenor, the model pictured in figure 2.1 arrays towns by their degree of response, whether inactive or active. Municipalities that comply with federal mandates but otherwise remain largely inactive fall close to the central compliance point, with increasingly active responses falling toward either the left- or the right-hand extreme.

Depending on the tenor of federal requirements for response to immigrants, inaction is in effect compliant, accommodating, or restrictive. Where federal policy prescribes no requirements for local response, inaction is equal to compliance. Since the United States requires no local government role in civic education for adult immigrants, inaction in this case is no different from compliance. On the other hand, where national mandates require municipalities to accommodate immigrants, inaction is tantamount to restriction. When localities fail to comply with federal language access mandates, as we will see in Yakima, inaction makes the locality more restrictive. Conversely, where federal mandates require or allow municipalities to restrict immigrants, inaction is a form of accommodation. Federal policies allow local law enforcement to check residents' immigration status upon a reasonable suspicion, but some localities have adopted an informal "don't ask, don't tell" practice with regard to immigration status. Here refraining from action creates a more accommodating environment for immigrants. Inaction can be an intentional form of resistance to federal requirements or a sign of lack of capacity, but it nonetheless deserves attention as a common mode of local response that contributes to making one municipality more accommodating or restrictive than another.

Bringing together the three key patterns identified in the cases, the model takes federal requirements as its baseline, identifies responses that go beyond them as either accommodating or restrictive, and takes into account the substantive importance of inaction. Towns then are arrayed on the model based on a combination of the tenor of their responses and their degree of activity. A greater number of accommodating practices moves the town toward the right-hand extreme, while a greater number of restrictive practices moves it toward the left-hand extreme. In this way the model classifies towns based on the number of practices they implement in response to immigrants rather than recognizing some practices as more influential than others in shaping the overall context of reception. Whereas policy activity can be readily quantified (e.g., a number of discrete ordinances, proclamations, appointments, etc.), policy effect cannot be so easily determined. Indeed, given the extant scholarship on local government responses, how far practices actually accommodate or restrict immigrant adaptation is not always visible at this stage.

Building on the example of the four case studies, the model implicitly assumes that towns tend toward either accommodation or restriction rather than actively pursuing both strategies—an assumption that the survey data presented in chapter 3 will bear out. Chapter 3 will further populate the model with examples of accommodating and restrictive responses measured in the survey, but first I turn to the evolution of response across the four case study cities, which explains where these cities fall on the model of response.

Municipal Responses across the Four Case Studies

In addition to revealing the key categories of compliance, inaction, accommodation, and restriction, the four case study cities demonstrate the trajectory of municipal response over time, as well as how responses differ in the two destinations that experienced substantial refugee resettlement. Lewiston, Wausau, and Elgin experienced prominent episodes of restriction, but these episodes ultimately resulted in intensified efforts to serve the immigrant group. Despite periodic restriction, for the most part the cities demonstrate a move toward greater accommodation over time.

Refugee destinations display a distinct trajectory of response from initial efforts to serve refugees to broader convening and mobilizing roles, and eventually efforts to include members of the immigrant ethnic group in decision making. As I will discuss further in chapter 4, local governments have additional responsibilities for serving refugees, since, unlike other immigrants, refugees are eligible for federal welfare benefits on arrival. Bearing in mind these differences in federal requirements, I first introduce the evolution of local response in the refugee destinations of Lewiston and Wausau, followed by the evolution of response in the primarily Latino immigrant destinations of Elgin and Yakima.

Lewiston: From Compliance to Accommodation

Turning first to Lewiston, the city's response to Somali immigrants demonstrates a clear transition from compliance—providing mandated services—to greater accommodation of newcomers. Yet Lewiston's response to the Somalis is best known for a letter written in October 2002 by then-mayor Laurier Raymond, which asked Somalis to slow their migration to the "maxed-out" city. Despite this restrictive episode, both before and after the infamous letter, Lewiston city employees were actively trying to accommodate Somali newcomers. Efforts to comply with civil rights legislation and to include Somalis in public roles only intensified following the controversy surrounding Mayor Raymond's letter.

Compliance with State Mandates

On arriving in Lewiston as secondary migrants from other US refugee resettlement sites, the first stop for many Somalis was the city's Department of Social Services (DSS). Maine municipalities must provide state-mandated General Assistance to anyone who expresses an intention to live locally and falls below an income threshold. While refugees are eligible for various federal programs, they often leave the support of their refugee resettlement agency behind when they migrate independently to a new city. Thus, on arriving, many Somalis turned to city hall. At first, however, Lewiston had no capacity to communicate with the newcomers. In part as a result, local government employees say that the early days of the Somali migration were characterized by "panic," "freaking out," "crisis mode," and "chaos." A city employee described the scale of the initial challenge:

> We effectively were starting from a base of zero. . . . There really wasn't a lot of experience in dealing with a population that had significant numbers of non-English-speaking people. Aside from not understanding the culture, aside from not understanding their religion, aside from not understanding why they dress the way they dress.

Lewiston administrators registered to use a phone-based translation service and gathered social service providers to learn about their responsibilities under federal law for serving non-English speakers. Relatively quickly, DSS administrators realized that, even with translation in place, existing staff could not respond to the full scale of Somali newcomers' needs. In May 2001 DSS hired a Somali caseworker, who also served as an interpreter.

As the Somali population continued to grow, Lewiston's resources became increasingly inadequate to meet the newcomers' needs. Lewiston public schools faced particular challenges. A high school teacher explained, "We were just getting [Somali] students all the time. . . . At first students were just showing up to class, and it was so disruptive because the kid would show up in class and I wouldn't know his level or anything." At the time, Maine was allotting annual English Language Learners (ELL) funding based on schools' needs two years earlier. Before the Somalis arrival, during the 2000–2001 school year, Lewiston's ELL program served just forty students. By the 2001–2002 school year, the program had expanded sixfold to serve 243 students. This rapid growth necessitated hiring three additional staff members and buying ELL materials, amounting to more than $168,000 of unanticipated expenses (Levesque 2002). The state eventually passed emergency funding for Lewiston, but not until midway through the fall of 2002, more than eighteen months after Somali students began requiring ELL services.

Over at Lewiston's Adult Education Center (AEC), administrators were facing similar pressures. When the Somalis first arrived the AEC had one ELL teacher on staff. With the arrival of the Somalis, the AEC was suddenly holding classes in the halls and the stairwell to accommodate the newcomers' needs. According to an AEC employee, "People were incredibly frustrated, screaming at one another. The American students stopped coming. The whole area was Somali. People were afraid to walk in. Somalis were afraid to walk in." In a 2002 report to Maine's governor, Lewiston city officials described the situation as "alarming" (Nadeau 2002a). Overwhelmed by the scale of need, AEC staff eventually "broke into" locker rooms in their building and turned them into additional classrooms. When I visited in late 2003, ELL classes were taking place in these makeshift classrooms, with posters decorating the bathroom stall doors.

As Lewiston implemented systems to address its immigrant population, these acute challenges became more manageable. Portland faced similar challenges with its burgeoning population of secondary migrants. The cities came together to apply for joint federal funding from the Office of Refugee Resettlement under an "unanticipated arrivals" grant. The 2002 grant created the Portland-Lewiston Refugee Collaborative, with the specific mission of serving secondary migrants through the respective cities' social service departments.

From Compliance to Accommodation

By early 2002, nearly a year into the Somali migration, Lewiston's response moved beyond providing required services to broader roles. The city expanded its efforts to serve as a convener, a mobilizer of resources, and a public educator about the growing presence of immigrants. It served in a key role on a local task force convened to coordinate response to the Somalis and generated a report to the governor aimed at mobilizing state resources. In addition, it took on educating the public, publishing a brochure on the Somali migration and holding an open meeting on the topic.

A local hospital administrator initially convened the task force on the Somali migration, which a city employee credits with "start[ing] the process of discussing how we were going to respond to this as a community." As the group evolved, the city began to take the lead. In May 2002 Lewiston submitted the report to the governor documenting the city's challenges and calling for state assistance. The city described its accommodating response as follows: "Countless individuals and organizations are working tirelessly to welcome the City's new population . . . and to embrace the benefits and challenges associated with being a culturally diverse community" (Nadeau 2002a). After this initial foray into convening local parties and mobilizing resources, Lewiston adopted an approach that involved cooperating with multiple partners. The city published monthly reports on responding to the Somali population, distributed to key city and state officials as well as to eighty-four individuals at other local, state, and federal agencies, civic and immigrant organizations, and state and national media outlets. Lewiston's embrace of this collaborative approach—convening internal and external stakeholders—succeeded in mobilizing resources to serve the Somalis, thereby lessening the costs to local government.

In early 2002 Lewiston also began to address local unease about the Somalis' presence, serving as a public educator. With fights erupting between Somalis and other students at the high school, local law enforcement, educators, and city officials gathered to discuss the need for "rumor control" (Nadeau 2002b). The police department advocated a proactive educational role, saying, "The opportunities for misinformation and miscommunication will continue if we do not find a mechanism to quickly and accurately answer, or otherwise address, these issues as they arise" (Minkowsky 2002). By spring 2002, Lewiston had developed a brochure for the public titled "Understanding Our Somali Community." The city also hosted a public meeting in May 2002 to respond to residents' concerns about the Somali population. A Lewiston senior citizen described the event:

> They had the Somalian [sic] community up on the stage with the Lewiston government. And then they opened the microphones on both aisles, and they had people get up and ask [questions]. . . . I bet we were there for four hours. It was unbelievable. And the people that were really angry about having [the

Somalis] here, they spoke, and then the people that were welcoming. . . . And they really aired their differences that night. And I think it really made a big difference, so that you got to understand both points of view and try to work through it.

Although the meeting did provide information, most city officials came away feeling that it exacerbated tensions among residents. Nonetheless the meeting typifies Lewiston's increasing efforts to accommodate immigrants.

Restrictive Rhetoric: The Mayor's Letter

Lewiston's collaborative approach to addressing the growth of the Somali population served the city well when a letter from its mayor prompted a major controversy. After several months of tension, in October 2002 Mayor Raymond sent a letter to a Somali community organization and the local newspaper asking Somali elders to "exercise some discipline" by slowing their arrival in the city. Lewiston, he wrote, was "maxed-out financially, physically and emotionally" (Raymond 2002). City employees, who had been working with the Somali community for months, including trying to discourage further migration, felt shocked and betrayed. One recounted, "We'll all admit that we cried the night the letter came out. Because you spent nine months trying to build the opposite reaction in the community and then in one letter the [mayor] legitimizes everything the community felt." In the aftermath of the letter, reporters from around the world descended to chronicle the story. A white supremacist group announced its plan to hold a rally in Lewiston supporting the mayor. City administrators responded by helping to convene the groups that united to hold a massive opposing rally, expressing Lewiston's welcome to the Somali population.

Intensified Accommodation: Incorporating
Immigrants in Decision Making

After Mayor Raymond's letter, Lewiston administrators and some elected officials intensified efforts to incorporate Somalis in local decision making. Mayor Larry Gilbert, elected in 2007, was particularly active in this respect. At his inauguration, he invited a rabbi to offer the opening prayer, a Catholic priest to give the invocation, and a Somali man "representing the Muslim community" to lead the closing prayer (Lewiston City Council Minutes 2008). Two months into his tenure, he took a controversial stand on including noncitizens on the Downtown Neighborhood Task Force. He recommended broadening eligibility from "registered voters" to "residents" to allow Somalis who had not yet attained citizenship to serve. The mayor's motion failed, but he appointed a Somali woman who was a registered voter and continued his efforts to appoint additional Somalis in other capacities.

Under Mayor Gilbert's leadership, local immigrant organizations also received their first funding from city hall. For the first three years that the African Immigrant Association requested funds for a Somali Independence Day festival, the request was denied, along with a quarter to a third of other applicants. In June 2007 Mayor Gilbert personally introduced the funding request for the group's fourth annual festival, which was approved at a slightly reduced level. Although it sparked debate, the city council renewed funding in subsequent years. In his second term, Mayor Gilbert issued Lewiston's Welcoming Proclamation, asserting that Lewiston aims to be a "community where all are welcomed, accepted and appreciated." Sixty more local leaders have since signed the proclamation, including current Mayor Robert Macdonald (Davis 2012).

Despite this affirmation, Mayor Macdonald, who took office in 2012, has made repeated controversial comments about Lewiston's immigrants, telling them to "leave your culture at the door," criticizing their behavior at public events, and decrying their perceived reliance on public assistance (Macdonald 2012a; Taylor 2012). On the other hand, Mayor Macdonald meets with immigrant leaders, attends their events, and twice appointed a Somali woman to a school committee vacancy. Although he feels strongly that immigrants should not accept public assistance and should rapidly assimilate, he also expresses pride in the accomplishments of Somali youth and says he hopes they will remain in Lewiston: "We're trying to build a community here, something for the future, and I hope they can be part of it" (Taylor 2012).

Moreover, though Macdonald continues to win narrow electoral victories, other Lewiston officials accommodate immigrants in spite of his vocal influence. The city council president has publicly disavowed the mayor's comments about immigrants (Canfield 2012), and in 2015 the majority of the city council endorsed his opponent, while no council members endorsed Macdonald (Shepherd 2015). Lewiston's comprehensive plan, which the city council approved in January 2017, acknowledges the role of Somali entrepreneurs in revitalizing the city's downtown and includes careful consideration of the valuable role immigrants will play in the city's future. Moreover, it includes promoting acceptance of immigrants as a key goal: "The overall health and functionality of the City is closely tied to . . . making this new population feel welcomed" (City of Lewiston 2017). The plan suggests that, regardless of Mayor Macdonald's comments and electoral popularity, most Lewiston officials intend to continue supporting immigrant residents.

Wausau: A Shared Path from Compliance to Accommodation

Hmong refugees first arrived in Wausau twenty-five years before Somalis migrated to Lewiston, yet the evolution of local response in the cities is quite similar, moving from compliance toward accommodation and continuing along that trajectory despite a key episode of restriction. In contrast to Lewiston, where city services far exceeded federal requirements owing to Maine State General Assistance policy, Wausau city hall was not intimately involved in the day-to-day details of serving the early Hmong refugees, who were sponsored by local churches. Marathon County social service agencies were more active in providing services, particularly once refugee benefits were exhausted. Nonetheless, like Lewiston, Wausau demonstrates a course from service provision to broader convening, mobilizing, and educating roles and to involving Hmong in local decision making. In Wausau, local foundations and nonprofit agencies led the initial mobilization to accommodate the Hmong, spurring later municipal accommodation.

From Compliance to Accommodation

Although the Hmong began to arrive in the late 1970s, efforts to accommodate the newcomers ramped up as they reached more than 5 percent of the population in the late 1980s, in part through secondary migration of Hmong refugees to Wausau from other cities. A coalition of organizations came together to seek grant funding from the Gannett Foundation, the charitable arm of the media conglomerate that owns the *Wausau Daily Herald*. The Gannett grant convened Wausau's elite stakeholders, including the mayor, county administrator, and school superintendent, to address the needs of the Hmong population. The project's final report credits the effort with "provid[ing] the catalyst for looking at the refugee issue in a systematic manner" and giving "other entities—the public sector and business—a focus for community activity" (Wausau Area Community Foundation 1989, 24).

In addition to the Gannett grant, in the early 1980s the federal Office of Refugee Resettlement began to channel postsettlement resources through refugee-run organizations, often called mutual assistance associations (Bloemraad 2006). Meanwhile, in Wausau refugee resettlement agencies, the County Department of Social Services, the schools, and the refugees themselves, were seeking more systematic means to serve the Hmong. Out of these various seeds for organizing and with the assistance of federal funding, Wausau's Hmong community established the Wausau Area Hmong Mutual Association (WAHMA) in 1984. City hall provided WAHMA with its first office space at no cost, until an anonymous donor stepped in to offer a building. Over time, WAHMA developed into the main service provider to local Hmong and the primary liaison between the Hmong and broader Wausau.

The Gannett project, the simultaneous efforts of local foundations, and the development of WAHMA mobilized local government and other organizations to address the Hmong migration. After the Gannett grant ended in the early 1990s, Wausau city and Marathon County took on a more intensive convening and mobilizing role. Even as the city began to engage more actively in accommodating the Hmong, a major controversy erupted surrounding a school redistricting plan.

Restrictive Response: The Partner Schools Controversy

In 1993 Wausau's school board voluntarily proposed a redistricting plan that would reduce the segregation of Hmong in downtown schools. Wausau's school desegregation plan, known as "partner schools," was announced at the June school board meeting in 1993 and set to take effect that fall. Almost immediately the decision raised a firestorm of protest. Reasons for concern ranged from outright racism to a desire to maintain neighborhood schools. A slate of livid parents circulated a petition to recall the maximum allowable number of school board members and advanced five of their own candidates to replace them. The recall candidates were new to politics and activism, but they rode the town's outrage to victory.

When it became clear that the new school board intended to repeal partner schools immediately, the school district's lawyer resigned in protest, saying that turning the system back would be a return to segregation and therefore legally objectionable. Initially, some new school board members wanted to place the Hmong in one ELL-related facility. But faced with legal pressure to maintain integrated schools even as they did away with partner schools, they developed an alternative plan.

The resulting redistricting was touted as an alternative to busing, but it in fact buses the Hmong and other low-income downtown residents to outlying schools. A proponent of the original partner schools plan describes the decision this way: "I don't know if they actually said it in these words, but, 'we don't want to put a burden on our [white] families to make them get their kids on a bus. So, okay, who's gonna bus? The minority.'" The controversy resulted in bitter local relations and attracted national media attention. Ultimately, however, even the new school board accepted the legal reality of the need to end segregation. Much like the mayor's controversial letter in Lewiston, the partner schools episode in Wausau was a departure from the city's generally welcoming response and reaffirmed the local government's efforts to accommodate immigrant newcomers.

Convening, Mobilizing, and Incorporating Immigrants in Local Decision Making

In the aftermath of the partner schools controversy, local government increased its efforts to accommodate the Hmong. Before the partner schools controversy, in 1992, the mayor and county administrator came together to establish a committee known as Wausau 2000, with the goal of implementing a plan to increase intercultural understanding and Hmong access to opportunity (City of Wausau, n.d.). Though the city and county had participated in earlier efforts, it was at this point that they became a leading force in convening stakeholders, mobilizing resources, and educating the public. From 1995 to 1999, the Wausau 2000 plan of action contributed to efforts to establish a walk-in clinic for the Hmong and hire additional Hmong police officers, social workers, health care interpreters, and ELL instructors. Even so, without dedicated staff time, progress toward the Wausau 2000 goals was slow. In the year 2000, the Wausau School District received a federal grant that enabled the hiring of a diversity affairs director. A Hmong insurance agent filled the role, providing staff support to a reenergized Wausau 2000 committee.

With the diversity affairs director in place, Wausau 2000 focused more on increasing Hmong involvement in local decision making. Projects included Hmong town hall dialogue meetings, a Hmong television news program, and most prominently the Hmong Leadership Initiative (HLI). Launched in 2003, the program produced an annual slate of twenty Hmong graduates ready to serve on local boards. A white municipal employee describes the thinking behind the program:

> We have our traditional community leadership program here; it's called Leadership Wausau. . . . We always have one or two Hmong in each class, but it was only once a year. And we thought, "Geez, it's gonna take us forty years to get enough [Hmong] leadership through this process. Why don't we start our own leadership classes?" So we did.

A brochure listed Hmong graduates of the program, allowing community organizations in search of board members to contact them. The organizer of the program estimated that by 2007 over a dozen Hmong individuals had been recruited to local boards and committees through the program. In addition, HLI encouraged two Hmong women to make bids for election to the school committee. Despite these successful efforts of the Diversity Affairs Department, in fall 2010 the City of Wausau and Marathon County eliminated the department over cost concerns, shifting these efforts to a joint city-county Diversity Affairs Commission (Dally 2010).

The elimination of the department in some ways reflects local Hmong progress. Members of the Hmong second generation now fill key local leadership roles, including a school board member, a doctor, lawyers, teachers, professors, and even the proprietor of a traditional downtown sports bar (Lawder 2015). In 2014 the Wausau Area Hmong Mutual Association changed its name to the Hmong American Center to reflect that it no longer serves refugees but primarily US citizens ("Wausau Area Hmong Mutual Association Changes Name" 2014). In September 2016, forty years after the Hmong initially arrived in Wausau, a war memorial honoring Hmong contributions to US forces during the Vietnam War was unveiled on the grounds of the Marathon County Courthouse, after a collaborative effort that included contributions from the local American Legion Post (Hertel 2015a, 2015b; Lee 2015).

Like Lewiston, Wausau has displayed an accommodating response to its immigrant population, which only intensified after the restrictive partner schools episode. Over time, the city and county's efforts expanded from convening, mobilizing resources, and educating the public to actively promoting Hmong participation in local decision making.

Elgin: A Trajectory toward Accommodation Despite Periodic Restriction

Suburban Elgin, with its growing Latino immigrant population, is in many ways quite different from Lewiston and Wausau. Even so, the evolution of its response to immigrants bears key similarities. When Mexican settlement in Elgin accelerated in the late 1980s and 1990s, leaders built on the limited civic infrastructure that had served the city's small Latino population since the 1970s. By the mid-1990s, however, existing systems were no longer effectively addressing Latino population growth. In particular, concerns about overcrowded housing led to more aggressive code enforcement. The city's restrictive enforcement garnered national media attention and brought a legal challenge from the Department of Housing and Urban Development. In the midst of the housing controversy, Elgin intensified efforts to accommodate local immigrants. After a decade of increasing accommodation, however, the city made some moves toward restriction in 2008, when the city council reluctantly bowed to pressure from a local anti-immigration group. Since then, officials interested in accommodation have managed to keep the issue off the public agenda while quietly maintaining accommodating measures.

Initial Civic Response

Unlike many new immigrant destinations, Elgin had in place some civic infrastructure to respond when the bulk of its immigrant population began to arrive in the late 1980s and early 1990s. In 1972 the city's small Latino population founded an immigrant multiservice organization, Centro de Información, which serves Chicago's far west suburbs. When newcomers began to arrive in substantial numbers, the organization gradually expanded. Centro now has an annual budget of more than $800,000 and serves more than 16,000 people a year (Phillips 2007; Casas 2015). In interviews with Spanish-speaking informants, nearly all mentioned Centro as a key place to turn for assistance.

Like WAHMA in Wausau, Centro de Información and other Elgin Latino civic organizations offer local government an effective interface with the growing immigrant population. In addition to Centro, local Latinos founded the Elgin Hispanic Network in 1987, which involves both Latinos and other residents in addressing the needs of the Spanish-speaking population.

Restrictive Response: Housing Code Enforcement

By the mid-1990s, however, Elgin was receiving widespread complaints from residents about overcrowded housing and related quality of life issues, which were attributed to the growing Latino population. In 1995 a house fire killed a family living in the basement of an overcrowded Elgin home (Spak 2002a). This event, along with growing complaints from residents, contributed to tougher housing enforcement. By the late 1990s, seven Hispanic families filed complaints of housing discrimination, which Elgin settled without admitting wrongdoing. Then in August 1999 a housing advocacy organization filed seventeen more complaints (Rozek 2000). A federal investigation alleged inconsistent application of codes, unjustified warrants, and unnecessary evictions. From 1995 to 1998, Hispanics occupied 20 percent of rental units and made up 8 percent of homeowners yet received 64 percent of the city's housing citations ("HUD Report Details Possible Housing Discrimination" 2000). In August 2002 the city settled the second round of complaints and agreed to pay up to $500,000, again without admitting culpability (Spak 2002b). Regardless of whether housing enforcement in the 1990s was a product of prejudice or public safety concern, since the lawsuits Elgin has backed away from enforcement. Moreover, the discrimination suits encouraged the city to develop systems to communicate more effectively with the growing Latino population.[3]

Intensified Municipal Accommodation

Though Elgin never admitted wrongdoing, after the housing discrimination suits the city initiated more targeted efforts to serve and represent Latinos. City hall formalized the position of Hispanic outreach worker. Not long afterward the police department hired a Hispanic outreach liaison. In addition to these Latino staff members, in the spring of 1999 the city council appointed Elgin's first Latino council member to a vacant seat. A city employee described these positions as sending a signal to immigrants: "City hall is for everybody. If you have to pay your water bill, you call me if you have any questions. You call to get your permit; people will help you. We'll have people available that can translate and make people feel comfortable." By 2008 a Latina employed by a local government agency saw this approach throughout Elgin's local government and at other local organizations: "Even city hall has a Hispanic outreach person. . . . I notice in general that pretty much every organization or service agency has done something for the Hispanic community."

Elgin also countered the embarrassment of the housing discrimination suits with the "DiverCity" advertising campaign described at the opening of this chapter. Over the years, the city has devoted several hundred thousand dollars to this Enhancing Elgin effort (Hitzeman 2008a). The city also sponsors and supports Latino organizations and cultural celebrations. Fiesta Salsa was one of the city's biggest local events and a way to "showcase Elgin." More recently, the city rolled together various sponsored cultural celebrations into an annual large-scale Elgin International Festival.

Recent Setbacks to Accommodation

As these various efforts demonstrate, Elgin's leaders have attempted to welcome immigrants, particularly in the aftermath of the housing enforcement controversy. Beginning in 2007, however, a growing grassroots anti-immigration movement undermined the city's efforts at accommodation. While the city did reluctantly make substantive concessions to these forces, it also continues trying to accommodate immigrants.

In 2006, national political debates surrounding unauthorized immigration filtered to the local level in Elgin. After the spring 2006 immigration rallies and the failure of federal immigration reform, local anti-immigration activists began attending city council meetings. Though immigration had not previously been prominent on the city council's agenda, in July 2006 the council asked the police chief to report on how the department addressed unauthorized migration. Unsatisfied with local officials' response, activists established the Association for Legal Americans (AFLA) to promote local immigration enforcement. The new organization developed a series of policy proposals for curbing unauthorized immigration and asked citizens to sign a petition of support. By January 2008 AFLA had collected over 2,700 signatures in support of these policies.

Initially, Elgin officials stonewalled the group. Then, when the *Elgin Courier News* asked the council to respond publicly to AFLA's proposals, the council presented a united front. Echoing talking points provided by the city's lawyers, councilors argued that immigration enforcement is a federal issue. Despite this firm stance, the national debate that spurred AFLA to action began to affect local officials' decision making. A month after the *Courier* piece, in January 2008, the mayor issued a press release highlighting new policies related to unauthorized immigration. The policies included using E-Verify (a federal system to determine legal eligibility for employment) in city hiring, instituting random audits of city contractors to ensure immigration compliance, screening foreign-born arrestees' legal status, and exploring further collaboration with ICE. The mayor emphasized that the policies aimed to enhance local efforts to prevent crime and would not racially profile or otherwise violate civil rights (Hitzeman 2008b). Even so, the city's sudden press release surprised many and suggested that AFLA was gaining ground. About the same time, the city asked the Hispanic outreach liaison to resign. The move reflected personnel issues, but the city rewrote the position as a special events coordinator in the Parks and Recreation Department.

In spring 2009 AFLA mounted a concerted campaign to elect a city council sympathetic to its cause, with some success. Two out of three AFLA-endorsed candidates were victorious, unseating incumbents John Walters, a twenty-two-year veteran of the council, and Juan Figueroa, the only Latino councilor. Figueroa's loss was emblematic of the changing tide of public support and of AFLA's influence. In 2005 he had won reelection with the most votes of any candidate, but in 2009 he was soundly defeated in a result some local observers attribute to AFLA's influence (Hitzeman 2009a).

Since the spring 2009 elections, however, Elgin has not carried through on most of its restrictive concessions. The AFLA-endorsed candidates remain on the council, and one periodically brings up contractors' use of E-Verify, but the city has not been actively conducting audits on contractors. Police involvement in immigration enforcement has been limited, but more consequential. Although the city did not pursue formal cooperation with ICE, when a new police chief took over in 2010 Elgin appointed a detective to serve on ICE's Gang Unit and participated with ICE in a sweep to execute outstanding warrants (Cox 2010; Hitzeman 2010). Though the city claimed its checking of arrestees' status focused on serious criminals, one analysis found that during the first eight months of the program 40 percent of those screened had been arrested for driving without licenses (Diaz 2009). Clearly the city's acquiescence to AFLA's demands created a more restrictive environment for unauthorized immigrants and other Latinos who might be mistaken as being undocumented.

Unauthorized immigration remained a campaign issue in Elgin through the 2011 elections, where long-term incumbent Mayor Ed Schock was defeated. Since then it has largely receded from the public agenda. The new mayor, David Kaptain, is more willing to discuss local responses to unauthorized immigration (Mathewson 2011) but is on record as supporting comprehensive federal reform (Gregory 2013). In May 2014 the city council majority, including one of the council members previously supported by AFLA, backed the appointment of the first Latina city councilor to a vacancy (Ferrarin 2014). Council member Rose Martinez won reelection in 2015, along with all the incumbents on the ticket. In the same election, Mayor Kaptain received the endorsement of Elgin's Latino Vote Committee over a fiscally conservative Latino opponent.

Most recently, in September 2015 a financial services company named Elgin the nation's twenty-seventh most diverse city. Reflecting its overall accommodating approach toward its immigrant population, the city celebrated this announcement on its website, and Mayor Kaptain touted it when speaking at a Hispanic Heritage Month event (Gathman 2015). Like Lewiston and Wausau, Elgin experienced a controversial restrictive episode followed by greater accommodation. Although it responded to increased pressure for restriction, particularly from 2008 to 2011, for the most part local officials have worked to minimize restriction and perpetuate accommodation. Elgin continues to support immigrant organizations and cultural celebrations as well as seeking to include Latinos in local decision making.

Yakima: Inaction Becomes Restriction

In contrast to Elgin, for many years Yakima did little to acknowledge or adapt to the growth of its Latino immigrant population. Officials demonstrated a lack of receptivity to Latino immigrants even as the Hispanic population grew to more than 40 percent of city residents. This inaction transformed into resistance when Yakima neglected federal mandates, taking action only when facing legal action. In 2006 a new slate of local elected leaders started trying to incorporate Latinos in public life, including appointing the city's first Hispanic city councilor to a vacancy. These overtures, however, were not lasting. Most recently, a federal judge ruled that Yakima's modified at-large city council voting system systematically disadvantaged Latino candidates, who had never won a seat on the city council. In November 2015—the first election under the newly mandated district election system—three Latinas were elected to the city council, ushering the city into a new era.

Inaction in the Face of Growing Immigration

Although Yakima has recently experienced this substantial change in Latinos' influence in local government, in the first decade of the twenty-first century nearly half of informants in the city reported that municipal leaders were doing little or nothing in response to the growing immigrant population. A non-Hispanic white woman who led a local nonprofit reported, "It's not that they're doing anything terrible; they're just not doing anything at all." A Latino city employee agreed, saying, "I am not aware of any huge effort by the political structure here to bridge the needs of the Latino community. . . . Obviously there's no plan." Three informants from different walks of life independently used the word denial in describing local responses to the growth of the Latino population, with one Latino clergyman explaining that the city "[wants] to pretend that this is not happening."

Even in public moments of tension over the growing immigrant population, officials and community leaders have not responded. In 1995 the *Yakima Herald Republic* ran a one-week series on Michoacán, Mexico, the home state of many of the Northwest's Mexican immigrants. The series attracted an overwhelmingly negative response, with many readers' comments connecting Mexican immigrants to crime, drugs, and a host of other ills. Despite the inflammatory comments, no one could recall any response to the upheaval from local leaders. In many cases, Yakima has ignored ethnic tensions rather than addressing them.

Yakima leaders' resistance to adapting to the presence of Latino immigrants was also evident in their attempts to safeguard the city's identity from association with Mexico. In 2004 a proposal to revitalize a section of downtown by building a Mexican-style plaza ignited local controversy. The business elite, trying to recast Yakima's image as the "Gateway to Wine Country," believed association with Mexico would hurt the city's economic prospects. Through political maneuvering, they made it clear to proponents of the project that they could build a plaza, but it could not be called a *Mexican* plaza.

Inaction Transforms into Resistance

As these controversies illustrate, Yakima officials largely preferred to disassociate themselves from the growing Latino immigrant population. As immigrant populations grow, this inaction can run afoul of federal requirements governing the treatment of ethnic minorities and those with limited proficiency in English. In such cases, lack of action becomes restriction. When the Spanish-speaking population reached 5 percent of county residents in the 1970s, the Voting Rights Act dictated that Yakima County election officials translate voting materials and provide bilingual poll workers. Despite repeated warnings, Yakima County failed to comply until the US Department of Justice brought suit. In July 2004, the department settled its suit, obliging the county to translate materials, employ bilingual poll workers, and hire a bilingual elections program coordinator, among other stipulations (US Department of Justice 2004).

Local resistance to providing Spanish-language translation was not limited to the Voting Rights Act. A Latino city employee said that local officials referred to posting multilingual signs at city hall as a "waste of money." Though this employee worked in a professional capacity unrelated to his bilingual skills, he received calls to interpret for Spanish-speaking residents up until roughly 2005, when more bilingual employees were in place. He explains:

> In the last couple years, I quit getting the calls . . . about coming down and, "Can you translate? Somebody's paying their water bill. Can you come to the front counter?" . . . And I didn't mind doing that. I mean probably what got me into that is because I would just see somebody struggling and stop what I was doing and go help them at the counter. And then I would remind folks, you need to get some [bilingual] people here who can help. And always resistance.

Although the city has recently increased its bilingual workforce, for many years Yakima's resistance to accommodating Spanish speakers resulted in a less hospitable environment for Latino immigrants at city hall.

Likewise, when accusations of police profiling emerged, the city proved reluctant to act. In August 2000 a dismissed Latino police officer filed a complaint alleging that the Yakima Police Department conducted racial profiling and discriminated against Latino officers (Nelson 2000). The city council appointed a panel to investigate the claims but then failed to act on its recommendations for more than a year, until the state pressured them to do so. Ultimately the city approved the creation of a citizens' committee to help the police department strengthen its relations with local ethnic groups and improve its system for collecting data on race (Nelson 2002a). Yet the city council resolution creating the committee misrepresented the panel's findings, stating that it had found no evidence of profiling (Nelson 2002b). After five years of little impact, in 2008 the city council disbanded the committee as part of a broader review of inactive council-commissioned groups (Bristol 2008). Despite the committee's demise, the controversy surrounding racial profiling put pressure on the city to respond to Latinos' concerns. When the police chief retired in August 2002 amid the profiling dispute, Latinos mobilized to push for consideration of Hispanic candidates. In 2003 Yakima hired its first Latino police chief, who served until 2010.

Although the city took few other steps to accommodate immigrants, hiring the Latino police chief, as well as a Latino superintendent of schools in 2000, contributed to a somewhat more hospitable environment, as I will discuss in chapter 7. Latino informants appreciated the effort to appoint Hispanic professionals to prominent roles. At the same time, Latino leaders report that they feel excluded as they cope with the perception that they were "hand brought in because they were Hispanic." Accounts from Latino leaders suggest that while Yakima may be attempting to recruit Hispanic leadership, the city is not successfully incorporating these leaders into the community.

Increasing Efforts at Accommodation

Since 2006, a new slate of local government leaders has intensified efforts to accommodate immigrants. Under Mayor Dave Edler, Yakima enhanced support for Latino activities and took further action to include

Latinos in public life. The local government's increasingly warm attitude toward Yakima's sister city, Morelia, Mexico, reflects this shift. In the early 1990s, several Latino community leaders began to advocate for a sister city relationship with a Mexican city. Yakima initially resisted, but after seven years of advocacy, in June 1999 the city council endorsed the Yakima-Morelia Sister City Association. Even once the association won approval, Latinos and their allies felt that Yakima was not sufficiently welcoming to delegations from Morelia. By 2007, however, the Latino leader of the organization spoke with pride about the city's embrace of the association, which included hosting meetings, providing funding, and welcoming delegations.

In addition to support for the sister city association, from 2006 to 2010 Yakima budgeted the same amount for the Greater Yakima Chamber of Commerce and the Hispanic Chamber of Commerce, treating the organizations equally in an economic development effort. Most prominently, in January 2009 Yakima's city council appointed its first Latino member to a vacant seat, despite competition from politically connected non-Hispanic residents. In nominating Sonia Rodriguez for the vacancy, Mayor Edler demonstrated his intent to improve representation for Yakima's Hispanics (Bristol 2009).

A Return to Resisting Change

Increasing efforts to accommodate immigrants did not fully take hold. In the subsequent election Rodriguez lost her seat, and when the new council was seated the councilors replaced Edler with a new mayor. In 2011 resistance to Latinos' presence again came to the fore when the Mexican government donated a bust of General José María Morelos to Yakima in honor of the sister city relationship. Only one city councilor voted against accepting the bust, citing traffic concerns related to its proposed installation site, but members of the public spoke out against a sculpture honoring a foreign leader. Another city councilor voted to accept the gift but commiserated with members of the public whose concerns about unauthorized immigration led them to protest the gift (Faulk 2011). While Yakima avoided outright rejection of the sculpture and similar restrictive actions, the city continued to struggle with acknowledging the place of its growing Mexican and Mexican American population.

In 2012, Yakima received a complaint from the American Civil Liberties Union (ACLU) alleging that its at-large city council system disadvantaged Latino voters. The council did not respond to the complaint, leading the ACLU to file a case against Yakima for violating section 2 of the Voting Rights Act. The city fought the allegations, but in August 2014 a federal judge ruled against Yakima in summary judgment and supported the remedy of an election system with seven city council districts. While the ruling does not claim the city intentionally discriminated against Latinos, it concludes that its voting system had that effect (*Montes v. Yakima*). The ruling cites examples such as appointed council member Sonia Rodriguez's loss to a non-Hispanic radio personality who had not even been able to campaign owing to an injury (Brunner 2011). Likewise, it points to another Latina's loss to a non-Hispanic white woman in a school board race even though the white woman had dropped out (La Ganga 2014).

The ruling further ordered Yakima to pay the ACLU's legal fees of $1.8 million in addition to the $1.1 million the city had already spent on its defense (Faulk 2015). Despite the mounting costs, Yakima appealed the decision and unsuccessfully sought to stay the ruling.[4] Under Washington State law, a change in local elections systems must be followed by a full election, meaning that all city council members would be forced to defend their seats under the new voting regime. Some argue that Yakima's elected officials appealed the decision more out of self-interest than in response to public resistance to Latino influence. The court allowed elections to go forward in November 2015, resulting in the historic election of three Hispanic members to Yakima's city council. In April 2016, the new city council officially abandoned the appeal (Faulk 2016). For many Yakima Latinos and others who support them, the election offered a chance to address the long-term neglect of Latinos' interests in the city.

Aligning the Case Study Cities with the Model

Having introduced the model of municipal response to immigrants and explained the evolution of each city's responses to immigrants over time, I now turn to arraying the cities on the model of municipal response, as displayed in figure 2.2. Tracing the responses to immigrants in Lewiston, Wausau, Elgin, and Yakima from 1990 to 2015 indicates that three out of four towns have implemented actively accommodating practices while one—Yakima—remained largely inactive in ways that made it substantively more restrictive. To be sure, Lewiston, Wausau, and Elgin

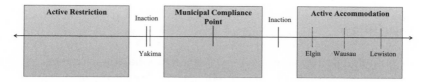

FIGURE 2.2. Categorizing response in four new destinations.

experienced prominent episodes of restriction. Their position on the model of local governments' response to immigrants did not remain static over time, exhibiting swings toward restriction. Nonetheless, the model calls for an aggregation of municipal activity over time to develop an overall picture of local context of reception for immigrants and provide a standard for comparison across cities.

Despite clear examples of restrictive response, Lewiston, Wausau, and Elgin all are characterized by largely welcoming responses. Lewiston falls farthest toward the right on the model because it actively provides services to refugee newcomers. While Wausau does not provide such extensive services to refugees within the city government, it does display the other key indicators of accommodating response, which I will elaborate further in chapter 3, such as engaging immigrants in municipal governance and supporting immigrant organizations. Thus, Wausau falls slightly to the left of Lewiston in the accommodating region of the model. The prevalence of accommodation in the two refugee destinations suggests that federal requirements surrounding service to refugees may prompt more accommodating responses to immigrants, a topic I will explore in chapter 4.

Looking beyond the refugee destinations, Elgin falls within the accommodating region, but still farther to the left since, unlike the two refugee destinations, it did not serve in a convening and mobilizing role in response to immigrants and because the city has displayed more restrictive responses in recent years. Though Yakima has recently become more accommodating, its long-term approach to immigration has been characterized by inaction, which at times transformed into restriction. I therefore place Yakima to the left of the municipal compliance point, indicating inaction that creates a less hospitable atmosphere for immigrants. While the actual placement of the cities on the model is somewhat impressionistic, the continuum allows researchers to aggregate local responses over time and compare cities with one another.

Conclusion

In sum, despite the prevalence of media and scholarly accounts of local government immigration restriction, analyzing local government responses across four case study cities demonstrates that restriction is not
the default local government response. In fact, across three out of four
cities—selected based on their demographic change characteristics and
not on their responses—accommodating responses predominated, while
one city remained largely inactive. Examining the trajectory of response
over time reveals commonalities across the four cases. In the refugee
destinations of Lewiston and Wausau, we see a progression of responses
from providing services, to broader convening around immigrant issues,
to incorporating immigrants into local public life. In three out of four
cities we see a restrictive response followed by intensified efforts at accommodation. While these four cities offer a detailed portrait of how
new destination local governments respond to immigrants over time, to
what extent do these findings extend to cities across the United States?

The case studies represent four previously homogeneous new immigrant destinations in largely Democratic-leaning states, suggesting that
their relatively accommodating examples might not represent immigrant
destinations nationwide. That said, we might have expected that these
new immigrant destinations would be the least receptive to newcomers,
given their lack of experience with diversity and the challenges associated with ramping up to serve immigrants. Yet all four cities produced at
least some accommodating responses. The cases also vary substantially
in their demographic, economic, and ideological characteristics, offering
no immediate explanation for why these cities would be distinctly more
likely to accommodate than other locales. Even so, the patterns found in
these four destinations bear testing on a broader sample of immigrant
destinations nationwide. Thus, in chapter 3 I apply the model of local
government response to analyzing responses to immigrants across a national sample of small to midsize destinations. Establishing what local
governments are doing in response to immigrants nationwide will then
allow me to turn to why they select these responses.

CHAPTER THREE

Municipal Responses Nationwide

Frequent Inaction, Substantial
Accommodation, Rare Restriction

Our community is seeking immigrants to add to our diversity. . . . Everyone benefits. Our region is actively seeking immigrants with skills to help us innovate. — City councilor, Michigan suburb

No one in the community seems to have an issue with legal immigrants. It is the illegal status of most immigrants that is at the heart of the anger and frustration along with the federal government's unwillingness to enforce immigration laws. . . . No one seems to care, and it is a problem that starts at the very highest office in the country and filters down to nearly every local jurisdiction. — Police chief, North Carolina suburb

We do not actively engage the issue. Until funding is available from the feds, it is unlikely that the city will institute proactive programs regarding illegal immigration issues. — City manager, Southern California suburb

The experience of Lewiston, Wausau, Elgin, and Yakima—four previously homogeneous new immigrant destinations detailed in chapter 2—suggests that local governments generally accommodate immigrants, though some remain relatively inactive. As the comments from the Municipal Responses to Immigrants Survey (MRIS) quoted above indicate, towns that participated in this nationwide survey of local governments' responses to immigrants run the gamut from accommodating to restrictive to inactive. What type of local responses to immigrants predominates in small to midsize immigrant destinations nationwide? Despite the popularity of restrictive policies among rural America's Trump voters and the reality that immigrant population growth can initially be costly to localities, both the case studies and the MRIS demonstrate that small to midsize local governments are far more likely to accommodate immigrants than to restrict their presence.

In this chapter I analyze data from the MRIS to demonstrate the frequency of a variety of practices in response to immigrants. Drawing on the model of municipal response developed through investigation of the case study cities and presented in chapter 2, I describe responses to immigrants in the categories of compliance, inaction, restriction, and accommodation. Synthesizing these practices, I introduce indexes of local accommodation and restriction that demonstrate the prevalence of inaction and accommodation and the dearth of restriction across towns nationwide.

Identifying Townwide Responses to Immigrants

Before turning to analysis of the 2014–15 MRIS (described fully in chapter 1), some brief methodological notes are necessary. A strength of the MRIS, which surveyed four officials in each town, resulting in responses from 598 officials across 373 towns, is that it provides information on local responses from different actors within towns, including both elected and appointed officials. Asking multiple officials within one town the same questions about their responses to immigrants allows for greater certainty about local response while also allowing me to identify when responses vary across different types of officials. To identify a townwide response, I generate average responses for each variable across officials in a town, thereby capturing the general tendency of response in each place.[1]

Of course, if certain types of officials are more likely to report certain practices, these practices will be overrepresented when only these officials respond in a given town. Indeed, across the thirty-nine practices analyzed, in five cases police chiefs report more accommodating practices than do city hall officials (city managers, city councilors, and mayors). In five separate cases, elected officials (city councilors and mayors) differ from appointed officials (city managers and police chiefs), though not in a systematic direction. In these cases the characteristics of an official's role—whether related to incentive structure or to knowledge base—affect how the official represents practices in his or her town (a topic I will discuss further in chapter 5). Where reported practices differ markedly across officials, I note these differences and summarize them further toward the end of the chapter. Nonetheless, the general findings presented here hold whether I analyze responses using townwide variables or instead analyze police chiefs, city managers, and elected officials separately. On the whole, the survey indicates substantial inaction, widespread accommodation, and extremely limited restriction across immigrant destinations.

In the analyses that follow, I present the unweighted survey results in order to preserve a focus on the more populous immigrant destinations to which the survey's sampling strategy give priority (see appendix C for further detail). That said, it is also useful to estimate the overall proportion of small to midsize towns across the United States that opt for restrictive versus accommodating or inactive responses to immigrants. Therefore, in summarizing my results at the end of the chapter I present results weighted back to the full sample frame, which includes a preponderance of small immigrant destinations.[2]

The MRIS and the Model of Local Response

Chapter 2 presented a model of municipal response to immigrants that grew out of the four case study cities and classified responses as compliant with federal requirements, independently restrictive or accommodating, or inactive in a manner that makes the locale either more restrictive or more accommodating (see fig. 2.1). In parallel with the model, each of the responses to immigrants queried in the MRIS can be considered compliant, accommodating, restrictive, or inactive. Figure 3.1 populates the basic model of municipal response with the specific practices measured in the MRIS. In the sections that follow I focus first on whether immigrant destinations nationwide are complying with federal mandates on language access and immigration enforcement. Then I turn to the prevalence of various independent restrictive and accommodating responses.

Municipal Compliance

As detailed in the introduction, local governments face federal requirements to serve immigrants in the realms of education, health care,

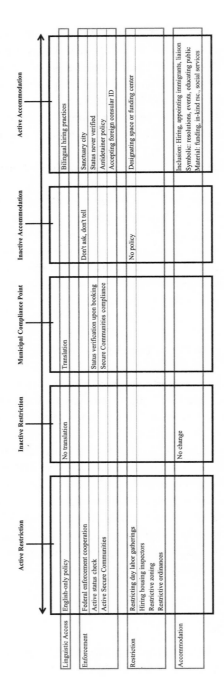

FIGURE 3.1. Detailed model of municipal response.

language access, and law enforcement. While educational and health care responsibilities toward immigrants are important, I do not focus on them in the MRIS for two primary reasons. With respect to education, school districts sometimes do not align with town jurisdictions, meaning educational decisions are not necessarily being made at the town level. With respect to health care, many towns, particularly the midsize towns in question here, do not have publicly operated hospitals and clinics. In contrast, city halls and police chiefs across these cities are centrally involved with language access and law enforcement.

LANGUAGE ACCESS.   As described in the introduction, federal regulations place language access requirements on all agencies that receive federal funding, encompassing the local governments of essentially all immigrant destinations. A local government that is host to a significant linguistic minority population must provide language access to non-English-speaking residents or face potential administrative action. For instance, as chapter 2 detailed, the Department of Justice took action against Yakima County for violating language access provisions of the Voting Rights Act. In the wake of the mayor's controversial letter in Lewiston, the Department of Justice's Civil Rights Office investigated whether Lewiston was complying with Title VI of the Civil Rights Act by providing language access to Somalis at city hall and in the schools.

Thus, translation and interpretation are identified on figure 3.1 as a key aspect of municipal compliance. Of course, not all towns comply with these regulations. Those that fail to do so, as Yakima did at times, have remained inactive in a manner that creates a more restrictive local context. A few towns also pursue actively restrictive language policies. While the United States as a whole does not have an official language, some states and localities have declared English their official or only language of business (Schildkraut 2005). In contrast, some towns, such as Elgin and Lewiston, seek to do more than comply with federal regulations, restructuring their hiring to attract bilingual employees. In sum, the federal government prescribes that localities with significant language-minority populations must provide language access, but local responses can run the gamut from active resistance to supererogatory efforts to provide access.

In the 2014 MRIS, more than three-quarters of small to midsize towns demonstrate clear compliance with language access mandates, while just under a quarter are relatively inactive in doing so. Very few towns actively restrict language access, and almost half pursue accommodating practices aimed at attracting bilingual employees. Officials were asked what would happen if a staff member needed to communicate with a non-English-speaking resident and did not speak the resident's language. They were asked to choose whether they would call on an interpreter employed by the municipality, use an external interpretation service the municipality contracts with, ask the resident's family member or neighbor to translate, or refuse service to the resident. In nearly half of towns (49 percent), officials reported that they would call on an interpreter on their staff. Another 30 percent said they would turn to an external contractor, such as a telephone-based interpretation service. Thus 78 percent of towns have some sort of formal interpretation capacity. Just under a quarter (22 percent) primarily rely on residents' kin to interpret. None of the 598 officials across 373 towns report that their municipality would refuse service to a non-English-speaking resident.[3]

The survey also asked how often city documents and informational materials were translated into languages other than English. Responses ranged along a five-point scale from "often" to "never" with "only upon request" as the middle category (Ramakrishnan and Lewis 2005). On average, towns report "sometimes" providing materials in languages other than English, though the modal response category is "often" providing translated materials, with 38 percent of towns selecting this response. Police chiefs report providing translated materials with systematically greater frequency than do other officials.

Very few towns had adopted concrete policies to restrict language access, with only nine towns (3 percent) reporting an "English-only" or "official English" policy. On the other hand, nearly half have bilingual hiring practices to provide language access. Here again police chiefs were more likely than city hall officials to report bilingual hiring.[4] In sum, we see high levels of compliance with language access mandates, although just under a quarter of towns report little action with respect to translation and interpretation. Moreover, while very few towns report restrictive responses in this sphere, nearly half report practices that promote hiring bilingual employees.

LAW ENFORCEMENT. Similar to language access, local law enforcement responses can run the gamut from compliance to active restriction and accommodation. As described in the introduction, how local officials should participate in immigration enforcement remains a hotly contested issue, and immigration enforcement initiatives remain in flux at the federal and local levels. For the most part, participation in immigration enforcement is voluntary, but policies such as Secure Communities implicate local police in enforcement efforts.

Figure 3.1 depicts the range of local law enforcement responses along the scale of restriction, compliance, and accommodation. As it indicates, local police are compliant with federal requirements when they run arrestees' information through FBI databases upon booking, which constitutes Secure Communities compliance.[5] Beyond this baseline compliance, some localities are actively restrictive, indicating that they cooperate with federal enforcement activities through programs like 287(g), check immigration status on any interaction with residents that raises a reasonable suspicion, or have policies that prescribe compliance with ICE detainers. Other localities are more accommodating, either by informally choosing not to act on immigration enforcement or by explicitly avoiding enforcement. In terms of inactive accommodation, some localities have informal, unwritten policies of not asking or sharing residents' immigration status. Other cities have actively pursued written policies that forbid immigration status checks or compliance with ICE detainers or that declare the city a sanctuary zone for unauthorized immigrants. Last, a number of local law enforcement agencies have decided to accept foreign consular cards as identification to make interaction with unauthorized immigrants easier (Varsanyi 2007).

Similar to language access, in the national survey roughly three-quarters of immigrant destinations report straightforward compliance with federal requirements for immigration enforcement. Towns that have taken action beyond federal requirements are more likely to accommodate than to restrict, though in the case of enforcement, relatively few towns have pursed either active accommodation or restriction. With respect to compliance, police chiefs were asked how they have implemented Secure Communities (Williams 2013). Of the 31 percent of responding police departments that operate jails and book prisoners, nearly three-quarters (74 percent) reported merely complying with Secure Communities. Nine percent reported a restrictive policy that "encourages active participation in Secure Communities," while 16 percent reported an accommodating policy that restricts compliance with Secure Communities, such as an antidetainer policy. On the whole, most towns merely complied with Secure Communities, but those that exceeded mere compliance were more likely to accommodate than to restrict.

The same trends apply to more general questions about local immigration enforcement. Roughly three-quarters of towns report no policy on unauthorized immigrants, and among the rest a larger proportion pursue accommodation than restriction. Officials were asked to choose a statement that best represents their approach to immigration enforcement. The four options ranged from whether their city could be described as "a 'sanctuary' city for illegal immigrants who are not engaged in criminal activities," whether their city "supports an informal policy of 'don't ask, don't tell,'" whether the city "encourage[s] local law enforcement to cooperate with federal authorities in enforcing immigration laws," or whether the locality has "no official policy vis-à-vis illegal immigrants" (Lewis et al. 2013).[6] As figure 3.2 indicates, more than three-quarters of towns (79 percent) reported they had no official policy. Eleven percent report an informal policy of not asking immigration status, and another 2 percent (six towns) identified as sanctuary cities. Nine percent of towns report policies of cooperating with federal authorities in immigration enforcement. Thus, though most towns profess no policy on unauthorized immigration, towns reporting practices that avoid enforcement exceed towns that cooperate in federal enforcement by four percentage points. Immigration enforcement, however, is an arena in which police chiefs represent local practices differently than do officials from city hall. Figure 3.2 demonstrates that while police chiefs and city hall officials did not differ in reporting policies at the extreme (sanctuary city or federal cooperation), police chiefs were much more likely to report a "don't ask, don't tell" policy.

In addition to this question on general enforcement, the survey asked police chiefs questions on police interactions with unauthorized immigrants. Specifically, they were asked if their department had "a written policy or procedural directive regarding when officers should verify immigration status" (Williams 2013). Sixty-three percent of police chiefs reported having no status verification policy. Just over a quarter report that immigration status is verified only on arrest and booking into jail, as Secure Communities requires. Another 3 percent report that status is never verified. Eight percent report that status is verified whenever the officer "has a reasonable suspicion that the person is . . . unlawfully present in the United States" (Williams 2013). Thus, among towns with status verification policies, police departments are more likely to avoid status

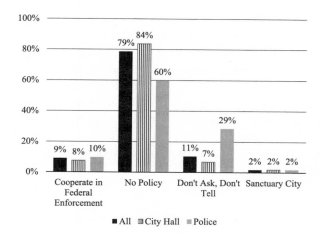

FIGURE 3.2. Immigration enforcement practices across local governments.

checks than to promote them. In this vein, many police departments have practices that make it easier for those without official documentation to interact with police, for instance, by accepting foreign consular ID cards. Eighty-one percent of police departments report accepting cards such as the Mexican *matricula consular* as identification. On the whole, the survey indicates that well over half of towns have not developed a policy on immigration enforcement, but that among those that have, accommodating practices are more common than restrictive ones.

Restrictive Initiatives

Having identified what constitutes compliance versus voluntary accommodation or restriction in terms of language access and immigration enforcement, I now turn to municipalities' independent restrictive initiatives, then to the independent accommodating initiatives. Following Monica Varsanyi (2010a), I divide restrictive initiatives into backdoor attempts to curtail immigrants' settlement through zoning policies and the like and more explicit restriction policies.

RESTRICTION THROUGH THE BACK DOOR. In an attempt to restrict local immigrants' presence or opportunities, some localities have pursued what Varsanyi (2008) refers to as "immigration policing through the backdoor." Typical forms of backdoor immigration restriction involve policies in other spheres that disproportionately affect immigrants. Among the most common are housing and zoning policies or efforts to curtail the presence of day laborers (Varsanyi 2008). "Facially neutral" housing or zoning policies may nonetheless disproportionately affect immigrants, who are more likely to live in overcrowded or otherwise substandard housing (Guzman 2010). Localities may hire additional housing inspectors to enforce existing codes more zealously (as occurred in Elgin), or they may introduce new ordinances that regulate "maximum occupancy" or define "family" in a narrow way that excludes extended family members.

Indeed, among immigrant destination towns that reported issues with housing, one in five reported having considered or passed housing or zoning ordinances in response to immigrants. Considering or passing such backdoor housing ordinances was the most frequent restrictive activity across immigrant destinations. Still, not all immigrant destinations report issues with housing. As figure 3.3 displays, most municipalities (59 percent) disagreed that overcrowded housing was a major local issue, with only 19 percent agreeing. On the other hand, a majority (56 percent) agreed that residents frequently complained about code violations such as poorly maintained homes or lawns. Just over a quarter of towns (26 percent) agreed that overcrowding and code violations were concentrated in areas where many immigrants live, while nearly half disagreed (46 percent) (questions modeled on Ramakrishnan and Lewis 2005). Immigrant destinations facing overcrowding or code violations tend to associate these issues with the presence of immigrants (Pearson's $r > .5$). Among towns reporting issues with either overcrowding or code violations, 41 percent agreed that these issues were concentrated in immigrant-heavy areas. Even so, four out of five towns with housing problems had not hired housing inspectors or considered housing ordinances in response to immigrants. Taking into account all responding towns, including those that did not report issues with housing, only 9 percent considered such ordinances and only 5 percent passed them. Likewise, only 5 percent of towns report having hired additional housing inspectors in response to immigration.

Similarly, not all towns report issues with day laborers, and among those that do, very few have pursued backdoor efforts to restrict their presence. Day laborers are employment seekers who solicit temporary work, typically in informal outdoor markets (Valenzuela 2003). Al-

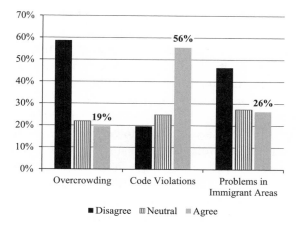

FIGURE 3.3. Perceptions of housing issues across local governments.

though their presence indicates a local demand for their services, often by construction companies, residents frequently complain about day laborers loitering in public spaces. The federal government does not prescribe what localities must do with respect to day labor. Some, however, have used antitrespassing or antisolicitation ordinances to restrict day labor gatherings (Varsanyi 2008). On the other hand, towns that do nothing in response to day laborers are in effect inactively accommodating their presence. On the actively accommodating side of the equation, other locales have used public funds or space to designate a place for day labor.

Officials in just over a third of towns (35 percent) reported that their town has one or more day laborer gatherings. Of these towns, 80 percent reported no policy in response to day laborers. Eleven percent said they had "designated an area or building" where day laborer gatherings were permitted (question from Ramakrishnan and Lewis 2005). Another 7 percent reported they had funded a day labor hiring center. Only three towns (2 percent) reported a policy to prevent day laborers from congregating. Thus, though most towns with day laborers have no policy in response, 18 percent provide a space where soliciting work is permitted, while only 2 percent of towns report restrictive action against day laborers' gatherings. On the whole, most immigrant destinations do not have issues with day labor, and among those that do, most have not established a clear policy.

EXPLICITLY RESTRICTIVE ORDINANCES. In addition to these backdoor practices and policies that nonetheless affect local immigrants' presence and opportunities, some localities have enacted ordinances explicitly aimed at deterring unauthorized immigrants, such as Hazleton, Pennsylvania's, Illegal Immigration Relief Act (IIRA). As discussed in the introduction, the incidence of these formal ordinances has been limited. Indeed, in the survey only 2 percent of towns (six towns) reported explicitly restrictive ordinances. In two more towns at least one official reported considering an ordinance, though other officials from the town did not. Interestingly, according to previously collected media reports and advocacy organization accounts (Fair Immigration Reform Movement 2007; Steil and Vasi 2014), seventeen of the cities responding here (5 percent) had considered or passed restrictive ordinances since 2006. As I will discuss in chapter 6, the disparity between lists of ordinances used by scholars in past analyses and reports by current officials raises questions about the true prevalence of restrictive municipal immigration ordinances. For now, however, it is sufficient to note that by either measure extremely few towns have pursued such explicitly restrictive ordinances.

Accommodating Initiatives

In contrast, more than four towns in five have implemented at least some efforts aimed at accommodating immigrants. Survey questions on accommodating initiatives drew from a review of the literature on local responses as well as from analysis of the four case study cities. Specifically, analysis identified three primary categories of accommodation. First, all four cities demonstrated active efforts to include immigrants and coethnics (US-born members of the immigrant ethnic group, such as the children of immigrants) in local government. A 2003 survey of California municipalities also identified the prevalence of these efforts (Ramakrishnan and Lewis 2005). In addition, the cities demonstrated varying levels of what Irene Bloemraad (2006) has referred to as symbolic and material support for incorporation. Symbolic support refers to statements and gestures by government that indicate support for immigrants and their incorporation, such as efforts to hold intercultural events. Material support refers to resources to support these efforts, such as funding for immigrant organizations. Figure 3.1 details accommodating practices measured on the survey in each of these three categories.

INCLUSION IN LOCAL GOVERNMENT. Across the four case study cities, the most common accommodating response was recruiting or hiring immigrants or coethnics to serve in local government. As I will discuss further in chapter 7, when local leaders and residents were asked what the local government was doing well and poorly, they often referred to efforts to hire immigrants or coethnics as local government employees or to appoint them to commissions and boards. Thus the survey asked city managers, city councilors, and mayors whether they have hired immigrants or coethnics as municipal employees in the past five years. Likewise, it asked officials whether they had attempted to recruit immigrants or coethnics to serve on boards or commissions over that period, as well as whether they had established an immigrant advisory council. Finally, city hall officials were asked whether they had ever appointed an immigrant or coethnic to a vacant elected position, as occurred in three of the four case study cities. All four officials, including police chiefs, were also asked whether they had a "designated employee who serves as a liaison with immigrant communities" (Williams 2013).

These practices were indeed common, as figure 3.4 indicates. Two-thirds of towns report hiring immigrants or coethnics as local government employees in the past five years. Fifty-seven percent of towns report recruiting immigrants or coethnics to serve on boards or commissions. Fully 19 percent of towns report appointing an immigrant or coethnic to a vacant elected position. Twelve percent had a designated employee who served as an immigrant liaison, a response that was more common among police departments than city halls. Last, 5 percent report establishing an immigrant advisory council.

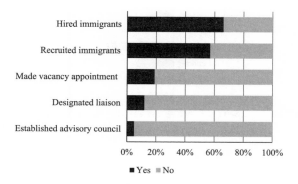

FIGURE 3.4. Prevalence of local government inclusion efforts.

SYMBOLIC AND MATERIAL INCORPORATION PRACTICES. Similarly, in questions asked of city hall officials only, towns report high levels of symbolic and material support for accommodation. Symbolic incorporation practices include hosting events, issuing resolutions, and providing information about immigrants to the public, all practices evident in the refugee destinations of Lewiston and Wausau. As figure 3.5 indicates, more than half of towns (56 percent) reported hosting an event to celebrate diversity or encourage intercultural interaction. A third (33 percent) reported issuing a resolution or proclamation in support of immigrants. Finally, 19 percent of towns report educating the public about local immigrants, as we saw when Lewiston distributed brochures and held forums to dispel myths about the Somali population. All together, 57 percent of towns report at least one symbolic practice, but 28 percent report two or more, and 9 percent report all three.[7]

Although we might expect that symbolic gestures would be more common than material incorporation practices because they do not require a substantial commitment of funds, many towns are also providing in-kind resources or direct funding to immigrants. Nearly half of towns (46 percent) report providing in-kind support for immigrant organizations or activities, such as allowing them to use municipal facilities free of charge. More than a quarter (26 percent) report providing direct funding. Twenty-one percent of towns report having developed new social service programs specifically for immigrants, while 17 percent report restructuring some existing social services to better accommodate immi-

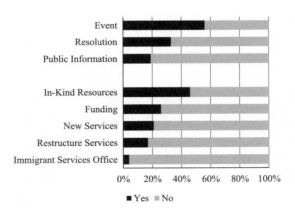

FIGURE 3.5. Prevalence of symbolic and material incorporation practices.

grants. Finally, 4 percent (eleven towns) report having established a local office for immigrant services. In sum, nearly half of towns (47 percent) report at least one material incorporation practice, and 16 percent report three or more.[8]

Examining the combined prevalence of symbolic and material incorporation practices reveals that 65 percent of towns—almost two-thirds—have implemented at least one symbolic or material incorporation practice. Nearly a quarter (23 percent) have implemented at least half of these practices—that is, four or more.

Given the prevalent image of municipal restriction in smaller American towns, this degree of accommodation in small to midsize towns and cities across the United States is remarkable. In addition, the interest in including immigrants in local government is notable and will be discussed further in chapter 7. Of the three accommodating practices adopted by more than half the towns, two involve inclusion in local government. Two-thirds of towns report hiring immigrants or coethnics, and 57 percent report recruiting immigrants or coethnics to serve on boards. The only accommodating measure that exceeds these is the frequency of accepting the *matricula consular* or other consular cards as identification, practiced by 81 percent of police departments.

Summarizing the Degree and Tenor of Response

The MRIS indicates that most towns clearly comply with federal language access and enforcement requirements, though roughly one in five remain inactive even with respect to these mandates. Very few towns have implemented restrictive initiatives, and more than four in five have implemented at least some accommodating initiatives. In this section I summarize the cumulative restrictive and accommodating initiatives across towns, focusing on indicators of voluntary accommodation and restriction rather than mere compliance. First I examine a simple count of accommodating and restrictive initiatives across towns, then I introduce two indexes that reflect what proportion of accommodating and restrictive responses a given town adopts. I consider differences in response across officials' roles and, finally, present a summary that explains the distribution of towns in relation to the model of local government response.

Counts of Restrictive and Accommodating Initiatives

The survey asked about seven distinct restrictive responses to immigrants and eighteen distinct accommodating responses. This imbalance does not reflect a bias inherent in the survey; rather, the survey asked about all restrictive and accommodating initiatives identified across the case studies and a comprehensive review of literature and media accounts. These reviews found more accommodating than restrictive initiatives. Given this imbalance, however, it is more appropriate to consider the proportion of accommodating or restrictive responses a given town embraced, which I will do in the subsequent section. For now, figure 3.6 displays the raw counts of restrictive and accommodating initiatives across towns. The count of restrictive initiatives includes English-only ordinances, cooperation with federal enforcement efforts, active immigration status checks by local police, backdoor restriction of housing and day labor, and explicitly restrictive ordinances.[9] As figure 3.6 indicates, 83 percent of towns report none of these restrictive responses. Seventeen percent report one or more, but only three towns (1 percent) report even as many as three restrictive responses—the maximum reported in the survey.

In contrast, only 15 percent of towns report none of the eighteen accommodating responses. These responses include bilingual hiring, acting as a sanctuary city or adopting a "don't ask, don't tell" approach to unauthorized status, never checking immigration status, designating

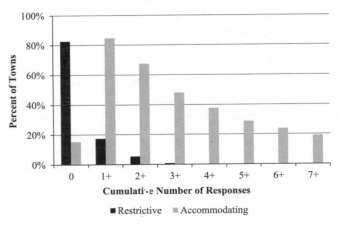

FIGURE 3.6. Cumulative proportion of towns reporting restriction and accommodation.

space or funding a center for day laborers, hiring and appointing immigrants or coethnics, having a designated immigrant liaison, and all of the symbolic and material accommodating practices.[10] Eighty-five percent of towns had implemented one or more of these practices, with nearly a quarter (24 percent) reporting six or more. Eight percent of towns report ten or more accommodating practices, with a maximum of fifteen reported by two towns. The modal number of accommodating responses is two, while on average towns report 3.5.

Proportion of Restrictive and Accommodating Initiatives

Figure 3.6 presents a clear pattern demonstrating the prevalence of accommodation and scarcity of restriction; however, a strict count of initiatives does not provide the most precise measure of the overall tenor of response. The counts could underreport the prevalence of restriction or accommodation since, as I will explain in greater detail, towns vary in the number of practices they could have reported based on which officials responded within a given town as well as how they responded to certain questions. I therefore construct indexes that measure the proportion of accommodating or restrictive practices towns report, allowing the denominator of the number they were asked about to vary. I first present these full indexes of accommodation and restriction, which measure the complete range of such practices across towns. These full indexes will be used further throughout the book, both in exploring what predicts accommodating and restrictive responses and in identifying how these responses shape local outcomes. In this chapter, in order to effectively compare the prevalence of accommodation and restriction, I present a more constrained accommodating index, which includes practices more directly comparable to the restrictive practices.

Figure 3.7 lists the practices included in the full accommodating and restrictive indexes, all of which extend beyond compliance with federal mandates. The restrictive index consists of three practices that all officials were asked about, listed at the bottom of figure 3.7 (English-only policies, explicitly restrictive ordinances, and cooperating in federal immigration enforcement); one practice that only police chiefs were asked about (immigration status checks); and two practices that only city hall officials were asked about (hiring housing inspectors and considering or passing zoning ordinances in response to immigration). Only towns that reported the presence of day laborers could respond to the ques-

Accommodating Index Practices
• *Design hiring to attract bilingual candidates.*
• *Sanctuary city or "do not ask, do not tell" policy regarding unauthorized.*
• *Designate employee to liaise with immigrants.*
• *Support hiring area or center for day laborers.* *
• *Immigration status checks not conducted by police (P)* *
• Recruit immigrant ethnic group to serve on boards (CH).
• *Appoint immigrant or coethnic to elected vacancy (CH).*
• Hire immigrants or coethnics (CH).
• *Establish immigrant advisory council (CH).*
• Issue resolutions in support of immigrants (CH).
• Host events celebrating diversity (CH).
• Host events promoting intercultural interaction (CH).
• Educate the public about immigrants (CH).
• *Provide funding for immigrant organizations or activities (CH).*
• Provide in-kind resources for immigrant organizations or activities (CH).
• *Develop social service programs for immigrants (CH).*
• *Restructure social service programs for immigrants (CH).*
• *Establish office for immigrant services (CH).*

Restrictive Index Practices
• English-only or official English policy.
• Consider or pass ordinance to deter unauthorized.
• Cooperate in federal immigration enforcement.
• Enforce policy forbidding day labor assemblages.*
• Immigrant status checks upon reasonable suspicion (P).*
• Hire housing inspectors in response to immigrants (CH).*
• Consider zoning ordinances in response to immigrants (CH).*

FIGURE 3.7. Accommodating and restrictive indexes.

Note: Practices marked with an asterisk were asked only of a subset of respondents, depending on their response to a previous question. Practices labeled (P) were asked only of police chief respondents, while those labeled (CH) were asked only of city hall respondents (city managers, city councilors, and mayors). Practices in italics are included in the constrained accommodating index.

tion about forbidding day laborers' gatherings, while only towns that reported housing-related problems could respond to the housing inspection and zoning questions. Thus the restrictive index consists of the proportion of restrictive practices the town reports, allowing the denominator to vary based on the number of restrictive practices the town was asked about.

Likewise, the accommodating index includes three practices that all officials were asked about (designing hiring to attract bilingual employees, having a "don't ask, don't tell" or sanctuary city policy, and designating an employee as a liaison for immigrants); one practice that only police chiefs were asked about (immigration status checks); and thirteen practices that only city hall officials were asked about. The accommodating index includes one practice—funding or hosting a day labor center—that only towns that reported having day laborers were asked about. In towns where both the police chief and at least one city hall official responded, which also had day labor presence (17 percent of towns), the accommodating index represents the percentage of the eighteen total accommodating practices the town reported. Otherwise the number of accommodating practices the town could have reported is less than eighteen. For instance, in towns in which only a police chief responded (21 percent), the town could report a maximum of five accommodating practices. In subsequent chapters I address the variation in the index, which is primarily due to which officials responded in a given town, by controlling for towns where only a police chief or only a city hall representative responded. For now, however, the indexes offer a gauge of towns' accommodating and restrictive practices that takes into account variation in what towns were asked about.

Looking first to the full accommodating index, 15 percent of towns report no accommodating practices, just under half report some accommodating practices (up to a quarter of those they were asked about), and 39 percent report more than a quarter of the accommodating practices they were asked about. On average, towns report 25 percent of the accommodating practices they were asked about, though the scale ranges from a low of zero to a high of 83 percent. Clearly the vast majority of towns engage in at least some accommodating practices, with nearly 40 percent accommodating immigrants relatively actively by implementing more than a quarter of practices they were asked about.

Before we can compare accommodating and restrictive activity, however, it is important to consider the imbalance in the number of accommodating and restrictive practices queried. This imbalance would be a particular problem if the accommodating initiatives were relatively easy to implement while the restrictive initiatives required greater capacity or effort. Indeed, some of the accommodating practices are more symbolic, such as hosting events, or could be carried out by a single official, such as recruiting immigrants to serve on boards or commissions. The restrictive practices, on the other hand, all require some deliberation and collective decision making. Thus, in order to allow for a fair comparison of the level of accommodating and restrictive activity across towns, for the rest of the chapter I will discuss a more constrained accommodating index, which includes only those eleven accommodating responses that arguably require an equivalent degree of deliberation and collective decision making. Thus I have excluded primarily symbolic gestures, such as holding events and issuing public information or resolutions, to concentrate on bilingual hiring practices, limited immigration enforcement policies, concrete hiring and appointments to advance immigrant inclusion (liaisons, vacancy appointments, and immigrant advisory councils), and the designation of funding or innovations to social service programs to serve immigrants or day laborers. In figure 3.7, italicized responses constitute the more constrained accommodating index.[11]

Figures 3.8 and 3.9 demonstrate the proportion of restrictive and accommodating practices reported. As figure 3.8 indicates, in total, 83 percent of towns report no restrictive practices, 11 percent report up to a quarter of those restrictive practices they were asked about, and only 6 percent report more than a quarter of them. In figure 3.9, by contrast, 43 percent of towns report none of the more strenuous accommodating practices in the constrained index, while just over a third report up to a quarter of the accommodating practices they were asked about. Eighteen percent report implementing more than a quarter but fewer than half of these accommodating practices, and 5 percent of towns report implementing half or more.

Yet as figures 3.8 and 3.9 also show, different types of officials report somewhat different degrees of restriction and accommodation. In two-sided t-tests, elected officials report marginally but statistically significantly greater restriction, with 23 percent of elected officials reporting at least some restrictive practices, compared with 15 percent of police chiefs and 12 percent of city managers. In keeping with earlier findings (Lewis and Ramakrishnan 2007), police chiefs report significantly higher levels of accommodation, with 39 percent reporting more than a quarter of accommodating practices compared with 27 percent of elected officials and 22 percent of city managers. These variations across officials are due in part to the construction of the indexes and in part to systematic differences in the way different types of officials responded.

Chapter 5 will explore in greater detail how responses to immigrants differ systematically across types of officials. For now, however, it is

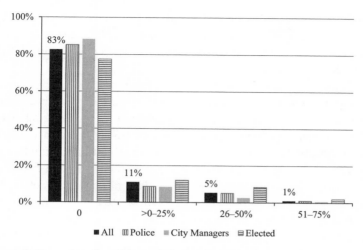

FIGURE 3.8. Proportion of possible restrictive practices reported.

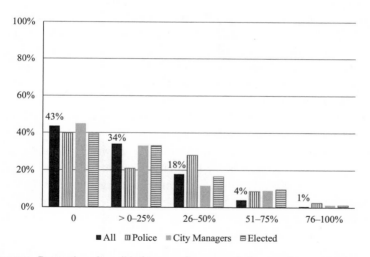

FIGURE 3.9. Proportion of possible (strenuous) accommodating practices reported.

worth noting that in two-sided *t*-tests police chiefs report statistically greater accommodation on five of thirty-nine response variables examined here. Police chiefs are more likely than city hall officials to report accepting foreign consular identification cards and more likely to say their town follows an informal "don't ask, don't tell" policy regarding unauthorized status. In contrast to city hall officials, they report translating materials more routinely and are more likely to have a designated immigrant liaison. They are also more likely to say they offer bilingual employees extra pay.

In contrast, elected officials differ from appointed officials (police chiefs and city managers) on five variables, but not in a consistent direction with respect to the underlying variables. Indeed, differing elected responses seem to be largely associated with lack of knowledge. Elected officials, particularly city councilors, expressed more uncertainty about responses to immigrants than did appointed officials. In one example of a differing elected response likely due to lack of knowledge, elected officials were more likely than appointed officials to report that their town operated a jail (as opposed to sending arrestees to a county facility). In responding to a subsequent question about Secure Communities, elected officials were systematically less likely to report having a local antidetainer policy and systematically more likely to report active participation in the program as opposed to mere compliance. In two-sided t-tests, elected officials were significantly more likely than appointed officials to report that bilingual job candidates received extra points in the hiring process but systematically less likely to report that bilingual staff members get extra pay. Since police chiefs and city managers deal more directly with facilities and hiring, it is likely that these discrepancies are due to a lack of knowledge among elected officials.[12]

For the most part, appointed city managers and elected city councilors and mayors reported similar levels of government inclusion and symbolic and material accommodation practices; however, elected officials were systematically more likely than city managers to report that their towns provided in-kind resources to immigrant organizations. In the aggregate, however, as figure 3.8 shows, elected officials were more likely to report at least some restrictive practices than were the appointed city managers and police chiefs.

These differences across officials will receive further attention in subsequent chapters. Nonetheless, the pattern of limited restriction and prevalent inaction and accommodation remains whether examining townwide responses or responses by type of official. Since police chiefs were more likely to respond to the survey and more likely to report accommodation, this analysis may somewhat overstate the prevalence of accommodation. Overall, however, the pattern of response across all officials is stark: substantial inaction, prevalent accommodation, and rare restriction.

Comparing Accommodating, Inactive, and Restrictive Responses

Clearly, towns are more likely to report accommodating practices than restrictive practices, regardless of the officials who respond in a given town. That said, examining accommodating and restrictive practices separately leaves some questions unanswered. What proportion of towns remain entirely inactive—pursuing neither accommodating nor restrictive practices? Are some towns actively pursuing both accommodating and restrictive practices? In addressing these questions, I employ the restrictive index and constrained accommodating index, since these indexes include only practices that require deliberation and collective decision making and thus allow for a fair comparison.

Figure 3.10 identifies towns that report only restrictive practices and no accommodating practices, towns that remain entirely inactive with respect to these restrictive and accommodating practices, towns that report only accommodating practices and no restrictive measures, and towns that report both accommodation and restriction. Towns reporting only restriction or only accommodation are divided into those reporting up to a quarter of that category of practices and those reporting more than a quarter. Reporting more than a quarter of accommodating or restrictive practices can be considered highly accommodating or restrictive, since the average level of restriction among towns that have implemented any restrictive activities is 27 percent, while the average level of accommodation for towns that have implemented some accommodation practices is 29 percent.

The figure demonstrates the low incidence of restriction and relatively high incidence of inaction and accommodation while also showing that relatively few towns report both actively restrictive and actively accommodating practices. Five percent of towns (twenty-two towns) report only restrictive practices, with 2 percent (nine towns) reporting more than a quarter of the restrictive practices they were asked about. The most restrictive among these highly restrictive towns, in Riverside County, California, reported hiring housing inspectors and passing housing ordinances in response to immigrants as well as passing another ordinance intended to deflect unauthorized immigrants from settling

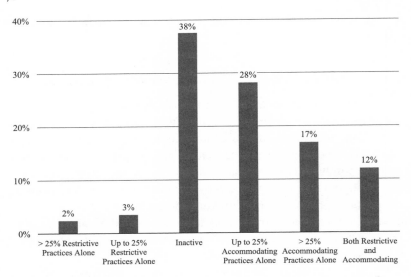

FIGURE 3.10. Distribution of inaction, accommodation, and restriction across towns.

there. This town has employees that can provide foreign-language interpretation and also reported hiring immigrants or coethnics in local government, but it had implemented none of the more strenuous accommodating practices.

Toward the right-hand side of the figure, a collective plurality of
45 percent (168 towns) reported only accommodating measures and no
restriction. Seventeen percent (sixty-three towns) reported more than
a quarter of the strenuous accommodating practices they were asked
about. One of the most accommodating among these highly accommodating towns was a city in the Boston metropolitan area that reported six
of the eleven strenuous accommodating measures as well as seven less
strenuous ones.

In addition to these solely restrictive and accommodating locales,
38 percent of towns (140 towns) report no restrictive practices and none
of the more strenuous accommodating measures. Keep in mind, however, that the constrained accommodating index includes only practices
that extend beyond mere compliance with federal requirements and also
require deliberation and collective decision making. Of the 140 towns
that report none of these practices, two-thirds had in-house interpretation capacities. Moreover, almost two-thirds (64 percent) reported at
least some of the less strenuous accommodating practices, such as host-

ing events or recruiting immigrants or coethnics to serve on boards. Though we see relatively high levels of inaction, officials in most of these towns are complying with federal regulations, and many are displaying some degree of accommodation. If we take into account the less strenuous accommodating measures, only 13 percent (fifty towns) report none of the accommodating and none of the restrictive measures.

Finally, 12 percent (forty-three towns) report both restrictive practices and some of the more strenuous accommodating practices. Just under half (twenty towns) are more accommodating than restrictive, eighteen are more restrictive than accommodating, and the rest report an equal proportion of accommodation and restriction. Taking into account the less strenuous accommodating measures, thirty towns are more accommodating than restrictive, while only thirteen are more restrictive than accommodating. Some of the towns pursuing both accommodation and restriction were accommodating cities in restrictive states. For instance, an Arizona town reported designing hiring to attract bilingual employees and developing social service programs for immigrants along with four less strenuous accommodating practices. At the same time, the town's police force conducts immigration status checks in accordance with Arizona's SB1070. In another example, a Georgia town reported providing funding to immigrant organizations, both developing and restructuring social services to meet immigrant needs, and eight other less strenuous accommodating practices. At the same time, however, the town reported hiring housing inspectors and passing housing ordinances in response to immigrant settlement. For the most part, towns that pursue both accommodation and restriction could be classified as leaning toward one or the other. Only nine towns (2 percent) report high levels of both accommodation and restriction, and only five (1 percent) are equally accommodating and restrictive.

Applying these proportions to the model of local government response in figure 3.11, 38 percent of responding towns fall between compliance and inaction; a cumulative 45 percent (168 towns) are solely accommodating; 5 percent pursue both accommodation and restriction but are more accommodating than restrictive; another 5 percent pursue both strategies but are more restrictive than accommodating; and only 5 percent (twenty-two towns) are solely restrictive. Another 1 percent (five towns) do not fit neatly into the categories presented here because they are equally accommodating and restrictive.

The shaded row in figure 3.11 presents the distribution of towns

High Restrict. Alone	Low Restriction Alone	More Restrict. than Accom.	Compliant to Inactive		More Accom. than Restrict.	Low Accom. Alone	High Accom. Alone
2%	3%	5%	38%		5%	28%	17%
4%	3%	4%	48%		3%	23%	14%

FIGURE 3.11. Distribution of inaction, accommodation, and restriction on the model of municipal response.

Note: The first row represents the unweighted results from the MRIS sample, while the second represents the results from the MRIS weighted back to the sample frame. The weighted results take into account the prevalence of smaller (often less active) towns and thte relative dearth of larger (often more active) ones. In each row, 1 percent of towns are not represented since they report equal proportions of accommodating and restrictive practices and therefore cannot be easily classified.

weighted back to the sampling frame. That is, these proroportions estimate the overall distribution of small to midsize towns' responses to immigrants nationwide, taking into account the relative prevalence of small towns.[13] Not surprisingly, smaller towns are less active in responding to immigrants, such that just under half of small to midsize immigrant destinations (48 percent) fall into the compliant to inactive category. Thirty-seven percent of towns remain solely accommodating. Restriction remains rare, with only 7 percent of towns reporting solely restrictive responses. Keep in mind, of course, that figure 3.11 draws on the constrained accommodating measure including only the eleven more strenuous accommodating practices. Many towns identified as inactive here are in fact implementing some of the less strenuous accommodating measures.

Conclusion

Part 1 of the book makes it clear that both the four case study cities and the nationwide MRIS indicate that US towns and cities are more likely to accommodate immigrants than to restrict them. Case study evidence suggests a general tendency toward accommodation over time across three new destinations—Elgin, Lewiston, and Wausau—despite episodes of restriction. Yakima, however, remained largely inactive in ways that made it substantively more restrictive. Examining small to midsize immigrant destinations nationwide, the MRIS demonstrates that towns are much more likely to accommodate immigrants than to undertake any restrictive practices. Nonetheless, many towns remain relatively inactive in response to immigrants, a situation that deserves greater attention. Lack of action to adjust to linguistic and cultural differences amid growing immigration can constrict the opportunities of local immigrants, as the example of Yakima demonstrates.

Many observers would have predicted that these small to midsize US towns and cities would be restrictive toward immigrants, particularly if they are new destinations like 36 percent of the towns surveyed here. These local governments are inexperienced in serving immigrants and may accrue short-term costs in doing so. Moreover, restrictive policies toward immigrants are popular among a substantial portion of the electorate, as Donald Trump's 2016 presidential victory demonstrates. Given these realities, why have so many localities chosen accommodation? Moreover, what kinds of towns pursue accommodation, and what distinguishes the small number of towns that pursue restriction? Finally, how do differences across local actors—police chiefs, city managers, and elected officials—affect the local context of reception? Part 2 turns to these questions in chapters 4 and 5. Of course, the MRIS findings represent only a snapshot of local responses to immigrants from 2014 to 2015. Examining the four case study cities and ninety-four once restrictive cities in chapter 6 allows me to identify when restrictive responses emerge and how they tend to be scaled back over time. In summary, however, part 1 illustrates that both the case studies and the survey data provide evidence that many local governments are choosing to accommodate immigrants while few attempt to exclude them.

PART II

Explaining Local Government Responses to Immigrants

CHAPTER FOUR

Federal Policies, National Politics, and Local Understanding of Immigrants

Mexicans were perceived as being here as cheap labor but not part of the social fabric and not welcome to be part of the social fabric. Here and gone. — Nonprofit executive, Yakima

Since the mid-twentieth century, Latino migrant workers have been a fixture in Yakima Valley apple orchards and hop fields. Over the years, farmworkers settled in the southern part of the valley, but until the mid-1980s the City of Yakima had a Hispanic population of only 5 percent. Even as the Latino population grew to more than a third of the city's population by 2000, the local government was so accustomed to the seasonal presence of Latino migrants that the growing resident immigrant population slipped "under the radar screen," as one businessman put it. In part as a result, Yakima remained largely inactive in response to its growing immigrant population. The city shifted to adopt some accommodating measures only as local leaders came to understand and define immigrants differently. As Yakima's Latino population grew and more skilled, bilingual, bicultural Latinos emerged, leaders transitioned from seeing Latinos as a transient workforce that was a "necessary evil" for the agricultural industry to defining the newcomers as valuable economic contributors.[1] Yakima's experience demonstrates that how immigrants are framed locally powerfully shapes municipal responses.

As immigrants disperse across the United States, some cities have actively welcomed them while others have actively sought to repel them.

Part 1 shows that accommodating immigrants is much more prevalent, but a few towns are restrictive and many remain inactive. What explains these disparate municipal responses to immigrants? Drawing on the theory described in the introduction, this chapter argues that municipal responses to immigrants depend on which frames surrounding immigrants are dominant among local officials (Williamson 2011; de Graauw, Gleeson, and Bloemraad 2013).

Theories across the social sciences emphasize that the ways groups are framed shape public views (Nelson and Kinder 1996; Chong and Druckman 2007). Social policies contribute to the framing of groups as deserving or undeserving, setting the stage for subsequent policy responses to these groups (Mettler and Soss 2004; Schneider and Ingram 2005). Given immigrants' liminal status, they are particularly vulnerable to elite framing that can cast them as clients or outsiders, contributors or lawbreakers (Newton 2005).

In both the case studies and the survey, state and federal policies and national political discourse are particularly influential in shaping frames of immigrants and directing the tenor of response (Hopkins 2010; Marrow 2011). In Lewiston and Wausau, local officials experienced federal refugee resettlement policies that define immigrants as clients of social programs and constrain officials to serve them, setting these towns on a path toward greater accommodation. In Elgin, national Republican political discourse surrounding the perils of unauthorized immigration defined local immigrants as "illegal aliens" and shifted responses somewhat toward restriction. But the influence of federal policies and national politics also depends on local demographic, economic, and partisan characteristics. In Yakima, for instance, national debates about unauthorized immigration did not reverse increasing moves toward accommodation, since the city's reliance on immigrant farmworkers made overtly restrictive responses out of the question. The juxtaposition of Elgin and Yakima, along with the other cases, reveals that external forces like federal policies and national politics interact with internal characteristics to influence definitions of immigrants and thereby shift responses.

Evidence from the MRIS further illustrates that how immigrants are framed locally shapes municipal practices, both in the degree of action and in the tenor of response. With respect to degree, definitions of immigrants shape *whether* local officials act in response. If members of the local foreign-born population are perceived as not residents or as not immigrants, action in response to immigrants is unlikely. Immigrants' visibility, along with local capacity, shapes whether local governments respond to them or remain inactive. As for the tenor of response, definitions of immigrants shape *how* local officials respond—with restriction or with accommodation.

These findings contribute in several ways to our understanding of municipal responses to immigrants. First, I move beyond analysis of what explains rare formal ordinances, at the extremes of local response, to analyze the factors predicting more prevalent informal practices in response to immigrants. Second, I identify a key mechanism that explains how various factors shape responses, namely by shifting local frames of immigrants. Third, I distinguish between factors predicting the degree of local response—whether municipalities are active in responding to immigrants—and factors shifting the tenor of response—whether accommodating or restrictive. Last, my findings help to resolve the debate surrounding whether local responses to immigrants stem from ethnic threat or from partisanship (Hopkins 2010; Ramakrishnan and Wong 2010; Walker and Leitner 2011; Steil and Vasi 2014; Gulasekaram and Ramakrishnan 2015), demonstrating that partisanship does shape responses but factors associated with ethnic threat do not.

I first describe these earlier debates, identifying factors other scholars have considered important in shaping local responses to immigrants. I then draw on evidence from the cases to demonstrate that the crucial mechanism in shaping municipal responses is how immigrants are framed locally. I show that federal policies and national political discourse are particularly influential in that process. Finally, I turn to the survey data, which allows to me to test these findings and identify the relative importance of various factors in defining immigrants and shaping municipal responses.

Previous Explanations of Local Government Response to Immigrants

Scholarship examining variation in local government responses to immigrants has concentrated largely on the incidence of restrictive or accommodating ordinances, which have been passed in only two hundred or so of the thousands of immigrant destinations nationwide (Steil and Vasi 2014). One point of view argues that places with more rapidly growing foreign-born populations are more likely to consider or pass restrictive ordinances, particularly when immigration is salient nationally (Hopkins 2010). In line with classic theories of conflict or ethnic threat (Key 1949; Blalock 1967), places with fast-growing immigrant populations may experience competition or challenges associated with immigrants that precipitate restrictive action. A contrasting school of thought argues that restrictive responses are a political matter largely unrelated to demographic change (Ramakrishnan and Wong 2010; Gulasekaram and Ramakrishnan 2015). These scholars argue that, particularly from 2006 to 2008, national political entrepreneurs strategically pushed restrictive efforts to the local level, where they were picked up in Republican strongholds. At least one article finds that both demographic change and partisanship contribute to the incidence of restriction (Walker and Leitner 2011). Others argue that while threatened responses are not inevitable amid growing ethnic diversity, in places with rapidly growing Latino populations officials can frame concerns about this population to support restrictive immigration ordinances (Steil and Vasi 2014).[2] The relative importance of ethnic demographic change and partisanship in prompting restrictive municipal responses remains a matter of debate.

With respect to accommodating ordinances, several studies agree that larger, more Democratic cities, in which the foreign-born and co-ethnics have more influence, are more likely to welcome immigrants (Ramakrishnan and Wong 2010; Steil and Vasi 2014). Thus, though not all accounts agree that Republican partisanship is associated with restriction, previous analyses generally concur that more Democratic places are more likely to accommodate. Previous analyses also offer an initial indication that city administrative capacity may matter in shaping local responses. Larger cities are more likely to pass both restrictive and accommodating ordinances (Ramakrishnan and Wong 2010; Steil and Vasi 2014; Gulasekaram and Ramakrishnan 2015).

Two studies examining local practices rather than formal ordinances underline that immigrant visibility shapes responses, though to varying degrees partisanship also plays a role. An examination of California immigrant destinations in 2003 found that larger cities with larger foreign-born populations were more likely to implement several accommodating practices, while more conservative cities were less likely to accommodate in some ways (Ramakrishnan and Lewis 2005). More recently, a 2008 survey of police chiefs in immigrant destinations of more than 65,000 residents found that a larger foreign-born population is associated with less restrictive police policies, while foreign-born growth is unrelated to local immigration policing. Partisanship is not a direct contributor to city policies; however, under mayor-council systems in more Republican places, police tend to enforce more restrictive policies. Proximity to the Mexican border also contributes to more restrictive policies, while the presence of Latino elected officials and police chiefs supports accommodation (Lewis et al. 2013). Recent studies of local police practices toward immigrants offer evidence that factors typically associated with ethnic threat, such as demographic change, unemployment, and crime, are not associated with restrictive responses and indeed, if anything, tend to be associated with more accommodation (Provine et al. 2016).

All these studies offer important insight into the factors shaping local responses, though most have focused only on ordinances—rare responses at the extremes. Several studies have hinted that how immigrants are defined locally plays a key role in shaping local responses, whether through the influence of national political discourse (Hopkins 2010), national issue entrepreneurs (Gulasekaram and Ramakrishnan 2015), or local political opportunists (Steil and Vasi 2014; see also de Graauw, Gleeson, and Bloemraad 2013). In the analysis that follows, the juxtaposition of the four case study cities and the survey allows me to explore how local understandings of immigrants develop and to test whether factors that are influential across the four cases apply on a national scale. In particular, the cases reveal that external cues from federal and state policies and national political discourse are especially influential in shaping the tenor of local response.

External Policies, Local Responses

The literature on "policy feedbacks" demonstrates that policies provide political actors with resources, incentives, and interpretive tools that influence their understanding of the world (Pierson 1993). Resources and incentives introduced by policies can encourage political actors to devote resources to a particular arena and develop capacity in it. The interpretations or frames conveyed by policies can define groups as insiders or outsiders, deserving or undeserving (Mettler and Soss 2004). Certain federal and state policies governing the local treatment of immigrants require municipal officials to devote resources to immigrants and build capacity to serve them while simultaneously framing them as clients.

At times federal and state policies provide local governments with resources or technical assistance, which enhances local capacity to serve
immigrants. Even more important, however, federal and state policies
that require service to immigrants provide a symbolic endorsement of
incorporation efforts and prescribe a role for local government. These
external policies both tell local officials what to do (instrumental message) and shape what they believe (symbolic message) (Schneider and Ingram 1997; Marschall, Rigby, and Jenkins 2011). The frames conveyed
by these policies can become institutionalized and persist over time in a
path-dependent fashion (Pierson 2000; Bleich 2002). In combination, the
requirements and symbolic endorsement of federal policies set localities
on a path toward accommodation. On the other hand, to the extent that
local officials are governed by restrictive policies toward immigrants,
these policies directly frame immigrants as nonclients and indirectly ac-
tivate regulatory roles, setting localities on a path toward inaction or restriction (Marrow 2011).

In the United States, immigrant legal status—whether refugee, legal
permanent resident, or unauthorized—strongly shapes local government
responsibilities toward newcomers. Comparing local government responses in refugee and nonrefugee destinations offers a key test of the
power of federal policies to shape local government responses. Since the
1980 Refugee Act, US refugee resettlement policy has allocated initial
direct payments to refugees and additional funds to states for providing
them with services. Refugee Cash Assistance gives direct assistance to
refugees for a limited time, now eight months. The federal government
reimburses states for the cost of educating and providing health care to
refugees and supplies some resources aimed at encouraging community
integration. States, in turn, contract out resettlement responsibilities to
voluntary agencies. Beyond these services, the federal Office of Refugee
Resettlement makes direct grants to refugee mutual assistance associations (MAAs) that provide linguistically and culturally specific services.
Through these programs, US refugee resettlement policy has created a
bureaucracy at the federal and state levels specifically aimed at integration, a network of voluntary agencies that support this aim, and a "grassroots infrastructure" of refugee MAAs (Bloemraad 2006, 132).

In addition to refugee-specific aid, refugees are often eligible for locally administered federal aid that even some legal immigrants cannot
access. Refugees' eligibility for programs and aid frames this subset of
immigrants as local government clients, thereby encouraging accommo-

dation. A variety of scholars have documented that federal refugee status prompts more receptive responses from local officials and the public (Pedraza-Bailey 1985; Horton 2004; Bloemraad 2006). Comparing the refugee destination of Portland, Maine, with the Latino immigrant destination of Danbury, Connecticut, Peggy Levitt and her colleagues found that service providers in Portland perceive refugees as a "deserving poor" in need of aid, while their counterparts in Danbury define nonrefugee immigrants as "cultural invaders who overuse services and resources" (Jaworsky et al. 2012).

Indeed, nonrefugee immigrants are often excluded from federal aid. Welfare reform in 1996 defined even legally present immigrants as ineligible for most forms of federal aid for their first five years of US residence unless states choose to cover them independently. Moreover, the United States lacks comprehensive programs aimed at nonrefugee immigrant incorporation (Gelatt and Fix 2007). Federal policies governing unauthorized immigrants are, of course, even more restrictive, with specific federal agencies working to apprehend them. Thus, immigrants' ineligibility for aid and the precarious position of unauthorized immigrants can frame nonrefugee immigrants as nonclients and spur local government inaction or restriction.

The influence of these federal policies in shaping local government responses is evident both across Lewiston, Wausau, Elgin, and Yakima and across agencies within the cities. If differences in federal policies toward refugees and nonrefugee immigrants shape local government responses, we would expect to see more active and accommodating responses in Lewiston and Wausau—refugee destinations—than in Elgin and Yakima, where primarily Latino immigrants live. Where federal policies mandate service to immigrants regardless of legal status, such as in the public schools, we would expect similar responses across the cities. Where federal policies prescribe different treatment for refugees and other immigrants, such as in social services, we could expect to find different responses across the cities. Further, if federal policies strongly shape the subsequent trajectory of local responses, we would expect more favorable responses in Elgin than in Yakima, since Elgin settled a small population of Laotian refugees in the late 1970s and early 1980s and this experience could "spill over" to affect nonrefugee immigrants locally (Anderson 2008). Indeed, these predictions fit the pattern of findings across the cases.

In Lewiston and Wausau, federal policies governing refugee resettlement encouraged local government administrators to become partners in incorporation efforts. The experience of serving refugees defined immigrants as clients and activated professional service norms that encouraged more accommodating responses down the line (see also Lewis and Ramakrishnan 2007; Jones-Correa 2008; and Marrow 2011 on bureaucratic incorporation). For instance, Wausau's Marathon County welfare office played a key role in serving the Hmong. A county employee described how her experience serving the Hmong through a federal program made her more active in accommodating refugees:

> When I took the job with county government I administered [an element of a federal program]. . . . And I saw it was essential that I learn a lot more. I knew some things about the culture. I'd done some reading, but I felt I really had to have a much deeper level of understanding of family structure, of culture, of history, and of current pressures on those families before I could direct a staff that would provide good services to them.

In Lewiston, both federal and state policies encouraged local government accommodation of Somalis. As I mentioned in chapter 2, Maine's General Assistance policy, which requires local aid to all residents who fall below an income threshold, meant that Lewiston's Department of Social Services played a key role in accommodating Somali newcomers. The combination of federal refugee policies and state rules governing General Assistance ensured that Lewiston officials were legally obligated to serve them. Once officials began to fulfill these requirements, they saw refugees as clients, and their professional norms led them to pursue additional accommodating strategies. One city employee described this transition from legal obligation to professional mission: "We have assumed that responsibility which is legally ours, and we want to do the best. We want to do more than just the legal minimum, because it isn't the legal minimum that's going to make things better in the long run."

In contrast, policies that excluded nonrefugee immigrants in Elgin and Yakima framed Latino immigrants as not being clients of local government agencies, particularly if they lacked legal status. In Elgin, other factors intervened to encourage accommodating responses without policy mandates. In Yakima, though, the lack of a mandated role for most local government agencies contributed to inaction.

Where federal policies define immigrants of all statuses as eligible for services, however, we see similar responses across the four cities. Since federal policy requires public schools to educate immigrants of all legal statuses, public educators across the destinations demonstrated a commitment to serving immigrant children related to both legal obligations and their professional service mission. For instance, an educator in Elgin said she acted in response to both professional obligation and federal policy mandates in establishing a school newcomer center for immigrants: "Not just because it's the right thing to do, but No Child Left Behind is now dictating." Similar accommodating responses in public schools across the four destinations demonstrate how inclusive federal and state policies define immigrants as local clients and set municipal agencies on a path toward greater accommodation.

The power of federal policies in shaping subsequent local responses is also evident in the way the presence of refugees affects the prospects of other local immigrant groups. In both Lewiston and Wausau, the institutional apparatus local governments were required to develop to serve refugees is now deployed to serve small Latino populations. Even in Elgin, where the size of the Latino population dwarfs that of the Laotian refugees, local leaders report that serving Laotians in the 1980s enabled later accommodation of Hispanic immigrants. Other studies have shown that refugee resettlement programs build local organizational capacity that "spills over" to support immigrants' broader political mobilization (Anderson 2008). Likewise, I find that the experience of serving immigrants through refugee resettlement spills over to encourage broader local government efforts at immigrant accommodation.

An advocate for the small Latino population in the Lewiston area observed that serving the Somali population had prompted the government to reach out to Latinos. Similarly, in Wausau and Elgin, serving refugees contributed to local capacity and willingness to accommodate Latinos. In 2006 Wausau's leaders worked with Latinos to develop a local Hispanic organization, which according to a white nonprofit executive was "patterned after the Hmong association here in town." A Wausau politician reported that the diversity commission developed to address Hmong refugee issues is now directing its attention to the Hispanic population. In Elgin, the adult ELL infrastructure developed to serve Laotians now caters to Latinos. Community outreach mechanisms created for Laotian refugees are also deployed to serve Latinos. A Latino civic leader explained:

The police department already had a Laotian outreach worker. And so there
was kind of a template, if you will, for community outreach from the Laotian side. . . . [T]he chief of police who saw success with the Laotian outreach
worker decided, you know what? I need one for Latinos.

Evidence of "spillover" from serving refugees into serving Latino immigrants provides compelling evidence that federal policies that involve localities in serving immigrants define the foreign-born as deserving clients and place localities on a path toward accommodation.

National Political Discourse, Local Restriction

In addition to the powerful role of federal policies in local definitions of
immigrants as clients, national political rhetoric is an additional external
factor shaping local responses (Hopkins 2010; Ramakrishnan and Wong
2010; Gulasekaram and Ramakrishnan 2015). In recent years Democratic and Republican members of Congress have diverged on immigration policy, with Republicans increasingly committed to immigration
restriction (Abrajano and Hajnal 2015). With the rise of the Tea Party
through to the presidency of Donald Trump, cracking down on unauthorized immigrants has increasingly taken center stage in the Republican platform (Skocpol and Williamson 2012; Parker and Barreto 2014).
Evidence from the cases allows me to consider how Republican political
rhetoric surrounding immigration affects localities with different partisan and demographic compositions. National political rhetoric proved
particularly influential in historically Republican Elgin, with its growing
Latino immigrant population.

While Elgin has historically leaned Republican, given rapid subur-
banization and redistricting the city recently shows some signs of shifting to the left. In the eight presidential elections from 1988 to 2016, Kane
County voters awarded a plurality of votes to the Republican candidate
in every year except 2008 and 2012, when they supported Illinois resident Barack Obama, and in 2016 when they supported Hillary Clinton
(CQ Voting and Elections). In terms of city offices, which are officially
nonpartisan, local historian Mike Alft (2000) reports that twenty-six of
the city's first thirty-three mayors were Republicans. Thus Elgin is historically Republican, with some evidence of a growing Democratic populace. Yakima, in contrast, has been and continues to be a staunchly

Republican city. In the eight presidential elections from 1988 to 2016, a plurality of Yakima voters supported the Republican candidate at a rate that exceeded the nation's by an average of seven percentage points (CQ Voting and Elections).

Wausau is a swing jurisdiction, influenced by both midwestern conservatism and Wisconsin's progressive elements (Cramer 2016). In the past eight presidential elections, Marathon County voters have supported the Democratic candidate four times and the Republican candidate four times, though in 2016 they were decisive in their support for President Trump, awarding him 56 percent of the vote. They likewise awarded Republican governor Scott Walker a clear majority in 2010 and 2014, suggesting a tilt toward the right (CQ Voting and Elections).

Lewiston has long been a Democratic stronghold, though it is showing recent signs of tilting Republican. In the eight presidential elections from 1988 to 2016, Androscoggin County voters supported Democrats every cycle save two: in 1988, when George H. W. Bush won by a slight margin, and in 2016, when President Trump captured 52 percent of the vote. Lewiston also supported native son and Republican governor Paul LePage in 2010 and 2014 (CQ Voting and Elections). Perhaps indicative of the overall move toward the GOP outside major metropolitan areas (Cramer 2016), Yakima is staunchly Republican, Elgin is historically Republican but trending Democratic, Wausau is a swing jurisdiction tilting Republican, while Lewiston is historically Democratic but trending Republican.

Only in Elgin, however, with its historically Republican leanings and its rapidly growing Latino population, did the increasing salience of national Republican political discourse on unauthorized immigration foreground definitions of immigrants as "illegal aliens." This shift in the predominant local frame ultimately pressured local officials to take some restrictive action. In December 2005 the US House of Representatives passed a controversial immigration bill that, among other provisions, aimed to make unauthorized immigration a felony. The bill ultimately failed to gain traction in the Senate, but the severity of its provisions prompted both widespread anti-immigrant rhetoric and massive Latino rallies in cities nationwide (Bada et al. 2006), including both Elgin and Yakima.

In the spring of 2006, Latinos in Elgin participated both in local rallies and in demonstrations in nearby Chicago. On May 1, for instance, 1,500 Latinos and allies marched in Elgin, and the city sent at least fifteen busloads to a larger rally in Chicago (Moyer 2006; Polansek 2006).

Grassroots anti-immigration mobilization followed in early summer 2006. Activists report that witnessing the rallies brought ongoing concerns about local immigration to the fore. A leader in the local anti-immigration effort explained:

> When they started taking to the street, I said, I really gotta research this, I gotta figure out for myself what's going on there, and that's when I started looking at it, and saying, wow, there are 12 million here. Maybe more. And looking at the demographics of Elgin, looking at the way things have changed in the school district, it was fascinating to me how much it had changed just in ten years. And then of course once you start looking at it, you start noticing everything else. You know, the cars, and you look at the identity theft things going on, and the crime reports, and so forth.

Those supportive of local immigrants also felt that the percolation of national issues to the local level was mobilizing anti-immigrant animus. A nonprofit leader noted,

> I think when this issue of the immigrant population became a national political issue, you began to see more press in the local newspapers, you began to hear more folks kind of talking about it. . . . I think the awareness was raised in a way that caught everyone off guard, because we kind of jumped on the national bandwagon, where we saw it as a problem.

A local politician further highlighted how national rhetoric affected local constructions of immigrants as "illegal aliens":

> [The national immigration debate] has given rise to folks feeling that it's okay now to say hateful things in the guise of it being about illegal immigration. . . . Where it was never okay to say hateful things about groups or other cultures, now it's okay. And people are whis . . . they're not even whispering it. I mean, they'll blatantly say. We got an e-mail the other day that said, "I don't have a problem with Mexicans who are here legally, it's the illegal Mexicans that I have a problem with. Unfortunately, you can't tell the difference."

As national political discourse increasingly framed immigrants as "illegal aliens," these definitions were applied to Latino immigrants across the board in Elgin, resulting in the period of more restrictive responses described in chapter 2.

While national political discourse can therefore influence local responses, it is not necessarily determinative. How far external frames surrounding immigrants influence local responses depends on local demographic, economic, and partisan characteristics. Highly Republican Yakima also experienced both immigrant and anti-immigrant mobilization during the nationwide rallies in 2006, but the region's economic reliance on immigrants as agricultural laborers defused the influence of anti-immigration mobilization. Latino immigrants and their allies held at least four substantial rallies in Yakima, including one on May 1, 2006, that drew an estimated 10,000 protesters (Ward 2006). A preexisting anti-immigrant group called "Grassroots on Fire" mobilized a small number of supporters to respond to the immigration rallies, but their efforts failed to raise the issue of immigration enforcement to the city's agenda. Local leaders attributed the lack of anti-immigrant response to the centrality of Yakima's agricultural economy and its need for immigrant workers. An elected official explained:

> Personally I think that most rational-thinking people in our community don't spend a whole lot of time thinking about [unauthorized immigration]. We recognize, again, the role of the immigrant in our community. We still have a substantial agricultural-based economy. And so, I mean, to be honest with you, I think that in a lot of ways, we'd like the country to leave us alone so that we can continue to do what we do up here.

Although Yakima is the most Republican of the four cities and therefore ostensibly the most receptive to Republican national rhetoric surrounding immigration, the predominant local definition of immigrants as essential workers lessened the influence of rhetoric that emphasized unauthorized immigrant status. National political discourse can prompt restrictive mobilization in agricultural economies, but it is less likely to result in restrictive action, as Ramakrishnan and Wong (2010) also found.

Whereas in Elgin national Republican political discourse brought unauthorized immigration to the local agenda and recast immigrants as "illegal aliens," in Yakima economic vitality requires not acknowledging or addressing its unauthorized population. Likewise, Lewiston and Wausau were less susceptible to national political rhetoric promoting definitions of immigrants as "illegal aliens" because their immigrant population was non-Hispanic and primarily has refugee status. Informants from

Lewiston in January 2007 and from Wausau in August 2007 agreed that the recent national debates over unauthorized immigration did not affect local responses to Somali and Hmong refugees, who were perceived as present legally. In Wausau one educator explained, "I really haven't seen it here. . . . See, the Hmong are here legally." A nonprofit executive agreed: "I think that's more related to the Hispanic community. . . . So I think we haven't had much conversation around the whole immigration issue because it's been less evident here."

These responses suggest that Elgin's particular susceptibility to national political discourse surrounding "illegal aliens" could be attributed to ethnic threat associated with its large and fast-growing Latino population (Hopkins 2010; Steil and Vasi 2014). But Elgin's susceptibility could equally well relate to its historically Republican partisanship (Ramakrishnan and Wong 2010; Gulasekaram and Ramakrishnan 2015). The four case studies do not allow me to judge how far demographic change or partisanship explains Elgin's restrictive responses, but evidence from the MRIS will subsequently address this debate.

In sum, previous analyses of local immigrant-related ordinances and practices, coupled with findings from the case studies, enable us to make several predictions about the factors shaping variation in local responses to immigrants. First, as my cases suggest, external factors such as state and federal policies and national political discourse are influential in defining immigrants and shaping local responses. Second, several accounts have discussed how these national factors, particularly national discourse surrounding unauthorized immigrants, interact with local characteristics such as demographic change and partisanship to shape responses. Third, these accounts offer some preliminary evidence that administrative capacity found in larger cities, as well as immigrant visibility, is associated with more active responses to immigrants. Finally, these accounts also suggest the need to consider how immigrant or co-ethnic political influence shapes accommodation, as well as the role of key local contextual characteristics such as form of government and economic characteristics.

Identifying Measures Predicting Local Responses

To what extent do these factors shape municipal responses to immigrants nationwide? The analysis that follows employs multivariate regression techniques to identify the influence of these various factors while holding other contributors constant. In particular I examine four key dependent variables generated from the MRIS to measure the degree and tenor of local response. For degree, I employ a variable accounting for whether a town has remained completely inactive. Thirteen percent of towns report none of the accommodating and none of the restrictive practices introduced in chapter 3, remaining completely inactive in response to immigrants. Therefore I first consider the factors associated with taking no action. The measure of inactivity is a dichotomous variable equal to one when the town has implemented no accommodating and no restrictive practices.

For tenor, I examine an index of restriction, the full index of accommodation, and a variable that measures towns' enforcement responses to unauthorized immigrants. Chapter 3 introduced indexes of accommodation and restriction, detailed in figure 3.7. Recall that the survey asked about seven distinct restrictive responses to immigrants and eighteen distinct accommodating responses. As I explained fully in chapter 3, I compare towns based on the proportion of accommodating or restrictive practices they report, allowing the denominator of the number of practices they were asked about to vary. The restrictive index ranges from a low of zero reported by fully 308 towns (83 percent) to a high of 67 percent. On average, towns report 5 percent of the restrictive practices they are asked about. The full accommodating index, incorporating all eighteen practices, ranges from a low of zero, reported by fifty-seven towns (15 percent), to a high of 83 percent.[3] On average, towns report 25 percent of accommodating practices they are asked about.[4]

The practices towns were asked about vary with which officials responded in a given town. Therefore I address this underlying variation in the indexes by controlling for which officials responded. Specifically, I include two dichotomous variables indicating whether only a police chief or only city hall officials responded in a given town. These controls allow me to account for police chiefs' being asked about fewer practices than are city hall officials. They also allow me to control for differences in response related to official role, since we know from chapter 3 that police chiefs are more likely to report certain accommodating practices than are city hall officials.

In addition to the accommodating and restrictive indexes, I also examine one variable that measures towns' police practices regarding unauthorized immigrants, which I will refer to as "enforcement practices."

The survey asks all officials to describe their municipality's "current position on illegal immigration," with response items ranging from declaring a sanctuary city to supporting an informal policy of "don't ask, don't tell," having no official policy, or developing policies to encourage cooperation with federal authorities. The scale ranges from one to four, with one indicating a sanctuary city and four indicating a city that cooperates with federal enforcement efforts. The dependent variable used in the analyses here represents the town's response to the question averaged across officials responding within the town. The average value across towns was a 2.89, corresponding to "no official policy." Twelve percent of towns report sanctuary or "don't ask, don't tell" policies, while 9 percent reported cooperating in federal enforcement.

The reason for examining this variable in addition to the indexes is twofold. First, local enforcement practices are arguably the most crucial factor in shaping the local context of reception for immigrants, since they affect whether immigrants and coethnics are treated as community members or as suspect interlopers. Second, since the accommodating and restrictive indexes vary in the questions asked across the towns, the enforcement practices variable provides a check on whether they are functioning properly. Because the enforcement practices variable was asked of all officials who responded to the survey, if the factors that predict enforcement line up with the factors predicting the accommodating and restrictive indexes, we can be more confident that the indexes are indeed capturing the tenor of local response.

To assess the factors associated with variation in inaction, accommodation, restriction, and enforcement, I employ multivariate regression analysis, controlling for key explanatory factors identified in my fieldwork and the preceding literature review: factors associated with ethnic threat, municipal capacity, immigrant visibility, external policy cues, partisanship, and foreign-born political influence, plus other contextual factors. Table 4.1 summarizes these independent variables and their predicted effect on the degree and tenor of response.

Ethnic Threat

To measure the effect of ethnic threat on local responses to immigrants, I first control for demographic change, specifically the percentage change in the foreign-born population from 2000 to 2012 (US Census 2000; American Community Survey 2008–12).[5] Since the foreign-born

TABLE 4.1. **Predicted effect of explanatory variables on degree and tenor of response**

		Degree	Tenor	Tenor
	Source of measure	Likelihood of inactivity	Predicted effect on accommodation	Predicted effect on restriction
Ethnic threat				
Percent change foreign-born, 2000–2012	US Census 2000, ACS 2008–12	↓	↓	↑
Percent foreign-born Hispanic	ACS 2008–12	↓	↓	↑
Percent foreign-born in poverty	ACS 2008–12	↓	↓	↑
Violent crime rate per 1,000 residents	FBI Uniform Crime Report 2013	↓	↓	↑
Percent homeownership	ACS 2008–12	↓	↓	↑
Local capacity				
Population 2012	ACS 2008–12	↓	↑	↑
Percent with BA degree	ACS 2008–12	↓	↑	↓
Percent change in median household income 2000–2012	US Census 2000, ACS 2008–12	↓	↑	↓
Immigrant visibility				
Percent foreign-born	ACS 2008–12	↓	↑	↑
External policy cues				
Refugee presence (= 1)	MRIS: town reports at least "small but visible refugee population"	↓	↑	↓
State-level immigrant policy score	Pham and Pham 2012	•	↑	↓
Within 100 miles of Mexican border (= 1)	Generated using GIS	↓	↓	↑
Within 100 miles of Canadian border (= 1)	Generated using GIS	↓	↓	↑
Partisanship				
Percent voting Romney 2012 (county)	CQ voting and elections	•	↓	↑
Foreign-born influence				
Latino elected official (= 1)	NALEO 2015 Report	↓	↑	↓
2006 protest (= 1)	Bada et al. 2006	↓	↑	↓
Immigrant-related organizations per 1,000	Guidestar	↓	↑	↓
Additional contextual characteristics				
Percent agricultural employment	ACS 2008–12	•	•	↓
Council-manager form of government (= 1)	ICMA 2011 Form of government survey	•	•	↓

Sources: ACS = American Community Survey; MRIS = Municipal Responses to Immigrants Survey; CQ Voting = Congressional Quarterly Voting and Elections; NALEO = National Association of Latino Elected and Appointed Officials; Guidestar; ICMA = International City/County Management Association.

population is ethnically diverse and Latino immigrants are especially prone to being defined as "illegal aliens" and therefore producing threatened responses, I also control for the proportion of the local foreign-born population that is Latino in 2012 (American Community Survey 2008–12). Further, I control for two factors that potentially abet negative definitions of immigrants: the proportion of the foreign-born population living in poverty (American Community Survey 2008–12) and the violent crime rate per 1,000 residents (FBI Uniform Crime Report 2013). Last, some studies have found that threatened responses are more likely in suburban destinations, where concerns over home values are heightened (Singer, Wilson, and DeRenzis 2009; Walker and Leitner 2011). Therefore I control for the proportion owning homes, expecting more restrictive responses in places with greater homeownership.

Capacity

Towns with greater administrative capacity likely will be better equipped to respond to immigrants. Holding constant other salient factors, town population (natural log of 2008–12 American Community Survey population estimate) serves as a proxy for administrative capacity, since larger cities have more staff and perform more functions locally (Dewees, Lobao, and Swanson 2003). Town population could affect local responses through a mechanism other than administrative capacity, but since the analysis holds constant so many other salient characteristics of towns, I argue that here it serves as a proxy for capacity. In addition to administrative capacity, more prosperous towns may have greater capacity and political leeway to accommodate immigrants. I therefore include two measures of local socioeconomic status: the percentage with a bachelor's degree or more in 2012 and percentage change in median household income from 2000 to 2012 (US Census 2000; American Community Survey 2008–12).[6]

Immigrant Visibility

In towns with larger foreign-born populations, issues related to immigration are probably more visible and likely to prompt responses. Therefore I control for the 2012 foreign-born proportion of the population (American Community Survey 2008–12). As I will discuss below, however, other factors may also relate to immigrant visibility. While I hypothesize that the proportion of the foreign-born population that is Hispanic or living in poverty may be associated with more threatened responses, immigrants' need or a larger Latino immigrant population may simply make immigration more visible locally, since lower-skilled Latinos are associated with immigration in the popular imagination (Brader, Valentino, and Suhay 2008; Chavez 2013). If threat is operative, we would expect towns to shift away from accommodation as foreign-born poverty or Hispanic dominance increases. On the other hand, if immigrant visibility is operative, we would see towns shift toward accommodation as the foreign-born Latino or foreign-born poor population increases.[7]

External Policy

Examples from Lewiston, Wausau, Elgin, and Yakima demonstrate that places exposed to federal refugee resettlement policies define immigrants as clients and produce more accommodating responses. Thus the survey asked officials about the size of their local refugee population. In the analyses below I include a dichotomous variable equal to one in the 18 percent of towns where officials report at least "a small but visible refugee population."[8] In addition, state-level policies can frame immigrants as clients or as outsiders and encourage local officials to move toward greater accommodation or toward greater restriction. To measure the tenor of state policy response, I use a variable developed by Pham and Pham (2012) known as the Immigrant Climate Index (ICI). The score summarizes state-level immigration legislation, ranging from −355 in Arizona, the most restrictive state, to 164 in Illinois, the most accommodating state.[9] Previous studies hypothesize that where state-level policy is more accommodating, local policies may also be more accommodating and vice versa (Ramakrishnan and Wong 2010; Steil and Vasi 2014).

In addition, I control for two dichotomous variables indicating whether a given city is within one hundred miles of the Mexican or Canadian border (Lewis et al. 2013). Owing to the massive presence of federal immigration enforcement officials, particularly on the US southern border, proximity to the border exposes local officials to enforcement policies that foreground frames of immigrants as "illegal aliens."[10] Proximity to the border also may be associated with threat or other factors, but I argue that it serves as a proxy for exposure to federal enforcement policies. If only proximity to the Mexican border increases restriction, that might suggest that the border is associated with ethnic threat related to Latino immigration, but if proximity to both the Mexican and Canadian borders increases restriction we can be more confident that these variables are capturing something other than threat—likely exposure to federal enforcement policies.

Partisanship

In a number of studies, a more Republican populace is associated with greater local restriction, while a more Democratic populace is associated with greater accommodation (Ramakrishnan and Wong 2010; Walker and Leitner 2011; Gulasekaram and Ramakrishnan 2015). I operationalize partisanship using the proportion of a county that voted for Republican presidential candidate Mitt Romney in 2012, drawing from the Congressional Quarterly Voting and Elections data. Although partisanship can vary within counties, town-level presidential results are not available for all states.[11] Thus most studies have employed county-level results as a proxy.

Foreign-Born Influence

The example of Yakima, plus some previous studies, suggests that accommodation increases along with the influence of the local foreign-born population (Ramakrishnan and Wong 2010). I operationalize foreign-born influence using three variables. First, I include a measure that indicates whether a town was home to a pro-immigrant protest in 2006, drawing on a database constructed by Xóchitl Bada and her colleagues (2006). In the wake of restrictive immigration legislation, immigrant protests took place in 166 towns nationwide, including smaller new immigrant destinations (Benjamin-Alvarado, DeSipio, and Montoya 2009). Protests took place in 25 of 373 towns (7 percent) that responded to the survey, as well as in both Elgin and Yakima.

In addition to protest mobilization, I include more formal measures of local immigrant influence: the number of immigrant-related organizations and the presence of Latino elected officials. I obtained the names of immigrant-related organizations in each town using Guidestar, a service that compiles 990 tax forms for registered nonprofit organizations and categorizes them. A research assistant identified immigrant-related organizations in the following categories: minority rights, civil liberties advocacy, civil rights advocacy for specific groups, ethnic/immigrant services, and relevant human service organizations. Sixty-five percent of towns (241 towns) had no registered immigrant-related organizations in these categories; 15 percent had one such organization; and the remaining 20 percent had two or more, with a maximum of twelve such organizations in one town. The variable included in analyses measures the number of immigrant-related organizations per thousand residents.[12] Finally, I include a dichotomous variable equal to one when the town had at least one Latino local elected official according to the 2015 National Directory of Latino Officials produced by the National Association for Latino Elected and Appointed Officials (NALEO). Fifteen percent of responding towns (fifty-six towns) have at least one Latino elected official.[13]

Additional Contextual Factors

In addition, I control for two characteristics of towns that may limit their susceptibility to national political discourse surrounding immigrants. As hypothesized from my fieldwork (and found by Ramakrishnan and his colleagues [2010; 2015]), places like Yakima that rely heavily on immigrant agricultural laborers may be less likely to have restrictive practices. Therefore I include a variable representing the proportion of the adult civilian labor force engaged in agricultural work (American Community Survey 2008–12). Similarly, places with a council-manager form of government, in which policy decisions are strongly influenced by an appointed city manager who is not as subject to political pressures, may be less likely to implement restrictive practices (Lewis et al. 2013). Places with city managers also may be more likely to carry out accommodating practices before official policy decisions by elected officials, as the bureaucratic incorporation literature suggests (Lewis and Ramakrishnan 2007; Jones-Correa 2008; Marrow 2009). I include a dichotomous variable equal to one when the city has a council-manager government, as indicated in the 2011 International City/County Manager Association Municipal Form of Government survey.[14]

All together, as table 4.1 summarizes, I control for factors associated with ethnic threat, anticipating that threat may increase the likelihood of restrictive responses and decrease the likelihood of accommodation. I control for municipal capacity because places with greater administrative ability and socioeconomic means may be more likely to accommodate immigrants. I also control for factors related to immigrant visibility, expecting that places with more evident immigrant populations may be more likely to take action. I control for accommodating federal and state policy cues, which may define immigrants as clients and promote a more accommodating local response, as well as for proximity to the Mexican or Canadian border, which may heighten associations of immigrants with "illegal aliens" through frames associated with federal enforcement policies. And I control for partisanship, since Republican-leaning places may be more sensitive to national Republican discourse surrounding un-authorized immigration. In contrast, immigrant influence may result in more accommodating local responses, and thus I control for protest ac-tivity, immigrant organizations, and Latino elected officials. I control for council-manager form of government and agricultural workforce be-cause these factors may reduce the likelihood of restrictive response and increase the probability of accommodation. Finally, as I explained ear-lier, I include controls for towns where only the police chief or only city hall officials responded, since official role affects both which questions officials were asked and how they responded. Table 4.2 presents the de-scriptive statistics for each of the key explanatory variables.

Evaluating Predictors of Municipal Response

To understand which factors shape municipal responses, I now evalu-ate how the variables described above affect the likelihood of local in-action, accommodation, restriction, and immigration enforcement, using multivariate regression analyses.[15] Appendix D presents the regression results (table AD1). The figures below employ the statistical software Clarify to display the predicted effect of the statistically significant vari-ables holding all other variables at their means (Tomz, Wittenberg, and King 2003). For continuous variables the predicted changes are for mov-ing from one standard deviation below the mean to one standard devi-ation above the mean; for dichotomous variables the change is from a value of zero to a value of one.

Factors Predicting Inaction

As I discussed in part 1, inaction is a frequent and substantively impor-tant local response, but it can make a city either more or less restric-tive. In some cases, as in Yakima, inaction is restrictive as localities fail

TABLE 4.2. **Towns' mean values for key explanatory variables**

	Mean value	Low value	High value
Ethnic threat			
Percent change foreign-born 2000–2012	83	−45	1,734
Percent foreign-born Hispanic	44	1	100
Percent foreign-born in poverty	19	1	53
Violent crime rate per 1,000 residents	3	0	19
Percent homeownership	62	14	96
Local capacity			
Population 2012	57,586	5,195	197,456
Percent with BA degree	32	3	77
Percent change in median household income 2000–2012	23	−13	64
Immigrant visibility			
Percent foreign-born	16	5	60
External policy cues			
Percent towns with refugee presence	18	0	1
State-level immigrant policy score	7	−355	164
Percent towns within 100 miles of Mexican border	6	0	1
Percent towns within 100 miles of Canadian border	5	0	1
Partisanship			
Percent voting Romney 2012 (county)	46	9	88
Foreign-born influence			
Percent towns with Latino elected official	15	0	1
Percent towns with 2006 protest	7	0	1
Immigrant-related organizations per 1,000	0.0	0.0	0.2
Additional contextual characteristics			
Percent agricultural employment	2	0	37
Percent towns with council-manager form of government	70	0	1
N	373		

to enact accommodating initiatives—even those that may be federally required—in the face of demographic change. In other cases inaction is accommodating, as cities choose inaction even when local residents are calling for cooperation with federal enforcement efforts, as Elgin officials attempted to do. Since inaction involves these crosscutting elements, we would not expect that the hypotheses related to tenor of response would apply directly to this initial analysis. The analysis does, however, provide a clear indication of the role of local capacity and immigrant visibility in moving a town from doing nothing—implementing none of the accommodating and none of the restrictive practices—to doing something. Moreover, it provides some indication that federal policy cues and potentially foreign-born influence play a part.

The findings demonstrate that places with a more noticeable immigrant presence and larger municipal administrations are more likely to act in response to immigrants. Specifically, population size, which serves as a proxy for local administrative capacity, is strongly negatively associated with inaction. As figure 4.1 displays, the model predicts that, all else constant, a small town of roughly 15,000 is 15 percent likely to be completely inactive (or a probability of 0.15). A larger city of just over 100,000 is only 6 percent likely to be inactive, a gap of nine percentage points. Towns with more Hispanic-dominant immigrant populations are also less likely to be inactive, by a statistically significant margin. A town in which 17 percent of immigrants are Latino is 16 percent likely to be inactive, while a town with a foreign-born population that is nearly three-quarters Latino is only 6 percent likely to be inactive—a gap of ten percentage points. As the dominant foreign-born group in the United States as a whole, Latinos are more visible as immigrants, leading to a greater likelihood of local response.

In addition to these two significant predictors of inaction, three variables fall out of the analysis because they predict inaction perfectly. First, none of the cities that report a visible refugee population is entirely

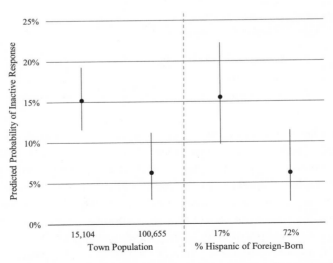

FIGURE 4.1. Predicted probability of inaction associated with key explanatory variables.

inactive in its response to immigrants, suggesting that accommodating federal policies may prompt more active local responses. Similarly, none of the cities within a hundred miles of the Mexican border is inactive, suggesting that proximity to federal enforcement may generate greater local response. Last, none of the cities that experienced a pro-immigrant protest in 2006 is entirely inactive, suggesting some relation between immigrants' mobilization and local responsiveness.

Factors Predicting Greater Accommodation

Having analyzed the factors associated with the degree of local response (whether active or inactive), I now turn to the tenor of local response. Looking first at factors predicting accommodation, we see that local capacity and immigrant visibility continue to play a role but that external policies and political discourse are also influential (fig. 4.2). Moreover, the analysis demonstrates that factors related to ethnic threat are not associated with less local accommodation. Considering local capacity and visibility first, both factors increase the proportion of accommodating practices a town reports. Holding all other variables at their means, moving from a town of roughly 15,000 to a city of more than 100,000 is associated with an increase in accommodating practices from 20 percent to 29 percent. Likewise, moving from 6 percent foreign-born to 26 percent foreign-born (all else constant) is associated with an increase in accommodating practices from 21 percent to 28 percent. The proportion of the immigrant population living in poverty was initially hypothesized to heighten local threat and depress accommodation, but results suggest that foreign-born need may heighten immigrant visibility and prompt greater response. All else constant, moving from a city in which only 8 percent of immigrants live in poverty to a city in which 29 percent of immigrants do is associated with a five percentage point increase in the proportion of accommodating practices.

While local capacity and foreign-born visibility are strong predictors of accommodation, external policy cues at the state and federal levels also are important. Looking first to the state level, moving from a state roughly as restrictive as Alabama to a state almost as accommodating as California is associated with a small but discernible four percentage point increase in the accommodating index. At the federal level, exposure to national policies that frame immigrants as clients, such as refugee resettlement programming, can bolster local accommodation,

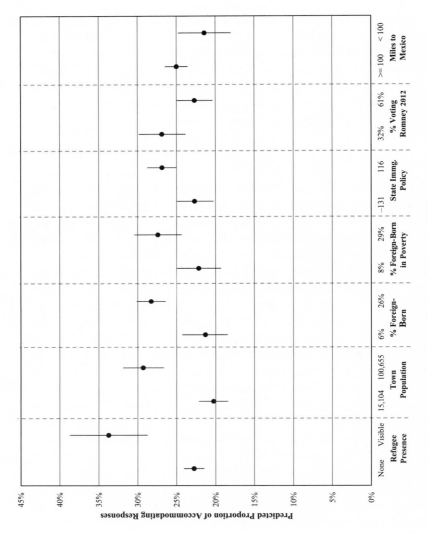

FIGURE 4.2. Predicted level of accommodation by key explanatory variables.

while exposure to policies that frame immigrants as lawbreakers, such as proximity to border enforcement operations, can hamper it. All else constant, reporting at least a "small but visible refugee population" was associated with an increase of eleven percentage points in the accommodating index, moving a town from reporting less than a quarter of practices to reporting more than a third. Proximity to federal enforcement operations near the Mexican border was associated with a four percentage point decline in the accommodating index.

Partisanship had a small but discernible effect on local accommodation. Moving from a county in which 32 percent of the population voted for Mitt Romney in 2012 to a county in which 61 percent of the population did so is associated with a four percentage point drop in the proportion of accommodating practices a town reports. In sum, local capacity, immigrant visibility, and accommodating external policy frames bolster accommodation, whereas Republican partisanship and restrictive external policy frames diminish accommodation. Factors standing in for ethnic threat were not associated with lower levels of accommodation, suggesting that demographic change may not determine local responses.

Factors Predicting More Restrictive Responses

Turning to restriction, the proportion of restrictive practices reported locally is not associated with local capacity, but it is associated with immigrant visibility (fig. 4.3). Moving from a town in which 6 percent of the population are foreign-born to a town in which 26 percent are is associated with a small but statistically significant increase of three percentage points on the restrictive index, holding all else constant. With respect to external policy cues, accommodating state and federal policies are not statistically associated with restriction, but proximity to US land borders and associated federal immigration enforcement is associated with an increase in restriction. All else constant, being within a hundred miles of the Mexican border is associated with a nine percentage point increase on the index of restriction, moving a town from 4 percent restrictive practices to 13 percent. Similarly, being within a hundred miles of the Canadian border is associated with an eight percentage point increase on the index of restriction. That proximity to both the Canadian and the Mexican borders is associated with greater restriction suggests that border proximity affects local responses through a mechanism other than ethnic threat, strengthening the argument that it serves as a proxy

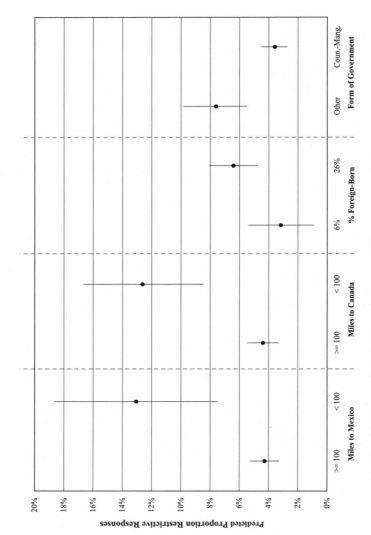

FIGURE 4.3: Predicted level of restriction by key explanatory variables.

for exposure to federal immigration enforcement policies that frame immigrants as "illegal aliens."

Republican partisanship is directionally associated with an increase in restriction, though not by a statistically significant margin ($p = 0.22$). On the other hand, local form of government plays a key role. All else constant, a community with a council-manager government, in which decision making is somewhat more insulated from political influence, is associated with a four percentage point decline on the restrictive index. Overall, restriction is not associated with local capacity, though it is related to immigrant visibility. It is not statistically associated with Republican partisanship, but restrictive policy cues and form of government have an effect, with proximity to US land borders associated with greater restriction and council-manager government associated with less. Once again, factors representing ethnic threat were not associated with greater restriction.

Factors Predicting Immigration Enforcement Practices

Finally, if we look specifically at immigration enforcement practices, local capacity and immigrant visibility continue to shape the likelihood of local response, as do external policy cues and partisanship. In addition to these factors, immigrants' political influence is a significant contributor to enforcement practices. Recall that the enforcement scale ranges from the accommodating extreme of operating as a sanctuary city (1), followed by having a "don't ask, don't tell policy" (2), to the restrictive extreme of cooperating in federal enforcement efforts (4). The mean value is having no formal policy (3).[16] Looking first to local capacity, population size is not associated with enforcement practices, but local socioeconomic status is associated with an increased likelihood of accommodating responses. All else constant, moving from a city in which 15 percent of the population have a bachelor's degree to a city in which 48 percent of residents do is associated with a decline on the four-point scale of 0.16 points, as displayed in figure 4.4. With respect to immigrant visibility, the proportion foreign-born is statistically associated with more restrictive responses to unauthorized immigrants, though the effect is small. All else constant, a twenty percentage point increase in the foreign-born proportion of the population is associated with an increase of 0.10 points on the four-point scale.

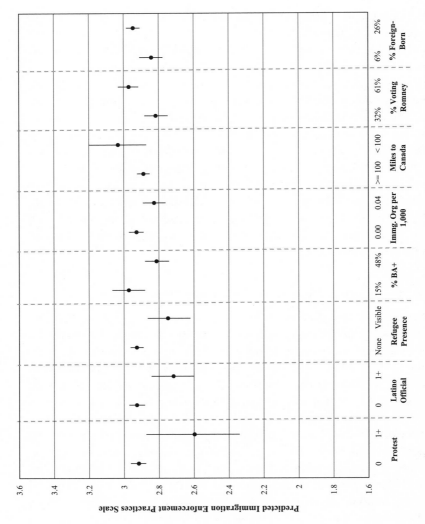

FIGURE 4.4. Predicted responses to unauthorized immigrants by key explanatory variables.

Federal policy cues also shape local responses to the unauthorized. Cities exposed to accommodating refugee resettlement policies are 0.18 points more accommodating on the four-point scale, all else constant. On the other hand, cities exposed to immigration enforcement practices near US land borders are more likely to take restrictive action against unauthorized immigrants, though the variable is significant only for the Canadian border. Cities within a hundred miles of the Canadian border rank 0.15 points more restrictive on the four-point scale. Republican partisanship also increases the likelihood of restrictive enforcement, with a twenty-nine percentage point increase in the proportion of the county voting for Romney associated with a 0.15 point move toward restriction on the scale.

Although foreign-born political influence was not a factor in shaping the proportion of accommodating or restrictive responses reported, it did shape enforcement practices. All else constant, experiencing a pro-immigrant protest in 2006 is associated with less restrictive responses to unauthorized immigrants by almost a third of a point on the four-point scale. Likewise, having at least one Latino elected official is associated with less restrictive responses by just over two-tenths of a point. Having more immigrant organizations proportional to a city's population is also statistically associated with less restrictive responses by a tenth of a point. Last, factors associated with ethnic threat did not influence local enforcement practices.

Visibility, Capacity, and External Cues, Not Threat

Table 4.3 summarizes the predicted effects of the explanatory variables and the actual effects found in the analyses. In sum, analysis of the nationwide MRIS demonstrates that local capacity and immigrant visibility shape the degree of local activity in response to the foreign-born, while external frames conveyed through state and federal policies and national political rhetoric powerfully shape the tenor of response. In both cases these mechanisms operate according to the way immigrants are defined locally.

Where immigrants are visible because they mirror popular conceptions of the foreign-born as low-skilled Latinos, localities are more likely to respond. In this way, local understandings of immigrants shape

TABLE 4.3. **Predicted and actual effects of explanatory variables on local responses**

	Degree		Tenor Accommodation		Tenor Restriction	
	Likelihood of inactivity	Effect	Prediction	Effect	Prediction	Effect
Ethnic threat						
Percent change foreign-born 2000–2012	↓		↓		↑	
Percent foreign-born Hispanic	↓	↓	↓		↑	
Percent foreign-born in poverty	↓		↓	↑	↑	
Violent crime rate per 1,000 residents	↓		↓		↑	
Percent homeownership	↓		↓		↑	
Local capacity						
Population 2012	↓	↓	↑	↑	↑	
Percent with BA degree	↓		↑		↓	↓ (enforcement only)
Percent change in median household income 2000–2012	↓		↑		↓	
Immigrant visibility						
Percent foreign-born	↓		↑	↑	↑	↑
External policy cues						
Refugee presence (= 1)	↓		↑	↑	↓	↓ (enforcement only)
State-level immigrant policy score	•		↑	↑	↓	
Within 100 miles of Mexican border (= 1)	↓		↓	↓	↑	↑
Within 100 miles of Canadian border (= 1)	↓		↓		↑	↑
Partisanship						
Percent voting Romney 2012 (county)	•		↓	↓	↑	↑ (enforcement only)
Foreign-born influence						
Latino elected official (= 1)	↓		↑		↓	↓ (enforcement only)
2006 protest (= 1)	↓		↑		↓	↓ (enforcement only)

TABLE 4.1. (continued)

	Degree		Tenor Accommodation		Tenor Restriction	
	Likelihood of inactivity	Effect	Prediction	Effect	Prediction	Effect
Immigrant-related organizations per 1,000	↓		↑		↓	↓ (enforcement only)
Additional contextual characteristics						
Percent agricultural employment	•		•		↓	
Council-manager form of government (= 1)	•		•		↓	↓

whether localities respond. Local definitions also shape *how* municipalities respond, with external frames playing an influential role in shifting responses toward accommodation or restriction. Where municipalities are exposed to more accommodating state and federal policies that define immigrants as deserving clients, municipalities are more likely to accommodate. Where they are exposed to federal enforcement policies along US land borders that emphasize immigrant illegality, they are more likely to restrict. Finally, where more residents are Republican, localities are more susceptible to Republican national political discourse that foregrounds definitions of immigrants as "illegal aliens," contributing to more restrictive responses.

Multivariate findings demonstrate that ethnic threat is not associated with more restrictive or less accommodating responses. Foreign-born growth, violent crime, and percentage of homeownership are not statistically associated with local responses. Hispanic foreign-born dominance and foreign-born poverty are associated with responses in some cases, though not in the anticipated direction. Places with more Hispanic-dominant foreign-born populations are less likely to be inactive, though not more likely to restrict. Places with a more impoverished immigrant population actually report a higher proportion of accommodating responses, holding other factors constant. These results suggest that Hispanic dominance and poverty increase immigrant visibility in ways that do not increase the likelihood of restriction but can increase the likelihood of accommodation.

Indeed, immigrant visibility is strongly associated with the likelihood of local response in these analyses. The proportion foreign-born in a city is associated with greater accommodation, but it is also associated with greater restriction and more restrictive responses toward unauthorized immigrants. Overall, as the proportion of foreign-born residents in a city rises, the city becomes more likely to respond, whether in an accommodating or a restrictive manner. One could argue that the positive relation between the proportion of local immigrants and restriction suggests that some degree of threat may be present, though restrictive responses remain extremely rare. Moreover, foreign-born presence is promoting both restriction and accommodation, suggesting not that the variable operates as an indicator of ethnic threat, but rather that a certain threshold of foreign-born population is necessary to warrant decisive action. Other typical predictors of threat also do not result in more restrictive responses, with some proposed predictors of threat (Hispanic dominance and foreign-born poverty) actually moving cities away from restriction.

These results show that where immigrants are more visible, municipal responses are more likely. Immigrant visibility depends on how large the foreign-born population is, but it also depends on whether immigrants are actually seen as immigrants. In Yakima, for instance, local officials remained inactive until they recognized that migrant farmworkers were settling permanently in the city rather than coming and going. Given stereotypes about immigrant characteristics, places with more Hispanic-dominant and less affluent foreign-born populations are more likely to implement practices in response to immigrants because they recognize their immigrant populations as such. Latinos are the largest foreign-born group in the United States. While 10 percent of foreign-born Latinos are college educated (Ryan and Siebens 2012), the popular conception of Latino immigrants is as low-skilled laborers. Thus towns where immigrants fit the popular conception are more likely to respond to the foreign-born.

In contrast, places where immigrants are largely non-Hispanic or high-skilled may not even define their foreign-born population as immigrants. In qualitative comments in response to the survey, an elected official in a wealthy northeastern suburb that is 17 percent foreign-born, but largely high-skilled Asian, reported that he thought of the city as diverse, but not as having immigrants. Likewise, an official from a wealthy northwestern community that is 9 percent foreign-born, but again largely Asian, replied to the survey saying, "I am not sure how we got on your list, but we really don't have any—I'll say any—immigrant population. . . . No real obvious immigrant issues or even persons to speak of." Hispanic ethnicity and immigrant poverty enhance foreign-born visibility and, rather than producing threatened responses, make action in response to immigrants generally more likely.

Predictors of local capacity also are positively associated with both acting in response to immigrants and accommodating them. City population size is associated with a lower likelihood of inaction and a higher proportion of accommodating responses. Residents' socioeconomic status, specifically the proportion with a bachelor's degree, is associated with greater accommodation and less restriction, though by a statistically significant margin only with respect to enforcement practices.

While immigrant visibility and local capacity shape whether municipalities respond to immigrants (degree of response), external cues affect how localities respond (tenor of response), pushing them toward accommodation or restriction. As both the four case studies and the survey demonstrate, exposure to federal refugee resettlement policies defines immigrants as deserving clients and is therefore associated with a greater proportion of accommodating responses as well as with less restrictive enforcement practices. Lewiston and Wausau were more accommodating toward immigrants given their experience with refugees, and in Elgin experience serving Laotian refugees spilled over into capacity to serve Latino immigrants. Similarly, living in a state with more accommodating statewide immigrant policies is associated with greater accommodation locally. On the other hand, exposure to federal immigration enforcement along US land borders foregrounds frames of immigrants as "illegal aliens" and is associated with less accommodation and greater restriction. Border proximity could also be considered an indicator of threat, though not of ethnic threat, since proximity to both the Canadian and Mexican borders prompts more restrictive responses. Since these variables operate differently than other predictors of threat in this analysis, I conclude that proximity to the border is associated with exposure to federal enforcement operations.

In addition to the important role of these external policy cues, national political discourse among Republicans shapes local definitions of immigrants and influences responses, as we saw in Elgin. Places with a more Republican populace report less accommodation as well as more restrictive enforcement practices. As the cases demonstrate, Republican partisanship is influential but not determinative in how national discourse shapes local responses. Local demographic and economic characteristics affect whether these external frames will resonate locally, as the example of Yakima's reliance on agricultural labor demonstrates.

Beyond these key predictors of local response, foreign-born influence plays some role, as Yakima's experience of growing accommodation in tandem with a rising immigrant second generation suggests. Places with Latino elected officials, immigrant protest mobilization, and immigrant organizations report less restrictive enforcement practices, though these factors do not affect overall indexes of restriction and accommodation. Yakima's experience also predicted that the proportion of agricultural workers would reduce the likelihood of restriction. A larger agricultural workforce was directionally associated with less restriction and less restrictive enforcement practices, though the coefficients fell just below conventional levels of statistical significance ($p = 0.12$, $p = 0.16$). Form of government is particularly influential in curtailing restrictive responses, though it is not statistically associated with greater accommodation. Systems with prominent appointed leadership seem less likely to produce restriction, an effect I will explore in more detail in chapter 5.

The type of official who responded to the survey within a given city does affect the tenor of response in some cases, though all the multivariate results presented here hold this factor constant. Towns where only police or only city hall officials responded are more likely to report inaction, while towns where both police and city hall officials responded report more active responses. Consonant with chapter 3, towns where only police officials responded report more accommodation, while towns where only city hall officials responded report more restrictive enforcement practices. While the officials who responded in a given town affect the construction of the accommodating and restrictive indexes, the results from these dependent variables are robust to the single variable measuring local enforcement practices, a question asked of all officials across the board. Results from the indexes and this single variable cohere to present clear findings on the predictors of local government accommodation and restriction, increasing our confidence that the indexes are reliable metrics of local response.

Conclusion

In combination, qualitative and quantitative data demonstrate that factors shaping municipal responses to immigrants operate by reshaping definitions of them. Local definitions of immigrants shape both the degree of response—measured here by whether towns act at all—and the tenor of response, whether accommodating or restrictive. Overall, cities become more likely to respond to immigrants when they are larger and have a larger proportion of foreign-born residents that are recognized and defined as immigrants by virtue of their similarity to stereotypes of immigrants as Hispanic and low income. Factors associated with threat therefore do not increase the likelihood of restrictive response; instead, Hispanic dominance and foreign-born poverty seem to increase immigrant visibility and prompt more accommodating responses. As the cases predicted, federal policy cues and national political discourse proved influential in shaping local definitions of immigrants and shifting responses toward accommodation or restriction.

On the whole these findings complement earlier work examining the factors predicting immigration-related ordinances, which also found local capacity and partisanship to be influential (Ramakrishnan and Wong 2010; Gulasekaram and Ramakrishnan 2015). At the same time, my findings advance our understanding of municipal responses to immigrants by showing that these factors shape not only rare ordinances, but also more prevalent informal practices. The central departure of these findings is that ethnic threat appears to play no role in shaping more restrictive responses. Several factors could account for this differing finding. First, not all scholars have found that ethnic threat shapes local responses; some argue that localities respond based on partisanship and not ethnic demographic change (Ramakrishnan and Wong 2010; Gulasekaram and Ramakrishnan 2015). Second, we would not necessarily expect that the factors influencing the likelihood of local ordinances—rare, formal responses at the extremes—would be the same as those shaping informal practices responding to immigrants. Third, perhaps the more recent period in which the survey was fielded differs from the height of restrictive ordinances in 2006–7.

Potentially, ethnic threat is operational only when immigration is salient nationally (Hopkins 2011). That is, we would see threat resulting in calls for more restrictive responses only when immigration is a topic of national discussion. In this case, however, the survey was in the field from summer 2014 to early 2015, a time of especially high national attention to immigration issues. The summer of 2014 was the height of child migrant arrivals along the US-Mexico border, with 51,705 unaccompanied Central American minors encountered at the border during fiscal year 2014, more than double the previous year's total (US Customs and Border Patrol 2016). In November 2014 President Obama announced controversial executive actions on immigration that intended to provide provisional status for up to five million unauthorized immigrants. If earlier results about ethnic threat continue to apply, we would expect that during the period the survey was in the field, local officials would have been facing enhanced calls for restrictive action.

Instead we see that, if anything, factors previously associated with threat tend to prompt greater accommodation. It is possible that threatened calls for restriction in late 2014 had not yet moved communities to change their policies toward immigrants. Since the bulk of restrictive local ordinances passed in 2006–7, the trend in communities has been toward greater accommodation, and perhaps the tide had not yet turned (Gulasekaram and Ramakrishnan 2015). Yet the survey does not suggest an incipient turn toward restriction. Indeed, according to local officials, Hispanic population growth is also not associated with the how controversial immigration is locally ($r = 0.07$), though the Hispanic dominance of the foreign-born population is moderately well correlated ($r = 0.36$).

Although the topic requires further exploration over time, the survey suggests that even when immigration was highly salient nationally, local officials were not responding to a growing foreign-born population with more restrictive policies. A substantial body of literature suggests that a growing ethnic minority population does produce threatened responses among residents (Key 1949; Blalock 1967; Glaser 2003; Enos 2014). Indeed, Brader, Valentino, and Suhay (2008) demonstrate that Americans feel more anxious about Latino immigrants than about white immigrants and are more likely to approach their officials with concern about immigration when the immigrants in question are Latinos. Certainly, in the four new destinations cases some residents do express feelings of competition and associated ethnic threat, as I will discuss in chapter 8. Yet the national survey of local government officials finds that municipal practices in response to immigrants are not determined by ethnic threat. Interestingly, Brader, Valentino, and Suhay (2008) found that white Americans feel less anxious about Latino immigration when they are presented with information countering stereotypes about these immigrants' costs and harm. As I will demonstrate in chapter 5, local government officials often have different sources of information surrounding immigrants and their economic role. Indeed, as the prevalence of accommodating responses suggests, local officials generally face strong incentives to serve immigrant residents, which may not be readily shared by the broader public—a situation I turn to in chapter 5.

CHAPTER FIVE

Beyond Bureaucrats

Elected and Appointed Officials'
Incentives for Accommodation

For those of us who believe in God, we are all children of God. Consequently, we are one humanity in that we are all brothers and sisters. The reality of life here in Lewiston and Auburn is that our refugee and immigrant neighbors will be here well beyond when we are all dead and gone. They will grow in number and sustain us as a community. — Mayor Larry Gilbert of Lewiston in the *Twin City Times*, 2011

I'm sick of hearing the Somalis don't feel welcome here. I'm sick of hearing Lewistonians must understand their culture and make exceptions towards them if their actions clash with American customs and laws. — Mayor Robert Macdonald of Lewiston in the *Twin City Times*, 2012

There could hardly be a greater contrast than that between Mayor Larry Gilbert, who served Lewiston from 2007 to 2011, and Mayor Robert Macdonald, who has served Lewiston since 2012. Mayor Gilbert advocated for Somalis' inclusion in local government and supported funding for Somali organizations. He traveled the country and testified in Congress, touting the benefits Somalis bring to Lewiston. Mayor Macdonald is not as consistently hostile to the Somali population as his periodic outbursts suggest, but he does insist that immigrants should not receive public assistance and should jettison their culture on arriving in the United States. Mayor Macdonald won his first term through what the *Portland Press Herald* referred to as "morbid luck." His Democratic opponent died before the runoff election; yet Macdonald still won by only seventy votes (Russel 2012). In his next race he decisively beat Mayor

Gilbert, who had returned to challenge him, in what some describe as a public referendum on Gilbert's approach to welcoming immigrants (Besteman 2016). In 2015 Mayor Macdonald beat progressive candidate Benjamin Chin despite Chin's much better funded and organized campaign (Shepherd 2015).

Across my cases, Mayor Macdonald is not the only elected official to capitalize on opposition to local immigration. In Elgin, two of three city council candidates fielded by an anti-immigration organization won in 2009 and held their seats in subsequent elections. That said, of the twenty-nine elected officials I spoke to in four case study cities that span the ideological spectrum, the overwhelming majority did not oppose immigrants' presence. Indeed, many were actively involved in efforts to accommodate newcomers. The same was equally true among the forty-one local government bureaucrats I spoke with across city administration, law enforcement, and the schools.

Still, the example of Mayor Macdonald and other restrictive local officials that have garnered media attention raises the question, If restricting immigrants' local presence and opportunities is potentially popular among the electorate, why do we see relatively little of it across immigrant destinations nationwide? Chapter 4 analyzed the contextual factors that predict local governments' responses to immigrants, finding in part that national politics and policies shape how local officials define and respond to local immigrants. Republican national rhetoric surrounding immigrants is more resonant and influential in places with a more Republican populace. But chapter 4 also presented evidence that cities with an appointed city administrator, rather than an elected mayor, as the local chief executive are less likely to pursue restrictive action, perhaps because they are less sensitive to political pressures. These findings suggest that both officials' role and their political ideology will influence their responses to immigrants. In this chapter I examine this topic further by analyzing which individual factors predict officials' attitudes toward serving immigrants. In particular, I test previous assertions that bureaucrats will be more likely to accommodate than will elected officials, and that Republican officials will be more likely to restrict.

I argue that while not all officials support immigrants all the time, local officials are predisposed to find favorable frames of immigrants more resonant and accessible, given the distinct legal and economic incentives associated with their position. As I discussed in chapter 4, some federal policies define immigrants as clients and require officials to provide certain educational, public safety, and language access services, at times regardless of immigrant legal status. In addition, as I will discuss in this chapter, local officials increasingly see immigrants as being a boon to their economy, whether by providing a desirable workforce, enhancing local entrepreneurship, or increasing their city's cultural vibrancy. Finally, as I will discuss further in chapter 6, when restrictive episodes arise, local officials are sensitive to external scrutiny that frames immigrants as a legally protected class and imposes reputational and legal costs associated with accusations of racism. In addition to these legal, economic, and reputational incentives, local officials tend to support immigrants based on their own higher socioeconomic standing, since on average better-educated people express more support for immigrants.

While local officials like Mayor Macdonald certainly exist and garner media attention with their outspoken criticism of immigrants, most local officials—both bureaucrats and politicians—hold favorable understandings of immigrants that contribute to a tendency toward accommodation among local governments. When immigration is politicized on the local level, elected officials, and particularly Republican elected officials, face countervailing incentives to restrict, as chapter 4 illustrated. Likewise, when federal policies constrain local officials to participate in restriction, these officials—particularly police chiefs who face pressure to participate in immigration enforcement—express greater concern about immigrant presence. On the whole, however, local officials' more favorable understandings of immigrants lead them to support immigrants more than the general public would choose. Indeed, evidence from the cases indicates that local officials often accommodate immigrants proactively—that is, before electoral demands to do so.

This chapter first considers earlier predictions about how officials' role and partisanship will shape responses to immigrants. I then turn to the cases to demonstrate that officials face distinct legal and economic incentives leading them to frame newcomers positively and to accommodate them, even prior to electoral demands. Using the MRIS, I test earlier predictions about how official role and partisanship will shape views on serving immigrants. Contrary to earlier predictions, I find that, on the whole, elected officials are not systematically different from bureaucrats. Politically conservative officials are less supportive of immigrants, though conservative ideology by no means predetermines a desire to restrict immigrants. Indeed, in the final section I show that local government officials in general—whether bureaucrats or politicians, conservative or otherwise—are distinctly more supportive of immigrants than is the general public.

Varying Responses by Local Official Role

Turning first to the influence of official role, according to bureaucratic incorporation theory bureaucrats will be more receptive to immigrants than elected officials will because bureaucrats' professional norms as service providers lead them to see immigrant residents as clients (Lewis and Ramakrishnan 2007; Jones-Correa 2008; Marrow 2009). Beyond this distinction between bureaucrats and elected officials, some scholars also distinguish between service bureaucrats, who possess a "client-serving ethic" (Derthick 1979, 21), and regulatory bureaucrats, who focus on maintaining adherence to rules (Jones-Correa 2008; Marrow 2009). Bureaucratic agencies can be arrayed along a continuum from strongly service-oriented institutions, such as schools, to more intensely regulatory agencies such as law enforcement. An agency's placement on this continuum shapes its responsiveness to immigrants (Marrow 2011). Bureaucratic incorporation theory predicts that bureaucrats will be particularly likely to respond to immigrants when federal policies such as refugee resettlement programs define immigrants as clients of local services (as discussed in chapter 4).

Where federal policies constrain local officials to participate in immigration enforcement, bureaucratic incorporation theory predicts that this regulatory involvement might shift officials' responses toward restriction. Since legislative changes in 1996, and particularly since the terrorist attacks of 9/11, local law enforcement has faced increased pressure to help enforce immigration laws, acting as "force multipliers" for the federal government (Provine et al. 2016, 2). Indeed, Secure Communities requires local police to interact with federal authorities, in that entering information on local arrestees in FBI databases automatically transfers the data to ICE as well. These policies have the potential to foreground officers' regulatory role toward immigrants by emphasizing definitions of immigrants as "illegal aliens" and involving local officers in enforcement (Donato and Rodriguez 2014). Along these lines, chapter 4 reported that towns within a hundred miles of US land borders, which were therefore more exposed to immigration enforcement operations, were more likely to take restrictive action toward immigrants. For police chiefs, the increasing devolution of immigration enforcement to localities could function in the same way, prompting greater restriction.

Despite these indications of law enforcement's increasing role in regulating immigration, the most comprehensive evidence of bureaucratic incorporation of immigrants comes from studies that compare local law enforcement's and elected officials' responses to immigrants. To date we have evidence from specific geographic locales that police are more likely to accommodate immigrants than are elected officials (Lewis and Ramakrishnan 2007), though this survey evidence from 2003 largely predates the rise in local immigration enforcement. We also have some limited evidence, again from specific places, that service-oriented bureaucrats are more accommodating than regulatory bureaucrats like police (Marrow 2011; Lucio 2013). But we lack a comprehensive nationwide investigation of bureaucratic incorporation theory that allows us to test the proposition that service-oriented bureaucrats will be most responsive to immigrants, followed by regulatory bureaucrats, and finally by elected officials.

Moreover, none of the previous studies have enabled direct examination of the mechanism underlying bureaucratic incorporation theory: that bureaucrats serve immigrants out of a sense of professional duty that elected officials lack. Most studies analyze reported policies rather than officials' attitudes toward providing services to immigrants. Given that bureaucratic incorporation theory is based on the premise that administrators' actions are shaped by their values (Meier and O'Toole 2006; Yang and Callahan 2007), it is important to measure not only the actions but also the underlying values. Indeed, without comparing the attitudes of elected officials and bureaucrats it is impossible to determine whether elected officials lack a sense of professional duty to serve immigrants. Some scholars have identified examples of politicians accommodating immigrants, though these tend to be presented as examples rather than as a systematic pattern (Ramakrishnan and Lewis 2005; Brettell 2008; Odem 2008; Price and Singer 2008; Frasure and Jones-Correa 2010; de Graauw 2014; Pastor, Ortiz, and de Graauw 2015).

While we tend to think of elected officials as "single-minded seekers of reelection" in Mayhew's (1974) famous phrase, studies at the local level suggest that municipal elected officials are often motivated by factors other than self-promotion, including a sense of civic obligation (Prewitt 1970) or a desire to advance specific causes or help local residents or organizations (Bledsoe 1993). As distinct from state and federal officials, local officials, particularly in smaller towns, may not harbor ambitions for higher office (Prewitt 1970; Bledsoe 1993; Lawless 2012).

In sum, while some scholars find evidence of elected officials' engagement, bureaucratic incorporation theory predicts that bureaucrats will be more likely to accommodate than elected officials owing to bureaucrats' professional duty to serve all local residents. Moreover, it predicts that service-oriented bureaucrats such as city managers will be more likely to accommodate than more regulatory bureaucrats like police chiefs. Thus I use the MRIS, a national survey of service bureaucrats (city managers), regulatory bureaucrats (police chiefs), and elected officials (mayors and city councilors), to assess these leaders' differing attitudes toward serving the foreign-born. In contrast to earlier theories, I draw on evidence from the cases to predict that both bureaucrats and elected officials face legal and economic incentives that lead them to embrace favorable definitions of immigrants and thus to accommodate them.

Varying Responses by Officials' Partisanship

Yet elected officials, especially Republican elected officials, are also subject to electoral pressures for restriction. Another strain of the literature suggests that partisanship will shape local officials' responses to immigrants, offering competing ideological incentives to restrict immigrants. At the national level, immigration advocacy group ratings clearly demonstrate the growing chasm between Democratic and Republican members of Congress on immigration policy (Abrajano and Hajnal 2015). Some have suggested that this partisan polarization extends to the local level (Gulasekaram and Ramakrishnan 2015), raising questions about my claim that local officials as a whole have a tendency toward accommodation.

In their analysis of renewed subfederal involvement in immigration policy since 2000, Gulasekaram and Ramakrishnan (2015) demonstrate that Republican partisanship is associated with an increased likelihood of restrictive state and local action. They argue that the rise of state and local restriction from 2004 to 2007 resulted from a coordinated strategy among national issue entrepreneurs. These entrepreneurs, from restrictionist advocacy organizations, national politics, and the media, framed immigration around security concerns in a post-9/11 world, emphasizing the purported danger and cost of "illegal aliens." At the same time, the issue entrepreneurs created model legislation and offered political advice and legal aid to states and localities willing to use it (Gulasekaram and Ramakrishnan 2015). Although restrictive towns claim their actions result from rapidly growing immigrant populations and federal inaction, Gulasekaram and Ramakrishnan (2015) demonstrate that restrictive action did not necessarily arise organically. For the most part Republican officials were not independently pursuing restriction at the local level; rather, they were more susceptible than Democrats to mobilization by restrictive issue entrepreneurs. Indeed, my own findings in chapter 4 indicate that more Republican-leaning places are less likely to accommodate and more likely to adopt restrictive enforcement practices.[1]

While Republican localities were statistically more susceptible to these negative definitions of immigrants, the fact remains that very few Republican localities actually pursued restrictive action. This evidence suggests that partisanship will be predictive but far from determinative of local responses to immigrants, with many Republican officials remaining relatively accommodating toward them. Nationally, and to some degree on the state level, it is hard for Republicans to deviate from a restrictive stance on immigration. At the local level, however, even some Republican elected officials will still support local accommodation because they are sufficiently insulated from public demands surrounding immigration, whether because immigration is not a salient voting issue locally or because local institutions shield them from public demands in general.

Local Officials' Motivations for Serving Immigrants

In sum, earlier studies suggest that bureaucrats will be the primary drivers of local accommodating responses to immigrants, while elected officials, especially Republicans, will be more subject to electoral incentives for restriction. In contrast, evidence from across the four cases suggests that both appointed and elected officials, even in politically conservative places like Yakima and Elgin, often proactively serve immigrants before electoral demands to do so because they see them as economic contributors, as deserving clients of municipal services, and as a group requiring protection from discrimination. In addition to these more favorable frames of immigrants, local officials are also predisposed to accommodate the foreign-born because of their own elevated socioeconomic standing.

Not surprisingly, local officials have more education than the average American (International City/County Managers Association 2012). Research on Americans' attitudes toward the foreign-born consistently finds that more educated people express greater support for immigrants, less because of self-interest and more because education is associated with less ethnocentrism and different understandings of immigrants' effects on society as a whole (for a review see Hainmueller and Hopkins 2014).[2] By virtue of their socioeconomic standing, local officials also have different experiences of immigration. Given their elevated status, local officials are more likely to choose when and where they interact with immigrants, offering a greater chance that these interactions are harmonious. A community organizer in Lewiston explained, "City professionals and folks in power would like to believe that [interethnic tensions] have sort of blown over. But they don't have to live downtown." In sum, local officials' greater education predisposes them to favorable views of immigrants, while their higher income often lets them be more selective in their interactions with immigrants, perhaps leading to greater harmony.

Beyond these socioeconomic differences, their own positions give local officials incentives to frame immigrants positively. Chapter 4 discussed how state and federal policies that define immigrants as clients set localities on a path toward accommodation. These policies are most influential in shaping bureaucrats' responses to immigrants, whom they are required to serve in their daily lives. That said, elected officials also are not immune to the influence of policies that define immigrants as clients, and they may well see serving them as an element of their duties, a proposition the MRIS allows me to test. Certainly elected officials are sensitive to civil rights policies and the costs of violating them (as I will discuss in chapter 6).

Moreover, municipal officials' economic development incentives lead them to see immigrants as economic contributors rather than solely as dependents. Across the socioeconomic spectrum and along several salient demographic characteristics, Americans prefer high-skilled, English-speaking immigrants who have entered legally and intend to work (Hainmueller and Hopkins 2015). While such immigrants are broadly preferred, I argue that municipal officials are more cognizant of immigrants' local role as valued workers and entrepreneurs. Public choice theories argue that local officials will not pursue "redistributive policies" that attract needy residents and drive out affluent taxpayers. Rather, cities will prioritize "developmental policies" that bolster the local economy (Peterson 1981). Some have argued that providing local services to immigrants flies in the face of these theories (Frasure and Jones-Correa 2010). Yet this claim depends on whether local officials see aiding immigrants as redistributive or developmental. I argue that officials often see accommodating practices as developmental, recognizing immigrants' contributions to the local economy. Given local officials' limited avenues for generating revenue, they often find themselves allied with business interests in a form of regime governance where businesses influence the policy agenda (Stone 1989). Through associations with local businesses, Chambers of Commerce, and economic development professionals, municipal officials are aware of immigrants' contributions to the local economy as workers, entrepreneurs, and consumers. What counts as redistributive versus developmental policy has always been a "coarse" distinction (Einstein and Glick 2016), but officials in the four new immigrant destination cities and beyond justify their efforts to serve immigrants as supporting economic development.

Across the four cases, both bureaucrats and elected officials report that their immigrant workforce not only contributes to existing industries but also might attract new businesses. Yakima's leaders have long recognized Latinos' contributions to the agricultural industry. More recently they realized that other businesses are attracted to Yakima precisely because of its bilingual, bicultural workforce. In 2006, major national retailers such as Whirlpool and Costco approached Yakima about setting up bilingual call centers. Yakima's economic development professionals spread the word about the national interest, and the message clearly impressed local leaders. As one elected official said, "Lately we've realized that our minus is a plus with the bilingual workforce." A Latino city employee recognized a similar shift in attitude:

> When I came here ten years ago and it was the old leadership, [a former leader would say] "Our workforce doesn't have any skills and they don't speak the language." . . . And now ten years later, boy, the number one thing we're promoting out there is a readily available workforce that's loyal and productive, and has bilingual capabilities when it comes to back-office stuff. . . . We've changed the outlook on what is it that the [Latino] community provides here.

In Lewiston local officials were excited about the contributions of Somali entrepreneurs. In a local newspaper column, former mayor Larry Gilbert wrote about the transformation of Lewiston's previously moribund downtown since the Somalis' arrival. Somali businesses now cover two city blocks on each side of Lisbon Street, Lewiston's main thoroughfare. Gilbert wrote, "These entrepreneurs are paying rent, taxes and circulating dollars in our community. They are contributing to life here in Lewiston" (2011). Even Mayor Macdonald has acknowledged Somali entrepreneurs' contributions, connecting the city's "multitude of small, diverse businesses" to Lewiston's turnaround (Macdonald 2014a).

Likewise, officials recognize immigrants' contributions as local consumers. An elected official in Yakima directly connected accommodating practices to immigrants' influence as consumers, saying, "The dollar really does drive a lot of what happens in communities, and the Hispanic community is more and more powerful, so that you have to truly reach them and cater them."

In addition to recognizing immigrants' contributions as laborers, entrepreneurs, and consumers, local officials across the four cases discussed how growing cultural diversity enhanced local economic competitiveness. An elected official in Elgin felt that diversity brought greater vitality: "Look, diversity's a plus. Yeah, it creates challenges, but it also creates excitement." Leaders in both Elgin and Wausau mentioned that ethnic diversity allows residents to "raise their kids to be competitive in this world." As its "DiverCity" advertising campaign attests, Elgin saw diversity as "a unique selling advantage." On a radio program, Mayor Ed Schock explained the city's embrace of the "DiverCity" slogan ("Chicago Matters" 2007):

Well, I think it starts with the basic belief and conviction that diversity is a factor that enhances the quality of life for everyone who lives in our community. That diversity—both economic as well as ethnic diversity—brings a richness to a community that homogeneity doesn't. So, we felt it was important to convey that message that this is a community that not only accepts diversity but welcomes it and embraces it.

Along the same lines, some elected officials had embraced the message of Richard Florida's *Rise of the Creative Class*, which argues in part that diversity supports the economic vitality of cities (Florida 2002). Florida even spoke in Lewiston in 2004, publicizing his message about the role of diversity in developing a "creative economy."

Increasingly, cities across the country see accommodating immigrants as a developmental policy that enhances their economic viability. Cities such as Baltimore, Detroit, and Pittsburgh have developed strategies specifically aimed at attracting immigrants (Pastor, Ortiz, and de Graauw 2015). As of 2014, as many as fourteen midwestern cities or metropolitan regions had developed formal initiatives intended to "recruit, retain, and welcome immigrants" (Kerr, McDaniel, and Guinan 2014). Former New York City mayor Michael Bloomberg founded Partnership for a New American Economy, which advertises itself as uniting "more than 500 Republican, Democratic, and Independent mayors and business leaders . . . in making the economic case for streamlining, modernizing, and rationalizing our immigration system" (Partnership for a New American Economy, n.d.). Similarly in Charlotte, North Carolina, the city's business elite has been influential in persuading local officials to maintain some accommodating responses toward immigrants in the interests of economic development, even as the state has swung toward greater restriction (Jones-Correa 2016).

While some localities trying to accommodate immigrants are large, politically liberal cities, the four examined in detail here are not. Even in these four cities with little previous experience of ethnic diversity, some of them politically conservative, local officials assert immigrants' economic value and see accommodating practices as contributing to local development.

These positive frames of immigrants as economic contributors motivate proactive municipal accommodation even in the absence of significant immigrant electoral power or interest group advocacy. Although bureaucratic incorporation theory posits that bureaucrats serve immigrants even without electoral pressure, some have argued that cities move toward accommodation only when pushed by immigrants' electoral clout (Dahl 1961; Browning, Marshall, and Tabb 2003) or by advocacy groups (de Graauw 2016). These factors are salutary in shaping accommodating responses, but my analysis demonstrates that they are not necessary conditions for accommodation. Across the four case study cities, we see examples in which both bureaucrats and elected officials proactively accommodate immigrants. Likewise, a recent analysis of responses in major metropolitan areas nationwide found that the share of immigrant voters did not directly predict local responses, though a vocal immigrant population did encourage accommodation in some cities (Mollenkopf and Pastor 2016).

Immigrants cannot exert electoral pressure until they are eligible to vote and exercise that power. Legal permanent residents (LPRs, or green card holders) generally may apply for citizenship after five years' residence in the United States. Unauthorized immigrants or those with non-LPR status are not eligible for naturalization (US Citizenship and Immigration Services 2016).[3] Among immigrants who obtained green cards from 1980 to 2012, nearly 8.8 million had not naturalized by January 2013, suggesting that roughly 30 percent of eligible immigrants from this period have not yet sought naturalization (Baker and Rytina 2014). Once immigrants naturalize they can participate in elections, but they register to vote and cast ballots less frequently than do native-born citizens (Ramakrishnan 2005). Thus there are multiple barriers to immigrants' electoral influence, including the exclusion of noncitizen immigrants, the time immigrants must wait before naturalization, and the fact that some eligible LPRs do not naturalize and some naturalized citizens do not register or vote.

Despite these barriers, across the four new destination cases, local officials were accommodating immigrants before the foreign-born were recognized as an influential voting bloc. By 2007 Lewiston, Wausau, and Elgin were already proactively accommodating immigrants, while Yakima was making some initial moves toward accommodation. In that year in Lewiston and Wausau, immigrants' political clout could not be a rational motivation for accommodation, since adult, naturalized or native-born members of the immigrant ethnic group made up only 2 percent of the electorate in each city. In Yakima and Elgin, though, Latinos made up 17 percent of the adult citizens in each city (American Community Survey 2005–7), a potentially influential portion of the electorate. In Yakima, however, elected officials did not perceive Latinos as voters. Even an elected official who championed accommodating immigrants reported that Latinos were not influencing local government because "they're not voting." Only in Elgin did any elected officials report responding to immigrants' electoral clout. One Republican state-level official whose district included Elgin reported,

> I represent a constituency, and I represent my entire constituency. And 42 percent of my district is Latino. I mean the majority of my district is minority. And when the Latino, the Lao, and the African American communi-

ties are here, you want to make sure that everyone has a voice, and I make sure I give rise to that voice. It also puts me on the firing line with some of the folks who don't feel that should be the case. . . . And the Latino community, contrary to popular belief, in this community votes and they get out the vote.

Other Elgin elected officials did not share this view. An elected city official who was otherwise relatively friendly toward immigrants echoed the views in Yakima, reporting flatly that "Hispanics don't vote" and attributing the situation to "more patriarchal cultures" with a "very difficult history of democracy." Thus, while Latinos exercised some political influence in Elgin, not all elected officials felt this influence. Likewise, only a few officials reported the influence of immigrant advocacy organizations, even though well-established ones were present in both Wausau and Elgin. Immigrants' political clout cannot be the complete explanation for accommodating policies, since all four cities implemented at least some accommodating policies and most did not see immigrants as politically influential.

In summary, the literature predicts that elected officials will be less likely than bureaucrats to accommodate immigrants. Further, to the extent that officials do accommodate immigrants, the literature suggests they will do so only along party lines, with Democrats more likely to accommodate and Republicans more likely to restrict. Drawing on the cases, however, I hypothesize that elected officials are also motivated to accommodate immigrants even in the absence of electoral incentives. While partisanship matters on the local level, I hypothesize that it is not determinative of local responses. Local officials, including Republicans, will be more accommodating toward immigrants than the general public would choose, signifying a municipal tendency toward accommodation owing to the officials' legal and economic incentives to embrace and act on favorable definitions of immigrants.

Testing Hypotheses about Officials' Attitudes toward Serving Immigrants

To test these hypotheses on a national scale, I turn now to the Municipal Responses to Immigrants Survey. In each town I surveyed two elected officials (the mayor and a randomly selected city councilor) as well as a regulatory bureaucrat (the police chief) and a more service-oriented bureaucrat (the city manager).[4] I selected these officials to capture the views of appointed and elected executives with similar levels of local influence and autonomy. While police chiefs fulfill both service and regulatory missions—protecting public safety and enforcing laws—their regulatory role with respect to immigration has been highlighted in recent years.

City managers also have both service and regulatory responsibilities—delivering programs to the public while also overseeing the implementation of local regulations—but are more typical of service-oriented bureaucrats and possess no specific regulatory duties with respect to immigrants. Studies of their duties show that city managers devote most of their time to their bureaucratic role of administering local services (Ammons and Newell 1989; French and Folz 2004; French 2005), and they increasingly spend time interacting with the public and attempting to build community (Nalbandian 1999; Nelson and Svara 2014). Although city managers regularly advise elected officials on policy matters, they cannot legislate independently, nor are they directly subject to voters' demands (Nelson and Svara 2014). For these reasons, bureaucratic incorporation theory predicts that service-oriented city managers will be most receptive and responsive to immigrants and regulatory police chiefs will be less so, trailed finally by elected city councilors and mayors.

The survey includes responses from 598 municipal officials across 373 cities representing the diversity in characteristics of city managers, police chiefs, and local elected officials. On average, local government officials are middle-aged, highly educated white men with considerable experience in local governance (table 5.1). Appointed officials average more than twenty years' experience, while elected officials average eleven to fifteen years of experience. Just under a quarter of city hall officials are women, while only 7 percent of police chiefs are women. Across all types of local government officials, more than 80 percent are non-Hispanic white, and a plurality describe themselves as politically conservative.[5] City managers are less likely than other officials to be ideologically conservative, as well as less likely to report Republican partisanship. Police chiefs are less likely to report liberal ideology or Democratic partisanship. These descriptive statistics suggest that if local officials differ in their views on immigration, we must ensure that these differences are not merely attributable to partisanship or ideology.

TABLE 5.1. **Local government officials' characteristics**

	All	Police	City manager	City councilor	Mayor
Average					
Age	55	52	54	58	60
Education	BA degree	BA degree	MA degree	BA degree	BA degree
Years of experience	21	29	24	11	15
Percent					
Women	18	7	22	26	21
Non-Hispanic white	85	86	84	82	86
Immigrant	3	1	3	4	4
Conservative	44	50	38	46	40
Liberal	24	12	26	29	34
Moderate	32	38	37	25	26
Republican	35	44	19	41	34
Democrat	31	21	28	36	44
Independent	31	33	48	22	18
N	598	196	154	128	120

Attitudes toward Serving Immigrants: Dependent Variables

The survey includes three key sets of questions on municipal officials' attitudes toward serving immigrants. First, the survey probed officials' motivations by asking how much they agreed or disagreed with several proposed reasons for serving foreign-born residents. As a direct test of bureaucratic incorporation theory, officials were asked whether serving immigrants was part of their professional duty and whether gaining immigrants' trust was a priority. Drawing on evidence from the cases, the survey further asked whether serving immigrants was important in order to welcome diversity, to maintain the local workforce, to bolster economic development, or to ensure compliance with federal regulations. Responses were measured on a five-point scale ranging from "strongly agree" to "strongly disagree." In the analyses that follow, the dependent variable is agreeing or strongly agreeing that these factors motivate the official's service to immigrants.

Second, the survey asked officials a variety of questions on the appropriate role of local government concerning immigration. One question asked, "What role should local governments play in immigration enforcement?" and respondents could check multiple options ranging from letting localities independently set their own immigration policies to protecting immigrant residents from federal enforcement. In the analyses that follow, I employ a binary variable that represents whether officials responded that "Local governments should not be involved in immigration enforcement." Another question probes officials' views on providing services to immigrants. I have constructed a five-point scale ranging from officials who believe local governments "should create programs and policies to help immigrants adjust to their new home" to officials who believe local governments "should restrict all immigrant access to programs, preserving benefits for native-born residents." In the analysis that follows I focus particularly on the likelihood of reporting that local governments should create programs for immigrants, as well as on the likelihood of reporting that local governments should restrict unauthorized immigrants' access to local services.

Third, the survey asked local officials eight questions often used in public opinion surveys to probe attitudes about the foreign-born, including whether immigrants drain local resources, raise taxes or crime, take jobs from other residents, or threaten the American way of life. Additional attitude questions include whether immigration to the United States should be reduced, whether immigrants contribute economically, and whether "there is a clear distinction in the contributions of legal and illegal immigrants." In multivariate analysis, I summarize immigration attitudes in an index that takes into account officials' views on all eight attitude questions. Each question is measured on a four- to five-point scale in which higher responses indicate greater concern about immigration.[6]

Identifying Predictors of Officials' Attitudes: Independent Variables

Together the three preceding sets of dependent variables allow me to assess how attitudes toward serving immigrants differ by official role and partisanship. In the analyses that follow, I first present descriptive statistics indicating differences across officials. I then turn to multivariate analysis to isolate the importance of official role in shaping these attitudes. In multivariate models, I control for the official's role, whether police chief, city councilor, or mayor, with city manager as the omitted category. Bureaucratic incorporation theory suggests that service-oriented city managers' views on serving immigrants will be consistently more receptive than those of other officials. Therefore if earlier theories

are correct, when controlling for other factors, police chiefs, city councilors, and mayors should express less interest in serving immigrants and
more concern about immigration.

In addition to these key explanatory variables identifying the officials'
roles, I control for officials' individual characteristics and political ideology as well as for contextual factors in their towns that may affect their
views on immigrants. At the individual level, analyses control for the official's age and education as well as for whether the official is a woman, is
nonwhite, or reports at least slightly conservative political ideology on a
seven-point scale ranging from very liberal to very conservative.[7] At the
contextual level, analyses control for the full range of factors identified
in past research as shaping municipal responses to immigrants, which
are described in detail in chapter 4. These factors include predictors of
ethnic threat, local capacity, immigrant visibility, external policy cues,
and immigrants' political clout.[8]

Municipal Accommodation across Official Roles

Table 5.2 illustrates responses to the three sets of questions broken down
by type of official. Looking to the first set of columns, in the aggregate
local government officials have concerns about immigration but express
a clear commitment to serving foreign-born residents. Nearly three-
quarters agree that serving immigrants is part of their professional duty
as well an important way to demonstrate "that our community welcomes diversity." Over half believe serving immigrants is important for
economic development and maintaining the local workforce, and nearly
half say gaining immigrants' trust is a local priority. Though a number of
officials select the neutral middle value on these five-point scales, very
few disagree with any of these statements. For instance, while just over
half agree that serving immigrants is important to maintaining the workforce, only 16 percent disagree with the statement, with the rest remaining neutral. On the whole, local officials are more motivated to serve immigrants than not.

Indeed, more than three-quarters of local government officials support providing services to immigrants, and more than half reject participating in immigration enforcement. Further, fewer than a quarter want
to impose restrictions on local services to unauthorized immigrants. Officials express some concern about immigrants, particularly in terms of
their taking jobs from other residents, but more than half also believe

immigrants contribute economically, and only 12 percent disagree that immigrants make economic contributions. While most of the immigration attitude questions at the bottom of table 5.2 are scored on a five-point scale on which officials could agree or agree strongly with the statement, the two variables on which they express the greatest concern (jobs and threat to American way of life) were scored on a four-point scale. The greater concern is because here officials are agreeing that these outcomes were at least "somewhat likely" compared with "not at all likely." Substantial proportions of officials express some reservations about immigrants, but a plurality disagree that immigrants raise taxes, increase crime, and drain local resources. As a whole, officials are far more likely than not to support providing services to immigrants, and on average they are motivated to serve immigrants in order to bolster the economy and signify welcoming diversity.

These aggregate figures, however, mask variations across types of local officials. Contrary to predictions of bureaucratic incorporation theory, bureaucrats are not systematically more likely to express interest in serving immigrants than are elected officials. Service-oriented bureaucrats (here, city managers) are more receptive to serving immigrants on most measures than are regulatory bureaucrats (here, police chiefs). However, police chiefs are also less receptive to immigrants than are elected officials (especially mayors) on many measures.

To demonstrate these patterns of response across officials in table 5.2, for each question the response most receptive to immigrants is highlighted in light gray, while the response least receptive to immigrants is highlighted in dark gray. Looking first at officials' inclinations for serving immigrants, more than half of all types of officials agree that serving immigrants is part of their professional duty, ranging from 58 percent of city councilors to fully 85 percent of police chiefs. This item roughly represents the anticipated pattern of response, with bureaucrats expressing a greater sense that serving immigrants is part of their professional obligation than elected officials do. Indeed, a two-sided test of proportions reflected in column (a) indicates that appointed officials are systematically more likely than elected officials to see serving immigrants as part of their professional duty.

Except for this item, however, responses to these questions do not follow the anticipated pattern. While 64 percent of police chiefs report that gaining the trust of immigrants is a priority, only 37 percent of city managers feel this way, similar to just over a third of city coun-

TABLE 5.2. **Local government officials' views on serving immigrants**

	All officials (%)		Appointed officials (%)		Elected officials (%)		Comparisons	
	Disagree all	Agree all	Agree - police	Agree - city manager	Agree - city councilor	Agree - mayor	(a)	(b)
Why serve immigrants?								
Part of my professional duty	8	74	85	79	58	65	****	
Important way to demonstrate we welcome diversity	8	71	70	78	62	74		**
Important for economic development	14	54	46	59	52	61		***
Important to maintaining workforce	16	53	46	49	48	61		***
Gaining immigrants' trust a priority	15	46	64	37	35	38	****	****
Important for maintaining compliance with federal regulations	14	37	39	37	36	38		
Local government role								
Local government should not enforce federal immigration law		53	47	66	45	56		****
Local government should provide access to existing programs		76	66	86	76	81		****
Local government should create programs to help immigrants		40	38	46	39	39		
Local government should restrict illegal immigrants' access to services		23	31	11	25	21		****
Immigration attitudes								
Immigrants contribute economically	12	53	46	58	55	57		**
Immigrants somewhat or more likely to take jobs		62	69	56	65	51		***
Immigrants somewhat or more likely to threaten American way of life		49	54	39	48	53		
Immigrants in community raise taxes	37	30	44	21	23	24	**	***

TABLE 5.2. **(continued)**

	All officials (%)		Appointed officials (%)	Elected officials (%)			Comparisons	
	Disagree all	Agree all	Agree - police	Agree - city manager	Agree - city councilor	Agree - mayor	(a)	(b)
Immigration to the United States should be decreased		28	30	26	26	27		
Immigrants in community increase crime	43	21	28	17	21	13		***
Immigrants drain local resources	49	17	21	11	22	14		***
Distinction in contributions of illegal immigrants	37	16	15	10	18	21	**	

Note: Column (a) represents two-sided difference of proportions tests comparing elected and appointed officials. Column (b) compares police chiefs and city councilors with city managers and mayors.
*p < .1
**p < .05
***p < .01
****p < .001

cilors and mayors. Here appointed officials are systematically different from elected officials, but only because police chiefs are such distinct outliers on this item. For the rest of the items, appointed officials are not systematically more likely than elected officials to say they are motivated to serve immigrants. Indeed, as column (b) demonstrates, a more evident pattern across the three sets of dependent variables is that city councilors and police chiefs are consistently less supportive of serving immigrants than are mayors and city managers (in two-sided tests of proportions). Contrary to bureaucratic incorporation theory, local officials' status as appointed or elected is generally not the primary factor driving their motivations for serving immigrants. That said, given differences in partisanship across official roles, multivariate analysis is necessary to sort out these competing explanations.

Multivariate analysis reveals that even holding constant officials' political ideology and the full range of individual and contextual characteristics, official role remains a strong predictor of motivations for serving immigrants, views on local government role, and attitudes toward immigrants in general. That said, official role does not operate the way bureaucratic incorporation theory predicted. Figure 5.1 uses the statistical software Clarify to predict the probability of agreeing that various factors motivate officials to serve immigrants while varying official role and holding all other variables at their means (Tomz, Wittenberg, and King 2003). As the top left panel indicates, police chiefs are the most likely to say that serving immigrants is part of their professional duty, with a predicted 90 percent agreeing with this view once other variables are held at their means. Their likelihood of agreeing exceeds city managers' by seven percentage points, a statistically significant margin, as indicated in regression table AD2 in appendix D. Elected officials, on the other hand, are statistically less likely than police chiefs and city managers to see serving immigrants as a professional duty, with 62 percent of city councilors and 66 percent of mayors agreeing with this statement, all else held constant.

Looking at the top right panel, agreement that gaining immigrants' trust is a priority displays a similar pattern. Here again police chiefs are the most likely to report that gaining trust is a priority. Chiefs (regulatory bureaucrats) exceed city managers (service-oriented bureaucrats) on this measure by thirty-three percentage points while holding other variables at their means. Elected officials are slightly more likely than city managers to say that gaining immigrants' trust is a priority, but not by a statistically significant margin.

On the whole, seeing service to immigrants as a professional duty somewhat follows the pattern anticipated by bureaucratic incorporation theory, with appointed officials more likely to agree with this statement than are elected officials. With respect to both variables, however, regulatory bureaucrats (police chiefs) report greater interest in serving immigrants than do service-oriented bureaucrats (city managers). Officials' views on gaining immigrants' trust also do not follow the anticipated pattern, since police chiefs see this as a strong priority and city managers respond much like elected officials.

Looking at the bottom left panel of figure 5.1, city managers are more likely to see serving immigrants as important to welcoming diversity than are those in either category of elected official. Here, however, police chiefs are not statistically distinct from city managers. Holding all other variables at their means, city councilors are eighteen percentage points less likely than city managers to agree that serving immigrants is important for welcoming diversity, while mayors are eight percentage points less likely to do so. In this case service-oriented bureaucrats express the greatest interest in serving immigrants, at a level statistically equivalent to police chiefs. That said, while the model predicts that 78 percent of police chiefs will agree that serving immigrants is important for welcoming diversity, it predicts that 77 percent of mayors will do so, demonstrating little gap between these regulatory bureaucrats and elected officials.

Finally, looking at the bottom right panel of figure 5.1, both police chiefs and city councilors were roughly ten percentage points less likely to agree that serving immigrants was important to maintaining the local workforce, while mayors were not statistically different from city managers. On whether officials saw serving immigrants as important for economic development (not shown), police chiefs were statistically less likely to agree with the statement than city managers were, while neither category of elected official differed from city managers. This pattern of results indicates that, contrary to bureaucratic incorporation theory, the salient distinction in motivations for serving immigrants is not whether officials are bureaucrats or elected officials.

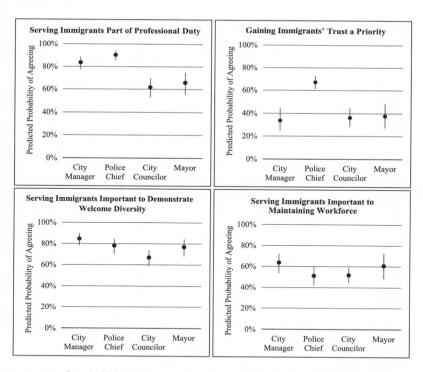

FIGURE 5.1. Local officials' predicted agreement with motivations for serving immigrants.

This finding extends to local officials' views on how municipalities should respond to immigration. Holding other variables at their means, a predicted 67 percent of city managers agree that local governments should not be involved in enforcing immigration law. Both police chiefs and city councilors are less likely to agree with this statement by a statistically significant margin (fig. 5.2). All else constant, just over half of police chiefs agree (52 percent), while just under half of city councilors agree (46 percent). Mayors are also directionally less likely to repudiate local immigration enforcement than city managers are, though not by a statistically significant margin. Police chiefs' regulatory role, combined with the devolution of immigration enforcement responsibility through Secure Communities, may make them less likely to eschew local enforcement. Moreover, contrary to bureaucratic incorporation theory, police did not express greater reluctance to enforce federal immigration laws than did elected officials.

Turning to views on serving immigrants, bureaucratic incorporation theory predicts that bureaucrats such as city managers and police chiefs

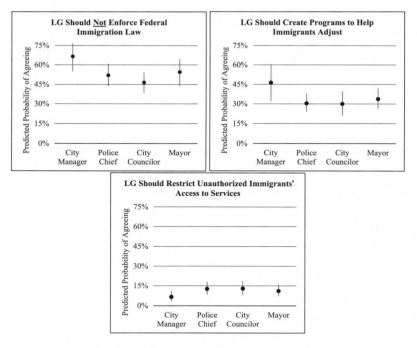

FIGURE 5.2. Local officials' predicted views on the municipal role vis-à-vis immigration.

will be more likely than elected officials to support providing services to immigrants. Here I present the predicted probabilities for supporting the creation of new programs for immigrants as well as the probabilities of wanting to restrict unauthorized immigrants' access to services, holding other variables at their means. As the top right panel of figure 5.2 indicates, even when holding ideology constant police chiefs are distinctly less likely than city managers to support creating new local programs to help immigrants adjust. With other variables held at their means, a predicted 46 percent of city managers believe municipalities should create new programs to help immigrants adjust, while only 30 percent of police chiefs agree—a gap of sixteen percentage points. City councilors' views on creating programs for immigrants are similar to police chiefs', while mayors' views do not differ statistically from those of city managers.

The same pattern is evident with respect to whether local governments should restrict unauthorized immigrants' access to programs. All else constant, a relatively small proportion of officials agree that local governments should impose these restrictions. Even when holding ideology constant, however, police chiefs are significantly more likely to agree with restriction, as are city councilors. Whereas bureaucratic incorporation would have predicted similarly receptive responses from bureaucrats and systematically less receptive responses from elected officials, these results indicate that city managers are distinctly more receptive to immigrants, while police chiefs do not differ markedly from elected officials.

Finally, a similar pattern emerges in officials' attitudes toward immigrants. Police chiefs are systematically less receptive, while elected officials do not differ significantly from city managers even when holding other individual and contextual variables constant. On the summative index of immigration attitudes, higher values represent greater concern about immigrants' taking jobs, raising crime and taxes, draining local resources, and other factors. The index ranges from a low of eight to a high of thirty-six, with an average among all officials of twenty. The top panel of figure 5.3 presents the predicted scores for each type of official on the composite index of immigration attitudes, holding all other explanatory variables at their means. All else constant, police chiefs register a predicted twenty-one on the composite index, compared with nineteen for city managers, a statistically significant 6 percent difference on the index.

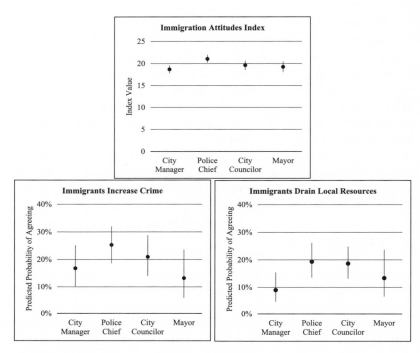

FIGURE 5.3. Local officials' predicted attitudes toward immigrants.

Compared with city managers, police chiefs consistently are directionally less receptive to immigrants and significantly less receptive on six of eight immigration attitude variables. Police chiefs are more likely to want a reduction in immigration and systematically express greater concern about immigrants' committing crimes, draining local resources, increasing taxes, and taking jobs. Likewise, police chiefs are more likely to acknowledge a distinction between the contributions of authorized and unauthorized immigrants. City councilors are also directionally less receptive to immigrants than city managers are, though only by a statistically significant margin on two of eight variables, once individual and contextual factors are taken into account. Finally, mayors are generally similar to city managers in their attitudes toward immigrants, differing by a statistically significant margin on only one variable.

In sum, the MRIS demonstrates relatively high interest in serving immigrants across both bureaucrats and elected officials. Although city managers and police chiefs are significantly more likely to say that serving immigrants is part of their professional duty, police chiefs otherwise express considerably less receptivity to immigrants. Elected officials, on the other hand, are not uniquely resistant to serving immigrants, with mayors generally expressing support for immigrants at levels similar to those of city managers. In total, multivariate analysis examined eight main variables—five motivations for serving immigrants, two variables regarding local government services to immigrants, and one composite variable measuring attitudes toward immigrants. Holding ideology and other salient factors constant, police chiefs were significantly more restrictive than city managers on five of these eight variables, though they were also the most interested in gaining immigrants' trust. City councilors were likewise more restrictive than city managers on five variables. Mayors differed from city managers by a statistically significant margin on only two of the eight variables.

Considerable case study evidence demonstrates that bureaucrats are actively accommodating immigrants even without political pressure to do so. My findings support the notion that local officials proactively try to accommodate, but contrary to bureaucratic incorporation theory, they indicate that elected officials also support accommodation. They also suggest that, despite their efforts to gain immigrants' trust, police officials have greater misgivings about immigrants' presence than do officials in other roles. Police views could be related to the increasing devolution of immigration enforcement tasks to the local level, bringing frames of immigrants as "illegal aliens" to the fore.

The analysis also validates predictions about the role of political ideology in shaping officials' responses. Conservative political ideology predicts less receptivity to immigrants across every variable examined here. Beyond official role and political ideology, relatively few variables serve as consistent predictors of officials' attitudes toward serving immigrants, though higher education is associated with more accommodating views toward immigrants on four of eight variables, underscoring the role of officials' socioeconomic status in shaping understandings of immigrants.[9]

Municipal Accommodation and Political Ideology

Although the preceding analysis demonstrates that many local officials feel motivated to serve immigrants, it remains true that not all officials are enthusiastic about doing so, and some want to actively restrict foreign-born presence. As predicted, these views break down along the lines of political ideology, such that conservative officials feel less motivated to serve immigrants. With conservative ideology being such a consistent predictor of concern about serving immigrants, it appears that polarization surrounding immigration extends to the local level, as some scholars predict (Gulasekaram and Ramakrishnan 2015). That said, how large are these effects? In this section I generate predicted probabilities to illustrate the effect of political ideology on attitudes toward serving immigrants, holding other factors constant. The analysis demonstrates that although partisanship is a strong predictor of officials' views, a substantial proportion of even conservative elected officials still support accommodating immigrants.

Since previous findings have emphasized the role of partisanship rather than ideology in shaping responses, it is worth briefly considering how my choice to control for ideology rather than partisanship affects my results. I chose that route because 21 percent of officials did not answer the partisanship question, compared with fewer than 9 percent declining the question on ideology. Conservative ideology and Republican partisanship are, of course, well correlated among officials (Pearson's r = 0.55). Of the conservatives who report their party affiliation, 65 percent are Republicans, 29 percent are independents, and only 6 percent (eleven officials) are Democrats. Ideology, then, serves as an effective proxy for partisanship. That said, as a robustness check, I reran all the preceding analyses controlling for Republican identification in lieu of conservative ideology. Doing so does not substantively change my conclusions about how official role shapes attitudes toward serving immigrants. Interestingly, however, Republican partisanship is a less consistent predictor of these attitudes than is ideology. Whereas conservative ideology was consistently associated with less support for immigrants on all eight dependent variables, Republican partisanship is a significant predictor on only four of eight variables. This discrepancy is due to the smaller sample size when controlling for party, as well as the fact that the contrast group "not Republican" is less precise, since it includes ideological conservatives who identify as independents but lean toward the Republican Party. For these reasons, in this case conservative ideology is a more effective proxy for partisanship than directly controlling for Republican identification.

The first panel of table 5.3 presents the predicted probabilities of attitudes toward serving immigrants for conservative officials versus those who are moderate to liberal, with other variables held at their means. In

TABLE 5.3. **Predicted attitudes toward serving immigrants by political ideology**

	Conservative officials	Liberal to moderate officials	Difference	Conservative elected officials	Liberal to moderate elected officials	Difference	Conservative elected officials in 62% Republican counties	Conservative elected officials in 33% Republican counties	Difference
Why serve immigrants? (%)									
Part of my professional duty	74	83	8 pp[a]	*60*	*66*	*6 pp*	*53*	*67*	*14 pp*
Gaining immigrants' trust a priority	40	50	11 pp	*35*	*35*	*1 pp*	*29*	*41*	*12 pp*
Important way to demonstrate we welcome diversity	66	85	19 pp	55	83	28 pp	41	67	26 pp
Important for economic development	43	67	24 pp	43	73	29 pp	34	52	18 pp
Important to maintaining workforce	42	67	25 pp	37	72	35 pp	37	*36*	*1 pp*
Local government role views (%)									
Local government should provide access to existing programs	45	42	3 pp	44	41	3 pp	41	44	*3 pp*
Local government should restrict illegal immigrants' access to services	16	8	8 pp	17	7	10 pp	22	13	9 pp
Local government should create programs to help immigrants	25	43	18 pp	21	43	22 pp	*14*	*28*	*14 pp*
Local government should not enforce federal immigration law	36	69	34 pp	33	65	31 pp	19	47	28 pp
Immigration views (%)									
Immigration attitudes index (score)	22	18	4 points	22	18	4 points	22	22	—
Immigrants in community increase crime	20	11	9 pp	21	9	12 pp	24	20	4 pp
Immigrants drain local resources	26	15	11 pp	28	6	22 pp	29	29	—

[a] Percentage points.

Note: In the second panel, results are italicized when conservative ideology is not a statistically significant predictor of attitudes. In the third panel, results are italicized when the proportion of the county voting for Romney is not a significant predictor of attitudes.

the second panel, because I predict that ideological differences are likely to be more pronounced among elected officials, I run the preceding analyses only for elected officials and generate predicted probabilities for conservative elected officials and others. Finally, in the third panel I generate the predicted probabilities among conservative elected officials in highly Republican counties and conservatives in counties with a low proportion of Republicans.[10]

While I expect to see differences between officials in general based on ideology (panel 1), I anticipate that these differences will be more pronounced among elected officials, who are more subject to partisan voter demands (panel 2). In panel 3 I test the combined effect of ideology and partisan context. In some cases we see wide partisan gaps among all officials, even wider gaps among elected officials, and gaps among conservative officials depending on the partisanship of the local electorate. Take, for example, the gap between conservative officials and others on whether providing services to immigrants is an important way of demonstrating openness to diversity. All else constant, conservative officials—both bureaucrats and elected officials—are nineteen percentage points less likely to say this is an important motivator for serving immigrants than are nonconservative officials. Among elected officials alone, the gap is even larger. Conservative elected officials are twenty-eight percentage points less likely than their nonconservative counterparts to see welcoming diversity as a motivator, with just over half of conservative elected officials agreeing with the statement. Conservative elected officials in highly Republican counties are even less likely to agree that welcoming diversity is an important motivator, at only 41 percent. In contrast, conservative elected officials in highly Democratic counties are 67 percent likely to agree with the statement, for a gap of twenty-six percentage points.

A similar pattern is evident with views on whether local governments should enforce federal immigration law. All else constant, roughly a third of conservative officials, whether bureaucrats or elected officials, agree that local government should *not* enforce federal immigration laws. Liberal and moderate officials, whether bureaucrats or elected, are over thirty percentage points more likely to agree with this statement, with roughly two-thirds eschewing local enforcement. Conservative elected officials in highly Republican counties are only 19 percent likely to agree with the statement, compared with conservative elected officials in highly Democratic counties, where 47 percent agree that local police should not be involved in enforcement—a gap of twenty-eight percentage points. In this case we see similar ideological gaps between all officials compared with only elected officials, as well as substantial gaps when partisan context is added to the picture. Thus partisan context is an important predictor of support for welcoming diversity as well as support for avoiding local enforcement. For the remaining variables, however, the partisan context is not a statistically significant predictor of conservative elected officials' views on these questions (as indicated in italics).

Indeed, among elected officials ideology itself is not always a predictor of differing views. As the second panel displays (in italics), there are only small, insignificant differences between conservative and nonconservative elected officials in seeing serving immigrants as professional duty or viewing gaining immigrants' trust as a priority. Even among conservative elected officials, a predicted 60 percent see serving immigrants as an element of their professional duty, while more than a third consider gaining immigrants' trust a priority. Larger gaps exist in conservative elected officials' views on other motivators for serving immigrants. Still, all else constant, substantial proportions of conservative elected officials say they are motivated to serve immigrants for these reasons.

On the single variable measuring officials' views on whether local government should provide or restrict services to immigrants, roughly equivalent portions of conservative and nonconservative elected officials agree that local governments should provide existing services to immigrants. Conservative elected officials are less interested than nonconservatives in creating new programs to aid immigrants, but a predicted 21 percent of them still believe local government should be generating such programs, all else constant. A greater proportion of conservative elected officials would like to see local governments restrict services for unauthorized immigrants. Still, all else constant, fewer than one in five conservative mayors and city councilors believe municipalities should implement these restrictive policies.

Last, with respect to attitudes toward immigrants, conservative officials hold more negative views than do nonconservative officials, though elected conservative officials are not substantially more negative than their nonelected counterparts. All else constant, 21 percent of conservative elected officials believe immigrants increase local crime, while 28 percent believe the foreign-born drain local resources. That roughly a quarter of conservative elected local officials hold negative views of

immigrants is no doubt consequential. Ideology is clearly a strong predictor of attitudes toward serving immigrants, even on the local level.

That said, even among conservative elected officials ideology is not determinative of attitudes. Among elected officials, conservatives and nonconservatives statistically are equally likely to see serving immigrants as
a professional duty, with a clear majority agreeing with this statement.
Likewise, ideology does not shape whether gaining immigrants' trust is a
priority, with more than a third of elected officials of all political stripes
agreeing with this statement holding other variables constant. Even
where we do see gaps between conservative officials and others, substantial proportions of conservatives—even among elected officials—remain
interested in accommodating the foreign-born. All else constant, from
one-third to more than half of conservative elected officials are motivated to serve immigrants in order to welcome diversity, support economic development, and maintain the workforce. A predicted 44 percent
want to give the foreign-born access to existing programs. On most measures, fewer than a quarter see immigrants negatively and want to restrict services to the unauthorized. The largest ideological gaps involve
local enforcement, but still, holding other variables constant, a third of
conservative elected officials do not believe local governments should
participate in federal immigration enforcement. In sum, while ideology
(and partisanship by proxy) is a strong predictor of local officials' views
on serving immigrants, even among conservative elected officials not every local official is operating from a partisan script. National partisan divides extend to the local level but are not entirely determinative of officials' attitudes toward accommodating immigrants.

Comparing Officials' Immigration Attitudes with Those of the Public

Moreover, while conservative officials are less receptive toward immigrants than are other officials, municipal officials on the whole have more
positive attitudes toward immigrants than the general public does, even
when taking into account these groups' differing demographic and ideological characteristics. The divergence between local officials and the
public on immigration is important because municipal accommodation
may not accomplish its aims if it meets resistance from the broader public. Table 5.4 illustrates the divergence in views on immigration between
local government officials and the general public. It compares data from
the MRIS with public opinion polls conducted at the same time using

similar questions. For instance, the 2014 General Social Survey (GSS), a long-running biannual national survey of Americans' views and habits, was in the field from March 31 to October 11, 2014, and the MRIS was in the field from July 2014 to February 2015. Likewise, a national Gallup poll was in the field June 5–8, 2014. All three surveys asked similar questions about whether immigration to the United States should be reduced.[11] A *New York Times* poll fielded May 7–11, 2014, included a question on local police enforcement of immigration law similar to the MRIS. In addition to these similar questions from polls fielded at the same time as the MRIS, a national survey conducted in February 2008 through Time-Sharing Experiments in the Social Sciences (TESS) contained three identical immigration questions (see Hopkins, Tran, and Williamson 2014). Although public opinion on immigration does fluctuate in response to events in the news and other factors (Hopkins 2010, 2011), comparing the MRIS with the GSS and with TESS data produces nearly identical results, suggesting that the 2008 survey can serve as a reliable point of comparison despite the time gap.

As table 5.4 displays, polls of the broader public reflect a greater interest in reducing immigration, with 41–50 percent of the public supporting a reduction compared with only 28 percent of local officials. Here the variable in question is the proportion of respondents reporting that immigration should be reduced, whether by a little or by a lot. Statistically significant gaps between officials and the public remain even when we control for available demographic and ideological predictors of immigration views. Looking first at pooled data comparing GSS and MRIS respondents, I control for education, age, and whether the respondent is a local official, Republican, conservative, female, or nonwhite (regression results in appendix D, table AD3). Being a local government official is strongly associated with a decreased likelihood of saying that immigration should be reduced. Indeed, the model predicts that a fifty-five-year-old college educated, conservative, Republican white man is 54 percent likely to report that immigration should be reduced, while a municipal government official with the same characteristics is only 41 percent likely to do so—a gap of thirteen percentage points. Conducting the same analysis using pooled data from the 2008 TESS survey and the MRIS produces very similar results. The predicted value for demographically identical TESS respondents is that 55 percent agree that immigration should be reduced compared with 44 percent of municipal officials—here, a gap of eleven percentage points. Not only are local gov-

TABLE 5.4. **Comparing local government official and public views**

	NYT 2014	GSS 2014	Gallup 2014	TESS 2008	MRIS All	Police	City manager	City councilor	Mayor
Immigration to the United States should be decreased (%)		44	41	50	28	30	26	26	27
Immigrants somewhat or more likely to take jobs (%)				89	62	69	56	65	51
Immigrants somewhat or more likely to threaten the American way of life (%)				75	49	54	39	48	53
Local government should not enforce federal immigration law (%)	39				53	47	66	45	56
N	1,000	2,005	1,027	566	410	196	154	120	128
Margin of error	+/– 4	+/– 3	+/– 4	+/– 5	+/– 4	+/– 7	+/– 8	+/– 9	+/– 9

Sources: NYT = *New York Times*; GSS = General Social Survey; TESS = Time-Sharing Experiments in the Social Sciences; MRIS = Municipal Responses to Immigrants Survey.

ernment officials more supportive of immigration than the general public, they are even more supportive than their demographic and ideological characteristics predict.

The gaps are similarly large when we consider the questions on whether immigrants "take jobs away from people already here" and whether "current and future immigration will threaten the American way of life." Questions are identical on the MRIS and TESS, with responses ranging on a four-point scale from "not at all likely" to "very likely." The variables analyzed here reflect whether the respondent believes these outcomes are at least "somewhat likely" as opposed to "not at all likely." Holding constant the same set of demographic and ideological characteristics, local government officials are significantly less likely to report that immigrants will take jobs and threaten the American way of life.

With respect to jobs, the model predicts that a fifty-five-year-old college educated, conservative, Republican white man is 91 percent likely to report that immigrants are at least somewhat likely to take jobs, while a municipal government official with the same characteristics is 74 percent likely to feel the same—a seventeen percentage point gap. Likewise, with respect to threats to American culture, the model predicts that a member of the public with these characteristics is 85 percent likely to feel that immigrants are at least somewhat likely to threaten the American way of life, while a demographically identical local government official is 72 percent likely to feel the same, for a gap of thirteen percentage points. Keep in mind that these are the predicted values for conservative Republicans. For demographically similar local officials who are not conservative or Republican, the predicted value is 47 percent support for the idea that immigrants are somewhat likely to threaten the American way of life and 62 percent support for the idea that immigrants are somewhat likely to take jobs. While this level of concern about immigrants may still seem high, it remains statistically distinct from most Americans, who are much more concerned about immigrants' presence.

If we instead control separately for each local government role, the responses of city councilors and city managers remain distinct from those of both GSS and TESS respondents. In the GSS data, police and mayoral responses are directionally less supportive of reducing immigration but fall just below conventional levels of statistical significance ($p = 0.13, p = 0.11$, respectively). However, the views of mayors and police may be less statistically distinct largely because these officials were less likely to answer the partisanship question and because including Republican as a control results in the loss of a number of cases. Controlling only for conservative and not Republican, the views of all four officials are statistically distinct from those of the public, even taking into account their demographic and ideological characteristics. Analysis of the TESS question on reducing immigration produces quite similar results when controlling separately for the local government roles. Here, however, even removing Republican from among the controls, police chiefs' views are not statistically distinct from the public's at conventional levels ($p = 0.18$). As the preceding analysis has indicated, local government officials' views are distinct from the public's, but among officials, police chiefs express the greatest concern about immigrants and therefore are the least distinct from the public, perhaps underscoring the influence of the devolution of federal enforcement policies. On the other questions analyzed here, however, all four officials express views that are statistically more favorable toward immigration than those of the general public, even holding other salient characteristics constant.

These gaps extend to views on how local governments should respond to immigration, with 53 percent of officials agreeing they should not enforce federal immigration law, compared with 39 percent of the American public opposing "local police taking an active role in identifying undocumented or illegal immigrants."[12] While these questions differ in important ways, in combination with the preceding comparisons they provide strong suggestive evidence that not only do local officials have more favorable views of immigrants, but they are also less willing to participate in federal enforcement than the broader public would like them to be.

Of course, we might expect local officials' views to differ significantly because they are a demographically distinct group—largely white, male, middle-aged, highly educated, and—at least in the MRIS—leaning toward conservatism and Republican partisanship. Data from both the 2014 GSS and the earlier TESS survey demonstrate that local government officials are more supportive of immigration even when holding these demographic and ideological characteristics constant. This analysis suggests that, on the whole, local government officials express more favorable views toward immigrants than the public does, not because of their demographic characteristics or ideology, but by virtue of their position and the incentives associated with it.

One might argue that gaps between officials and the public result from some form of social desirability bias, since officials answered these questions more carefully on a survey in which they were representing their town rather than acting as individuals. In the event that officials behaved this way, their caution only underlines my broader point. When discussing and responding to immigration, local officials face incentives distinct from those of the general public. As evidence from the cases and survey demonstrates, local officials' legal and economic incentives lead them to frame immigrants as deserving clients, economic contributors, and a legally protected class. In response, they express less concern about immigrants than the broader public does and have a greater interest in serving immigrants locally. Although partisan divides extend to the local level and shape responses, municipal officials, including elected officials, remain more supportive of immigrants than their demographic and ideological characteristics would predict.

Conclusion

Previous literature suggested that bureaucrats will accommodate immigrants while elected officials, particularly Republican elected officials, will not. Interviews with bureaucrats and elected officials across four new immigrant destination suggest that local officials in general tend to embrace favorable definitions of immigrants, contributing to a tendency toward municipal accommodation. The MRIS confirms these findings, demonstrating that substantial majorities of both elected and appointed officials see serving immigrants as a professional duty and an important way to demonstrate that they embrace diversity. Bureaucrats do not differ systematically from elected officials in their views on immigrants, suggesting that the distinction between bureaucrats and politicians is not the most salient factor shaping their responses. Political ideology represents a much starker dividing line shaping officials' views. Nonetheless, comparing officials' survey responses with polls of the American public demonstrates that local officials are distinctly more likely to support immigrants, even taking into account demographic and ideological differences between these populations. Even politically conservative elected officials are systematically more supportive of immigrants than are ideologically and demographically similar members of the public. As a result, proactive efforts to serve immigrants often extend beyond bureaucrats to a more encompassing municipal incorporation.

These findings provide limited support for bureaucratic incorporation theory, but they also raise key questions. The central tenet of the theory—that bureaucrats are more likely than elected officials to serve immigrants owing to unique professional incentives—earns support, with city managers and police chiefs systematically more likely to report that they serve immigrants out of a sense of professional duty. Beyond this question, however, officials' attitudes do not fit the pattern suggested by bureaucratic incorporation theory. The theory predicts that not only will bureaucrats be more responsive to immigrants than elected officials will, but that service bureaucrats will be systematically more responsive than regulatory bureaucrats. This nationwide survey of 598 officials in small to midsize towns does not identify a pattern in which bureaucrats are consistently more receptive to immigrants. Rather, city managers and mayors tend to be more receptive while police chiefs and city councilors tend to be less so. Police chiefs express the greatest motivation to serve immigrants out of a sense of professional duty and a desire to gain their trust. Beyond these two questions, however, police chiefs tend to be less receptive than service-oriented city managers but not more so than elected officials. Indeed, police chiefs express the highest concern about how immigrants will affect the community—exceeding both city managers and elected officials.

While police officers are more politically conservative than other officials, these findings remain true even when controlling for individual political ideology and other potentially confounding variables. Political ideology is a strong and consistent predictor of less interest in serving immigrants and more concern about foreign-born presence. Beyond the official's political ideology, official role was the only significant predictor of these attitudes across all eight variables examined.

The findings raise several key questions that warrant examination in future work. First, this chapter measures officials' attitudes rather than their actual policies toward immigrants. Previous studies of bureaucratic incorporation have tended to investigate policies rather than attitudes. These studies present evidence that police departments are more active in responding to immigrants than are city halls (Lewis and Ramakrishnan 2007). Indeed, as chapter 3 details, the MRIS also demonstrates that police chiefs report more accommodating policies toward immigrants than both city managers and elected officials. Police chiefs are more likely than city hall officials to report accepting foreign consular identification cards and more likely to say their town follows an informal "don't ask, don't tell" policy on unauthorized status. In contrast to city hall officials, police chiefs report translating materials more routinely and are more likely to have a designated immigrant liaison. Likewise, they are more likely to say they offer additional compensation to attract bilingual employees.

Although police departments are more active, this chapter suggests that these accommodating law enforcement policies do not stem from a unique enthusiasm for serving immigrants or from distinct goodwill toward them. More research is necessary to definitively determine what factors contribute to this disjuncture between police chiefs' less receptive attitudes toward immigrants and their more active efforts to serve them. Evidence presented in chapter 4 about the influence of federal policies in shaping local responses suggests that the increasing devolution of immigration enforcement to local police may play a key role. Scholars have demonstrated how policies that restrict immigrants' rights or increase the salience of definitions of immigrants as "illegal aliens" can make bureaucrats less responsive to them (Marrow 2009; Donato and Rodriguez 2014). Increased federal devolution of immigration enforcement since 2001 foregrounds police officers' regulatory role with respect to immigrants, making negative frames more accessible and resonant. At the same time, police officers also have a service-oriented role to serve and protect local residents, which leads them to give priority to gaining immigrants' trust. Elected county sheriffs provide an interesting contrast to appointed police chiefs on this count. Some findings suggest that sheriffs are both more exposed to federal enforcement because they are more likely to operate jails and more motivated by partisanship because they are elected (Farris and Holman 2017). Nonetheless, further investigation is necessary to better understand the countervailing pressures federal policies place on police chiefs' practices toward and attitudes about immigrants.

Additional investigation is also necessary to understand why mayors often are more receptive to immigrants than city councilors are, even when controlling for ideology and other factors. Mayors' role as the public representatives of their cities may make them uniquely interested in cultivating a receptive image compared with more parochially focused city councilors.

This chapter also identifies the importance of ideology in shaping both elected and appointed officials' attitudes toward immigrant residents. Chapter 4 argued that local officials' responses to immigrants reflect federal policies that both require service provision and condition them to see the foreign-born as clients. Chapter 5 demonstrates that the effects of these policy frames vary based on the official's ideological background. Officials' responses therefore are shaped both by the socializing effect of their role and by their own characteristics (Oberfield 2010).

Political divisions are stark and determinative at the federal level, but at the local level ideology predicts but does not determine municipal officials' attitudes toward serving immigrants. A substantial proportion of even conservative elected officials remain interested in providing services to local immigrants. When immigration is not politicized at the local level, officials are insulated from national partisan debates surrounding immigration. In Elgin and Yakima, Republican local officials went so far as to appoint Latinos to vacant elected positions, claiming it was a means to represent the growing immigrant community.

A final piece of evidence underlining local government officials' distinct incentives for serving immigrants stems from comparing attitudes toward immigrants among the public versus among municipal officials. Local government officials are systematically more supportive of immigrants than the public is, even holding constant differences in demographic and ideological characteristics. As chapter 8 discusses, this disjuncture means that accommodating policies can contribute to backlash against both immigrants and the officials who support them.

Ultimately, this chapter does not fully corroborate the claims of bureaucratic incorporation theory because it does not find that bureaucrats are systematically more receptive to immigrants than are elected officials. On the other hand, it does provide strong evidence that many local officials—both bureaucrats and elected officials—support serving immigrants. Looking across all categories of officials, more than three-quarters say that local governments should give immigrants access to local services. Likewise, almost three-quarters see serving immigrants as part of their professional duty. While officials express some misgivings about immigrants' perceived toll, particularly in taking jobs, more than half of officials see serving immigrants as an important component of maintaining their local workforce and supporting economic development, and few disagree with these statements. As a whole, these findings suggest that while bureaucrats may not be uniquely receptive to immigrants, local officials in general often support accommodating them even before electoral demands to do so. Indeed, local officials appear more supportive of immigrants than the general public would choose. As a result, elected officials at times pursue restrictive policies more closely aligned with public opinion in order to garner support. Chapter 6 discusses what happens when such restrictive responses arise and demonstrates that even in these cases local officials ultimately face strong legal and reputational incentives to scale back restriction and move toward accommodation.

CHAPTER SIX

The Civil Rights Legacy, External Scrutiny, and Reining in Restrictive Response

We're not gonna be like Selma, Alabama; we're gonna make sure that this works. — Civic leader, Wausau, Wisconsin

In 1993 local turmoil over Wausau's school desegregation plan garnered national attention, with unflattering portrayals in major media outlets. Local leaders insisted they objected to the redistricting because it did away with neighborhood schools, not because their children would be integrated with Hmong refugees. Nonetheless, some saw the concerns as racist, and it became clear that turning back the desegregation plan ran afoul of federal civil rights law. Responding to external scrutiny from the media and advocacy organizations, local officials adopted a modified desegregation plan and ramped up efforts to demonstrate that they welcomed the Hmong. The community leader quoted above linked these local efforts to a desire to disassociate Wausau from America's history of racial prejudice. As this quotation suggests, local officials are sensitive to accusations of racism and often respond to external scrutiny of restrictive responses by reining in restriction and even pursuing compensatory accommodation to mitigate association with racism.

Chapters 4 and 5 identify the power of federal policies and national political discourse in shaping local definitions of immigrants and shifting the tenor of local response. In combination, these chapters argue that local government officials are more likely to accommodate than restrict resident immigrants because they are subject to federal policies and economic incentives that frame immigrants as clients and contributors. Readers familiar with the current tenor of political debate surrounding immigration as well as with some highly publicized examples of local government restriction of immigration may be surprised by these conclusions. Although this book demonstrates that local government restriction is not prevalent, what about these highly visible cases of opposition to immigrants, as we saw in Hazleton and also in three of the four cases?

In this chapter I analyze what happens when local governments pursue restrictive action toward immigrants. I find that even in small, previously homogeneous new immigrant destinations local officials are sensitive to definitions of immigrants as a protected class under civil rights law and in some cases have internalized antidiscriminatory norms associated with these protections. As a result, external scrutiny of restrictive responses from the media and advocacy organizations leads officials to scale back restriction and even promote compensatory accommodation. Drawing on evidence from the cases as well as an original database that reveals the current status of responses to immigrants in ninety-four once restrictive cities, I demonstrate that the federal civil rights legal framework tends to set municipalities on a path toward accommodation over time.

The Civil Rights Legacy and Immigrant Incorporation

When local governments respond restrictively to immigrants, they often attract scrutiny in the form of federal regulators, advocacy organizations, and media coverage. The civil rights movement established antidiscrimination policies governing the treatment of ethnic minorities and institutionalizing antidiscriminatory norms. Increasingly, these policies designed primarily to serve native-born ethnic groups are aiding in the incorporation of immigrants (Graham 2001; Skrentny 2001; Kasinitz et al. 2008). Among other examples, the 1974 Supreme Court case *Lau v. Nichols* drew on the "national origin" clause of the 1964 Civil Rights Act to require public schools to accommodate immigrant children with ELL instruction (414 U.S. 563 [1974]). Likewise, the language provisions of the 1965 Voting Rights Act provide non-English-speaking immigrants with access to the polls. And the 1968 Fair Housing Act ensures that local policymakers face consequences when housing code enforcement disproportionately affects ethnoracial minorities, including many immigrants. Indeed, an international index comparing nations' immigrant integration policies identifies the United States' antidiscrimination infrastructure as among the most comprehensive in protecting immigrants (Migration Policy Index 2015, as noted in Bloemraad and de Graauw 2012).

The United States lacks a comprehensive immigrant integration strategy, but federal civil rights law contributes to moving local governments toward accommodation. Where towns' restrictive immigration practices violate federal policies and associated antidiscriminatory norms, the media and advocacy organizations can frame immigrants as a legally protected class experiencing discrimination. To be clear, civil rights regulations do not protect immigrants as a group per se. Rather, they prevent discrimination based on race, ancestry, or national origin, among other categories. Local officials curtail restriction when regulators, the media, and advocacy organizations frame immigrants as a protected class experiencing discrimination along one of these dimensions.

Federal intervention alone does not explain the far-reaching influence of civil rights regulations in shaping local government practices. Although no comprehensive count of federal civil rights investigations and prosecutions is readily available, recent reports from the Department of Justice's Civil Rights Division provide some sense of the scale of these interventions. From 2009 to 2013, the Office of Civil Rights and associated federal civil rights regulatory agencies reported on fifty-seven civil rights enforcement matters pursued against local governments. Of these fifty-seven, eleven dealt with violations of immigrants' or immigrant ethnic groups' civil rights, with five related to language access for students or voters and six related to the rights of immigrant ethnic groups, such as disproportionate discipline against Somali students in a Minnesota school district (US Department of Justice, Civil Rights Division, 2013a, 2013b). Given that the report highlights matters involving only fifty-seven local governments over a five-year period, the federal government's direct civil rights regulation efforts have relatively little reach. Moreover, as I will discuss at the end of this chapter, civil rights investigations have been dramatically scaled back under the Trump administration, raising questions about the role of these policies in shaping local responses (Bazelon 2017; Huseman and Waldman 2017).

That said, regardless of the scale of federal civil rights investigations, the infrastructure of institutions that have developed in response to federal civil rights regulations has more far-reaching influence. Title VI of the Civil Rights Act included provisions allowing the federal government to withhold funding from local agencies that violated its mandates. Revoking funding proved politically unworkable, but federal courts demonstrated their willingness to issue injunctions against local authorities in response to suits brought by private parties. Subsequent reforms increased the monetary damages and attorney fees that parties could seek in bringing suit, enabling the further development of legal and advocacy institutions for civil rights (Melnick 2014a, 2014b).[1] While the reach of the US federal government appears weaker than that of European advanced democracies, federal influence is strong through private actions pursued in the courts (Melnick 2014b). Together, federal law and civil rights organizations have been influential in developing antidiscriminatory norms, leading some to describe the federal government as "administratively weak, but normatively strong" (Dobbin and Sutton 1998, 441).

Through the combination of antidiscriminatory institutions and norms, external scrutiny of local governments can rein in restriction in three ways. For those who have internalized antidiscriminatory norms, association with bigotry is personally embarrassing (Gilens, Sniderman, and Kuklinski 1998; Fazio and Hilden 2001). As literature on explicit racial appeals indicates, non-Hispanic whites tend to reject messages with clear racial content, in response to the violation of egalitarian norms (Mendelberg 2001; Huber and Lapinski 2006; but see White 2007; Hutchings, Walton, and Benjamin 2010). Even for those who resist antidiscriminatory norms, their broader influence makes deviating costly in two ways. Civil rights regulators and advocacy organizations may bring lawsuits that place fiscal strain on localities. More broadly, the reputational effects of association with discrimination threaten loss of business and other economic consequences. Along these lines, Charles Epp (2009) has argued that local government officials adopt reforms in several policy spheres in response to the "'carrot' of professional legitimacy" coupled with the "'stick' of legal pressure." For some officials, professional embarrassment associated with racism serves as a crucial motivator, while for others the threat of legal costs and consequences is more potent.

Despite some portrayals of new immigrant destinations as backward and even racist, I find that local officials in these settings demonstrate concern about damaging professional legitimacy through association with bigotry. Where policymakers have internalized antidiscriminatory norms, the values underlying these norms—emphasizing common humanity, respect for difference, and equal treatment—can both prevent negative treatment of immigrants and encourage positive treatment. Restrictive episodes followed by external scrutiny can act to redraw the boundaries of local community (Wong 2010), emphasizing immigrants' status as "us" over their status as "them." Not all places are sensitive to the antidiscriminatory norms that can prompt these reconceptualizations of community. Yet even where local leaders have not embraced such norms, the existence of civil rights policies and the advocacy organizations that have grown up to protect them can frame immigrants as a legally protected class and thereby propel or compel localities to scale back restriction and even promote accommodation. These processes are evident in Lewiston, Wausau, and Elgin, as the next section details, but they can also be seen in a quantitative analysis of ninety-four once restrictive locales in the section that follows it.

External Scrutiny, Scaled-Back Restriction, and Compensatory Accommodation

After months of simmering tension, in October 2002 Lewiston mayor Laurier Raymond wrote his infamous letter to the growing Somali community, asking them to slow their migration because Lewiston was "maxed-out" (Raymond 2002). In the aftermath of the letter, reporters from around the world descended to chronicle the story, and a white supremacist group announced it would hold a rally in Lewiston supporting the mayor's message. In the four months from October 2002 to January 2003, coverage of the mayor's letter and the rallies included thirty major US and Canadian newspapers and all three major television networks' nightly news, plus CNN, NPR, and Voice of America. At least three federal agencies and the state attorney general's office investigated claims of civil rights violations. Several national advocacy groups sent representatives to weigh in on the controversy, including the Somali Justice Advocacy Center, the ACLU of Maine, the Portland branch of the NAACP, and the National Coalition Building Institute.

The external scrutiny mobilized local government administrators to more actively accommodate Somalis. Local officials helped to convene the Many and One rally, which protested the white supremacist event and expressed Lewiston's welcome to the Somali population. One city employee explained how media attention catalyzed local efforts to respond to Somalis:

> The media has blasted us up every chance it could. I think [the mayor's letter] was a turning point in that it brought the attention. It certainly brought the Many and One Coalition and the rally. And that showed the rest of the state and the rest of the county, and the rest of the world, I guess, . . . that Lewiston and its residents are not a bunch of racist people.

Lewiston's deputy city administrator Phil Nadeau directly attributed a variety of subsequent efforts to serve Somalis to the external scrutiny, writing, "Much of the local, state, or statewide activity . . . correlated directly to the public attention" (Nadeau 2003b, 34).[2]

In part the city's intensified efforts to serve Somalis stemmed from concerns about the legal costs of civil rights violations. Nadeau commented that the "ever-present threat of litigation elevated the need for a rapid and professional response" (Nadeau 2003b, 29). After Justice Department inquiries, the city invited the department's Civil Rights Division to assist with local compliance. As part of this effort, the city initiated community dialogues to address intergroup conflict, which were endorsed publicly by the City Council.

But local leaders were also concerned about the reputational consequences of appearing discriminatory. A business leader expressed his concern about the effect: "It's all part of image. . . . You've got this issue flared up and skinheads coming to town and making us look nasty and like all the racists in the world are in Lewiston, Maine." The Lewiston-Auburn (L-A) Economic Growth Council and the Androscoggin Chamber of Commerce launched a public relations campaign to combat the image of Lewiston as backward and racist. The effort mobilized seventy-one businesses to fund a series of newspaper advertisements that included the headline "Strength through Diversity: An L-A Tradition" (Scott 2003).

A city employee summed up how the external scrutiny changed the tone of local discourse: "After the [mayor's] letter you had this pendulum of people who swung really far to the side of 'we-don't-want-the-Somalis.' But when the supremacists showed up they didn't want to be seen as racists, so things swung back a bit." While not all local officials and residents became proponents of the Somalis after the mayor's letter, the unwanted attention from white supremacists defined the Somalis as a legally protected racial group and made it politically infeasible to openly criticize them.

Likewise, as the opening to this chapter details, external scrutiny following Wausau's debate over school desegregation resulted in a retreat from restriction and intensified efforts at accommodation. In the midst of the desegregation controversy, Wausau was the subject of an influential piece in the *Atlantic Monthly* and an unflattering profile on *60 Minutes* (Beck 1994; CBS News Transcripts 1994), along with coverage in a dozen major US newspapers. Though the desegregation battle and the resulting school board recall deeply divided Wausau, both opponents and proponents of the original redistricting plan shifted their behavior in response to scrutiny.

Facing lawsuits alleging school segregation, the newly elected school board retreated from its stance against redistricting and approved a plan that bussed Hmong children throughout the district. Other officials ramped up efforts to respond to the Hmong, through a local task force that enhanced efforts to incorporate them in public life. A local nonprofit leader explained further:

> I know that the community got some bad publicity out of [the schools controversy] on a national level and that became a catalyst. . . . The city fathers, the people with money, the people that owned things, were real sensitive to that and wanted to do something about it. . . . I kind of feel like there's two chapters to the story. The one chapter leading up to the whole bussing thing. And then the healing process I feel like that took place after that, that made it possible for this community to welcome a second wave of refugees. . . . I kind of feel like the community did a lot of work to compensate for that experience.

For both opponents and proponents of the original school desegregation plan, the disparaging press coverage and accusations of racism were difficult to handle. More than a decade after the episode, a local journalist recalled how the coverage "cut people. It really hurt." A businessman involved in recalling the school board described how the legacy of the negative coverage heightened sensitivity to antidiscriminatory norms: "You got a community that's been open arms and everything else, but I think there's so many people that walk on pins and needles because they figure they're gonna be called a racist or something if they say something that's just not right."

An elected official similarly emphasized the resultant local sensitivity to accusations of racism:

> I think that in the leadership of the community it's not acceptable to be a racist. You're just not gonna express those kinds of ideas overtly and get a majority of support, because people understand that that's a toxic thing. And so, yes, there are some folks like that, but they're not in the leadership, and they're not in a position where they can really comfortably say stuff like that without being shouted down by thoughtful folk.

Community leaders agree that after the school desegregation episode "fear of embarrassment," as one leader put it, motivated bureaucrats and elected officials to accommodate the Hmong and belie accusations of racism.

Elgin leaders also sought to dispel perceptions of racism after the housing discrimination controversies, which first brought attention from advocacy organization and later media scrutiny. Under the pall of complaints filed with the federal Department of Housing and Urban Development from October 1998 to May 1999 ("Elgin, Illinois, Will Revamp" 1999), in early June 1999 Elgin's city council appointed its first Latino member. When a seat on the council became open, local politicians worked through back channels to advertise that they hoped to appoint a Latino resident (Bailey 1999). Of the eight residents who applied for the vacancy, five were Hispanic (Hantschel 1999a). The candidate ultimately appointed had a professional background in affordable housing loans and cooperated with the city in improving outreach to Latinos on housing issues. In his first year in office, he hosted an affordable housing fair—an event he committed to when he was appointed (Hantschel 1999b). Politicians in Elgin used Councilor Figueroa's appointment to tout their commitment to cultural diversity amid continuing external attention over housing enforcement practices (O'Konowitz 2003).

The federal fair housing investigation and ongoing external scrutiny succeeded in defining local immigrants as a legally protected class and narrowed local officials' range of palatable responses, removing restriction from the menu and intensifying efforts to accommodate immigrants. In 2000 and 2001 the *Washington Post* and *ABC Nightly News* chronicled Elgin's ongoing housing discrimination cases, with the *Post* story displaying Elgin in a particularly unfavorable light (Fletcher 2000; "Suburbs Becoming More Ethnically Diverse" 2001). The story highlighted a Hispanic woman who, at eight months pregnant, was evicted from her home by Elgin housing inspectors during a December rainstorm. After the negative media exposure, in 2002 Elgin formed the Enhancing Elgin committee, and in 2004 it launched its DiverCity image campaign.

As happened in Lewiston and Wausau, Elgin officials expressed sensitivity to the way accusations of racism hurt the city's reputation. An Elgin elected official explained his frustration with federal regulators and his "deep resentment about the fact that communities like ours are portrayed as racist when it comes to housing." The effects of external scrutiny were apparent even years after the bulk of the coverage. In the spring 2009 local elections, where immigration was a central campaign issue, incumbents stressed that anti-immigrant ordinances would harm the city's reputation. One explained:

> There are perceptual things that are important. We talked about, for example, the global economy and us trying to bring more investment here from outside of the country, and frankly if you have an English-only provision, it makes you look like you're stepping out of the backwoods. And frankly it's insulting when you're dealing with people who are at least bilingual and in many cases multilingual from Asia and from Europe. It doesn't make you look like you're very forward thinking.

Referring to neighboring towns ensnared in anti-immigration controversies, a local journalist commented, "The Elgin city council members and the mayor specifically have said a number of times, 'We don't want to be another Waukegan, and we don't want to be another Carpentersville.'" A businesswoman agreed that Elgin's being accused of housing discrimination curbed the restrictive impulse evident in Carpentersville:

> The town north of us, Carpentersville, . . . I don't want us to become that. And, I think in some ways that we won't. I think, if anything came out of the HOPE [Fair Housing Center] lawsuits, that we'll be able to manage our situation in a more rational way.

For many years after the housing controversy, Elgin's leaders avoided restrictive responses and accommodated immigrants in order to deflect the damage from association with racial discrimination. Beginning in 2007, however, Elgin's emergent anti-immigration organization advocated "giv[ing] our society permission to talk about" illegal immigration (Hitzeman 2009b). Even this group worried about the racial content of its messages, however. One activist explained, "We thought long and hard about whether or not to use the 'H word.' Do we talk about Hispanic or don't we? And that's really where the numbers are, that's where the demographics are, but the label of racist is gonna come into play."

Ultimately their messages did associate Latinos with unauthorized immigration, in part because he and his compatriots were "getting tired of just this political correctness." The tenor of Elgin's responses to immigrants changed only when this restrictionist group emerged to challenge local constructions of immigrants as a legally protected racial class. As discussed in chapters 2 and 4, this group did shift Elgin toward somewhat greater restriction in the short term, though most local officials still endeavor to promote accommodation and avoid association with racism.

Like the three other destinations, Yakima is somewhat sensitive to external criticism. In 2002 the city council finally took up the recommendations of a police racial profiling task force after nearly two years' delay when it received pressure from the state and statewide Latino groups. Although it did not accede to all of the task force's recommendations, the external scrutiny may have contributed to the move to hire a Latino police chief in 2003. Even so, Yakima did not receive the far-reaching media scrutiny and widespread perceptions of discrimination that the other destinations experienced. Perhaps as a result, its response was less substantial and shorter-lived. Even in 2012–15, when Yakima became the subject of the ACLU Voting Rights Act complaint, the city received relatively little scrutiny from national media, with an article in the *Los Angeles Times* only following the judge's ruling in the case. The differing response in Yakima suggests that the amplified reputational consequences of widespread media portrayals of discrimination could be key in mobilizing compensatory accommodating responses.

Across the cases and over time, evidence suggests that external scrutiny of local responses can rein in restriction and encourage accommodation. Lewiston, Wausau, and Elgin each received substantial negative attention over a controversial restrictive response. This external scrutiny made explicit the discriminatory and racially charged nature of the response, thereby constructing local immigrants as a legally protected class. In each city, local governments ramped up accommodation in an effort to avoid legal challenges and the negative effects of accusations of racism. Even in new destination cities with little previous experience of racial and ethnic diversity, many local officials have internalized antidiscriminatory norms such that external accusations of bigotry motivate compensatory accommodation. Yet even where policymakers resist such norms or reject constructions of immigrants as a legally protected class, concerns about the costs of thwarting these policies and norms can result in a similar move away from restriction. As I will describe below, some towns that once considered and passed restrictive local ordinances subsequently proved sensitive to the legal and economic costs associated with violating antidiscriminatory policies.

Since the heightened national political salience of immigration in 2006 and certainly since the campaign and election of Donald Trump, constructions of immigrants as "illegal aliens" have become increasingly influential in many immigrant destinations. Given the Trump administration and the widely publicized restrictive responses to immigrants in states like Arizona and localities such as Hazelton, Pennsylvania, Farmers Branch, Texas, and Fremont, Nebraska, some may be surprised by my argument about the power of external scrutiny to rein in local restriction through antidiscriminatory norms. Indeed, since policymakers in my cases generally demonstrate an internalized sensitivity to such norms, the characteristics of my cases limit my ability to conclusively generalize about why some places appear less susceptible to external scrutiny. For that reason I now turn to analysis of an original database of responses to immigrants in towns that previously considered or passed restrictive ordinances.

Testing the Role of External Scrutiny in Curtailing Restriction

In 2014–15 I compiled a database examining towns that considered or passed restrictive ordinances in 2006–7. The database records the current status of these restrictive ordinances as well as identifying the scale of scrutiny the town encountered from external media and advocacy organizations. To identify restrictive municipalities, I used a list compiled by Steil and Vasi (2014) through both advocacy organization records and extensive media searches. From Steil and Vasi's list of ninety-seven cities that had passed restrictive ordinances from 2000 to 2011, I considered all fifty-seven city ordinances passed from 2006 to 2007.[3] Since Steil and

Vasi analyzed only cities that had passed ordinances, I supplemented this list by randomly selecting another thirty-seven municipalities that had considered or passed ordinances during this period according to the Fair Immigration Reform Movement (FIRM), for a total of ninety-four cities. In addition, to examine the fate of accommodating ordinances over this period, I investigated all twenty-one cities identified as passing pro-immigrant ordinances from 2006 to 2007 according to Steil and Vasi.

To determine the current status of ordinances, research assistants used a systematic method to search municipal codes, media accounts, court documents, and advocacy organizations' websites. Using search terms recommended by Steil and Vasi (2014), they first searched municipal codes to see if the ordinance in question was still on the books. Then they searched for the town and state name and "immigration" on Lexis-Nexis and Google. They counted the total number of articles and court documents recorded on LexisNexis from this search and then reviewed these sources to identify the number of articles relevant to the ordinance and its aftermath. Using Google, they identified and counted immigration advocacy organizations that mentioned the town's ordinance (employing a "site:.org" search). In the analysis that follows I will refer to national advocacy groups that seek to constrain immigrants' presence or opportunities as "restrictionist" and to groups that aim to expand them as "expansionist." Where these methods proved insufficient to determine the ordinance's current status, we identified articles in local newspapers, searched municipal websites, and reviewed city council meeting minutes for evidence that an immigration ordinance was in effect. In sum, these methods provided up-to-date information on ordinances in eighty-five of the ninety-four towns.

In addition, the technique provided counts of newspaper articles and advocacy organizations that serve as a metric to judge the scale of external scrutiny. Once we had researched one-third of the towns, we drew on our findings to create a systematic coding system. Thereafter we coded the subject of each ordinance, its current status, how much external media and advocacy organization attention it received, and, if the ordinance was no longer in force, the factors that led to its demise. Four coders were trained in the coding scheme, including coding the same cases to ensure intercoder reliability. I reviewed all ninety-four cases for coding consistency before analysis.

Although media and scholarly attention give the impression of a wave of local immigration enforcement, towns that have been counted as re-strictive actually are relatively rare, geographically concentrated, and in some cases not particularly restrictive. Of the ninety-four cities exam-ined here, twenty-six (more than a quarter) are in Pennsylvania, near Hazleton, the epicenter of the restrictive ordinance movement. More-over, not all of the towns included on advocacy organization lists are particularly restrictive. According to FIRM, for instance, of the 113 mu-nicipalities it identifies as having considered ordinances, only thirty-seven (one-third) passed them. As I will demonstrate, many of these have been struck down or repealed since that time. Other scholars find a higher number of ordinances that passed during this period (Steil and Vasi 2014), but it remains clear that many cities did not pass the ordi-nances they considered. Indeed, among the towns that only considered ordinances, several merely had a single discussion in a city council meet-ing, with no further vote or action. In sum, while advocacy organization lists provide an easily quantified metric of local response, examining solely these lists exaggerates the true extent of local restriction.

Of the fifty-seven towns Steil and Vasi identify as having passed or-dinances in 2006–7, as well the thirty-seven FIRM identifies as hav-ing considered or passed ordinances, I find that fifty-eight ordinances passed and thirty-six were considered but never passed. Of the ordi-nances that initially passed, I found evidence that in twenty-three towns an ordinance remains in effect. In an additional seven towns I found that the ordinance had passed but could find no evidence of its current sta-tus. At the bottom of table 6.1 I count these indeterminate ordinances as remaining in effect. Thus ordinances remained in effect or potentially in effect in thirty towns, or just over half of the fifty-eight that initially passed restrictive ordinances.

Table 6.2 displays the subject of the thirty-two ordinances across thirty towns that remain in effect and enforced (or potentially in effect and enforced). Nine aim to prevent businesses or municipal contractors from hiring unauthorized immigrants, and six are English-only reso-lutions. Five are housing ordinances that either require tenants to reg-ister and present limited forms of official US identification or regulate maximum occupancy in a way that targets immigrants' extended fami-lies. Five others are Illegal Immigration Relief Acts (IIRA) of the type passed in Hazleton, which include an English-only ordinance and pun-ish business owners who hire unauthorized immigrants and landlords who rent to them. In all likelihood these IIRAs are no longer in effect

TABLE 6.1. **Current status of ninety-four ordinances examined**

	Number	Percent
Considered, not passed	36	38
Tabled or rejected, internal reasons	18	19
Tabled or rejected, external reasons	16	17
Considered, status unclear	2	2
Passed	58	62
In effect	13	14
Less restrictive version in effect	10	11
Repealed or not enforced, internal reasons	7	7
Repealed or not enforced, external reasons	21	22
Passed, status unclear	7	7
Total in effect (or potentially in effect)	30	32
Total reined in, internal reasons	25	27
Total reined in, external reasons	37	39
Total	94	

TABLE 6.2 **Subject of ordinances that remain in effect**

Type of ordinance	Number of ordinances
Regulates businesses or contractors hiring unauthorized immigrants	9
English-only ordinance	6
Illegal Immigration Relief Act	5
Maximum occupancy or tenant registration ordinance	5
Restricting day laborers' presence or solicitation	4
Impounding cars of unlicensed, uninsured, or out-of-state drivers	3
Total	32

given the court ruling striking down Hazleton's ordinance, but we could find no evidence one way or the other. Finally, four towns restrict day laborers' presence or solicitation, and three impound the cars of suspected unauthorized drivers.

As table 6.1 indicates, however, among the thirty towns where ordinances remain, ten have less restrictive versions in effect than originally intended. Some passed a less restrictive version after debate, and others later amended the ordinance so as to scale back restriction. In two towns, for instance, a full Hazleton-style IIRA was proposed, but only a relatively mild business ordinance ultimately passed. In two more towns, full IIRAs were proposed but only nonbinding English-only resolutions passed. Though the numbers indicate that half of the ordinances that passed may remain in effect, several are largely symbolic.

Having established that some towns have reined in restriction since 2006–7, the question remains whether they did so in response to external scrutiny that defined local immigrants as a legally protected class. While investigating the status of current ordinances, research assistants identified any reasons local decision makers gave for scaling back restriction, whether in media reports or meeting minutes. In addition to coding the various reasons offered, they assessed whether officials scaled back restriction internally or in response to external pressure from media coverage or advocacy organizations. Towns where decision makers explicitly referred to external attention from media or advocacy organizations or fear of such attention were counted as curbing restriction in response to external scrutiny. Decision makers offered explicit mentions of external pressure in sixteen of the thirty-six ordinances that were only considered (44 percent) and in twenty-one ordinances that passed but were ultimately repealed or unenforced (36 percent of initially passed ordinances). All together, media coverage and other sources provide direct evidence that external scrutiny affected local decisions to scale back restriction in a total of thirty-seven cases, or 39 percent of all ninety-four towns.

In these thirty-seven towns and seventeen others, local decision makers offered specific reasons for scaling back restriction, particularly fears of litigation, concerns about legal costs and loss of business, and worries about appearing discriminatory or racist. As table 6.3 indicates, three

TABLE 6.3. **Reasons for reining in restriction**

Reason ordinance reined in	Number of towns
Legal pressure	33
Reputational concerns	12
Legal cost concerns	11
Economic or fiscal cost	7
Federal, state, or county decision	5
Court ruling or settlement	3
Total	71

Note: Some towns offered multiple reasons for scaling back restriction.

towns no longer enforce their ordinances because they were formally struck down in court or rescinded in settlement agreements: Escondido, California, Farmers Branch, Texas, and Hazleton, Pennsylvania. Even these places, which the *Washington Post* ("Arizona Demonstrates the Lunacy of Mass Deportations" 2011) described as "stake[ing] out a reputation . . . as a citadel of intolerance," with the "explicit purpose" of deflecting unauthorized immigrants, were ultimately forced to set aside restriction owing to litigation sponsored by expansionist advocacy organizations. Federal civil rights policies (combined with legal strategies emphasizing federal preemption) constrained even the most restrictive towns to temper their policies. Five more towns were forced to scale back local restriction because of administrative decisions at the county, state, or federal level. For instance, Prescott, Arizona, voted to sign a 287(g) agreement to partner with federal immigration agents, but the federal government chose not to pursue an agreement with the town. In another case Mission Viejo, California, was forced to repeal its ordinance mandating that local contractors use E-Verify when the California General Assembly passed legislation forbidding local entities to require use of the employee verification system.

Witnessing legal action in other locales, thirty-three towns scaled back their ordinances in part out of concerns about litigation. In Frackville, Pennsylvania, for instance, the council president reported that the town had planned to advance a Hazleton-style ordinance but reconsidered in view of Hazleton's legal challenges. "Our solicitor put it on a wait-and-see situation," he explained (Malcolm and Turano 2006). Likewise in Larksville, Pennsylvania, the council president reported that they were not considering an ordinance further because "our attorney told us to stay out of it for now" (Mocarsky 2007).

Eleven other towns cited legal costs as a factor in turning away from their restrictive ordinances. For example, in Newton, New Jersey, town officials posted a notice on their website announcing, "Due to the preemption in federal law, and as a cost saving measure to Newton taxpayers, the Town Council has made an economically-wise decision to table this issue until resolution of the existing litigation in Hazelton, Pennsylvania" (Karczweski 2007). In seven towns local officials expressed concern about the effects restrictive ordinances would have on local businesses. In Avon Park, Florida, business owners reported losses after a restrictive ordinance was proposed. Some were concerned that Latino customers would leave, while others said they had encountered clients who no longer wanted to do business with Avon Park (Bouffard and Rodriguez 2006).

Finally, in twelve towns local leaders explicitly cited reputation in explaining that they scaled back restriction to avoid an appearance of discriminatory or racially biased motive. Riverside, New Jersey, a town of 8,000, passed an Illegal Immigration Relief Act, but within a year it reversed its ordinance in the face of mounting legal fees and the closing of local businesses (Martinez 2011). Mayor George Conard, who originally voted for the ordinance, supported the repeal out of concern over local costs and damage to the town's reputation. In an interview with the *New York Times*, Conard regretted that the ordinance had put the small town "on the national map in a bad way" (Belson and Capuzoo 2007). Similarly, Mayor David Smith in Friendswood, Texas, opposed an English-only ordinance that was ultimately withdrawn, saying, "This is not the light in which I want the community of Friendswood to be seen by the rest of the world" (Evans 2007). In Allentown, Pennsylvania, a Latino city councilor was influential in framing an ordinance restricting immigrants' rights in terms of race and civil rights. Citing an Anti-Defamation League report that the Ku Klux Klan was using anti-immigrant sentiment to recruit new members, the councilor asked his colleagues whether they wanted an "Allentown filled with Ku Klux Klan members" (Kraus 2007). Likewise, Lancaster, Pennsylvania, voted down a restrictive ordinance in part over concerns about appearing discriminatory and a month later passed an ordinance condemning local immigration enforcement and supporting earned legalization. As council president Jessica Dickson explained, "We're formalizing the position that Lancaster is a welcoming community that values diversity" (Harris 2007).

While few towns performed a 180-degree turn comparable to Lancaster's, external scrutiny forced proponents of restrictive ordinances to confront accusations of racial prejudice. Indeed, media coverage in half of the cities (forty-six of ninety-four) referred to the restrictive ordinances as racist, nativist, intolerant, bigoted, or prejudiced. Thus, even where the competing construction of immigrants as "illegal aliens" was strong, supporters of restrictive ordinances took pains to deny that their motives were racist. A resident of Lake Havasu, Arizona, insisted, "I don't hate these people. I'm not a racist," telling a local reporter that "legal immigrants are just fine" (Hays 2007). These competing constructions are also clear in Taneytown, Maryland, which scaled back a more restrictive proposed ordinance and passed a nonbinding English-only resolution. A journalist covering the town's deliberations described Taneytown as feeling "both afraid it might be overwhelmed by poor Hispanics who are in the country illegally and ashamed it might be tarred as racist and intolerant" (Constable 2008).

The preceding analysis shows that even in those towns labeled as restrictive, antidiscriminatory policies that impose legal and financial costs and antidiscriminatory norms that impose reputational costs at times succeed in defining immigrants as a legally protected racial class and checking further restriction. These findings suggest the substantial influence of federal civil rights policies in constraining local response. Yet was the propensity to limit restriction associated with the prevalence of external scrutiny? To investigate this question, we collected several measures of external scrutiny, including the count of articles mentioning the city's ordinance and its aftermath on LexisNexis and the number of national expansionist and restrictionist advocacy associations involved in opposing or supporting the ordinance according to media reports and advocacy organization websites. For twenty of the ninety-four towns (21 percent), not a single relevant article was indexed on LexisNexis. At the other extreme, 299 articles discussed Hazelton's ordinance and its aftermath. On average, just over twelve articles archived on LexisNexis covered each city's ordinance and its aftermath. Eighteen towns garnered attention from major national newspapers such as the *New York Times* and the *Washington Post,* and twenty more were mentioned in major national newspapers in conjunction with more prominent restrictive cities.

With respect to attention from advocacy organizations, forty-nine of the ninety-four towns (52 percent) received no attention from national organizations on either side (apart from being cataloged on lists of restrictive towns). The other towns received attention from one to five national expansionist organizations (e.g., the ACLU, Latino Justice, MALDEF, and LULAC) and from one to five restrictionist organizations (e.g., FAIR, NumbersUSA, and the Immigration Reform Law Institute). The involvement of expansionist advocacy organizations ranged from filing suit against the ordinances, to sending joint letters threatening legal action, to hosting events or protest actions in the town. Restrictionist advocacy organizations helped towns draft ordinances, defended challenges in court, raised money to defray legal expenses, and also hosted events or protests. On average, towns received attention from 0.78 national expansionist organizations and 0.46 national restrictionist organizations. Twenty-nine towns experienced the direct involvement of national expansionist advocacy organizations, while seven more received attention in conjunction with more prominent cases. Likewise, twenty-four towns experienced the direct involvement of national restrictionist advocacy organizations, with seven more receiving some attention.

To develop a measure of the strength of external scrutiny, we ranked the attention from media and expansionist advocacy organizations in each town, differentiating between towns that received national-level attention, those that received only passing mentions in national media in conjunction with more prominent towns, and those that received no national attention. Media and advocacy organization attention are ranked on a 1–3 scale with 1 representing no national attention, 2 representing "spillover" from more prominent cases, and 3 representing national attention. A summative 2–6 index of external scrutiny ranges from the forty-two towns (45 percent) that received no attention from national media or expansionist advocacy groups to eighteen towns (19 percent) that received passing mention by either national media or advocacy organizations, to thirteen towns (14 percent) that received national attention from one source or the other, seven (7 percent) that received national attention from one source and spillover attention from the other, and finally fourteen (15 percent) that received attention both from national media and from advocacy organizations.

To analyze how external scrutiny shapes responses, I now turn to the fifteen towns that passed ordinances (and therefore displayed an initially equivalent commitment to restriction) and for which the current status of ordinances is known. The seven towns for which the current status is unknown received very little media or advocacy attention, so including them in the analysis as though the ordinance were in effect would bias findings in favor of my hypothesis that towns with less external scrutiny were more likely to maintain ordinances. These towns do, however, demonstrate that it is not the severity of an ordinance alone that garners scrutiny resulting in retraction or restraint. Among these jurisdictions that received virtually no attention, three passed Hazleton-style Illegal Immigration Relief Acts, and another three passed ordinances that included a key component of IIRA ordinances—fining or revoking the licenses of businesses that hire unauthorized immigrants.

In the twenty-three towns where we have concrete evidence that restrictive ordinances are still in effect and enforced, seventeen received little to no national external scrutiny, five received national attention from at least one source, and only three received attention from both (table 6.4). In total, the average combined external scrutiny score for the twenty-three currently restrictive towns is 3.04 on the 2–6 scale. In contrast, among the twenty-eight towns that passed ordinances that are no longer in effect, ten received little to no national attention, nine received national attention from either advocacy organizations or the media, and nine received national attention from both the media and pro-immigrant advocacy organizations. In total, the average external scrutiny score among towns that passed ordinances no longer in effect was 4.21 on the 2–6 scale.

Table 6.4 displays the results of two-sided *t*-tests examining whether the amount of external scrutiny received by towns where ordinances passed and remain in effect was statistically distinct from the scrutiny in towns where ordinances passed but are no longer in effect. The greater than one-point difference in external scrutiny between these categories of towns is statistically significant. Likewise, if we focus on the number of relevant media mentions among towns that rescinded versus maintained their ordinances, we see that the towns that maintained their ordinances had an average of six relevant articles on LexisNexis compared with twenty-seven for towns that rescinded them, a statistically significant difference. Similarly, we see that towns that maintained their ordinances received attention from an average of 0.48 expansionist advocacy

TABLE 6.4. **Differences in external scrutiny where ordinances are not in effect**

	Passed, in effect	Passed, not in effect	Difference	*p*-value
Number of towns	23	28		
Average media mentions	5.78	27.39	21.61	0.07
Average expansionist advocacy attention	0.48	1.46	0.98	0
Average restrictionist advocacy attention	0.39	0.86	0.47	0.12
Average external scrutiny score	3.04	4.21	1.17	0.01
Average local expansionist advocacy attention	0.35	0.54	0.19	0.44
Average state expansionist advocacy attention	0.35	0.25	−0.1	0.63

organizations, whereas towns that rescinded them received attention from, on average, 1.56, a statistically significant difference.

The scrutiny influential in reining in local responses was truly national rather than state-level or local. National organizations' influence is associated with curbing restriction, whereas involvement of state and local organizations is not. We tracked the counts and influence of state and local organizations in each town, finding that fewer of them played an evident role in responding to restrictive ordinances. Among the fifty-one towns, at least one national expansionist organization was involved in twenty-nine. By comparison, according to media accounts, state organizations were involved in only eleven towns and local organizations in fifteen. Whereas the number of national expansionist organizations and the degree of national organizations' focus was associated with a lower likelihood that ordinances remained in effect, state and local organizations' numbers and influence were not statistically associated with a lower likelihood that ordinances remained in effect (see table 6.4). External scrutiny from the national level—not advocacy activity in general—played the key role in turning back local restrictive policies, underscoring the role of external frames surrounding immigrants in shaping local responses.

The table also provides evidence that external scrutiny from expansionist organizations was effective in scaling back restriction, while attention from restrictionist organizations did not bolster restriction. Towns that maintained their ordinances did *not* do so with the assistance of restrictionist organizations. Rather, towns that rescinded their ordinances received greater attention from restrictive advocacy organizations, though the difference falls just below conventional levels of statistical significance. Overall, bivariate investigation provides clear support for the hypothesis that external scrutiny from the media and expansionist advocacy organizations is associated with a greater likelihood of reining in restriction.

Multivariate analysis bears out these impressions. Regression table AD4 in appendix D indicates that external scrutiny is statistically associated with a decreased likelihood that ordinances remain in effect, even when controlling for the major predictors of local response, identified in chapter 4. Probit models hold constant the proportion foreign-born, the percentage change in the foreign-born population from 2000 to 2012, the proportion of immigrants who live in poverty, the proportion of immigrants who are Hispanic, the natural log of the town's population, the proportion of homeowners, the percentage change in median household income, whether the town has a council-manager form of government, the percentage of the county voting for Romney in 2012, and an index of state-level immigration policy.[4] Model one examines the effect of the number of relevant articles on LexisNexis, finding that more media attention is associated with a decline in the likelihood that the ordinance is in effect, even holding these other factors constant. Model two examines the effect of the number of expansionist advocacy organizations involved in a town, finding that more expansionist advocacy attention is likewise associated with a decline in the likelihood that the ordinance is in effect. Model four controls for both media and expansionist advocacy organization attention. While both are negatively associated with the likelihood that an ordinance remains in effect, the coefficient on advocacy organization attention falls just below conventional levels of statistical significance ($p = 0.14$), suggesting that perhaps media attention plays a more decisive role, as the example of Yakima suggests. Model five examines the effect of the aggregate measure of external scrutiny, finding that greater attention from national media and advocacy organizations is associated with a decline in the likelihood in that an ordinance remains in effect.

Although this analysis is primarily interested in the effect of external scrutiny, other contextual factors are associated with whether restrictive ordinances remain in effect. As the proportion of the foreign-born population increases, the likelihood that restrictive ordinances remain in force declines. Likewise, as the proportion of the foreign-born population living in poverty increases, the likelihood that restriction remains in place also declines. Similar to chapter 4, immigrant visibility and need can be associated with less restrictive responses. On the other hand, in these analyses the proportion of the immigrant population that is Hispanic is associated with an increased likelihood that the ordinance remains in effect. A more rapid increase in the foreign-born population is also associated with an increased likelihood that restrictive ordinances remain in force in three of the five models. These factors suggest that in already restrictive locales, Hispanic immigrant predominance and rapid demographic change are associated with more lasting restrictive initiatives. While these factors did not prove decisive when examining the low propensity for restriction among towns in the national survey, among already restrictive towns, Hispanic predominance and rapid diversification likely increase the salience of constructions of immigrants as "illegal aliens," thereby increasing the likelihood that restriction remains in force.

Figure 6.1 presents the predicted probabilities associated with moving from no external scrutiny (media, advocacy, or aggregate) to external scrutiny one standard deviation above the mean level while holding all other independent variables at their means (Tomz, Wittenberg, and King 2003). As the dotted line displays, moving from no media mentions on LexisNexis to twenty-seven articles is associated with a decrease of fifty-three percentage points in the likelihood that the ordinance remains in effect.[5] In other words, all else constant, a place with no media mentions is 65 percent likely to have its restrictive ordinance still in effect, while a place with twenty-seven media mentions is only 12 percent likely to do so. Similarly, as the dashed line shows, moving from no attention from expansionist advocacy organizations to attention from 2.24 organizations is associated with a thirty-eight percentage point decline in the likelihood that the ordinance remains in effect. That is, all else constant, a place with no advocacy organization attention is 59 percent likely to still have its restrictive ordinance in force, while a place with attention from just over two advocacy organizations is only 21 percent likely to do so. Last, the solid line illustrates that moving from no national attention to national attention from either media or expansionist

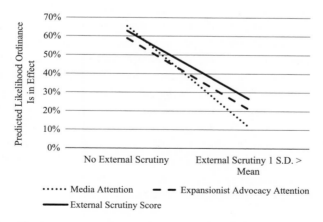

FIGURE 6.1. Likelihood that ordinance remains in effect by external scrutiny level.

organizations is associated with a thirty-six percentage point decline in the likelihood that a restrictive ordinance remains in effect. Holding other variables constant, a place with no national attention is 63 percent likely to have its ordinance in effect, while a place with national attention from at least one source is only 27 percent likely to do so. In sum, even when controlling for other key predictors of local response such as capacity, immigrant visibility, and partisanship, external scrutiny continues to play a strong role in curtailing restriction.

Finally, the multivariate analyses also reinforce the finding that while attention from expansionist advocacy organizations is associated with declines in restriction, attention from restrictionist organizations has not bolstered restriction. In fact, all else constant, restrictionist advocacy attention is actually associated with a decline in the likelihood that a restrictive ordinance is in effect (table AD4, model three). On the whole, the same places received attention from both restrictionist and expansionist advocacy organizations (Pearson's r = 0.59), but expansionist organizations were more successful in achieving their aim of scaling back restrictive ordinances. The case study evidence presented above suggests that media coverage and attention from advocacy organizations are influential in prompting public embarrassment and shifting local responses. Even in towns that have passed restrictive ordinances, federal civil rights policies influence outcomes through media attention and sophisticated civil rights advocacy. The combination of laws and associated norms exerts powerful pressure, often curtailing restrictive action.

While the preceding analysis has demonstrated that many restrictive ordinances were scaled back from 2007 to 2015, is it possible that restrictive cities were not unique in shifting their policies over this period? Perhaps towns that passed accommodating ordinances were targeted by restrictionist organizations and conservative media, leading them to reduce their efforts to welcome immigrants. To investigate this possibility, I also examine the list of twenty-one cities that Steil and Vasi (2014) identify as having passed accommodating ordinances in 2006 or 2007. Thirteen of these cities proposed resolutions limiting local participation in immigration enforcement; seven combined such resolutions with declarations supporting expansive federal immigration reform; and one passed only a resolution supporting comprehensive federal reform. Of these twenty-one accommodating proposals, one appears never to have passed (National City, California), one was repealed largely owing to state pressure (Chandler, Arizona), and one was repealed after a change in municipal leadership (Albuquerque, New Mexico). The remaining eighteen are still in force. Thus, while twenty-eight of fifty-one restrictive ordinances (or 55 percent) are no longer in effect, only two of twenty accommodating ordinances that passed have been scaled back since that time.

Moreover, the staying power of local accommodating ordinances is not due to an absence of external pressure. Rather, accommodating cities from this period have maintained their policies despite external pressure from restrictionist groups. Since passing their accommodation measures, the twenty cities have received attention from zero to seven restrictionist advocacy groups, for an average of more than three groups per city. The cities also experienced scrutiny from external media, with an average of thirteen relevant articles on the town's immigration policies found in LexisNexis since 2006. Media and advocacy attention often followed crimes allegedly committed by unauthorized immigrants. Critics argued that the crimes were the result of city policies that accommodate the unauthorized, echoing the recent sanctuary city debate. After a 2007 incident in Newark, New Jersey, for instance, congressman and presidential candidate Tom Tancredo (R-CO) visited Newark to argue that its policies limiting immigration enforcement led to dangerous crimes. Then Mayor Cory Booker decried "folks [who] descend from out of town to protest in front of City Hall" (Fahim 2007). Likewise, some accommodating cities have faced legal action. After a crime committed by an unauthorized immigrant in Los Angeles, the national restrictionist organization Judicial Watch partnered with a Los Angeles resident to sue the city. The suit protested Los Angeles' use of taxpayer funds to block cooperation between local police and federal immigration enforcement efforts. A judge dismissed the case, ruling that Los Angeles' policy did not violate federal law or constrain intergovernmental communication (Steinhauer 2008).

Despite this external pressure, with few exceptions Newark, Los Angeles, and other cities stuck with their accommodating policies. Therefore the scaling back of restrictive policies from 2007 to 2015 was not a simple matter of general flux in policies over time but was evidence that cities were responding to external scrutiny of restrictive policies and modifying them out of concern over legal costs and damage to reputation. Chandler, Arizona, however, bears consideration as a city that has been pulled toward both accommodation and restriction over time. After a controversial restrictive episode in the late 1990s, Chandler curtailed restriction and moved toward accommodation (Walker 2010). In July 1997 Chandler's police department cooperated in a federal immigration raid. During a five-day period, the operation arrested 432 undocumented immigrants, but it also detained US citizens and legal residents ("Immigrant Phobia" 1997). The events, which became known as the Chandler Roundup, incited a federal investigation and generated considerable national media scrutiny. In the face of lawsuits and widespread criticism, Chandler issued a 1999 separation ordinance forbidding the police to participate in further immigration enforcement and establishing a municipal Human Relations Commission.

Two scholars separately concluded that Chandler took compensatory accommodating measures to "rebuild its reputation" (Walker 2010; Varsanyi 2010b). Responding to this controversial restrictive episode set Chandler on a path toward greater accommodation until pressure from the state of Arizona resulted in a reversal of the separation ordinance in 2010. Chandler's new policy, which preceded Arizona's similar statewide law (SB 1070) by two months, allows local police to check residents' legal status upon a reasonable suspicion of unauthorized status. As chapter 4 suggested, towns in more Republican counties and in states with more restrictive policies will be less likely to accommodate. As the example of Chandler illustrates, experiencing external scrutiny and reining in restriction may not always be permanent, particularly in places where the competing construction of immigrants as "illegal aliens" is more likely to resonate. The role of state policies in shaping Chandler's course away from accommodation is particularly salient at a time when the Trump administration is emphasizing unauthorized immigration and attempting to penalize sanctuary cities that avoid participating in federal enforcement.

Conclusion

The experience of Chandler, Arizona, makes it clear that municipal restriction has not vanished since its height in 2006–7. Indeed, Steil and Vasi (2014) identify another forty restrictive municipal ordinances that passed from 2008 to 2012. Likewise, as I will discuss further in the book's conclusion, at least a few localities have embraced Trump's reintroduction of the 287(g) program that deputizes local police to serve as immigration agents (US Immigration and Customs Enforcement, n.d.b).

That said, this analysis demonstrates that, overall, restriction is rare, and where it occurs it is often curbed through external scrutiny.

In combination, chapters 4, 5, and 6 demonstrate that external forces like federal policies and national partisan politics are particularly important in shaping local responses to immigrants because of their influence in framing local definitions of the foreign-born. Chapter 4 demonstrates that towns exposed to federal resettlement policies defining refugees as clients of local services are considerably more likely to implement accommodating policies. It also shows that national discourse among Republican leaders defines immigrants as "illegal aliens" and influences local responses, with Republican-leaning locales becoming less likely to accommodate immigrant residents. Chapter 5 additionally proposes that federal policies that involve local police officials in immigration enforcement may explain why police chiefs have more concerns about immigrants' presence, even though they also value serving immigrants and gaining their trust. Finally, chapter 6 provides evidence that federal civil rights policies and associated antidiscriminatory norms generate external scrutiny that defines immigrants as a legally protected racial group and encourages officials to curtail restriction out of concern over legal and reputational costs.

Both case studies and analysis of an original database of once-restrictive towns suggest that many places respond to external scrutiny by scaling back restriction. Only twenty-three, or just under a quarter, of the ninety-four restrictive cities examined here remained impervious to these forces. Moreover, it is worth noting that ten of the twenty-three scaled back their restrictive plans in some way before passing the ordinances in question. In this way federal civil rights policies and associated organizations and norms constrain localities to temper restriction and at times promote compensatory accommodation. As the case studies and the comments of officials in other cities demonstrate, in some places the embarrassment of association with bigotry is sufficient to prompt retraction. Here media scrutiny may be particularly influential in shaping responses. In other places the threat of fiscal consequences and legal action limits restriction. Here scrutiny from expansionist advocacy organizations plays a powerful role. Even so, in a small subset of cases policymakers continue to support restriction even in the face of costly external scrutiny.

Scholars have described the civil rights movement of the 1960s as "creat[ing] a repertoire of ideas, institutions, and organizational forms for challenging racial subordination" (Kasinitz et al. 2008). The role of external scrutiny in scaling back restriction suggests that despite abiding racial inequalities, when immigrants are racialized they are included in a protected category instantiated in federal policy. When they are defined primarily as "illegal aliens," they do not have access to the same federal protections and associated norms and are therefore more vulnerable.

In its early months, the Trump administration has both emphasized defining immigrants as "illegal aliens" and sought to lessen the federal government's role in promoting civil rights protections (Bazelon 2017; Huseman and Waldman 2017). The media and civil rights advocacy organizations have responded with considerable scrutiny, contributing to efforts that forced the administration to scale back targeting sanctuary cities and to initially retract restrictions on travel from certain Muslim-majority countries. In the conclusion to the book I will discuss these events along with their implications for the future of municipal responses to immigrants.

PART III

Local Government Responses and Consequences for Immigrant Incorporation

CHAPTER SEVEN

The Select Few

Municipal Accommodation and Elite Collaboration

In late summer 2001 Mr. Farhan, a Somali international development professional, arrived in Lewiston to join his family, who had migrated there from their original resettlement site. Within a week of his arrival, a Somali acquaintance who worked at city hall introduced Mr. Farhan to the school superintendent. The superintendent offered Mr. Farhan a job on the spot and, given the man's fluent English and professional experience, immediately elevated him to an intermediary position as a liaison between the schools and the Somali population. In new immigrant destinations, local officials often seek out immigrant intermediaries like Mr. Farhan in response to urgent communication challenges. In Elgin, where immigrants are a more established presence and communication mechanisms are in place, local officials nonetheless sought out intermediaries to represent immigrants in local affairs. In spring 1999, for instance, Elgin's city council appointed its first Latino councilor, Juan Figueroa, to a vacant seat.[1]

Hiring and appointing immigrant intermediaries like Mr. Farhan and Councilor Figueroa was the most common response to immigrants across the four new immigrant destination cities as well as among the most common responses to immigrants described in the MRIS among a random sample of immigrant destinations nationwide. Two-thirds of towns report hiring immigrants or members of the immigrant ethnic group as local government employees, and 57 percent report recruiting immigrants or coethnics to serve on local boards or commissions. Part 1 of the book demonstrated that accommodating responses along these lines were common across US towns and cities. Part 2 showed that local government officials have unique incentives to support immigrants, contributing to the prevalence of proactive accommodation—that is, implementing accommodating practices before immigrant or electoral demands. In part 3 I ask how municipal accommodation affects immigrant incorporation—with respect to both immigrants' adaptation and their broader public acceptance. In this chapter, I turn to the way local government accommodation affects political incorporation, focusing particularly on how the prevalent practice of identifying immigrant intermediaries shapes immigrants' ability to take part in politics and have their voices represented.

Proactive efforts to accommodate immigrants may bolster immigrant incorporation by building avenues for participation and showcasing official support for foreign-born inclusion (Bloemraad 2006). Looking beyond immigrants, positive interactions with government boost Americans' sense of efficacy and subsequent engagement (Soss 1999; Mettler 2002; Campbell 2005), while negative interactions suppress them (Soss 1999; Weaver and Lerman 2010; Epp, Maynard-Moody, and Haider-Markel 2014). Municipal accommodation therefore may offer immigrants positive impressions of government that encourage further political incorporation. On the other hand, proactive efforts to incorporate immigrants could suppress immigrants' need to mobilize (Okamoto and Ebert 2010). Threatening restrictive policies, while troubling in other ways, have been shown to generate immigrant mobilization that contributes to efficacy, support for immigrant-friendly policies, and even identification as Americans (Pantoja, Ramirez, and Segura 2001, 2003a; Benjamin-Alvarado, DeSipio, and Montoya 2009; Wallace, Zepeda-Millán, and Jones-Correa 2014; Branton et al. 2015; Silber Mohamed 2017). Given these conflicting findings, it is crucial to evaluate how far municipal accommodation efforts actually advance immigrant political incorporation. Therefore I turn to examining how the prevalent practice of hiring or appointing immigrant intermediaries to roles in municipal government affects immigrants' local political engagement.

I begin by defining what I mean by intermediaries and identifying their central role in representing immigrant interests. I then use the MRIS to demonstrate that local government officials in small to midsize towns nationwide often rely on individual immigrants for gathering information on foreign-born residents and sharing information with these groups. The survey further demonstrates that in places that more actively accommodate immigrants (including identifying intermediaries), officials report more interaction with the foreign-born and have more positive impressions of immigrants' civic participation. Of course this cross-sectional survey data cannot demonstrate a causal link between accommodation and positive perceptions of immigrants' civic contributions, since causality could run in the opposite direction, from more positive views on immigrant contributions to greater municipal accommodation. At the very least, however, the quantitative data demonstrate that the relation is positive, while the qualitative data show that municipal officials are trying to accommodate immigrants proactively, even before immigrant organization advocacy or electoral influence.

Finally, I return to the qualitative data from the four cases studies to demonstrate the benefits and pitfalls of proactive municipal accommodation when it relies on individual intermediaries. Immigrant intermediaries can open productive communication channels between officials and immigrant leaders as well as sometimes engaging additional coethnics in local civic life. That said, municipal officials' efforts to identify immigrant intermediaries do not necessarily achieve broad-based immigrant incorporation. Officials are not always cognizant of heterogeneity within immigrant ethnic groups and may choose intermediaries who are detached from immigrants or otherwise ill suited to represent them. Local officials frequently expect individual immigrant intermediaries to speak for entire immigrant groups, an unrealistic expectation given differences in language, nationality, generation, and other factors within ethnic groups. Local government officials' distinct incentives to accommodate immigrants may establish productive relations among immigrant and nonimmigrant elites but will not necessarily advance efforts to include immigrants more broadly in civic life.

Immigrant Intermediaries in the Literature

The concept of the intermediary is not new, though intermediaries' influence in local political incorporation remains understudied in the United States. A substantial literature in several fields explores the role of intermediaries, "middlemen," or "brokers" in studies of ethnic entrepreneurship and political anthropology (e.g., Bonacich 1973; Light 1984; Lewis and Mosse 2006). The literature on cultural competence and cultural brokers in public health, social work, and education also touches on issues related to immigrant intermediaries (e.g., Fandetti and Goldmeier 1988; Martinez-Cosio and Iannacone 2007). In Western Europe a growing literature explores government-sponsored immigrant intermediaries. For instance, in Spanish Catalonia, since the late 1990s the regional government has endorsed an integration program with a prominent role for "intercultural mediators," typically immigrants hired by local government agencies or nongovernmental organizations (NGOs) to help negotiate intercultural tensions (Agusti-Panareda 2006). In France and Italy similar initiatives exist, with immigrant intermediaries known as *femmes relais* or "linkworkers" (Agusti-Panareda 2006; Scales-Trent 1999).

In the United States, studies of immigrant destinations in both the traditional gateway state of California and in new immigrant destinations have highlighted the role of select individual intermediaries. In a 2003 California survey, appointing individual immigrants to committees and boards was a common response by local government to the foreign-born (Ramakrishnan and Lewis 2005). An edited volume of new immigrant destination case studies comments on the crucial importance of individuals "willing to act as liaisons" and calls for more study of this unique role in shaping incorporation processes (Zúñiga and Hernández-León 2005, xix).[2]

Often, however, studies of incorporation in the United States focus less on individual intermediaries and more on immigrant or coethnic organizations. Scholars argue that immigrant organizations serve as a crucial engine of local incorporation amid the decline of unions, parties, and other civic organizations and the concomitant increase in privatizing social services. These organizations have the potential to teach immigrants civic skills, to mobilize them for political action, and to act as their representatives (Bloemraad 2006; de Graauw 2016). Scholars describe how local officials fund immigrant organizations or enter into partnerships with them to provide services (Frasure and Jones-Correa 2010; de Graauw, Gleeson, and Bloemraad 2013).

Immigrant organizations no doubt are crucial to incorporation where they have strong civic presence or influence (Ramakrishnan and Bloemraad 2008). Yet evidence from both the new destinations and the survey suggests that immigrant organizations often are absent or lack influence. Local officials often rely on individual immigrant intermediaries for learning about immigrants or sharing information with them. How does the tendency to rely on individuals—one of the most prominent responses to immigrants across small to midsize destinations nationwide—affect incorporation processes?

Defining Immigrant Intermediaries

The term immigrant intermediary refers specifically to foreign-born individuals or persons from the same ethnic group (coethnics) that serve as formal or informal liaisons between immigrants and established residents. As the examples of Mr. Farhan and Councilor Figueroa suggest, intermediaries facilitate communication, but they are also expected to represent their ethnic group to local officials. While residents who are not coethnics do at times serve as liaisons, intermediaries are coethnic individuals often sought out as descriptive representatives of their group. The term descriptive representative refers to an individual who is "in some sense typical of the larger class of persons whom they represent," often along the lines of race or gender (Mansbridge 1999, 629). Political theorists argue that including descriptive representatives from marginalized groups is necessary for the legitimacy of democratic institutions (Phillips 1991; Mansbridge 1999), though some question whether descriptive representatives are necessary to speak for the interests of these groups (Pitkin 1967). While intermediaries are not always effective in representing immigrants' interests, I will argue that local officials seek out intermediaries in part to bolster the legitimacy of institutions through descriptive representation in the face of growing ethnic diversity.

Descriptive representation typically refers to elected representatives, but I use it more broadly here to refer to intermediaries who are asked to speak for immigrants. In *The Good Representative*, Suzanne Dovi encourages us to broaden our conception of democratic representation to include all those engaged in democratic advocacy. As she points out, a wide variety of unelected, informal representatives "speak for" constituencies as business lobbyists, union organizers, and leaders of NGOs. Dovi writes that in evaluating representation, "what matters is not a political actor's official title or her specific political office, but what she does" (Dovi 2007, 2).

As such, intermediaries may be employees of local government, like Mr. Farhan, appointed or elected officials, like Councilor Figueroa, heads of immigrant organizations or traditional leadership structures, or private residents who are recruited or self-select into the role. In Lewiston and Elgin Mr. Farhan and Councilor Figueroa were most frequently described in interviews as playing this local liaison role. In Wausau the most frequently mentioned intermediary was the head of the Wausau Area Hmong Mutual Association, demonstrating that immigrant organizations can play this role where they are present and influential. In Yakima, where the local government was initially less active in seeking out intermediaries, the one most frequently mentioned was a local activist who was described by Latinos and others as having self-selected into her role.

In these new immigrant destinations, the everyday necessity of communicating with people who do not share a language often drives the initial search for intermediaries. For local governments to function, officials must convey information about services and expectations. Likewise, officials require information from immigrants to shape the provision of services. Bilateral information sharing is necessary for placing children at the correct grade level in school, determining eligibility for benefits, enforcing traffic rules, and keeping the streets safe from criminals. Employing and appointing intermediaries helps local governments gather such information while "lower[ing] the transaction costs associated with overcoming language and cultural barriers" (as Frasure and Jones-Correa [2010] have argued about partnerships with immigrant organizations).

As immigrant populations grow, local leaders incorporate intermediaries not only to address the logistics of communication barriers, but also to maintain the legitimacy of institutions. In Elgin and Yakima, which are now 45 percent Latino, several non-Hispanic white leaders commented that it seemed wrong to have all-white leadership in places with large Latino populations. A non-Hispanic white businessman and civic leader in Yakima described how concerns about fairness led him to support the appointment of a Latino school board member:

> It doesn't seem fair. When 40 percent of the adult population is Hispanic, and 65 percent of the students are Hispanic, there ought to be Hispanic leadership involved in getting an effective job done. I wasn't offended by what the school board was doing, but if there's five white people there, they have trouble making the right decisions for the Hispanic population because they don't know the culture that well.

Along with most leaders in Yakima, this man identifies as politically conservative but still demonstrates an internalized sense that institutions are not legitimate if they do not include descriptive representatives of groups that make up a substantial proportion of the population.

Similarly in Elgin, an elderly white businessman and civic leader explained his motivation for diversifying the civic boards he serves on:

> I've been chair of the nominating committee in a number of organizations in the community. While it seems crass, you sort of target sometimes, because you say, "Okay, this board is made up of 90 percent men. What about introducing a woman?" Then you say, "Our organization is 50 percent Hispanic, how about a Hispanic woman?" You see? It's about awareness. And one of the persons that we asked to serve was [a Hispanic woman], and she serves on that board. Now it doesn't mean that she's a token individual. It means that as a board we realized we needed to be more than we were, and how could we become that?

Elgin's city hall takes a similar approach to municipal hiring, as a key administrator described: "What we've attempted to do is really aggressively hire. Our goal is to have the city workforce reflect the community's demographics."

For institutions in Elgin and Yakima, as the Latino population continues to grow, incorporating immigrants is seen as essential to remaining legitimate amid shifting demographics. Local officials' attention to descriptive representation may involve self-interest in an attempt to remain relevant as the local population changes. Including intermediaries may be a way to convey the local government's agenda to immigrants, gain substantive input from immigrants, or promote an appearance of welcoming diversity. Elected officials may be attempting to attract voters or perhaps to cultivate future voters. In the literature on racial and ethnic politics in US cities, white politicians have at times incorporated representatives of ethnic groups as a means to bring the ethnic group into the coalition as a junior partner, while still maintaining dominance (see, for instance, examples from Chicago in Dominguez [2016, 81]).

As the analysis in chapter 5 indicates, however, electoral interest is not the central driver for attempts to bolster the descriptive representation of immigrant groups in these new destinations. In Lewiston and Wausau, naturalized adult members of the immigrant ethnic group do not yet constitute a sizable voting bloc, while in Elgin and Yakima

Latinos are numerous but have not consistently been seen as electorally influential. Across the four sites, local officials report that they initially seek out intermediaries to address communication challenges and later use them to demonstrate inclusion of immigrant voices as the immigrant ethnic group grows.

Intermediaries and Immigrant Representation

In these new immigrant destinations, where relatively few individuals possess the bilingual, bicultural skills necessary to connect immigrants with other local residents, intermediaries take on disproportionate influence in incorporation because of their unique position in local networks. In social network theory, an individual can increase her influence when she mediates interaction between two disconnected groups. Her advantage disappears when the disconnected groups link with one another independently (Burt 1992). Given linguistic and cultural barriers, immigrant and nonimmigrant groups in new destinations often cannot link without intermediaries. For this reason intermediaries play a decisive role in shaping interaction between immigrants and the receiver society. Intermediaries are a central lens through which native-born elites understand immigrants' needs as well as through which immigrants learn about the receiving society's institutions.

While it is not unusual for select individuals to be influential in shaping local opinions, democratic societies generally aim to arrange institutions so that representatives are accountable to those they speak for. Ideally, intermediaries use their privileged position to effectively connect immigrants with local officials and other long-term residents. Where intermediaries deviate from effective representation, in an ideal world immigrants can hold them accountable. In new immigrant destinations, however, the need for intermediaries often precedes the development of an infrastructure of immigrant-serving institutions. As in Mr. Farhan's case, local leaders may choose intermediaries rapidly based on their English skills, offering no guarantee that they understand immigrant residents and can effectively represent them. Since intermediaries may be recruited by long-term residents or self-selected, immigrants may not have access to formal accountability mechanisms to ensure effective representation.

Comparing intermediaries to brokers in the business world is instructive. A broker's "core currency" is trusting relationships through which information and goods can be exchanged. In recognition of this powerful role, in which brokers can selectively filter information and manipulate exchange, brokers typically must comply with licensing standards and professional codes of ethics (Briggs 2003). Immigrant intermediaries, prevalent across new destinations and beyond, follow no such formal code. Often immigrant intermediaries are in the odd position of being unelected representatives of nonvoting constituents. Attention to intermediaries is therefore essential, since we cannot rely on institutions with formal accountability mechanisms to ensure that desirable representation emerges (Dovi 2007, 8). Ineffective or unethical representatives can damage confidence in government, particularly influencing immigrants by providing negative early impressions of US institutions.

Even in the typical scenario where intermediaries are ethical and well intentioned, differences between intermediaries and the immigrants they serve are almost inevitable, given that possessing bilingual, bicultural skills is a hallmark of relatively privileged socioeconomic status or of more time and experience in the United States (Dovi 2007, 51). Descriptive representation is justified because along some dimension (race, gender, sexual orientation) members of marginalized groups face shared obstacles. At the same time, however, descriptive representation presents challenges because, despite common barriers, members of marginalized groups are not homogeneous along other dimensions and often have different interests. As a result, elevating some members of historically excluded groups can, in effect, marginalize other members of those groups (Dovi 2007, 35). Cathy Cohen (1999) refers to this as "secondary marginalization," in which the relatively more privileged members of marginalized groups have a say over the less privileged members of the group. In this way intermediary selection can benefit immigrant elites but does not necessarily aid immigrants more broadly.

In view of similar concerns, some theorists have been skeptical that mere descriptive representation will achieve the substantive representation of marginalized groups' interests (e.g., Pitkin 1967). Nonetheless, the empirical literature largely confirms the hopeful predictions about the potential of descriptive representation to aid in incorporating immigrant ethnic groups. The presence of descriptive representatives has been found to increase Latino voter turnout (Barreto 2007; Rocha et al. 2010) and reduce alienation (Pantoja and Segura 2003b). With respect to immigration issues specifically, the presence of larger Latino caucuses in state legislatures is negatively associated with restrictive immigration legislation (Filindra and Pearson-Merkowitz 2013). These findings extend to the local level with respect to descriptive representation on school boards and city councils (Leal, Martinez-Ebers, and Meier 2004; Marschall 2005), though the results on mayoral descriptive representation are more mixed.

With respect to unelected representation, a related literature on representative bureaucracy suggests that the appointment of descriptive representatives can provide similar benefits to marginalized groups (Dolan and Rosenbloom 2003). The empirical literature on the local level seems to confirm these benefits (Meier and Stewart 1992; Meier 1993; Meier, Wrinkle, and Polinard 1999; Rocha and Hawes 2009; Shah 2009). The presence of a Latino police chief is among the strongest predictors of less restrictive local immigration policing practices, suggesting that efforts to make police forces (and potentially other local bureaucracies) more representative of immigrant populations "may have effects that are more than cosmetic" (Lewis et al. 2013, 20).

Thus the empirical literature on descriptive representation offers hope that local officials' efforts to appoint intermediaries may support the political incorporation of immigrants. At the same time, however, the political theory literature offers some reason for concern. Local officials' appointment of intermediaries in new immigrant destinations offers no guarantee that these intermediaries will effectively connect immigrants with local officials, nor does it provide accountability mechanisms to ensure that they speak for immigrants' interests. As I will discuss, where immigrant organizations serve as intermediaries there is a greater chance that they are both connected to immigrants and accountable to their interests. Yet evidence from the new destinations suggests that local officials are often relying on individual intermediaries rather than turning to immigrant organizations, which may be absent or lack influence.

In the following section I investigate how much local officials in small to midsize cities nationwide rely on individual intermediaries, as well as exploring officials' views on immigrants' local civic presence in general. Finally, I test the hypothesis identified through the case studies: that proactive inclusion of immigrant intermediaries promotes collaboration between officials and immigrants as well as offering some immigrants an entrée to participation. Specifically, I test whether greater accommodation of immigrants is associated with more interaction between immigrants and officials and more positive perceptions of immigrants' civic presence.

Intermediary Prevalence and Effects Nationwide

The MRIS offers several indications that municipal officials beyond the four new destinations often rely on individual intermediaries rather than turning to immigrant-serving organizations. First, whereas more than half of towns report hiring or recruiting individual immigrants, only 26 percent report funding immigrant organizations or activities. Of course it is conceivable that towns interact with immigrant organizations they do not sponsor. Yet 65 percent of the destinations have no formal immigrant organizations according to Guidestar, a database that collects information on nonprofit organizations through the tax forms they submit.[3] Relying on tax forms provides an undercount of immigrant organizations, since religious organizations and those with revenues of less than $25,000 are not required to submit the forms (Gleeson and Bloemraad 2013). Even so, it remains apparent that many small to midsize immigrant destinations do not have prominent immigrant-serving organizations they can rely on as intermediaries. Indeed, even towns with large foreign-born populations may not have prominent immigrant organizations. More than half of respondent towns where one in five residents are foreign-born (53 percent, a total of sixty-one towns) have no immigrant-related organizations reported on Guidestar.

In addition to the apparent dearth of influential immigrant organizations, local officials report that they often rely on individual immigrants when seeking information about immigrants or conducting outreach. The survey asked officials to rank the resources they use "when seeking information on local immigrant groups," with possible responses ranging from federal, state, and municipal agencies to social service nonprofits, churches, immigrant/ethnic nonprofit organizations, and also "individual contacts within the immigrant community." As table 7.1 displays, local officials were most likely to rank federal government agencies first (including the US Census), with 21 percent placing this source first. Immediately following, however, was "individual contacts in the immigrant community," which 19 percent of officials ranked first. Only 10 percent of officials ranked ethnic organizations first.

TABLE 7.1. **Most commonly used sources of information on local immigrants**

	Number	Percent
Federal government agencies, including the Census	101	21
Individual contacts within the immigrant community	91	19
Churches, faith-based organizations	59	12
Local school district	46	10
Immigrant/ethnic nonprofit organizations	46	10
Municipal departments	40	8
Social service nonprofit organizations	38	8
State government agencies	31	6
Other	14	3
Local newspapers	7	1
Professional associations	5	1
	478	100

Individual immigrant contacts are also the resource most likely to be ranked in the top three sources of information about immigrants, with 44 percent of officials ranking individuals as one of their top three sources. General social service nonprofits, local schools, and faith-based organizations were the next most likely to be ranked among officials' top three resources, followed only then ethnic organizations, which just over a third of officials ranked in their top three. Local newspapers and professional associations were not common information sources. Overall, the results clearly demonstrate that local officials in small to midsize US immigrant destinations are more likely to rely on individual contacts than to turn to immigrant or other nonprofit organizations when seeking information on resident immigrants.[4]

Individual immigrant contacts not only are key in providing information to officials, they are also relied on to convey information to immigrant residents. After the question about sources of information, local officials were asked to list which specific groups or individuals they would turn to "if there were an issue or government program that you thought local immigrant residents should be aware of." Across the 317 officials who responded to the open-ended question, eighty-one named at least one local ethnic or immigrant organization, while fifty-five named at least one nonimmigrant local nonprofit. Only ten officials felt comfortable enough to list the names of individuals they would contact for outreach to immigrants, but sixty-six officials reported they would use individual contacts in the immigrant community for outreach. For instance, an official in a Minnesota town said he would contact the "head" of the local Somali population; an Illinois official reported that for outreach to Asians "it would be an individual who's their spokesperson"; and an official in a Virginia town said he would seek out "generally people known to me in the particular community." In addition to mentions of government agencies and specific organizations and individuals, twelve officials reported they would use ethnic media for outreach to immigrants, ten said they would use landlords or housing associations, five reported they would contact a local consulate, and four said they would rely on ethnic businesses.

Although local officials were reluctant to name specific people, individual contacts clearly remain a key resource when reaching out to immigrants. Yet this question also demonstrates that where ethnic or immigrant organizations are available, local officials are likely to turn to them for assistance with outreach. In all, 22 percent of officials listed an immigrant or ethnic organization as an avenue for outreach, while 18 percent referred to individual contacts.

In terms of both seeking information and conducting outreach to immigrants, local officials are highly likely to rely on individual immigrants or coethnics. Moreover, relying on individuals does not seem to be limited to newer immigrant destinations, which we would expect to lack immigrant-serving infrastructure: 16 percent of new destination respondents report that individuals were their top source of information about immigrants, and 20 percent of officials outside new destinations do the same. Likewise, 45 percent of officials in new destinations and 43 percent outside new destinations report relying on individual contacts among their top three sources of information.[5] Interestingly, officials in new destinations also are no less likely to rely on immigrant or ethnic NGOs, with 37 percent of those in new destinations citing ethnic NGOs as among their top three sources of information and 32 percent of other officials doing the same. As other studies are increasingly finding, the time frame when immigrants have been in a place does not necessarily determine that place's responses (Mollenkopf and Pastor 2016; Chambers et al. 2017; but see de Graauw, Gleeson, and Bloemraad 2013). In new immigrant destinations and beyond, local officials are frequently relying on individual immigrants as intermediaries.

Perceptions of Immigrant Civic Presence

Not surprisingly, given the limited influence of immigrant organizations across these destinations, very few officials report that immigrants are prominent contributors to local civic life. In this section I report on officials' perceptions of immigrants' civic presence before turning to whether accommodation is linked with more positive perceptions. Three sets of questions gauged local officials' perceptions of immigrants' civic presence. First, officials were asked several questions about immigrants' ability to participate and their interest in doing so. Second, they were asked how well key racial and ethnic minority groups were represented on local boards and commissions. Third, in an attempt to assess how much local officials' networks intersect with those of immigrants, officials were asked how much they interact with immigrants outside the office.

In interviews across the four new immigrant destination case studies, a common refrain among officials and other residents is to attribute immigrants' lack of participation to time pressure, lack of qualifications, and a desire to remain insular. Immigrants, informants explain, are too busy working multiple jobs with inflexible schedules to participate in local civic affairs. Too few immigrants speak English or have the professional qualifications needed to participate, others argue. Last, some assume that immigrants' perceived lack of participation shows they want to remain separate, often citing cultural factors. For instance, a media representative and civic leader in Yakima reported, "There is a banding together and preserving of cultural ties in the Hispanic community, so it may be that they are more comfortable in their community."

On the whole, these perceptions are less prevalent, though by no means absent, among officials surveyed nationwide. The survey probed these beliefs directly, asking city hall officials (but not police chiefs) whether immigrants and coethnics are vocal and well organized, whether they lack the skills to participate, whether they are too busy to participate, or whether they "would prefer to keep to themselves." While only 13 percent of officials feel that immigrants were "vocal and well organized in civic matters," few attribute immigrants' lack of influence to time pressure or lack of skills, as table 7.2 displays. Only 17 percent of officials agree that immigrants are too busy to participate, while more than a third (36 percent) disagree with this sentiment. Likewise, 19 percent agree that immigrants and coethnics lack the skills to participate,

TABLE 7.2. **Officials' perceptions of immigrants' and coethnics' civic presence**

Immigrants and coethnics	Agree %	Disagree %	Neutral %
Are vocal and well organized in civic matters	13	53	34
Are too busy to participate	17	36	47
Lack language or skills to participate	19	42	39
Would prefer to keep to themselves	37	25	38

while 42 percent disagree with the statement. On the other hand, officials are more likely to agree than disagree that immigrants "would prefer to keep to themselves and not participate," with 37 percent agreeing and only a quarter disagreeing.

These numbers demonstrate that most officials do not see local immigrant groups as influential in the local civic scene. Officials generally feel that immigrants have the time and skills to participate, but more than a third believe they prefer not to do so. Large numbers of officials also choose the neutral middle category, indicating neither agreement or disagreement, suggesting some ambivalence about these assessments. Interviews with local officials suggest that some would prefer to differentiate between immigrants and coethnics or among immigrant ethnic groups in making these assessments. On the whole, however, the results suggest that officials do not necessarily question immigrant groups' ability to participate in civic affairs, but more than a third doubt their motivation to do so.

Similarly, when asked to assess the representation of local racial and ethnic groups, few officials see these groups as well represented in local civic leadership. All local officials were asked how well Hispanics/Latinos, African Americans/blacks, and Asians/Pacific Islanders are currently represented on local boards and commissions (question from Ramakrishnan and Lewis 2005). On average, towns report that Latinos and African Americans are somewhat represented, while Asians have marginal to no representation. As figure 7.1 indicates, 44 percent of immigrant destinations think Latinos are marginally represented on local boards, while only 22 percent feel they are well represented. The distribution is similar for African Americans, though officials consider this group slightly better represented. In contrast, 66 percent of towns report marginal to no representation of Asians, while only 7 percent report that Asians are well represented.

Admittedly, perceptions of how well these groups are represented depend on how officials see the relative population size of these ethnic groups, as well as whether they equate proportional representation with being represented "well." For the moment, however, it is worth noting that as the local proportion of the ethnic group increases, the likelihood of seeing the group as well represented also increases.[6] Along the same lines, a 2003 California survey found that the perceived degree of representation increased with the size of the ethnic group (Ramakrishnan and Lewis 2005, 31).

With respect to interaction between immigrants and local government officials, officials were asked how frequently they see immigrants, hear residents speaking a foreign language, and have conversations with immigrants in their daily lives outside their offices. A five-point response scale ranges from never to every day. Almost three-quarters of officials (73 percent) report that they see immigrants outside the office once a week or more (table 7.3). Sixty-nine percent report that they hear a foreign language spoken outside the office once a week or more, and 42 percent report having conversations with immigrants outside the office once a week or more. Officials tend to estimate that the average non-immigrant resident has less substantive interaction with immigrants than the officials themselves do. Officials estimated that just under a third

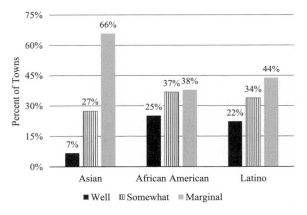

FIGURE 7.1. Officials' perceptions of group representation on local boards.

TABLE 7.3. **Intergroup interaction in immigrant destinations**

	Percent agreeing
Official sees immigrants in community once a week or more	73
Official hears residents speaking a foreign language once a week or more	69
Official has conversations with immigrants once a week or more	42
Average resident has conversations with immigrants once a week or more	31

of native-born residents (31 percent) have at least weekly conversations with local immigrants. On the whole, officials report relatively frequent passive interaction with immigrants—seeing and hearing them—but relatively little active engagement in their daily lives. Indeed, more than a third of officials report that outside the office they have conversations with immigrants less than once a month.

In sum, the survey demonstrates that municipal officials indeed look to individual intermediaries when seeking information and conducting outreach. Likewise, it confirms that officials do not see immigrants and coethnics as particularly well organized and well represented, though they are more likely to attribute this state of affairs to immigrants' preference than to a deficit in skills or availability. Last, they report relatively infrequent active engagement with immigrants both for themselves and for average residents in their communities.

Case study findings from Yakima, Elgin, Lewiston, and Wausau indicate that where officials actively accommodate immigrants, more productive intergroup collaboration and greater opportunities for immigrant engagement can emerge. The question then arises, among the towns surveyed nationwide, Do those that more actively accommodate have more positive perceptions of civic presence and interaction with immigrants? Conversely, in places that implement restrictive practices, are perceptions of civic presence and interaction less positive?

Accommodation and Perceptions of Civic Presence

I examine these questions using multivariate regression analysis that evaluates how much local accommodating and restrictive policies influence perceptions of civic presence and interaction, while holding other relevant factors constant. The cross-sectional analyses that follow cannot provide definitive evidence that accommodating immigrants has improved civic presence and interaction. Indeed, it may be that perceptions of immigrants' civic presence have led to greater accommodation. Nonetheless, these analyses identify that a positive association exists between efforts to accommodate immigrants and officials' perceptions of immigrants' civic presence. Evidence from the new destination case studies demonstrates that even previously homogeneous, politically conservative destinations are proactively accommodating immigrants before feeling pressure from immigrant voters or organizations. The case study findings therefore suggest that the arrow of causality could run from accommodation to immigrant civic engagement rather than entirely vice versa. If implementing accommodating practices were not positively associated with officials' perceptions of civic presence, it might indicate that accommodation was dampening or complicating immigrants' civic engagement. As it stands, the analysis does not rule this out, but it provides initial evidence that accommodating practices are not backfiring in a way apparent to local officials.

To evaluate this relationship, I rely on three sets of dependent variables. I first examine the four questions on immigrants' civic presence, measured on a five-point scale ranging from 1, indicating strong disagreement with the statement, to 5, indicating strong agreement. Second, the three questions on whether immigrant ethnic groups are well represented in local civic life are measured on a three-point scale ranging from marginally represented to well represented. Third, the two questions measuring officials' and residents' interactions with immigrants rely on a five-point scale ranging from never to every day. While residents' perceived interaction with immigrants is measured on this five-point scale, officials' interactions with immigrants are rolled into a summative scale that combines responses to the questions regarding seeing, hearing, and conversing with immigrants.[7] Each of these dependent variables represents an average of answers to the given question from responding officials within the town.

The key explanatory variables in these analyses are the full accommodating and restrictive indexes. While this chapter focuses largely on one type of accommodating practice—including immigrant intermediaries in municipal affairs—I use the full accommodating index in analyses for two reasons. First, it is interesting to see whether my observations about the benefits of intermediary inclusion extend to other forms of accommodation. Second, using the accommodating index rather than a more specific measure of efforts to include immigrants in local affairs produces very similar results, suggesting that efforts to include immigrants in municipal affairs affect perceptions of immigrant civic presence similarly to accommodation efforts more generally.[8]

Since factors that influence local practices toward immigrants may also affect officials' perceptions of them, these analyses hold constant largely the same set of factors identified in chapter 4: those associated with ethnic threat (percentage change in foreign-born population, percentage of the foreign-born population in poverty, violent crime rate, and percentage of homeownership), local capacity (natural log of population, percentage of residents with a BA degree or greater, and the percentage change in median household income), immigrant visibility (percentage foreign-born), external policies (state immigrant policy score, refugee presence, and locations within a hundred miles of the Mexican or Canadian border), partisanship (percentage of county voting for Republican Mitt Romney in 2012), foreign-born influence (presence of a Latino elected official, presence of a pro-immigrant protest in 2006, and immigrant organizations per thousand residents), and other contextual factors (percentage of agricultural employment and council-manager form of government).

One variation in these analyses is that rather than controlling for the proportion of the foreign-born population that is Hispanic, here I include three variables controlling for the proportion of the overall local population that is African American, Latino, or Asian. Including or excluding these measures did not make a difference in the analyses in chapter 4, but including them here is important since the proportion of local Latinos (and other ethnic groups) is almost certainly related to whether these groups are seen as well represented locally, as well as to other perceptions of civic presence.[9] To illustrate the effect of accommodation on immigrant civic presence, I generate predicted outcomes when varying the accommodating index from reporting no accommodating practices to reporting half of the accommodating practices asked about, while holding all other independent variables at their means (Tomz, Wittenberg, and King 2003).[10]

Before turning to how accommodation affects perceptions of immigrants' civic presence, it is worth noting that how much a town restricts immigrants' presence or opportunities is not associated with perceptions of civic presence or levels of interaction. The restrictive index is not a significant predictor of any of the aforementioned nine dependent variables. It is not necessarily surprising that restrictive policies do not affect perceptions of immigrants' civic presence in a clear direction. First, restrictive practices are relatively rare, so it may be difficult to identify patterns in how restriction affects outcomes, given the limited variation in the restrictive index. Second, threatening policies have been found to generate both immigrant mobilization (Pantoja and Segura 2001, 2003a; Benjamin-Alvarado DeSipio, and Montoya 2009) and immigrant withdrawal (Jones-Correa and Fennelly 2009; Furuseth and Smith 2010; Menjívar and Abrego 2012). Given these crosscutting effects, it stands to reason that local officials do not systematically perceive immigrant participation differently in more restrictive locales. In contrast, the accommodating index is significantly associated with more positive impressions of immigrant civic presence for seven of the nine dependent variables.

Looking first to the questions about perceptions of civic presence, officials were more likely to perceive immigrants as well organized and civically active in places that had implemented a greater proportion of accommodating practices. Specifically, moving from zero to 50 percent accommodation was associated with an increase of 0.36 points on the 1–5 scale measuring perceptions of immigrants' civic presence, all else constant. Likewise, in places that were more accommodating, officials were less likely to see immigrants as lacking in linguistic and other skills necessary to participate. Moving from zero to 50 percent accommodation was associated with a 0.4-point decline on the 1–5 scale. Finally, officials were less likely to claim that immigrants preferred to "keep to themselves" in places that implemented a greater proportion of accommodating measures. An increase from zero to 50 percent accommodation was associated with a quarter-point decline in the likelihood of agreeing that immigrants prefer to remain insular, holding other variables at their means.[11]

Places that report a greater proportion of accommodating practices also report that Hispanics and African Americans, though not Asians, are better represented locally. As figure 7.2 demonstrates, holding other variables at their means, a town that implemented no accommodating measures ranked a quarter point lower on the three-point scale of perceived Hispanic representation than did towns that implemented half of their possible accommodating measures. A nearly equivalent difference in perceived African American representation was noted between towns

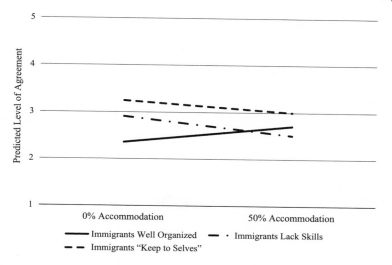

FIGURE 7.2. Accommodation and perceptions of immigrants' civic presence.

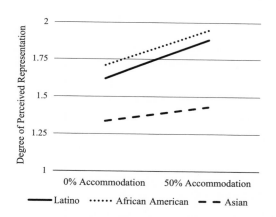

FIGURE 7.3. Accommodation and perceptions of ethnic group representation.

that did not accommodate versus towns that were 50 percent accommodating. Accommodation was directionally, but not statistically, associated with perceived levels of Asian representation, perhaps because Asian populations were typically small across the towns surveyed, with an average of 6 percent Asian residents compared with 21 percent Hispanic and 11 percent African American.

Last, implementing more accommodating practices was associated with more interaction between immigrants and officials as well as greater perceived interaction between immigrants and other average residents. Moving from no accommodating practices to half of accommodating practices, all else constant, is associated with an increase of 1.5 points on the twelve-point scale aggregating local officials' interaction with immigrants outside the office. Put simply, officials in towns with no accommodating practices reported interacting with immigrants roughly one to three times a month, while officials in towns that had implemented half of their possible accommodating measures reported interaction close to weekly.[12] Likewise, moving from zero accommodating practices to half of possible accommodating measures (all else constant) is associated with a half-point increase in perceived interaction among immigrants and local residents on the five-point scale.

In sum, higher levels of municipal accommodation are associated with more positive perceptions of immigrants' local civic presence as well as greater interaction. Keep in mind that this finding is not a simple matter of places with more immigrants, certain types of immigrants, or more active immigrants having both more accommodation and more interaction. These predicted probabilities are generated while holding constant the proportion of foreign-born and ethnic minority residents as well as other key predictors of local response such as foreign-born residents in poverty and indicators of immigrants' political clout. As table AD5 in appendix D indicates, aside from the accommodating index, the proportion of foreign-born residents is the most consistent predictor of perceptions of immigrant civic presence. The proportion of foreign-born residents serves as a predictor of greater interaction with officials and average residents as well as a lower likelihood of reporting that immigrants are too busy or too unskilled to participate. The proportion of local Hispanic residents is also a predictor of greater civic presence for three variables: greater interaction with officials, more representation of Hispanics locally, and a greater likelihood of seeing immigrants and co-ethnics as well organized civically. On the other hand, where the Latino population is larger officials are also more likely to say immigrants are too busy to participate. City population size also serves as a predictor of greater immigrant civic presence on three variables, with larger cities more likely to report that Hispanics, African Americans, and Asians are well represented.

Interestingly, the accommodating index is a much better predictor of perceptions of immigrants' civic presence than are the actual measures of their influence: the presence of Latino officials, immigrant organizations, and immigrants' protest activity. All else constant, the presence of Latino officials is associated with a greater likelihood of seeing Latinos as well represented and immigrants and coethnics as well organized in civic life. On the other hand, where Latino elected officials are present, towns are also more likely to report that immigrants are too busy to participate. A greater presence of immigrant organizations is associated with a lower likelihood of seeing immigrants as unqualified to participate; but for reasons that are unclear, immigrant organizations were also associated with a lower level of interaction with officials and a lower likelihood of African American representation. Finally, where immigrant protests took place in 2006, towns were more likely to report that immigrants lack the skills to participate. Clearly, further investigation is necessary to sort out the relation between these measures of immigrants' civic influence and officials' perceptions of their influence. For now, however, it is clear that the level of local accommodation is more of a predictor of officials' perceptions of immigrant civic presence than are these limited measures of actual immigrant engagement.

Benefits and Pitfalls of Proactive Immigrant Intermediary Selection

Analysis of the nationwide survey indicates that officials often rely on individual intermediaries and do not see immigrants as influential in local matters. Where towns are actively accommodating, however, officials are more likely to see immigrants as civic contributors and more likely to interact with them regularly. Although this analysis cannot confirm the direction of causality, the findings match evidence from the case studies, which suggests that where officials proactively include immigrant intermediaries, more productive collaboration and greater opportunities for immigrant engagement emerge. Even so, the quantitative data cannot reveal how these processes play out on the local level. Likewise, the quantitative data illustrate the relationship between accommodation and officials' impressions of immigrants' civic presence but do not capture the potential pitfalls of municipal accommodation.

Although officials may experience more productive collaborative relations with immigrant elites, these outcomes do not necessarily extend to immigrants as a whole. Officials tend to select immigrant intermediaries who suit their own needs but who may not effectively represent the immigrant population more broadly. Thus officials' impressions of immigrants' civic presence may not tell the whole story about immigrant incorporation. In the rest of the chapter I consider the benefits and pitfalls of municipal leaders' efforts to incorporate intermediaries, concluding with recommendations for how they might do so more effectively by fostering immigrant organizations rather than relying on individuals.

Benefits of Proactive Municipal Intermediary Selection

The benefits of proactive efforts to include immigrant intermediaries are evident in the contrast between incorporation processes in Elgin and in Yakima. For many years, Elgin employed Hispanic outreach liaisons in the police department, city hall, and, more recently, the local school district, in addition to appointing Councilor Figueroa to a vacancy in 1999 and Councilor Rose Martinez in 2014. In Yakima, local officials initially did not hire immigrant intermediaries in the police department or city hall. Although three city council vacancies arose in the late 1990s and early 2000s, local officials appointed a Latino to a vacancy only in 2008. Yakima officials did recruit a Latino police chief and superintendent of schools, but neither of these high-level officials could focus primarily on serving as an intermediary. In Elgin the presence of dedicated immigrant intermediaries recruited by local officials enabled productive collaboration between the immigrant ethnic group and officials, as well as building immigrant civic networks. In Yakima, local inaction resulted in self-selected intermediaries' stepping forward and using adversarial tactics to be heard, setting a conflictual tone to local intergroup relations.

Elgin's experience demonstrates that incorporating Latino intermediaries creates cooperative systems the community can rely on when issues arise. When problems occur in Elgin, Hispanic civic leaders and other local officials know how to work together. When the school district begins the process of hiring a new superintendent, the district's Hispanic liaison reaches out to Latino civic leaders as a matter of course as well as seeking the input of an established bilingual parent advisory council. Likewise, Hispanic leaders know that if they have concerns the mayor and the chief of police are willing to sit down with them. After a spate of gang shootings in summer 2007, Councilor Figueroa took the initiative to organize a gang prevention task force and appointed a local Latino judge to chair the committee. A Latina civic leader describes how the collaboration came about:

> [The Latino judge] called a meeting, and you had people from the different Latino organizations, but you also had [non-Hispanic] people from the other neighborhood groups that were concerned about what's going on. And the [non-Hispanic] police chief came along with a couple of their gang leaders and members of the team to talk to us and address questions on what do we need to do. And then from that they created a task force. So if there are serious issues that come up, we can reach out to all those people that we network with. The nice thing I think about is, yeah, we're Latino, but we still communicate with a lot of different people.

As this example demonstrates, when incidents occur involving the Hispanic population in Elgin, intermediaries that were recruited by local officials can connect immigrants and nonimmigrants to get things done.

The presence of dedicated intermediaries also offers a way to mobilize other members of the immigrant ethnic group. Councilor Figueroa played a key role in incorporation efforts through Latino voter registration drives, the establishment of the Elgin Latino Political Action Team (ELPAT), and efforts to get Hispanics appointed to local boards and commissions. In addition, two Latina leaders in Elgin credit their civic participation to appointed intermediaries, who identified the women's interest and connected them with opportunities. One describes how she became involved when she began working in Elgin:

> [The city's Hispanic outreach coordinator] sent me an e-mail. He's like, "Hey, I'm the short Puerto Rican guy you met the other day." . . . So that's how we connected, and that gentleman, he's still a very good friend of mine, he was the one who introduced me to like the whole Hispanic world. . . . [H]e just saw, "Wow, female Latina with a big title—she's gotta be something. She's gotta be well-connected." And so he approached me.

The second Latina, who went on to win elective office, recalled:

> I met [the city's Hispanic outreach coordinator and the Hispanic city councilor] and then I asked them, "Hey, how do I get involved more?" They were excited, because there [were] younger people that wanted to get involved, but

they needed more. And they gave me different ideas. [The Hispanic outreach coordinator] brought me to participate in [a Latino event] in 2005. . . . And then the following year I ended up chairing the whole thing.

For both of these women the presence of a readily accessible Hispanic outreach worker who was dedicated to connecting Latinos to opportunities enabled their easy entrée into local participation. Including intermediaries in local affairs has the potential to enhance immigrant participation and develop systems through which immigrants and established elites can cooperatively address local issues. Other scholars have also found that government-appointed coethnic leaders can encourage immigrant incorporation, serving as "access points" into politics (Bloemraad 2006, 161) or "improv[ing] communication flows and get[ting] more immigrants involved in local affairs" (Ramakrishnan and Lewis 2005, vii).

Conversely, the absence of proactive municipal efforts to involve immigrant intermediaries has consequences for immigrant incorporation. In Yakima, where officials remained inactive in this sphere for many years, self-selected immigrant intermediaries stepped forward to advocate. For instance, the most frequently mentioned intermediary in interviews in Yakima was Ms. Vasquez, a Mexican American woman who reports she was fired from a job soon after arriving in the city, in part because "they didn't like the fact that I was assertive. I was not a shy farmworker." Ms. Vasquez chose to stay in Yakima and establish a nonprofit organization. In the absence of municipal action to incorporate intermediaries, Ms. Vasquez and a handful of other self-selected intermediaries used adversarial approaches to advocate for other Latinos.

On my first visit to Yakima in 2003, non-Hispanic informants often spoke about "divisive," "aggressive" Hispanic leaders. All the same, if any Latinos were invited to serve on boards and participate in local affairs, these were the Latinos that local officials were familiar with. Over time, officials' resistance to inclusion and the intermediaries' adversarial response exacerbated tensions between Latinos and non-Hispanic whites as well as among Latinos. Even as the bilingual, bicultural second generation has become increasingly prominent, for many years the legacy of this standoff complicated political incorporation in Yakima.

Self-selected intermediaries in Yakima used confrontational approaches to break down officials' resistance to incorporating immigrants. Nonetheless, these intermediaries have been blamed for the resulting antagonism and accused of not having immigrants' best interests at heart. First-generation Mexican immigrants, younger Mexican American leaders, and non-Hispanic whites almost invariably describe the self-selected intermediaries as "having their own agenda." A Mexican businessman described the conflict in this way (differentiating himself, a Mexican immigrant, from Mexican Americans):

> Mexican Americans sometimes think different than we think as a migrant people, so to make those connections are not easy. And some people who have been here years and years and years have a lot of hard feelings or hurt feelings about the white people and racism back in the sixties. You know, that famous Chicano movement. . . . They don't trust. So it's hard. Sometimes I feel myself in between these [non-Hispanic] people who are really trying to help us, or do I need to listen to this [Mexican American] person who is telling me, don't trust [this non-Hispanic], he is going to hurt you.

Regardless of the legitimacy of the self-selected intermediaries' claims, their oppositional approach initially reinforced local resistance to change and, for a time, continued to hinder local political incorporation.

Yakima's example demonstrates that failure to incorporate immigrant intermediaries can have pitfalls. While it remains possible that Yakima's experience is somewhat unique, it stands to reason that without municipal attention to immigrants, intermediaries may have to use adversarial techniques to gain attention, potentially complicating local intergroup relations. In contrast, Elgin's experience suggests that proactive intermediary recruitment has important benefits, but it also has drawbacks. Relying on individual intermediaries is often inadequate to address the interests of immigrant ethnic groups more broadly.

Pitfalls of Proactive Municipal Intermediary Selection

Particularly in new immigrant destinations, relatively few immigrants or coethnics have both the desire and the bilingual, bicultural skills necessary to serve as effective intermediaries. The limited availability of such intermediaries overburdens existing intermediaries and frustrates established officials. Moreover, their small number gives these intermediaries substantial local influence in shaping the information flow and relations between established residents and immigrants. This influence becomes a problem when intermediaries are not effective representatives. Since local officials in new destinations are ill equipped to understand cultural dynamics within immigrant communities, sometimes the intermediaries whom established officials select lack the ability to speak effectively for their coethnic community. Indeed, the select individuals identified to speak for immigrants may represent immigrant elites while failing to mobilize immigrants more broadly.

OVERBURDENED INTERMEDIARIES.   Given the challenges of recruiting immigrant intermediaries and keeping them engaged, a talented immigrant or coethnic who comes to local officials' attention often ends up overburdened with invitations and commitments. A non-Hispanic business leader in Elgin explained: "There used to be one person, the only Latino businessperson that people actually knew and had conversations with, so that person was put on every board." The non-Hispanic head of an Elgin NGO agreed, saying: "We're competing. See, we're all trying to go after the same Hispanic leaders to serve on our board." The situation is similar in Wausau, as a social service administrator described it: "A few people get identified as leaders, and then they become the 'go-to' people. And there's no way that they could spread their talents as much as people want them to."

A Mexican immigrant businessman in Yakima reflected this reality:

> I mean I don't like to say this, but people consider me maybe a leader, so there are very few of us [Latinos] with maybe a little bit more education because we had the opportunity to have it. So we are very few. It's very interesting that, I mean not every other day, but at least once a month, somebody calls me to be part of their board. I say "Okay." So I'm serving on ten boards right now.

This man's situation is common among the limited pool of identified immigrant intermediaries in new immigrant destinations. As a result of the tremendous demand for their services, these intermediaries can run out of steam. This scarcity causes problems not only for the harried intermediaries but also for local officials, who complain that overcommitted intermediaries fail to follow through on promises. A social service administrator in Lewiston described this challenge:

> To be fair to the [Somali] leaders, they're being pulled in every direction. The service providers need input and counsel, and at the same time [Somalis] are supposed to know and speak for their whole community, but they're still trying to formulate legitimacy and at the same time open businesses. I wish they

would be more honest and set limitations, but because they don't want to be perceived negatively they say, "Well, we'll help out with everything." But they can't deliver.

With multiple organizations relying on a handful of immigrant intermediaries, capacity for outreach is limited. This scarcity overburdens existing intermediaries, but it also offers them substantial influence because of their unique ability to connect immigrants with nonimmigrants.

DISCONNECTED INTERMEDIARIES.   Local officials rely on immigrant intermediaries for much the same reason they rely on other sources of political information such as preferred newspapers and advocacy organizations. Accessing information about politics and interpreting it is costly in time and mental energy (Huckfeldt and Beck 1994). Amid cultural and linguistic barriers, gathering information about immigrants is particularly difficult. Thus local officials rely on a handful of intermediaries who are willing and able to provide what is seen as "the immigrant perspective." Finding one person to represent all immigrants is unrealistic given the diversity among immigrants along many dimensions, though some individuals will represent the dominant immigrant population more effectively than others. Interaction and information flows between immigrants and established officials are compromised when officials choose ineffective or ill-suited intermediaries. When established officials incorporate immigrants, they tend to select people who suit the officials' interests, often without attention to dynamics among members of the immigrant ethnic group.

Skillful intermediaries communicate well with both immigrants and established officials, understanding the needs of both. In describing a skillful intermediary in Wausau, a white nonprofit leader pointed to the fine line an ideal intermediary must walk: "He's slightly bicultural, but not overly bicultural. So he's trusted by the Hmong community, and he's bicultural enough that he's easy for [us] to befriend." Ideal intermediaries represent immigrants to local officials while remaining part of the immigrant community. Intermediaries who lack authentic knowledge of immigrant communities are, in effect, a bridge to nowhere. Local officials rely on them for information that the disconnected intermediaries cannot credibly provide.

Particularly in Latino destinations where coethnic leaders may be third-generation Americans and beyond, coethnic intermediaries may feel distant from new arrivals. The second-generation Latina leader of an Elgin Hispanic organization told me she had little contact with recent immigrants and relied on the non-Hispanic head of the Salvation Army for information on their needs. A Yakima Latina leader also recognized her distance from immigrant experiences:

> I'm half Hispanic and half white and grew up with my [white] mom, so I really was never exposed to discrimination or anything. And it wasn't until I got to be more involved in Hispanic issues . . . and was recognized as Hispanic because of my last name . . . that I started seeing that.

A Hmong educator in Wausau who came to the United States as an infant said even she sometimes feels disconnected from the Hmong community:

> [Two of the older Hmong leaders] might be able to talk more about the traditional Hmong and the Hmong community than I could. I feel like I'm kinda out of it. You know, out of the Hmong, because, I don't know, sometimes I feel like I'm totally outside. I have to relearn what Hmong is.

Intermediaries who are disconnected from recent immigrants in this way may or may not have the ability or desire to mobilize immigrants more broadly.

INATTENTION TO HETEROGENEITY.   Incorporation can also be compromised when officials select informants without attending to heterogeneity within the immigrant ethnic group. In Elgin, for instance, several prominent intermediaries recruited by local officials are Puerto Rican, even though 88 percent of Elgin's Latinos are Mexican. Puerto Ricans are only 6 percent of Elgin's Latinos (American Community Survey 2010–14), but they hold disproportionate local influence in intergroup relations. Since Puerto Ricans are US citizens and are more likely to have bachelor's degrees and to speak English than Mexican immigrants (Motel and Patten 2012), Elgin's established officials think they are choosing the most qualified candidates. Even so, selecting Puerto Ricans over Mexicans ignores the significance of national origin among Latinos. A first-generation Mexican American professional described the tension these appointments create:

There is some resentment out there because a lot of people feel that Mexicans/Mexican Americans are the overwhelming majority of Hispanics. The [Puerto Rican] councilman there was originally picked for a vacancy; he wasn't elected. . . . The [Puerto Rican] person who works for the city as a liaison was picked by the city. So the city, had it been a little more sensitive or thoughtful about what they were doing and wanted someone who was really representative of the population they're serving, might have taken that into account. The same with the head of the bilingual program, which is made up overwhelmingly of Mexican/Mexican American kids, is a Puerto Rican lady, and culturally and linguistically there are some significant differences.

In addition to the city councilor, Hispanic outreach coordinator, and bilingual program head, in the 2000s Puerto Ricans led the local Latino political advocacy group and Centro de Información, Elgin's multiservice immigrant nonprofit agency. In May 2008 this trend continued when Elgin's school district hired a superintendent of Puerto Rican descent (Calandriello 2008).

Inattention to Latino heterogeneity leads to both intra-Hispanic and interethnic mistrust. At public events, Mexican Americans say that non-Hispanic politicians spend more time with Puerto Ricans. A first-generation Mexican immigrant journalist explained, "When you ask [the politicians] to participate in a Mexican activity, they really don't mingle with us. If it's a Puerto Rican group, they are more inclined to participate." A non-Hispanic woman who works closely with Latino newcomers believes tensions between Mexicans and Puerto Ricans stem in part from officials' inadvertent favoritism toward Puerto Ricans. She explains,

[Non-Hispanic leaders] still don't do a real good job with not putting all Hispanics in one big pot. Because there's a definite minority Puerto Rican community that have a lot of power. And the Anglo community doesn't understand that stuff. So because they don't have to mess with immigration [paperwork] with Puerto Ricans . . . we have people being hired for positions that culturally are very different from the people perhaps they're working with.

While inattention to heterogeneity often generates problems, in some cases a panethnic spirit emerges to embrace Latino leaders.[13] Although the appointment of Puerto Rican city councilor Figueroa stirred initial controversy among local Mexicans/Mexican Americans, a decade later Latino leaders commented that he seemed to rise above intra-Hispanic divisions. Part of his acceptance may be attributable to his relatively recent arrival in the continental United States and his firsthand familiarity with new immigrants' challenges. When he arrived from Puerto Rico in 1992, Councilor Figueroa's English was not fluent, and he worked his way up from his first job as a bank teller. Given his recent migrant experience, he may have more in common with the bulk of recent Mexican immigrants in Elgin than initially meets the eye. Councilor Figueroa's case demonstrates the inherent multidimensional heterogeneity among immigrant ethnic groups in terms of immigrant generation, socioeconomic status, and national origin. To some degree, officials' categorizing Latinos as a cohesive group helps to "bring the group into being" (Itzigsohn 2009, 168); yet attempts to address Latinos as a group may have little effect unless the group already has an underlying sense of shared identity (Garcia Bedolla 2005). In this way, since established officials in new destinations usually fail to attend to heterogeneity within immigrant groups, the intermediaries they recruit may or may not be effective representatives of local immigrants.

In Lewiston the schools department was fortunate in hiring Mr. Farhan, who connected effectively with both established officials and Somalis. For instance, he brought Lewiston officials and Somali elders together to address challenges around Muslim students' prayer schedule, the observance of Ramadan, and an exception to the high school's "no hat" policy that allows Somali girls to wear the hijab. Another city department was less fortunate in its hiring. The very first person the city hired was a young Somali intermediary who served as a caseworker and advocate for Somali newcomers. Although he had relevant experience, spoke good English, and befriended colleagues, traditional Somali elders saw this caseworker as "young and flashy." Thus, while he was able to connect effectively with established residents, his youth and less conservative demeanor made him unacceptable to many Somalis. The Somali community's concerns about him were particularly pressing since he was in a position to supply or deny public benefits. At first, given how few Somalis could communicate with them, other city employees were unaware of the problems. About a year after the caseworker was hired, however, the city was receiving regular complaints that he was biased in his decisions. Initially none of the allegations could be substantiated, but tensions over his role continued to rise. Ultimately the Somali community's concerns proved real when the caseworker resigned in the spring of 2004 after being charged with soliciting sex from a social services client (LaFlamme 2004). A Somali NGO leader described his frustration with the city's initial reliance on this individual: "They was trying to refer that you hire one person and then you know the whole community. . . . So that's one mistake I think the city done."

The experience of hiring Somali intermediaries in Lewiston demonstrates how the urgency of communication needs in new destinations can prompt rapid and uninformed selection of intermediaries by established officials. In an atmosphere of urgent needs and limited information, city officials often simply relied on the Somalis they could most easily understand—relatively educated English speakers. Writing about the experience, a local government official explained, "The ability to speak English often dictated which Somalis spoke to the press and represented the Somali community at meetings with local, state and federal officials" (Nadeau 2003b).

Indeed, new destination leaders with little experience of ethnic diversity may not be equipped to recognize heterogeneity within newcomer groups. In fact, the need to consider differing interests and relationships among immigrants does not immediately occur to some establishment leaders. For instance, a white NGO representative in Lewiston reported,

> What I've gotten to know about the Somali community is they're really no different than anybody else around here. You have your subgroups that argue among themselves just like any other subgroups around here. But people tend, because they're foreigners, I guess, to think of them as a lump sum.

A second white NGO representative had a similar learning curve. She reported,

> One thing that kept on coming up is we would have different Somali folks saying, "I'm speaking for the entire Somali community," and as we moved forward and talked with different people, I just realized that kind of statement is like someone saying, I'm speaking for the entire Irish American community or whatever. There's so many communities within.

Lewiston's immigrant population has become even more diverse over time as a growing number of Somali Bantus and asylum seekers of other national origins make the city their home. The city was not consistently sensitive to distinctions between the groups, initially employing Somalis to translate for school meetings with Somali Bantus, who speak a different language and have been persecuted as ethnic minorities within Somalia. The example of Lewiston therefore demonstrates that officials' selection of intermediaries inadvertently risks further elevating privileged immigrants (Cohen 1999; Gilbert 2009). While proactive recruitment of intermediaries can have important benefits, it can also lead to problems when established officials choose the intermediaries they are most comfortable with, without regard heterogeneity within the immigrant group.

INEFFECTIVE INTERMEDIARIES AND INCORPORATION. Choosing ill-suited intermediaries has important consequences for incorporation. Since many officials in new destinations lack experience with cultural diversity and interact with relatively few immigrants, the behavior of intermediaries disproportionately shapes their views on local immigrants. Intermediaries who do not serve as effective representatives also can damage immigrants' nascent confidence in government and civic organizations.

In Wausau, for instance, negative impressions of an early Hmong intermediary contributed to broader generalizations about the Hmong population as a whole. In 1992 a Hmong man I will call Mr. Moua won a seat on the school board in an uncompetitive election and later ran unopposed for the Wausau City Council and the Marathon County Board of Supervisors in the late 1990s. Initially, local Hmong and their allies were excited about his victories. Established elected officials, however, were uniformly unimpressed with Mr. Moua's efforts and also mistrusted his motives. A former elected official explained:

> The first Hmong councilperson and I shared seats next to each other. And unfortunately, I think it was the wrong person to pave that new path. He was more interested in himself and in gaining notoriety than in issues that affected how to better open doors and just deal with Asian culture.

Another former elected official agreed: "Tell you the truth, he had a high opinion of himself. It didn't go over too good." Others complained that Mr. Moua failed to participate actively and took unpredictable positions on issues. Ultimately a local political operative saw the man's vulnerability amid tax troubles and other rumors and mounted a successful write-in campaign to oppose his reelection.

Just as Mr. Moua's initial election was a victory for local immigrants, his fall from grace had implications beyond himself. Some established residents generalize from his actions to draw conclusions about Hmong leadership in general. Especially in places with little experience with ethnic diversity, early intermediaries play a major role in shaping perceptions about the immigrant group and setting the stage for future civic and political incorporation. Ineffective intermediaries like Mr. Moua and the troubled caseworker in Lewiston can shake immigrants' confidence in local institutions. As these examples suggest, despite their local influence, intermediaries may not always be authentic or effective representatives of immigrant communities.

INTERMEDIARIES AND ELITE MOBILIZATION.   A final pitfall in relying on individual intermediaries is that even where these intermediaries are effective, their efforts may establish collaborative relations between immigrant and nonimmigrant elites but will not necessarily mobilize immigrants more broadly. The example of Elgin offers evidence that immigrant intermediaries selected by established officials can at times mobilize immigrants broadly. As I described above, Councilor Figueroa held Latino voter registration drives, and the Hispanic outreach official brought additional Latinos into leadership roles, but this broader-based incorporation is not guaranteed. Since bilingual, bicultural immigrants are typically more privileged, even conscientious intermediaries question their own ability to understand the problems of more recent immigrants. For instance, a Latino educator in Yakima explained,

> I do think there's some issues with really trying to figure out what our valley, our community needs, when you don't have that [Hispanic] population represented at the table. And I'm not even sayin' I'm the right person, because I'm middle class now. I'm not low income. However, I am still Hispanic. But I'm not always necessarily representing with the right voice, the group that's underrepresented at these meetings.

Some scholars suggest that national government immigrant integration programs help to counteract this elite bias in civic engagement by mobilizing immigrants more broadly. Where formal national immigrant integration programs exist, not only are community advocates more numerous, but these intermediaries are more diverse in their socioeconomic backgrounds. Without national government-supported programs, the immigrant leaders who emerge tend to be businessmen and others who were prominent in the home country. National government integration programs can generate broad-based mobilization because when diverse advocates achieve formal leadership positions they continue to support immigrant political incorporation by employing coethnic staff and serving as an access point and pathway to leadership for others (Bloemraad 2006).

Proactive immigrant intermediary selection on the local government level offers similar potential benefits. As often as not, however, the intermediaries that local officials select suit the officials' own interests rather than necessarily representing immigrants more broadly. When established civic leaders are recruiting immigrants or coethnics to serve on local boards or government commissions, they seek English-speaking professionals with flexible work schedules that let them attend meetings. These appointments contribute to descriptive representation and offer the potential to substantively bring immigrant interests to the table. These intermediaries may go on to involve other immigrants, but their elite status offers no guarantee that they will. As the quotation above suggests, even the intermediaries may question whether they can speak for the interests of recent immigrants given their own relative privilege.

Fostering Intermediary Organizations

What, then, should local officials do if they want to include immigrant intermediaries while also promoting incorporation? Evidence from Wausau suggests that fostering immigrant organizations has the best potential for developing intermediaries who are both connected to immigrants and accountable for representing their interests. The example of Wausau also suggests that local governments and other civic leaders can play a key role in fostering the development of strong immigrant organizations capable of fulfilling the intermediary role.

Though Wausau has not been immune to the struggles of other new immigrant destinations, over time the city has developed a highly functional system to manage local intergroup relations. Relatively soon after the Hmong arrived in Wausau, local leaders and philanthropists worked with them to establish an organization that provides services to refugees and mediates between the Hmong and the community at large. Wausau has been uniquely successful in identifying and employing intermediaries because it created a mechanism through which immigrant-selected leaders can collaborate and communicate with established community leaders. Since identifying intermediaries is difficult and established leaders lack information about immigrants' culture, establishing a parallel process through which immigrants can select leaders who then communicate with established officials ensures that intermediaries are both connected to and accountable to immigrant communities.

In the 1980s Wausau's established leaders supported the Hmong in developing the Wausau Area Hmong Mutual Association (WAHMA) (now the Hmong American Center). Frustrated by the difficulty of communicating with local refugees and seeking a mechanism for channeling funds and services to the Hmong, local leaders mobilized to provide extensive support to WAHMA. By providing technical assistance, local foundations and leaders expressly aimed to create an "institutional bridge" and "unifying voice" for the Hmong community.

In assisting with WAHMA, local leaders proved impressively perceptive about the heterogeneity within the Hmong community. An established community leader found that the younger, English-speaking refugees knew little about Hmong culture because they had grown up in refugee camps. He explains how he navigated this scenario:

> My approach on this was I never wanted to rely on a person who could just speak English because I didn't think that necessarily meant that they knew a lot about the culture. So when we were trying to do stuff, my plan was to always talk to people at different ages, different lengths of time in the camp, and I would just ask people, who would you talk to about this issue, who might have an idea how folks would think about it?

In contrast to many established residents in new destinations, this man and a handful of others in Wausau recognized the folly of relying on a select few individual intermediaries.

Rather than choosing a Hmong individual who suited established leaders to run WAHMA, the man quoted above and others worked with the Hmong to write bylaws that established a board of directors composed of one member from each of the fourteen Hmong clans present in the city. This system of identifying leaders generated a process that had legitimacy in the eyes of both established elites and Hmong traditional leaders. From the perspective of local elites, here was a registered NGO that could formally accept grants and serve as a go-to when issues arose concerning the Hmong. Gaining the endorsement of Hmong traditional leaders took longer, but it helped that WAHMA had a clear interface with the clan structure.

Through established leaders' assistance and increasingly capable Hmong leadership, WAHMA came to serve as a bridge and voice for the Hmong. As early as the late 1980s, when local government officials encountered issues related to the Hmong population, they turned to WAHMA for assistance. An elderly former elected official described how he involved WAHMA in resolving an interethnic dispute about a park in his district. Facing complaints from constituents that Hmong men were urinating in the park, he contacted WAHMA's executive director, who in turn gathered the relevant clan leaders. Discussions mediated by WAHMA convinced city officials that the park was a crucial gathering point for the Hmong. In response, the city installed porta potties to address constituents' concerns while still accommodating the Hmong. In this way WAHMA serves as a crucial bridge between the Hmong and established institutions in Wausau.

Identifying immigrant-selected intermediaries need not be limited to cultures with recognized clan structures. In Yakima a group of Latino leaders developed the Hispanic Professionals Group, which identified and nurtured local Latino leaders to serve as an alternative to the self-selected intermediaries. Over time the group has supported Hispanic candidates for elected office and helped established civic organizations to identify Hispanic board members. Like WAHMA, it offers the promising possibility of identifying a pool of immigrant- or coethnic-supported leaders that established officials can recruit as intermediaries.

This type of parallel leadership identification that links immigrant-selected intermediaries with established elites offers the best chance to ensure that intermediaries are connected to immigrants and accountable to their interests. The examples from these four cities indicate that proactive effort by established officials can contribute to immigrant political incorporation in new destinations. But relying on organizational intermediaries such as WAHMA makes it more likely that intermediaries will have some legitimacy among immigrants. Unlike individual intermediaries, organizations need to involve multiple parties and demonstrate a member or client base to maintain credibility. For this reason local governments would be well served to not only identify individual intermediaries but also help to develop credible immigrant organizations. Nonprofit organizations themselves may not always be accountable to the communities they serve (Marwell 2007) but they offer a greater probability of connection and accountability than appointing select individual intermediaries.

Conclusion

Seeking out immigrant intermediaries is among the most common local government responses to immigrants found both in new destination case studies and in the national survey of small to midsize immigrant destinations. Relying on individual intermediaries enhances collaboration among immigrant and established elites and offers the chance to encourage civic participation by more members of the immigrant ethnic group. Often, however, reliance on overburdened or ill-suited individual intermediaries compromises both local officials' perceptions of immigrants' civic presence and immigrants' perceptions of local government. Immigrant organizations, in which immigrant-selected intermediaries are more likely to be connected and accountable to their communities, are more likely to generate broad-based political incorporation. Developing immigrant organizations takes time and is unlikely to be an immediate solution to the early communication challenges that face new immigrant destinations. Given the benefits and pitfalls identified in this chapter, should local officials recruit select individual intermediaries when developing organizations is not an immediate possibility?

Elgin's and Lewiston's more active approach to identifying immigrant intermediaries, with designated outreach employees in several city agencies, has some benefits for ensuring that newcomers have an entrée to local institutions. It also contributes to productive collaboration between immigrant and nonimmigrant elites. In Elgin it has helped to encourage Latinos' participation beyond the intermediaries themselves. But relying on recruited intermediaries has crucial pitfalls, especially when established leaders fail to recognize heterogeneity within immigrant groups. Hiring Puerto Ricans to represent Mexicans resulted in intraethnic tension in Elgin. In Lewiston the rapid hiring of English-speaking Somalis without attention to their connection to other Somalis at times caused resentment toward the city. Established leaders in new destinations face a real dilemma in that they rely on intermediaries to negotiate cultural differences yet often know too little about immigrant cultures to understand whether those chosen are authentic representatives of their ethnic communities. The relatively privileged individual intermediaries they select may reinforce socioeconomic divisions within the immigrant ethnic group rather than mobilizing immigrants more broadly.

That said, failing to use any intermediaries also has serious consequences for local incorporation. In Yakima local leaders chose a reactive approach, expecting Latino newcomers to organize themselves. As a result, self-appointed Latino activists filled the void with an oppositional approach intended to overcome established officials' inattention. The long-term standoff between Latino activists and established decision makers left scars on both intra- and interethnic relations in the city. Despite this fraught history, by 2016 Yakima had much greater formal immigrant political representation than the three other cities. Perhaps as a result of the long-term local inaction, immigrants were forced to mobilize. Initially, adversarial techniques appeared to impede collaboration between the immigrant population and local elites. More recently, however, the confrontational challenges—cooperating with the ACLU and the National Voting Rights Advocacy Institute in filing suit against Yakima—ultimately brought more rapid transformation. After Yakima's at-large city council election system was struck down in 2014, three Latinas were elected to the city council in 2015. Indeed, for much of 2016 Yakima's mayor was the daughter of one of the original self-selected intermediaries. In Elgin, where local officials have been far more accommodating, city council elections are still held at large, and the only Latino city councilor is an appointee who recently won reelection.

Yakima's recent transformation suggests that the relation between local accommodation and immigrant political incorporation is not simple. While proactive intermediary selection can enable productive relations among elites and provide some immigrants with an entrée into participation, Yakima's experience underlines earlier findings that threat (or perhaps inaction) is also a potent force for mobilization and solidarity (Pantoja, Ramirez, and Segura 2001; Pantoja and Segura 2003a; Benjamin-Alvarado, DeSipio, and Montoya 2009; Wallace, Zepeda-Millán, and Jones-Correa 2014; Branton et al. 2015; Silber-Mohamed 2017).

Previous theories of ethnic and racial political incorporation have argued that to avoid co-optation, marginalized groups should organize from within rather than accepting elite concessions (Piven and Cloward 1979). From this perspective, appointing intermediaries bolsters the legitimacy of established officials at the expense of broader mobilization of immigrants. Appointing intermediaries to unpaid positions may be an inexpensive symbolic gesture that lets established officials off the hook without providing real resources to support incorporation. Meanwhile the symbolic gesture itself can reinforce inequities by accepting into the local power structure immigrant elites who do not have genuine ties to immigrants in need.

Survey data demonstrate that officials have more positive impressions of immigrants' civic presence where officials are more actively accommodating. It remains unclear, however, whether immigrants on the whole have greater opportunities for political incorporation where accommodating practices are prevalent (Frasure and Jones-Correa 2010). Because local officials act on their own distinctive legal and economic incentives to accommodate immigrants, they tend to accommodate in ways that advance their own interests and do not necessarily encourage immigrants' participation or represent immigrants' interests. Since federal policies frame immigrants as local government clients and encourage officials to accommodate them, municipal accommodation may incorporate immigrants as clients rather than as full citizens. Likewise, federal civil rights policies may rein in restrictive responses and encourage compensatory accommodation (as discussed in chapter 6), but these antidiscrimination policies do not always empower the victims of discrimination and could incorporate immigrants as members of marginalized groups rather than on their own terms (Bumiller 1992; Bloemraad 2006).

Thus one productive avenue for future research is examining the long-term consequences municipal accommodation has for immigrant incorporation. Do accommodating practices sap movements for immigrants' inclusion or do they further empower them? In previously homogeneous destinations, contact between immigrant and nonimmigrant elites seems to foster productive responses, but it is unclear how much these elite relations will shape grassroots incorporation in the long term. Since accommodation is more prevalent than restriction, it is crucial that scholars devote greater attention to assessing how proactive accommodation promotes the participation of immigrants beyond the elite level.

CHAPTER EIGHT

Municipal Accommodation

Generating Welcome or Backlash?

On a weekday morning in 2003, a Somali woman waited outside Lewiston's city hall preparing to translate for another Somali who was visiting a city agency. As she stood there, a white woman emerged and screamed at her, "They won't give me my Medicaid because of you people!" The Somali woman was not surprised at the incident; she said that struggling Lewiston residents "need someone to blame." As the white woman's comment demonstrates, however, this established Lewistonian perceived two culprits for her inability to access aid. She screamed at the Somali newcomer for using up resources she perceived as rightly hers. But she also railed against the city authorities who allowed the purported situation to occur. Chapter 7 analyzed how municipal accommodation affects immigrants, and this chapter investigates how it shapes the views of established residents. As this incident suggests, municipal accommodation of immigrants can spur established residents to resent both newcomers and the local leaders who serve them.

Since incorporation involves both immigrants' adaptation and their acceptance by society, it is crucial to understand how municipal accommodation affects the public's views. Much of this book portrays local government officials as receptive to elite framings of immigrants in federal policies and national political rhetoric, but local officials also convey frames about immigrants. Indeed, because elite framing shapes public views of immigrants (Hainmueller and Hopkins 2014), local officials can be crucial to cultivating receptivity among local residents. Some argue that providing government support and resources can grant legitimacy to the incorporation of immigrants, furthering both their advancement and their societal acceptance (Bloemraad 2006). Others argue that multicultural policies have brought backlash, contributing to less expansive policies toward immigrants as well as the popularity of far-right parties in Europe (e.g., Vertovec and Wessendorf 2010; Banting and Kymlicka 2013). In the United States, some observers interpret Donald Trump's rise and the broader shift of whites to the Republican Party as evidence of such backlash against immigrants and elites who support them (Abrajano and Hajnal 2015; Klinkner 2017; Sides 2017). These divergent findings raise the question, Will municipal accommodation serve as a cue that encourages the public to welcome immigrants or as a wedge that generates backlash?

At least in the four new destinations examined closely here, accommodation at times spurs resentment toward immigrants and leaders who support them, suggesting how white backlash may play out on the local level. Since the public is not necessarily exposed to officials' incentives to serve immigrants, established residents may resent their leaders' efforts. Findings from the MRIS indicate that in US towns and cities under 200,000 both accommodating and restrictive practices are associated with greater local discussion of immigration, and to some extent controversy on the topic. Local government responses to immigrants—regardless of their tenor—can promote strong feelings among established residents.[1]

Largely white places like the four cases examined here, which are experiencing ethnic diversity for the first time in living memory, let us observe both how local responses develop and how these responses shape community relations between and within ethnic groups. In this way the findings here intersect with a literature on how growing ethnic diversity affects social connectedness (Allport 1954; Blalock 1967; Putnam 2007). In this chapter I draw on this literature to argue that municipal accommodation can prompt greater animosity toward the out-group (immigrants) as well as within the in-group (through tensions between established residents and their leaders). Local officials are seen as part of the problem when they support immigrants, undermining overall trust in government and support for redistributive policies.

Local officials accommodate immigrants because their incentives make them receptive to framing immigrants as clients and contributors. Yet when they try to convey these frames to established residents, these positive understandings often fail to resonate. Efforts to make the case for immigration using facts and figures or generic praise for diversity are

usually ineffective and, at least in these new destinations, appear counterproductive. Assuming that simply bringing residents together will create greater interethnic harmony—what one official called the "just add
water" approach—is equally misguided. In new destinations, local governments advanced societal acceptance of immigrants when they coupled their support for interaction with opportunities for immigrants and
other residents to interact in meaningful ways (Allport 1954).

In the pages that follow I introduce three schools of thought on how
relations operate among diverse groups: the conflict, contact, and constrict theories. I then describe how accommodating immigrants can
heighten interethnic tensions in line with the predictions of the conflict
theory. Frustration with immigrants, however, is intertwined with anger
at local government for serving the newcomers. I demonstrate that tensions among established residents over accommodation contribute to the
broader declines in social connectedness amid diversity predicted by the
constrict theory. Next I turn to the MRIS, finding suggestive evidence
that both accommodating and restrictive practices are associated with
greater local controversy over immigration. Last, I evaluate how existing
accommodation efforts introduced in part 1 affect inter- and intragroup
relations, then make recommendations for what local governments can
do to minimize harm to inter- and intraethnic relations when accommodating immigrants. In essence, I find that institutions can enhance societal acceptance of immigrants by encouraging meaningful cross-ethnic
interaction that replicates the conditions proposed by the contact theory.

Before proceeding to these findings, it is worth noting that responses
to municipal accommodation may differ in important ways beyond these
new destination settings. Traditional immigrant gateway cities have long
been engaged in immigrant accommodation, and we would not necessarily expect backlash to operate similarly there. Some larger new immigrant destination cities like Atlanta and Nashville are making sophisticated efforts to increase public receptivity toward immigrants (Pastor,
Ortiz, and de Graauw 2015). These carefully planned efforts may not
succumb to the same pitfalls evident in smaller, previously homogeneous
destinations.

Even so, that local government responses are associated with public controversy over immigration in the nationwide MRIS suggests we
should entertain the possibility that accommodation can diminish public receptivity. Indeed, in a democratic society, in which public views can
shape future policies, those who want to promote immigrant incorpora-

tion need to consider how their efforts shape acceptance of immigrants. Since we have very little evidence on how municipal accommodation affects intergroup relations and public support for immigrants, my findings are likely to be of interest beyond these midsize new destinations.

Conflict, Contact, and Constrict Theories

Social scientists have long debated how interaction across ethnic boundaries affects group relations. Adherents of the conflict theory argue that increasing ethnic diversity results in out-group prejudice and in-group solidarity as the in-group bands together to compete for resources (Key 1949; Blalock 1967; Glaser 2003; Enos 2014). In contrast, contact theory argues that interaction amid diversity results in out-group harmony as narrow in-group identification diminishes (Allport 1954; Pettigrew and Tropp 2006). Both theories assume that intra- and interethnic ties are inversely related (Putnam 2007). Conflict theory argues that the threat of an out-group's presence enhances in-group solidarity, while contact theory claims that a growing embrace of the out-group attenuates in-group preferences. Recent empirical findings, however, suggest that ethnic diversity results in an overall constriction of social connectedness within both in-groups and out-groups (Alesina and La Ferrara 2000, 2002; Costa and Kahn 2003; Putnam 2007; Schaeffer 2014). Americans hunker down amid diversity, displaying less intra- and interethnic trust, a proposition referred to as the "constrict theory" (Putnam 2007).[2]

Although some see the conflict, contact, and constrict theories as competing, they are by no means mutually exclusive. Contact theory does not naively suggest that simply gathering different ethnic groups together will promote interethnic harmony. Indeed, Gordon Allport (1954, 261, 263), who introduced the theory, writes that such "sheer" contact "does not dispel prejudice; it seems more likely to increase it." Rather, the theory argues that to achieve improved relations through interethnic contact, interacting groups must possess the same level of status, work cooperatively toward a shared goal, and have the blessing of relevant authorities. Not surprisingly, these conditions are hard to replicate in the real world of diverse communities, especially since ethnic divisions are often associated with differences in social status. Without these conditions, both Allport and conflict theorists seem to agree that amid ethnic diversity conflict and competition often result.

Along these lines, in the new immigrant destinations examined here, established residents feel they are competing with immigrants, often complaining that immigrants take more than their fair share of local resources. Local government accommodation of immigrants can exacerbate these concerns, abetting perceptions that immigrants are receiving preferential treatment. Thus, at the same time that accommodation heightens competition and conflict with immigrants, it can also intensify tensions between established residents and their leaders. This conflict between residents and leaders suggests one mechanism through which constrict theory operates. As diversity increases, disagreements emerge within the in-group over how to respond to the out-group. In-group trust diminishes as people grapple with challenging questions: Do people like me disagree with me? Are my community members no longer on my side?

Although it is unlikely to be responsible for the constrict effect as a whole, this alternative mechanism explains prevailing constrict theory findings better than previously proposed mechanisms did (Williamson 2015).[3] Indeed, relations between local elites and the general public are implicated in the constrict theory. Along with lower levels of trust, increasing ethnic diversity has been associated with less faith in local leaders, the local media, and local, but not national, government (Putnam 2007). In this way, in new immigrant destinations with growing diversity, municipal accommodation of immigrants can act as a wedge promoting backlash against both immigrants and local leaders.

Municipal Accommodation and Backlash

As detailed in chapter 5, leaders have incentives that encourage positive understandings of immigrants, leading them to accommodate. Long-term residents of newly diverse neighborhoods, on the other hand, feel they are competing with immigrants for resources and express considerable concern that the newcomers are consuming more than their fair share. As a result, residents see leaders as giving immigrants preferential treatment. For their part, leaders complain about residents' negative views of immigrants. As diversity increases, divisions among established residents become more evident, decreasing in-group trust.

Given the variation across the four case studies, we would expect to see stronger evidence of tensions among established residents in the more accommodating refugee destinations, specifically Lewiston and Wausau, followed by accommodating Elgin and then inactive Yakima. Indeed, as I will demonstrate below, such tensions were most evident in the refugee destinations. Tensions were particularly evident in Lewiston, where some refugees still rely on public assistance, as well as historically in Wausau, where the same was true until the mid-1990s. Likewise, conflicts between residents and leaders were most common in the destinations where leaders proactively accommodated immigrants: Lewiston, Wausau, and Elgin. That said, across the four cities, even the minimal accommodations required by US law, such as English-language education in the public schools, heightened resentment toward immigrants and led to perceptions that leaders were giving them preferential treatment.

Conflict and Competition

In Lewiston and Wausau, residents expressed misgivings about how much aid immigrants deserved, if not outright suspicion about their abuse of public aid. Whereas federal policies encourage local officials to see immigrants as clients, many established residents are not exposed to this favorable framing and see immigrants as undeserving outsiders. For instance, an unemployed Lewistonian reported, "For me the biggest thing is coming to another nation and expecting that nation to bend over backward for you." He shared the suspicions of many Lewiston residents that Somalis had come to Maine primarily to take advantage of the state's generous welfare benefits. Similarly in Wausau, accusations of welfare abuse were the unifying theme of criticisms against the Hmong in letters to the editor during the 1980s and 1990s (Duffy 2007). Observers described welfare as a "primary element fueling inter-ethnic tension within the Wausau community" (Koltyk 1998). Criticisms of Hmong welfare abuse have receded as the Hmong gain economic independence, but they are not entirely absent from contemporary discourse. Even at a coffee klatch in 2007, a few Wausau small-business owners complained that the Hmong rely on public "handouts" yet still frequent casinos.

That refugees qualify for some targeted government aid contributes to outlandish rumors that build resentment. In Lewiston, erroneous claims that Somalis receive large sums of money, free groceries, and free cars were routinely presented as fact in interviews. One Lewistonian told me that a Somali man drives around town in a flashy SUV with the license plate U BOT IT, suggesting a flagrant abuse of public resources.

The same claim appeared on the local newspaper's online comment page (comments on Taylor 2008). A hairdresser told me, "When [the Somalis] went up to buy their groceries, all they had to do was say their name and the cashier looked through a little box and it was charged. We're not sure to who." A law enforcement official corroborated the ubiquity of these rumors: "I don't know how many times that I was either at dinner parties or restaurants or out with friends, and the $10,000 [voucher to the Somalis] thing would come up." During her extensive fieldwork with Somali Bantu refugees in Lewiston, anthropologist Catherine Besteman (2016) profiled the most common rumors, finding that the five most prevalent ones involved Somalis' receiving free services and refusing to work in return.

In reality, spending on Somali refugees has declined since the early years of their presence and was never a large portion of the municipal budget. In 2002 Somalis made up 52 percent of local General Assistance rolls, gradually falling to a low of 16 percent in 2009 (Cullen 2011). Since that time, General Assistance spending has fluctuated, with a more recent increase due to the arrival of asylum seekers of various national backgrounds, who cannot legally work while their asylum claim is adjudicated. In 2015, 48 percent of the General Assistance budget was spent on foreign-born residents, though only 11 percent of that went to Somali refugees (Seelye 2015).

Clearly there are areas in which Somalis do require services. For instance, 23 percent of Lewiston's schoolchildren are now English language learners (Washuk 2013). Somalis make up more than half of residents in housing facilities designed for larger families but are only 10 percent of overall Lewiston Housing Authority clients. The housing authority director felt the need to emphasize this to the local newspaper: "All applicants are on an even playing field. We've never given special treatment to Somali families" (Cullen 2011). In addition to these expenses, the city has received more than $9 million in grants from the federal government and other sources since the Somalis arrived in Lewiston (Besteman and Ahmed 2010). Nonetheless, that some Somalis and other foreign-born residents do receive municipal services has contributed to rumors that are substantially out of line with reality.

Concern over immigrants' economic impact can be double-edged. Residents protest perceived dependency on public services, but they also become suspicious when immigrants seem prosperous. In Wausau during the 1990s, Hmong economic progress raised suspicions and contributed to rumors about welfare abuse. White residents reported seeing Hmong residents buying minivans and homes and wondering how they could afford such expenses while purportedly not working. A letter to the local newspaper commented, "I see many of them always dressed up with built up shoes, gold chains around their necks, driving new cars and vans with six or ten children on food stamps. . . . We the taxpayers cannot absorb all the extra taxes" (*Wausau Daily Herald* 1993, as quoted in Duffy 2007, 174).

Resentment over immigrants' use of public benefits is less pronounced in Elgin and Yakima, since fewer nonrefugee immigrants qualify for public assistance. As in Lewiston and Wausau, however, accommodating immigrants in the schools and through translation contributes to resentment of the newcomers' presence. In Yakima, residents resented the need to translate signs and materials for immigrants. A city employee in Yakima explained, "Five or six years ago, there was a great concern about doing dual language signs on the city's part. [People said,] 'It's a waste of city money. Why are you reaching out to do that? Learn English!'" A letter to the editor in Elgin expressed a similar sentiment: "Signs and phone answering systems often give the illegal immigrants living here information in their native Spanish language. They are here illegally; we should stop catering to them" (Abbs 2007). As these comments suggest, anger at immigrants is often intertwined with frustration with local elites for accommodating the newcomers.

Municipal Accommodation and Tensions
between Residents and Leaders

Clearly, established residents of newly diverse neighborhoods feel competition with immigrants over government services. Yet they also blame local leaders for efforts to serve immigrants, which they frequently characterize as preferential treatment for undeserving outsiders. This ingroup mistrust is not a one-way street: some leaders disdain those who resent immigrants. Thus, municipal accommodation of immigrants engenders not only animosity toward newcomers, but also tensions between established residents and their leaders.

In Lewiston, where some Somalis continue to rely on public assistance, these tensions are once again particularly evident. Several white women described how encountering Somalis at social service agencies increased their resentment toward both the newcomers and the local authorities serving them. One young mother complained,

> I was sitting there for forty-five minutes with both of my kids, and I was in there to see if I could try to get emergency food stamps or anything like that, and one [Somali] woman came in and I was number 83. They called 97 before 83 and this [Somali] woman who just walked in went in. I asked the receptionist and she said, "Well, it depends on which caseworker is not busy at the moment." Whatever. That's stupid. I was here first; I should get in first.

Displaying both animosity toward Somali women and contempt for the local government, another young mother concluded, "If you need help, you need to have ten kids and wear a sheet on your head."

Residents of Lewiston and Wausau exhorted the local government to care for established residents first, or at least equally. A sixty-year-old Lewistonian who relies on public assistance resented the more generous benefits she believes Somalis are granted:

> We pay the taxes and somebody's getting special treatment that's not us. I worked at [a resort] for twenty years, and I don't want somebody getting something better than I am when I'm the one who's been paying in the taxes. . . . I'm not sure why it's being done. But if there's some reason, it would behoove them [the city government] to tell us what it is. I mean, it's our damn money, and they act like it's not.

In Wausau, a letter to the editor railed against the government for the injustice of providing aid to undeserving Hmong. A long-term white resident wrote,

> Everyone in Wausau needs some answers . . . [about] how Asians can afford to buy new cars and $80,000 houses. What kind of unjust system do we have? Well just the other day I saw a family member that just bought that $80,000 house buying food at the grocery store with . . . you got it! Food stamps! (*Wausau Daily Herald* 1992, as quoted in Duffy 2007, 182)

In each of these comments we see how services to immigrants intensified distaste for the newcomers as well as contempt for the government agencies that served them. It follows that in both Lewiston and Wausau, social service workers report being harassed through phone calls and public haranguing by white residents concerned about preferential treatment of immigrants. Other scholars have similarly found that in cases of perceived "distributive injustice," public employees themselves may become a target of resentment (Cramer 2016).

Even federally mandated accommodation measures such as translation can raise resentment not only toward immigrants, who are criticized for failing to adapt, but toward leaders who are seen as catering to them. A politician in Elgin explained established residents' objection: "Their feeling is that we're now kowtowing to a group of immigrants because they refuse to speak English." To avoid such criticisms, a school administrator in Yakima printed separate English and Spanish documents rather than bilingual forms and strenuously tried to avoid sending the wrong language to the wrong parents. He also struggled with concerns over preferential treatment when he provided child care and a meal for a Latino parent meeting through a targeted federal grant but did not have the funds to do the same for the general population.

At a time of growing economic inequality and mistrust in government, municipal accommodation unintentionally exacerbates polarization between the long-term resident public and local leaders. In effect, helping the immigrant out-group places local officials on the side of that out-group in the minds of some residents. In Lewiston, the city's simultaneous support for the Somali refugees and aggressive downtown redevelopment has heightened distrust between disadvantaged downtown residents and city elites. Downtown residents resent that the local government "dumped" Somalis in their neighborhood. For some the Somalis' arrival is part of a conspiracy to raise rents, demolish vacant buildings, and evict poor residents. Downtown residents feel excluded from the city's progress. Whereas local officials see immigrants as a boon to the economy, many local residents have yet to be convinced that diversity is good for economic development. As Lewiston's elites push this message and move forward with their urban development agenda, the Somalis' presence heightens mistrust between established residents and local leaders.

While some established residents complain about the elite's accommodation of immigrants, some local leaders complain about residents who resent the immigrants' presence. In discussing local animosity toward immigrants, leaders tend to scapegoat low-income or less educated residents for holding these views. In Wausau, for instance, a local

government administrator explained, "I think you'll find the more educated segment of the community is less likely to be ignorant of the situation. Let's put it that way. You've got your blue collars that tend to
react not very informed. They don't mind writing nasty letters to the
editor." A Wausau politician agreed that working-class residents were
more likely to dispute the Hmong's presence: "Let's face it; if you already have some amount of success, [the Hmong] are not your competition, all right? . . . You're not standing in line in back of them for a tee
time or something like that."

Even Mayor Macdonald in Lewiston, who gets into hot water for his
own hasty comments about Somalis, blames the less fortunate for animosity toward immigrants. In a 2011 letter to the editor he writes sarcas-
tically, "Who could have foreseen unrest breaking out between Somalis
and our downtown state wards over the shrinking welfare pie?" At the
same time, however, Mayor Macdonald positions himself in the middle
of the dispute, between disadvantaged long-term residents and other local elites, who are making what he sees as unreasonable demands for accommodation of immigrants. In a newspaper column he writes,

> Almost all Lewistonians welcomed [the Somalis]; that is, with the exception
> of those living in the neighborhood in which the Somalis were settled. These
> new neighbors looked upon the Somalis as interlopers, fearing they would
> cut into their portion of the welfare pie. Their solution? Make it uncomfort-
> able for the Somalis. The result? All Lewistonians were branded as racists,
> creating a divide—not by the Somalis, but by the white do-gooders and car-
> petbaggers. . . . The demagoguery and hypocrisy coming from a small num-
> ber of extremist white liberals and their African surrogates seeking to cast
> Lewiston in a bad light is unconscionable. (Macdonald 2012b)

Here Macdonald simultaneously denigrates disadvantaged Lewiston residents for their reactions to Somalis and castigates "white do-
gooders" who expect Lewiston to do more to accommodate newcomers. That most local elites are interested in accommodation while much
of the public is not exacerbates existing tensions over socioeconomic inequality. Politicians like Macdonald can exploit this latent mistrust to
win electoral victories over officials who support accommodation.

In Elgin, the city council's disdain for those concerned about unauthorized immigration precipitated a major local conflict that contributed
to some councilors' ouster. In 2007 a local anti-immigration group, the

Association for Legal Americans (AFLA), issued a series of proposals aimed at deflecting unauthorized immigrants from settling in the city. When the council acceded to pressure to respond to AFLA's proposals in the local newspaper, their tone was often pedantic, if not outright contemptuous. Former councilor Mike Powers did not soft-pedal his criticisms, writing of the restrictive proposals,

> Such a law would be patently offensive to any number of my friends and acquaintances, including an Indian doctor, an Iranian florist, a Mexican attorney, a Belgian chef, and a Danish businessman. . . . I find such laws are typically the product of uninformed xenophobia. (As quoted in Brooks and Johnson 2007)

In view of the councilors' comments, long-term residents concerned about unauthorized immigration expressed mistrust toward local authorities. A letter to the editor read, "Instead of honest and truthful responses, all we got from any of them was what sounded like a well-rehearsed monologue. They seemed more worried about staying popular with the Spanish citizens of this city than upholding their oaths to the lifelong residents of Elgin" (Brunschon 2007). Another letter writer commented, "I finally came to the conclusion that these guys are either in denial or they have forsaken all common sense and now worship at the altar of political correctness" (Froberg 2007). A third letter stated, "It appears that there is a real disconnect and distinct separation between the will/voice of the people and the powers of the establishment" (Sowers 2007). As these comments suggest, the city council's accommodation of immigrants by refusing to consider local enforcement efforts contributed to both animosity toward immigrants and mistrust between residents and elites.

Local officials' differing incentives with respect to accommodation of immigrants therefore exacerbate tensions between local leaders and the broader nonimmigrant public. These tensions clearly shake the foundations of trust among established residents. In addition to declining intragroup trust, conflicts among established residents lead some to withdraw socially. As predicted, these tensions are particularly evident in cities where leaders actively accommodate immigrants, such as Lewiston, Wausau, and Elgin. In Wausau, two white social service providers separately noted that they stopped attending their churches during the controversy related to school desegregation because, as one man put it: "I couldn't believe the people that I really liked and respected in so many ways, on this [issue] would miss the boat." Another Wausau leader on the opposite side described how the same controversy had turned her and others away from community participation:

> They're not tuning out because they don't care; they're tuning out because it's just too painful to go through all the crap that's attached to it. . . . I know in this town there are a lot of very caring people that are very concerned about Wausau. . . . But to climb through all the crap—nobody does it any longer. They retreat. Because it's painful. You know, you take some of that seriously and you get to a point where it's like, yeah, enough.

Similarly in Elgin, contentious battles over the city's stance against immigration enforcement caused some residents to lessen their engagement in local affairs. Two women, a city employee and a social worker, found themselves tuning out local affairs because of ugly immigration-related conflicts. The city employee explained,

> Every, every day, you hear the same things about immigration, immigration, immigration. I think that whether people are right or wrong or indifferent, I think it just fuels the fire and either people are doing too much, or they're not doing enough, or the police aren't acting appropriately, or the city's not responding appropriately. You know, at some point you just get tired of hearing it all.

The white social worker said the vitriolic coverage made her want to hide: "Just the whole idea of fighting over that kind of stuff turns me off so much that I guess I want to hide my head in the sand and think that they're just kind of loony people and they're gonna go away." Conflicts related to perceived preferential treatment of immigrants have led her to see even some members of her own ethnic group as "loony" and as such inherently untrustworthy.

Across these four cases, municipal accommodation of immigrants is often perceived as preferential treatment for undeserving newcomers, contributing to resentment toward immigrants and mistrust of local leaders. Evidence from other case studies of new immigrant destinations points to similar tensions over accommodation. Observers of a Georgia carpet-producing town with a growing Latino population commented on how elite accommodation complicates local relations: "What is most notable in the case of Dalton is that Latino immigration has fostered a split between different sectors of the white population" (Hernandez-Leon and Zuniga 2005, 270). Evidence from new destinations suggests that the challenges of navigating relations with the out-group contribute to schisms within the in-group.[4] In this way, municipal accommodation can contribute to backlash against immigrants and the officials who support them.

Accommodation and Perceptions of Local Controversy

If accommodation prompts tensions between residents and their leaders, perhaps officials nationwide will report that immigration is discussed more frequently and is more controversial where officials are implementing more accommodating practices. In this section I report the results of multivariate analyses that examine the effect of accommodating and restrictive policies on the degree of local interest in and controversy over immigration, while holding constant the typical predictors of local responses to immigrants used throughout the book (and detailed in chapter 4). These analyses cannot determine whether accommodating or restrictive policies are causing greater controversy over immigration, since the arrow of causality may run in either direction—places with greater controversy may be leaning toward certain types of practices in response. That said, if I can show that places that accommodate are also experiencing greater controversy over immigration, that would at least demonstrate an association between accommodation and local ferment over immigration, providing suggestive evidence for the effect identified through the case studies.

Indeed, I find that both restrictive and accommodating practices are associated with greater discussion of immigration locally. Both types of policies are also associated with a greater likelihood of controversy over immigration, though the association between accommodation and controversy falls just below standard levels of statistical significance. Holding constant the size and characteristics of the immigrant population as well as local partisanship and other factors, municipal responses to immigrants are associated with strong reactions among local residents.

The analysis here centers on two questions. First, the MRIS asks officials to characterize "the conversation on immigration in your community," offering options to say that immigration is discussed frequently, occasionally, or rarely. Responses are averaged across officials who respond within a given town. Across the 373 towns responding, more than half (55 percent) report that immigration is discussed only occasionally, with an additional 22 percent reporting that it is rarely discussed. Just under a quarter (23 percent) report that immigration is discussed frequently. The analysis uses a dichotomous variable indicating whether, on average, the town reports that immigration is discussed frequently.

Second, the MRIS asks officials, "How controversial would you say local immigration is in your community?" Response options range on a three-point scale from very controversial to not at all controversial, with somewhat controversial as the middle value. Again, responses are averaged across officials within towns. Only 5 percent of towns report that local immigration is very controversial. An additional 46 percent report that local immigration is at least somewhat controversial, for a total of just over half reporting at least some controversy surrounding local immigration. Analyses here use a dichotomous variable indicating whether the town reports, on average, that immigration is at least somewhat controversial.[5]

The key explanatory variables in question are the full indexes of accommodation and restriction introduced in chapter 3. The accommodating index, for instance, reports the proportion of accommodating practices a town has implemented out of the practices officials from the town were asked about. Regression results are presented in table AD6 in appendix D. In the analyses that follow, I employ the statistical software Clarify to predict the degree of local interest or controversy when towns have reported no accommodating or restrictive measures compared with half of the accommodating or restrictive measures they were asked about, while holding all other independent variables at their means.

Both accommodation and restriction are associated with more local discussion of immigration. All else constant, towns with no accommodating practices are only 11 percent likely to say immigration is discussed frequently, whereas towns that have implemented half of the accommodating measures are 32 percent likely to report that it is a topic of frequent discussion—a jump of twenty-one percentage points, as displayed in figure 8.1. Similarly, towns with no restrictive measures are 18 percent likely to report that immigration is discussed frequently, while towns that have implemented 50 percent of restrictive measures are 40 percent likely to report that immigration is discussed frequently, for a difference of twenty-two percentage points.

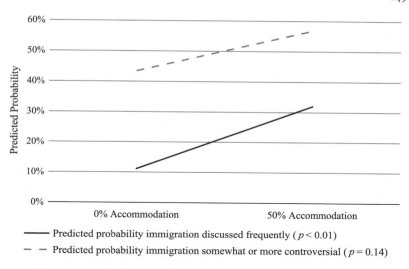

FIGURE 8.1. Accommodation and local discussion and controversy over immigration.

The same basic pattern is apparent in local controversy over immigration. The degree of local restriction is statistically associated with the degree of controversy, while the degree of accommodation is directionally associated, though it falls just below conventional levels of statistical significance. Holding other factors at their means, towns that reported no restrictive measures were 47 percent likely to report that immigration was a somewhat controversial topic locally, while towns that reported half of their possible restrictive measures were 76 percent likely to say the same—a difference of twenty-eight percentage points. Likewise, towns that reported a greater proportion of accommodating measures were also more likely to report local controversy over immigration, though not by a statistically significant margin ($p = 0.14$), as indicated in figure 8.1.

In sum, these analyses provide evidence that where local leaders have taken a firm stance on how to respond to immigration—whether with restriction or with accommodation—immigration is a more frequent topic of conversation and, to some extent, more controversial. Since we are holding other salient factors constant, this association would not be due to the size of the immigrant population, its growth, the socioeconomic or ethnic characteristics of immigrants, or a variety of other contextual factors, including local partisanship. Rather, the multivariate analysis isolates the association between the types of policies a town implements and the degree of local interest or controversy. It does not allow us to say definitively whether the tenor of local response causes local conflict over immigration, but it does indicate that where local leaders are taking a more evident position, immigration is of greater interest and perhaps more conflictual. These results also provide an important reminder of the challenges facing local officials in responding to the foreign-born amid public ferment over immigration. Both accommodating and re-strictive responses are associated with greater turmoil, underlining the public's ambivalence and perhaps explaining why many localities choose to remain inactive rather than taking action that is bound to offend one side or the other.

Structuring Accommodation to Promote Incorporation

If local governments seek to promote incorporation but accommodation precipitates backlash, what are they to do? Any efforts to accommodate immigrants represent a balancing act. To reduce resentment toward im-migrants, officials must challenge the view that the foreign-born do not deserve local aid. To lessen resentment toward local leaders, they must refute the claim that immigrants receive preferential treatment. In ef-fect, local officials must find ways to make positive frames of immigrants as deserving clients and as contributors more accessible and meaning-ful to established residents. To achieve this, they must move beyond two unrealistic expectations. First, simply making the case for immigration is not enough to change the hearts and minds of most members of the public. Second, officials cannot take a "just add water" approach to in-terethnic relations, as one Lewiston official said he learned. In the short term, unmediated interethnic contact is not likely to result in harmoni-ous relations.

The cases indicate that the conditions of the contact theory provide useful guidance on reducing interethnic resentment. Where possible, lo-cal governments can structure accommodation efforts so that when es-tablished residents and immigrants encounter one another they share equal status, work cooperatively on projects, and have the express bless-ing of authorities for their collaboration. Meaningful interethnic contact structured in accordance with these conditions of the contact theory has the potential to suspend stereotypes about the out-group, making room for more positive understandings (Allport 1954). Reducing animosity toward immigrants may lessen anger at leaders as well, by combating perceptions that undeserving immigrants receive preferential treatment.

Addressing both immigrants' advancement and their societal acceptance requires local governments to walk a fine line. Implementing the conditions of the contact theory requires careful application, which may perpetuate perceptions that officials are exerting undue effort on behalf of immigrants. Given these perceptions, would local governments be better off reducing the public profile of immigrant accommodation in order to stave off backlash? Should officials offer services that bring established residents and immigrants together with the aim of structuring encounters to promote harmony? Or should they provide services to immigrants out of the public eye, minimizing the potential for competition over resources and perceived preferential treatment? Even if the local government does not pursue a proactive strategy of accommodation, it must consider these questions as it fulfills its obligations to immigrants under US law. For instance, should the schools serve English language learners in separate classes or as part of the mainstream curriculum? Should towns hold interethnic public hearings with a translator or separate events for separate languages?

While it is tempting to believe that quiet efforts to serve immigrants will best calm public concerns, this logic is flawed for two reasons. First, outrage over preferential treatment toward immigrants is typically about perception, not reality. As the preceding discussion indicates, local residents often are angry over unfounded rumors of public assistance for immigrants rather than the reality of this assistance. Efforts to serve immigrants quietly and separately may well increase suspicions about preferential treatment. Second, this approach contravenes two conditions of the contact theory and may further hamper societal acceptance of newcomers. If municipalities separate immigrants to provide culturally or linguistically specific services elsewhere, officials are missing opportunities to encourage meaningful interethnic contact. Moreover, a key condition of the contact theory is the express sanction by authorities for interethnic collaboration. If local governments attempt low-profile accommodation, they miss the opportunity to express their support for the enterprise.

That said, the stringent conditions required for interethnic contact to bring harmony suggest that mere pro-diversity rhetoric and cosmetic changes will do little to encourage intergroup trust and may undermine it, along with trust in local government. Thus local governments will be better served by promoting meaningful interethnic contact as a general operating principle than by holding one-off diversity events or simply paying lip service to the value of immigration. Such events and rhetoric may have other benefits, such as dispelling a reputation for discrimination, but evidence from across the cases suggests they do little to improve interethnic relations and may undermine them. To advance inclusion and societal acceptance of immigrants, officials must go beyond mere talk to make positive understandings of immigrants more meaningful for the population as a whole.

Common Accommodation Practices and Social Relations

Part I introduced several common categories of local accommodation efforts, including resisting federal enforcement, providing language access, offering symbolic and material support to immigrants, and supporting immigrants' inclusion in local government. The effects of policies that avoid cooperation with federal enforcement are investigated elsewhere (Provine et al. 2016). Providing language access, although often controversial, in certain scenarios is legally mandated under civil rights regulations. Research indicates that even limited exposure to written Spanish can cue more restrictive responses to immigrants among those who hear Spanish more frequently in their daily lives (Hopkins, Tran, and Williamson 2014). While language access efforts therefore might precipitate backlash among some segments of the public, under many scenarios municipal governments legally must provide these services. Failing to do so can also be dangerous when newcomers cannot communicate with police officers, firefighters, or other key personnel. Barriers to language access also impede immigrants' access to education and other services that help them adjust, perhaps perpetuating perceptions that immigrants fail to assimilate. Because providing translation and interpretation is often a legal and public safety imperative, and since failing to do so is arguably counterproductive, here I do not further assess the effects of language access on inter- and intragroup relations. Instead I concentrate on common accommodating practices for providing symbolic and material support and advancing immigrants' inclusion in local government.

SYMBOLIC SUPPORT AND INCORPORATION. Local government's symbolic efforts to support immigrants—educating the public, issuing public affirmations, and holding related events—have the potential to support both immigrants' mobility and their societal acceptance. After all, Americans base their attitudes about immigrants on perceptions about how the foreign-born affect the nation as a whole—perceptions that are often sensitive to elite framing (Hainmueller and Hopkins 2014). Symbolic support is an opportunity for local governments to convey positive frames of immigrants that cue the public to welcome newcomers. To do so, however, officials must move beyond intellectual efforts to make the case for immigration and undertake more direct efforts to encourage meaningful interethnic contact.

To avoid tensions among established residents and their leaders over accommodation, the benefits of immigration must be more broadly evident. This suggests a public education role for local government. Indeed, as chapter 2 detailed, Lewiston, Wausau, and Elgin engaged in public messaging about the value of local immigration. Likewise, 19 percent of towns in the MRIS report having educated the public about immigrants, while a third report issuing resolutions or proclamations in support of immigrants. Nonetheless, across the four new destinations, typical means of providing public information did not succeed in dispelling rumors about preferential treatment. In Lewiston, brochures from the city and a well-attended public forum failed to reduce suspicions, since residents did not trust local government to provide an honest account. In May 2002, a bit more than a year after the Somalis arrived in town, Lewiston hosted a forum to provide information and respond to residents' questions. An elected official described how the public forum failed to counter prevalent rumors about preferential treatment for Somali residents:

> We did have a public meeting. People stood and asked these questions of our superintendent, and he's a real straight shooter and he would answer these questions as honestly as he could and said that this was not the case and said if there was other information would they please contact him so he could look into it, and nevertheless these stories were still out there. Even though he said it wasn't true, people still wanted to believe it.

The forum not only failed to assuage public concerns, it raised Somalis' worries about public antipathy toward their presence (Voyer 2013, 51). Similarly, Elgin officials' fact-filled, legalistic responses arguing that the city should not pursue restrictive practices backfired with concerned members of the public, as described earlier in this chapter.

As these examples suggest, when educating the public and providing symbolic support consist simply of arguments and rhetoric in favor of diversity, they are likely to exacerbate both inter- and intraethnic tensions. Officials are aware of the need to foster receptivity toward immigrants but, at least in smaller new destinations, may not consistently have the resources or skills to do so.

Beyond these destinations, large cities and national organizations undertake more strategic efforts to make the case for immigration. Several mayors' offices of immigrant affairs, especially in new immigrant destinations, were founded specifically to reduce interethnic tensions and foster receptivity toward immigrants (Pastor, Ortiz, and de Graauw 2015). Partnership for a New American Economy, a Bloomberg-supported coalition of mayors and business leaders, aims to "make the case for sensible immigration reform as a way to boost economic growth and create jobs for Americans" (Partnership for a New American Economy, n.d.). For Welcoming America, a national organization that works with communities aiming to become more inclusive toward immigrants, making the case that immigration contributes to shared prosperity is an explicit part of the process. Welcoming America presents a sophisticated plan for developing messages that are "rooted in values rather than a transactional or numbers-first approach to communications" and offers guidance on meeting the audience where they are and maintaining an awareness of established residents' economic insecurities (Welcoming America 2013).[6] While some cities and organizations are taking this careful approach to making the case for immigration, efforts across the four cities examined here suggest that officials at times present the case for immigration in a way that backfires, contributing to greater resentment toward immigrants and local leaders.

Two common tacks in making the case for immigration involve emphasizing America's immigrant heritage and relating the economic benefits of immigration. These economic benefits encourage municipal officials and similar local elites to support immigrants, as chapter 5 details. Whether local residents doubt the veracity of claims or lack the associated economic incentives, they do not necessarily respond positively to claims about immigrant heritage and economic benefit.

Even in Lewiston, with its early twentieth-century experience of large-scale Franco-American immigration, harking back to the town's immigrant past did not consistently spur support for immigrants. While some residents did connect their support for Somalis to their immigrant heritage, resentment of such comparisons was also a common refrain both in my interviews and in the findings of other researchers (Besteman 2016). A second-generation Franco-American merchant explained it this way:

> You can't compare them. Can't compare. [Franco-Americans] went here and went to work and did what they had to do to make a living and raise a family. They weren't collecting welfare. So that irks me a little bit when they compare them. Saying things like that, they make us dislike them.

As this comment suggests, a shared immigrant heritage did not always translate into sympathy for the Somalis in Lewiston. Moreover, analogies between Franco-Americans and Somalis increased animosity toward both Somalis and those who drew such comparisons: "Saying things like that, they [the elite messagers] make us dislike them [the Somalis]." Though these concerns were particularly evident in Lewiston, to the extent that residents across the other destinations drew on immigrant heritage in discussing contemporary immigration, their inferences were equally mixed. Evidence from the new destinations suggests that simply providing symbolic support for immigration by drawing connections to America's immigrant heritage will not consistently enhance receptivity.

Making the case for immigrants' economic value may be more effective, but local residents' perceptions seemed to evolve over time through contact with immigrants rather than in response to presentations of facts and figures. The forum in Lewiston did little to shift residents' views. Many Lewistonians were angered in 2006 when *Newsweek* published a piece titled "Lewiston, Maine, Revived by Somali Immigrants," pointing to Somali entrepreneurs' contributions (Ellison 2009). In other cases officials focused less on economic facts and figures and more on diversity's inherent value. This rhetoric alone, without broader efforts to reduce resentment toward immigrants, can perpetuate perceptions of preferential treatment and further distance local officials from the populace. In Elgin, the English-language DiverCity campaign may have offered a symbolic welcome to immigrants who were aware of it, but it did little to promote acceptance of immigration among the population at large and may, in fact, have undermined both intra- and interethnic connections. Similarly, the *Yakima Herald Republic*'s series highlighting the city's growing ties to Michoacán, Mexico, intended to celebrate increasing local diversity but was met with complaints that the paper was "shoving Mexicans down our throats" ("Readers Sound Off on Mexico Project" 1995).

While claims of immigrant value and contributions might be met with incredulity, actual contact with immigrants over time enabled residents to perceive and value their contributions. A Lewiston health care professional explained it like this:

> The feelings are still out there, . . . however, as the Somali community have shown that they're willing to work within the community, they've become part of the community in regards to they've set up businesses, they're not all on welfare anymore. You know, they're starting to buy homes, they're starting to become part of the community. And they're part of the workforce. And I think that's the biggest thing when they start working side by side with people and the people start seeing that hey, look, these individuals do good work, then it really functions as a way of breaking some of the stuff.

Residents report recognizing immigrants' contributions over time, in part through contact with them rather than directly in response to symbolic statements. Symbolic support—making the case for immigration—achieves one condition of the contact theory by signaling the local government's support for interethnic harmony. Yet facts and figures or sweeping statements delivered through forums, brochures, the media, and official releases did little to raise support for immigrants and at times prompted backlash against the newcomers and the officials supporting them.

Lewiston also offers a more positive example of municipal efforts to educate the public about immigrants beyond simple symbolic statements. In the Lewiston schools, a successful program involved white and Somali students in becoming peer educators on diversity issues. Teachers reported that residents were more likely to believe that Somalis do not get free cars when they hear this information from a friend rather than from a local official's denial. Training peer educators also may take accurate information viral, using the same mechanisms to spread truth that initially propagated rumors.

In addition to these attempts to educate the public about immigrants and provide positive messages, local governments often hold events to celebrate diversity or promote intercultural contact. Indeed, in the MRIS, more than half of towns report doing so. Often, one-off events involve self-selected participants who already feel warmly toward immigrants. Nonetheless, examples across the cases demonstrate that it is possible for one-off events to promote contact that lessens interethnic resentment. Neighborhood activities where participants share a similar status and common interests have the potential to reduce tensions. At Lewiston's Hillview housing project, an annual Neighbor Night first broke the ice between Somalis and white residents. A worker in Hillview's resource center now sees interactions among Somali and white mothers, who attend one another's baby showers and worked together to make a wedding dress. In Lewiston's downtown, both established residents and Somalis enjoyed Neighbor Nights organized by local VISTA volunteers. A white nonprofit employee reported that the events were productive, even dispelling common rumors. A lifelong downtown resident told me she was surprised to see that many of her white and Somali neighbors voluntarily gathered for a New Neighbor Night during which they drew pictures of their families and discussed traditions of family life in their cultures. Through symbolic support, municipal governments can play an important role in setting the tone for discussions of immigrants. But to be effective these symbolic statements must be coupled with opportunities for contact.

Indeed, sociologist Andrea Voyer (2013) argues that Lewiston tried to advance Somalis' incorporation by setting and enforcing the bounds of local discourse to emphasize the community's welcome. This welcoming stance had a downside, however, in that the official messages silenced those concerned about the Somalis' presence without helping them work through their concerns. For instance, diversity training for employees in Lewiston asserted that staff should appreciate diversity but did not effectively respond to employees' questions on how to navigate difference. An employee wondered, for instance, how to respond to a Somali neighbor who appeared unfriendly from his perspective. The training insisted he should value his neighbor but offered no guidance on how to interact. In this way, symbolic support for immigrants that aims to be inclusive can exclude those who are struggling to negotiate newfound diversity (Voyer 2013).

Ultimately, symbolic support for inclusion through educating the public, inclusive rhetoric, and events has the potential to enable immigrants' inclusion and societal acceptance, but it has important pitfalls.

Where it focuses on making the case with facts and figures and accla-
mations of diversity, it often falls flat in these new destination settings.
At a time of growing mistrust of government, municipal officials' claims
about immigration's benefits can seem like one more manipulation. On
the other hand, where municipal efforts to provide symbolic support involve person-to-person strategies that encourage interethnic contact, a
greater opportunity emerges to make positive understanding of immigrants more accessible and meaningful for the broader public.

MATERIAL SUPPORT FOR INCORPORATION.   Similarly, providing material
support for immigrants can promote public backlash, but it can also encourage productive interethnic contact. Local governments must weigh
short-term tensions against the long-term benefits of developing immigrants' capacity. After all, perceiving immigrants' economic mobility
can improve residents' receptiveness toward the foreign-born. Enhancing immigrants' capacity also increases the chances that same-status
groups of immigrants and residents can interact, another condition of
the contact theory.

One in five towns responding to the MRIS report developing new social service programs for immigrants, while others report restructuring
social services to better serve the foreign-born. Clearly, providing social
services to immigrants can become controversial. The waiting rooms of
aid agencies provide little opportunity for meaningful interaction and
much potential for animosity. Local governments could choose not to
provide services to immigrants beyond those mandated at the state and
federal level, but it would be misguided to imagine that lack of material support will support long-term incorporation by avoiding short-term
backlash. Alternatively, local governments could choose to minimize
contact between immigrants and residents, perhaps by serving immigrant clients in a different place or at a different time. This form of separate accommodation, however, can strengthen rumors about preferential treatment. Rather than shying away from contact, in some cases
local administrators actively attempted to promote interethnic contact
through their programs. Administrators' position of authority offers the
opportunity to replicate the conditions of contact theory among same-
status clients of different ethnicities.

Educational settings offer a particularly valuable opportunity to reduce interethnic tensions, in that an authority figure can mandate a
shared task and encourage respect for difference. In Elgin the public

schools capitalize on youth interethnic contact to bring parents together for events like international potlucks, pizza and bingo, and a "math night" (Malone and Dillon 2004). Youth extracurricular activities can be used to encourage parents to collaborate across ethnic lines. In Lewiston, a white nurse had her first positive interaction with a Somali mother when they both served on the parent booster group for their children's basketball league. She comments, "When you see them helping out on the basketball team with their daughter, you see that there are some really nice people. Kids are really good kids and moms are really good moms, just like we are." Local government recreation departments and parent resource centers can build this type of interethnic collaboration into their programming. Though language barriers present challenges, first-time mothers' groups or cooperative play groups offer the opportunity for cross-ethnic interaction among individuals with similar status and a shared task.

Beyond schools and youth programming, institutions of higher learning and adult education centers provide ample opportunities for meaningful contact between groups. Classes at Lewiston-Auburn College and Yakima's private Heritage University provide some of the most successful examples of interethnic bridging, since students at the same level participate in a shared endeavor sanctioned by a professor. At Heritage University, which is on the Yakama Nation reservation and divided roughly evenly between Native Americans, Latinos, and whites, students must take a communications class that includes instruction on intercultural communication and complete a community service project with a diverse team. The college conscientiously gives equal billing to all groups in its activities, decor, and curriculum. Heritage further builds community among faculty and staff through monthly activities that promote interethnic interaction. Assigned to "care groups" of ten diverse members, staff members engage in discussion and activities at monthly breakfasts. Through these efforts, Heritage University is playing a crucial role in promoting positive interethnic relations in Yakima. Although Heritage is a private institution, public adult education institutions offer similar opportunities to generate meaningful contact.

At Lewiston's adult education center, a current events class brings advanced students of English, many of them Somali, together with former Lewiston millworkers who are seeking their GEDs. Though interactions are not always cordial, the teacher can structure shared tasks and encourage thoughtful discussion among those of different ethnic backgrounds.

An adult educator says the course offers an opportunity for residents to talk about shared challenges such as scarcity of low-wage jobs. On the day I visited, the instructor led the class in a discussion about the September 11 attacks, as an excerpt from my field notes describes:

> [The teacher] asks them what they remember about September 11th, and they respond with their personal reflections. . . . The most active student and best reader, an elderly white man with an oxygen tube stretching from his nose, asks [a Somali student], how he felt about the attacks since he knew what war was like in his own country. [The Somali student]'s halting English does not allow him to fully respond. A couple of thirty-something women toward the head of the table pipe in. "Remember that Somali girl who was in our class last year? She told us about the fighting." They all struggle to remember and pronounce the girl's name. Later in the discussion, a tense middle-aged woman claims that shortly after September 11 a Somali man who worked at Cumberland Farms near Portland was arrested in a covert operation and locked up in New York because he had something to do with the attacks. Other students nod, and [the teacher] changes the subject.

Although connecting across language barriers and suspicions is a challenging task, the teacher guided the class toward shared interests and away from potential conflicts. The students showed interest in one another across ethnic lines and had established a relationship with the Somali former student they mentioned.

Beyond public social service and educational programs, more than half of towns in the MRIS report providing in-kind support to immigrants' activities or organizations, for instance, by allowing organizations to use public facilities for meetings at no charge. More than a quarter reported direct funding along these lines. All four case study cities also provided both in-kind aid and funding to immigrant organizations. While social service programs were the target of public ire, few residents seemed to have noticed municipal funding for immigrant organizations. Material support for such groups thus offers a means to increase immigrants' capacity with less chance for public backlash.

Funding can also be directed toward stimulating interethnic contact. The City of Yakima provides a venue for the Yakima-Morelia sister city meetings as well as modest financial support. The organization leads semiannual delegations from Yakima to Morelia as well as welcoming a delegation from Mexico each year. These trips have led to exchanges of orchestra conductors between Morelia and Yakima and Mexican crafts exhibitions at the Yakima Valley Museum. Arts leaders feel these efforts are doing a great deal to build understanding and enhance respect for Mexican culture, if largely among the Yakima elite. Two other initiatives may have a broader local impact. Yakima firefighters have established a relationship with their counterparts in Morelia. Two Mexican firefighter apprentices spent a year training with the Yakima crew. In recognition of this developing relationship, the sister city organization purchased two surplus fire trucks to give to the city of Morelia. Although cultural exchange is still the most active component, a subcommittee including elected officials is working on an economic development initiative that involves sharing agricultural technology and exporting crops.

Material support for immigrants' activities also can increase opportunities for productive contact down the road. In the case of the Wausau's Hmong Leadership Initiative, providing support to a Hmong-specific activity developed the capacity of more Hmong to serve on local boards with established residents of equal stature. In making funding decisions, local officials can consider evaluating how proposed projects would contribute to meaningful interethnic contact.

INCLUSION IN LOCAL GOVERNMENT AND INCORPORATION. As chapter 7 discussed, efforts to include immigrants and coethnics in local government contribute to more productive interethnic relations among elites, though these benefits may not extend to average immigrants and other residents more broadly. Among established residents, hiring and appointing immigrants may also raise suspicions about preferential treatment. In an e-mail communication shared with me, an anti-immigration activist in Elgin expressed his disdain for the city's Hispanic outreach position:

> The city has an open head count now that [the Hispanic outreach liaison] has resigned. They can't really replace the Hispanic outreach worker without creating other outreach positions for all segments of the population. . . . [M]arried people are a huge segment of the population. Do we have a Married Person outreach worker?

While some established residents may find such hiring and appointments suspect, efforts to hire immigrant workers also offer opportunities for meaningful contact, especially among municipal workers. Likewise, efforts to establish cross-class boards contribute to broader meaningful interethnic contact.

Municipal workplaces reach a relatively limited portion of the population, but they offer a worthy starting place. Reducing interethnic tension among local government employees may carry over into cross-ethnic interactions with clients. At Lewiston's Department of Social Services, for instance, administrators tried to build camaraderie among Somali and white caseworkers. Colleagues collaborated to plan a fellow employee's office birthday party. In the Wausau public schools, administrators have structured collaboration among Hmong teachers and others by requiring that all kindergarten through fifth grade teachers receive ELL certification. An advocate of this approach explained the benefits:

> What's really nice about having the classroom teachers have that ELL certification is it's no longer "your kids" aren't doing this, and what's the matter with "your kids"? Now, they're all *our* kids. And so that ownership is there.

Opportunities for public participation in local government also may allow meaningful contact between groups. Task forces or committees that meet repeatedly with a shared goal present chances to encourage intergroup harmony. More often than not such opportunities are limited to elites, but this need not be so. In Yakima, two early childhood education efforts involve parents and community members in overseeing programming. An interpreter who provided translation for meetings of one parent advisory committee was impressed to see that over the course of a year low-income Latino parents began to feel comfortable speaking up and communicating across ethnic lines. Planning for the Gates Foundation's Thrive by Five initiative in Yakima has involved multiple planning committees. Some committees that were meant to be interethnic split because translation made meetings unwieldy. For those that persevered, however, concerted efforts have promoted valuable cross-ethnic connections and learning. Several Yakima leaders commented on how the Thrive by Five meetings transformed business leaders' attitudes toward Latino parents. An educator described the evolution of events:

> A year and a half ago when I started talking with the white business leaders about this project, their language was very much about us and them . . . and I

was very clear—as were the Gates folks at the time—that isn't the way it's going to be. At the table, there'll always be parents, there will always be providers, and there will be businesspeople, and we will learn for the first time to really work together. And now those business leaders are talking more inclusively than I've ever heard before. . . . And that all happened within the last eighteen months. We've got a ways to go, but that's a perfect example of the power I attribute to bringing divergent, different people together to work on a common thing.

A politically conservative Yakima businessman confirmed this version of events. At one meeting he says he expressed disbelief that Latino parents in the target neighborhood did not take advantage of a month of free pre-kindergarten: "We all know that education is the first priority for parents, so how can that be true?" A Hispanic mother on the board spoke up, saying that her peers' top priorities are food, housing, clothing, and not getting deported, adding, "Education may make it in the top ten." The businessman was struck by the comment, and the episode strengthened his support for parents' participation in meetings. As he said, "How can I devise a plan for people when I don't understand how they think?" While interethnic boards are hard to negotiate, this example illustrates their value.

In sum, offering symbolic and material support as well as encouraging immigrants' inclusion in municipal affairs can precipitate backlash, but when implemented carefully it has the potential to improve local receptivity. Rhetoric that aims to make the case for immigration with facts and figures does little to change public views and, amid inequality and mistrust in government, can even exacerbate tensions between established residents and their leaders. Material support in the form of social services can raise complaints about preferential treatment of immigrants. Attempts to bring immigrants in or foster intercultural interaction offer promise, but too often they take place only among elites or those who self-select.

All that said, across the cases we also see examples in which local government accommodation, when done effectively, can both aid immigrants and foster societal acceptance. The best opportunities for local governments to encourage harmony through interethnic contact occur where the city has the authority to require regular attendance, structure shared tasks, and sanction collaboration (Allport 1954; Pettigrew and Tropp 2006). In municipal workplaces and educational settings, for instance, leaders can structure an even playing field among students or workers at the same level. Neither setting offers a guarantee of harmony, but examples from across four new immigrant destinations suggest that in these settings leaders can create opportunities for bridging interethnic divides. In other settings, for the most part, the local government has less control over the status of participants and less authority to promote collaboration and regular attendance. Nonetheless, local government committees and other chances for public participation let leaders structure meaningful contact. Hosting and sponsoring community events also can promote interethnic harmony, when the occasions encourage meaningful interaction.

As these examples suggest, carefully structured interethnic contact mitigates the discomfort of demographic change while revealing the potential benefits of immigration to the general populace. In this way local officials can make positive frames of immigrants as deserving contributors more accessible and meaningful. Though such efforts will require careful planning, they need not involve substantial municipal expense. Lewiston, for instance, has effectively deployed VISTA volunteers to run programs that partner Somalis and other residents for English-language conversation and to host Neighbor Nights and other collaborative community programs.

Conclusion

This chapter demonstrates that municipal accommodation can heighten interethnic tensions by raising concerns that immigrants unduly tax local resources. Further, because established residents generally do not share officials' experiences and incentives, accommodation can increase tensions between the established residents and authorities by encouraging a perception that immigrants get preferential treatment. Across the case studies, tensions among established residents are more evident in destinations that more actively accommodate immigrants, especially in new refugee destinations, where local authorities are tasked with providing refugees with federal benefits. Even where municipal leaders do not actively accommodate immigrants, simply complying with federal guidelines surrounding English-language education and translation can contribute to tensions between established residents and elites.

The MRIS provides evidence that tensions associated with accommodation may extend beyond the new destinations examined here. Among a random sample of immigrant destinations nationwide, accommodating practices are associated with greater interest in and, to some extent, greater controversy over immigration on the local level. An alternative interpretation of these findings could argue that where immigration is salient and controversial, local officials are forced to act. Although the data available here cannot sort out the direction of causality, at the very least, accommodating policies do not seem to resolve local interest in or controversy over immigration.

These concerns are familiar to anyone who followed the 2016 presidential campaign. President Trump successfully capitalized on concerns about immigrants to increase his popularity (Ahler and Broockman 2016; Klinkner 2017; Sides 2017). Even before Trump's rise, whites had been shifting toward the Republican Party, in part as a backlash against immigration (Abrajano and Hajnal 2015). This chapter offers a sense of how these dynamics play out locally, especially in new destinations. At the same time, the cases demonstrate that municipal governments can craft policies that address both immigrants' advancement and their societal acceptance. Promoting substantive interethnic contact that engenders positive conceptions of immigrants offers the best chance for reducing tensions over aid to newcomers.

These findings make several contributions to the broader literatures on immigrant incorporation and intergroup relations amid diversity. First, since we know very little about how local accommodating practices affect interethnic relations, these findings of backlash are a cautionary tale worthy of further examination in future work. Second, the process that unfolded in these newly diverse destinations suggests a mechanism through which constrict theory may operate. Amid growing diversity, established residents experience divergent preferences over how to respond to immigrants, decreasing trust (Williamson 2015). Third, these findings identify how growing diversity may increase existing tensions over socioeconomic inequality. Differences between elite and public views on how to respond to immigration offer a frustrated public another reason for mistrust. Perceptions of distributive injustice erode trust in government officials and offer populist leaders like Trump an opening to play on resentment toward groups perceived as undeserving (Cramer 2016).

That said, the finding that elite accommodation may contribute to resentment toward immigrants and local leaders by no means automatically suggests that accommodation should be curtailed. Disagreements over how to respond to out-groups may break down in-group solidarity, serving as a precondition for promoting eventual interethnic harmony. Indeed, where social capital (or solidarity) remains high, racial and ethnic minorities may experience greater inequities (Hero 2007; Hawes and Rocha 2011). Cleavages within the in-group that are associated with attempts to accommodate diverse newcomers may ultimately aid incorporation. In the most optimistic prognosis, in-group mistrust amid diversity could be a sign of the diminishing salience of ethnic boundaries and progress toward incorporation of out-groups.

How people conceptualize their community (or in-group) affects their political views and behavior, including their willingness to provide aid to outsiders. But these conceptualizations of community are not fixed (Wong 2010). Evidence from new immigrant destinations suggests that increasing diversity disrupts existing definitions of "in-group," contributing to declining trust even among coethnics. In the short term this disruption of the in-group can be challenging. In the long term, however, it might pave the way for more expansive conceptualizations of community (Putnam 2007). When our older, narrower understanding of our in-group is shaken up, it may then be possible to develop a newer, more inclusive understanding of community.

CHAPTER NINE

Conclusion

The idea that small cities and towns across the United States are generally welcoming to immigrants may seem to defy reason in the early months of the Trump administration. One need only look at the county-level results of the 2016 presidential election to see that President Trump and his dominant campaign message of restricting immigration captured the votes of most places beyond large liberal cities. Since taking office, Trump has restricted travel from several Muslim countries, targeted federal funding for sanctuary cities, increased arrests of noncriminal unauthorized immigrants, and endorsed legislation to drastically reduce even legal immigration. While my findings about municipal accommodation may seem surprising in this political environment, they are in fact quite consistent with Trump's rise. The disjuncture between elite and public views on immigration—visible even among municipal officials and residents in smaller cities—contributes to a backlash against immigrants and established leaders and attracts support for anti-immigration leaders like Trump.

Given Trump's rise, however, what will happen with municipal accommodation of immigrants? A central argument of this book is that local officials accommodate immigrants in part because of federal policies that frame them as clients or as worthy of civil rights protections. With Trump at the helm of the federal government and Republicans in the majority in Congress, can the trend toward local government accommodation of immigrants persist? In this conclusion, I provide an update on the case study cities, review the book's key findings, and then turn to this crucial question of the future of municipal accommodation, followed by discussion of broader questions about accommodation, intergovernmental relations, and immigrant incorporation.

Municipal Accommodation and
Incorporation in Four Small Cities

While this book demonstrates a clear tendency toward accommodating immigrants in small to midsize US cities nationwide, the four case studies also demonstrate that local government accommodation of immigrants is not a seamless march toward greater welcoming and greater incorporation. In recent years each city has experienced some challenges in its efforts to accommodate immigrants, whether from internal resistance or from struggles to adapt to President Trump's new tone and policies. Moreover, accommodating policies do not always yield the greatest advances toward immigrant political incorporation.

Elgin continues to be largely accommodating toward immigrants, with its anti-immigration organization falling quiet about 2011. Indeed, since Trump took office Mayor Kaptain responded to constituent demands by asking Elgin's Human Relations Commission to study sanctuary city policies. Elgin's police chief held a Spanish-language forum to reiterate that while the city complies with Secure Communities, it does not otherwise ask for immigration status. Elgin police directly reach out to ICE only when it comes to serious offenders—just thirteen of more than 3,500 arrests in 2016. Jaime Garcia, the longtime executive director of Centro de Latino, Elgin's main immigrant-serving organization, reported that under Trump immigrants' fears have intensified but Elgin has responded to these concerns effectively (Ferrarin 2017). Despite these largely accommodating policies, Elgin is now 45 percent Hispanic, yet only two Latinos have ever been elected to the at-large city council, and both were initially appointed to vacancies. Only one serves at present, meaning that Latinos make up 45 percent of Elgin's residents but only 11 percent of its elected city council.

In contrast, Yakima has long been inactive in responding to immigrants in ways that sometimes transformed into restriction. With the help of external advocacy organizations, local Latinos mobilized to challenge the at-large city council structure that prevented them from gaining electoral traction. Since a judge's 2014 ruling establishing a district-based council structure, three Latinas now serve on the city council. Yakima is 45 percent Hispanic, and its elected leadership is now 43 percent Hispanic. But making the city more openly accommodating toward immigrants is an uphill battle. In March 2017, in response to the federal immigration crackdown, the city council agreed to draft a policy on inclusive policing that would codify the police department's informal "don't ask, don't tell" policy on immigration status. At the April meeting, the four non-Hispanic white members of the council voted to terminate discussion of the proposed ordinance. Under a legal challenge for violating open meetings statutes, the council agreed in June to reopen discussion on the ordinance, which it then tabled in July (Bain 2017). Yakima's Latinos now have a prominent seat at the decision-making table and are bringing new topics to the agenda; yet they still face resistance in effecting change.

In 2016 Wausau celebrated forty years of Hmong progress toward incorporation, highlighted by the recent election of Hmong leader Mary Thao to the school board. At the same time, Wausau's Hmong were angered that one of their own, sixteen-year-old Dylan Yang, was tried as an adult for a murder that some consider a case of self-defense. That Yang's actions were automatically attributed to gang participation suggests that stereotypes of the Hmong persist in Wausau. The Hmong responded by mobilizing hundreds for a protest march, demonstrating the group's increasing political visibility (Xaykaothao 2016). County administrator Brad Karger joined the march but later was suspended for a month without pay by the elected board, which saw his participation as a criticism of local law enforcement (Schulte and Wasson 2016).

In 2016 Lewiston was touting its successes in accommodating Somali newcomers as communities around the country looked to its example when considering whether they would welcome Syrian refugees (Dritschilo 2016). By all indications, many Somalis are prospering in Lewiston, playing on championship soccer teams and revitalizing wide swaths of downtown. At the same time, President Trump's rise stirred animosity toward Somalis and other asylum seekers in Lewiston. In August 2016 Trump visited Portland, Maine, and claimed that Somalis presented a security threat and brought increasing crime to the state. Although the data entirely contradict his assertions—crime in Lewiston has declined substantially since the arrival of the Somalis—Trump's comments heightened quiet misgivings among established residents (Cook 2016). Consonant with municipal officials' tendency toward accommodation, even Mayor Macdonald, who supports Trump and at times criticizes immigrant residents, contradicted Trump's claim, saying, "We have no problems with anybody. We're a very safe community" (MacQuarrie and Wang 2016). He also spoke out strongly against harassment of Somalis in the days following the presidential election (Waugh 2016).

In three of the four cities examined here—Lewiston, Wausau, and Yakima—a majority of voters supported Trump in 2016. Support for Trump in Wausau's Marathon County exceeded national averages by ten percentage points. In Lewiston's Androscoggin County, voters supported the Republican presidential candidate for the first time since 1988. Although this analysis cannot definitively tie local support for Trump to his anti-immigration message, broader studies of voters' motivations suggest that immigration played a central role (Klinkner 2017; Sides 2017). Journalistic accounts in Lewiston draw the same conclusion (Galofaro 2017; Hinckley 2017). Despite Trump's local popularity, municipal leaders in both Lewiston and Yakima have spoken out against his statements or taken action to limit the effects of immigration enforcement on the local level.

Even so, this snapshot from 2016 clearly demonstrates that municipal accommodation does not always directly further immigrant political incorporation. Yakima's resistance may have been more effective in spurring immigrants to mobilize than Elgin's accommodation. In Lewiston and Wausau, successful efforts to aid refugees are not consistently matched by widespread societal acceptance.

Explaining Municipal Accommodation and Its Incorporation Outcomes

This book has presented a theory to explain why local governments accommodate immigrants, and also why their efforts do not consistently achieve their aims. Drawing on four comparative case studies and a national survey of local officials, it demonstrates that local governments tend to accommodate immigrants because municipal officials—both bureaucrats and elected leaders—face legal and economic incentives that inculcate positive understandings of newcomers. Part 1 demonstrates that among small- to midsize cities responding to the nationwide Municipal Responses to Immigrants Survey (MRIS), more than four in five local governments have implemented some accommodating practices, while fewer than one in five have implemented any restrictive ones. A substantial proportion of localities also remains inactive, though towns with greater administrative capacity, where immigrants are more visible, are more likely to act in response.

Part 2 addresses why local governments tend toward accommodation, finding that external forces—particularly federal policies and national politics—are crucial to shaping the tenor of local response by shifting the way officials define immigrants. Federal policies constrain municipalities to provide immigrants with K-12 education, language access, and in some case emergency health services. Federal refugee resettlement policies further constrain localities to serve newcomers. Federal and state policies that require local officials to serve immigrants define the foreign-born as clients of local services, directing municipal responses toward accommodation (Lewis and Ramakrishnan 2007; Jones-Correa 2008; Marrow 2011). In Lewiston, the combination of federal refugee resettlement policies and Maine's state General Assistance policies set the city on a path toward active accommodation. Nationwide, towns that are home to refugees are systematically more accommodating. Likewise, towns in states with more accommodating policies are themselves more accommodating, even holding constant a host of other factors.

Of course federal policies also influence local responses when they require local officials to participate in immigration enforcement. The increasing devolution of enforcement to the local level through programs like 287(g) and Secure Communities—now bolstered by the Trump administration—gives local officials the message that immigrants are lawbreakers, at times encouraging restrictive responses on the local level. Towns most exposed to federal immigration enforcement efforts—those along the Mexican and Canadian borders—are more likely to implement restrictive policies. Likewise, local police, who are more exposed to these policies than are city hall officials, face countervailing pressures. Their service-oriented mission encourages them to gain immigrants' trust in order to maintain public safety. Their regulatory mission, brought to the fore by these federal programs, encourages them to enforce immigration law (Marrow 2009; Donato and Rodriguez 2014). Perhaps as a result, police nationwide are more likely than city hall officials to provide some services to immigrants, but also more likely to be concerned about their presence.

Given the mixed messages coming from federal policies, emphasizing both services to immigrants and enforcement, why would municipalities tend toward accommodation? Traditional theories of urban politics would predict that towns will avoid costly redistributive efforts to help immigrants in order to keep taxes low (Peterson 1981) or will at least wait until immigrants have achieved some electoral clout (Dahl 1961; Browning, Marshall, and Tabb 1984; Stone 1989). Often, however, local officials see efforts to serve immigrants not as costly redistributive policy, but as vital to economic development. Because of their positions and the fiscal constraints that make them rely on business interests, officials encounter definitions of immigrants as valued workers, entrepreneurs, and consumers. More than half of local officials therefore agree that serving immigrants is crucial for economic development, and extremely few disagree with this statement.

Even where restrictive responses emerge, federal civil rights policies play a central role in defining immigrants as a protected class based on race or national origin, thereby curtailing restriction and encouraging compensatory accommodation. US civil rights policies provide incentives for private parties to bring suit against local governments that violate regulations. The presence of these policies has developed both an infrastructure of civil rights advocacy associations and associated antidiscriminatory norms (Melnick 2014a, 2014b). Across three of four case studies, external scrutiny from the media and advocacy organizations led local officials to rein in restriction to avoid legal costs and embarrassing association with racial bigotry. Nationwide, a substantial majority of towns that passed restrictive ordinances in 2006–7 have since retreated from restriction. Towns that received more scrutiny from advocacy organizations and the media were particularly likely to rescind their ordinances out of concern over costs and damage to their reputations. Federal policies that define immigrants as clients and as a group worthy of civil rights protections, combined with local economic factors that define them as contributors, tend to set municipalities on a path toward accommodation.

Yet national partisan politics also plays a key role in shaping local responses to immigrants, at times defining immigrants not as a group worthy of protection from discrimination but as "illegal aliens." The Republican Party has increasingly staked out a position hostile to some forms of immigration, particularly if immigrants are unauthorized (Abrajano and Hajnal 2015). Thus places with a more Republican-leaning electorate are less likely to implement accommodating practices and more likely to pursue restrictive law enforcement policies. National ideological divides on immigration extend to the local level, with politically conservative officials expressing greater concern about immigrants' presence and less interest in serving them locally. Municipalities where politics plays more of a role in local policymaking—those with an elected mayor at the helm rather than an appointed city manager—are more likely to implement restrictive policies. That said, partisan divides are not entirely determinative of responses or views on the local level. Even among conservative elected officials—the group most subject to partisan demands for restriction—more than half see serving immigrants as part of their professional duty.

Indeed, local government officials have systematically more favorable views of immigrants than does the general public, even holding constant demographic and partisan differences between these populations. Theories of immigration policymaking have long argued that an elite consensus surrounding the benefits of immigration bolsters expansionary policies and keeps criticism of immigrants off the public agenda (Freeman 1995; Tichenor 2002). Even as that elite consensus seems to be crumbling on the national level, the disjuncture in views between municipal officials and the broader public suggests that it still exists on the local level.

Part 3 examines the consequences of municipal accommodation for immigrant political incorporation. That municipal officials' distinctly favorable views of immigrants spur accommodation structures how this accommodation shapes incorporation. When local government officials proactively accommodate immigrants, they may establish productive relations between immigrant and municipal elites, but they will not necessarily generate more broad-based incorporation of immigrants. In addition, the fact that the broader public does not necessarily share officials' incentives to serve immigrants means that efforts to accommodate can precipitate nativist backlash. Whereas most local officials see immigrants as clients, some established residents see them as outsiders. Where most local officials tout immigrants' economic contributions, some residents emphasize costs. And while most local officials recognize that immigrants are in some ways protected by civil rights laws, some residents emphasize definitions of immigrants as lawbreakers. At a time of deep-seated mistrust in government institutions, officials' efforts to make the case for immigration can fall flat when they rely on facts, figures, and exhortations about the value of diversity. That said, evidence from Lewiston, Wausau, Elgin, and Yakima demonstrates that municipal accommodation can foster both immigrants' advancement and their societal acceptance when officials focus on creating opportunities for meaningful interethnic contact that make positive understandings of immigrants more resonant.

These findings stem from four case studies and a national survey of municipal officials in small to midsize cities, but their implications have broader reach. Although my investigation excludes the 109 immigrant destinations in the United States with populations of more than 200,000 (American Community Survey 2008–12), there is ample evidence that the tendency toward accommodation I describe extends to these larger cities (Pastor, Ortiz, and de Graauw 2015). Although my survey took place at a time when cities and states were moving toward greater accommodation (Gulasekaram and Ramakrishnan 2015), complementary findings from the case studies over the period 1990 to 2015 suggest that these trends are not limited to this moment in time. Nonetheless, will the Trump presidency's changes in tone and policies disrupt the general trend toward municipal accommodation?

The Future of Municipal Accommodation in the Trump Era

The Trump administration's policies and rhetoric have the potential to undermine municipal accommodation in three key ways. First, President Trump's executive order revoking funding for sanctuary cities and reinstating Secure Communities and the 287(g) program amplifies local police departments' role in immigration enforcement. Second, Attorney General Sessions's efforts to scale back civil rights investigations lessen the chances that local officials will face consequences for restrictive immigration practices. And third, President Trump's continued rhetorical attacks on immigrants raise the salience of negative understandings of immigrants as dangerous "illegal aliens" and increase the likelihood that immigration issues will be politicized on the local level. Thus far, however, numerous cities—both large and small—have continued to support or even enact policies supporting immigrants. Similar to processes I describe on the local level, some of the more restrictive elements of the executive orders have been stayed through civil rights advocacy and legal action. To gauge how President Trump will affect municipal accommodation of immigrants, I consider how cities have responded to changes in policy on sanctuary cities, the 287(g) program, and civil rights investigations in the first six months of his tenure.

Thus far the Trump administration has been unsuccessful in withdrawing funding from sanctuary cities. San Francisco and Santa Clara County successfully sued in federal court to stay the revocation of funds, except for one law enforcement grant program. Chicago has now filed suit against new guidelines to exclude sanctuary cities from that grant program (Kenning and Ax 2017). Among major cities, only Miami has repealed its sanctuary policy since Trump came to power (Bernal 2017). But how are sanctuary cities outside the national limelight responding?

While there is no one definition of "sanctuary city," the label typically applies to places that in some way limit police participation in immigration enforcement. Given the lack of a standard definition and given that some cities that limit enforcement do not embrace the term sanctuary, there is no definitive list of cities with sanctuary policies. Drawing on several sources, I compiled a list of 250 sanctuary cities and reviewed responses in a randomly selected one-third of them since Trump's election in November 2016.[1] Of the ninety-three cities reviewed, twenty-seven appeared on lists of sanctuary cities, but we could find no evidence in the media or in statements by the city that they had ever had policies limiting police participation in law enforcement.[2] Since Trump's election, four of these cities have publicly denied their sanctuary status. Of the remaining sixty-six cities with some sanctuary policy in effect, seventeen had enacted their policies after Trump's election and twenty-six had affirmed their existing policies since the election. Five cities had made statements officially disavowing the term sanctuary, but all of these appeared to have policies in place that limit participation in enforcement. Thus, of the sixty-six cities that actually had policies limiting enforcement, close to two-thirds have enacted or affirmed their policies since Trump's election, 29 percent appear to have maintained their policies but not publicized them further, and only 6 percent have taken any steps that indicate they might scale back their policies. Among sanctuary cities, President Trump's efforts to crack down on immigration generally are not weakening local resolve to accommodate. As I will discuss in the following section, however, state-level efforts to impede sanctuary cities in Texas and elsewhere may be having more of an immediate effect in scaling back efforts to limit police participation in enforcement.

Although sanctuary cities, which lie at the extremes of accommodation, are not retreating from their welcoming stance, it remains possible that Trump's policies will stir interest in restrictive policies in other jurisdictions. For instance, will cities embrace the renewed 287(g) policy, which deputizes local police to carry out federal immigration enforcement? Drawing on several sources, I compiled a list of 106 jurisdictions that have had 287(g) memoranda of understanding with the Department of Homeland Security: thirteen state agencies, seventy-seven counties, two regional departments, and fourteen cities.[3] Of these, forty-seven agreements (44 percent) are no longer active. Thirty-one earlier agreements (29 percent) were renewed in 2016–17, and twenty-eight jurisdictions (26 percent) have signed new agreements in 2016–17, twenty-six of them since Trump's election. Of the fifty-nine agreements currently active, nearly all (fifty-three) are at the county level, with only two in city police departments that renewed earlier agreements (Mesa, Arizona, and Carrollton, Texas). That twenty-six counties have signed 287(g) memoranda of understanding since Trump's election is evidence that there is some appetite for subfederal immigration restriction, though most of the interest is in counties, with elected sheriffs, rather than in city police departments, which typically have appointed leaders.

The county-level dominance of the 287(g) program is not necessarily surprising, since it primarily involves immigration enforcement in jails, and many smaller cities send arrestees to county facilities, making the program less relevant on the city level. Yet the pattern also reflects this book's argument. Local government officials—both appointed police chiefs and city managers, as well as elected city councilors and mayors— are able to pursue their legal and economic incentives to accommodate immigrants because they usually are insulated from partisan debates over immigration. At the county level, elected sheriffs have greater incentive to attract votes by capitalizing on public concerns about unauthorized immigration (Farris and Holman 2017).

A key question, then, is whether immigration will become more politicized in cities under Trump. Evidence from the case study cities and from other scholars suggests that, at a time when immigration is of increased national salience, the topic will be more politicized on the local level, leading to greater public cries for restriction (Hopkins 2010, 2011). In Elgin in 2006–8, national debates over comprehensive reform and subsequent immigrant marches mobilized local anti-immigration activists who succeeded in shifting the tenor of response somewhat toward restriction. In Lewiston, local leaders report that President Trump's false comments about Somalis and crime have brought concerns among established residents into the public discussion. Indeed, even places with essentially no immigrant populations have experienced bitter local debates over immigration since President Trump's election. In Homer,

Alaska, a town of just over 5,300 with only eighty-nine foreign-born residents (American Community Survey 2011–15), three city councilors faced a recall election after supporting a proposed resolution declaring Homer a welcoming community for unauthorized immigrants (Reed 2017). They held their seats in the recall, but local acrimony continues (Downing 2017).

Before Trump's rise, local officials were able to accommodate in part because they were relatively insulated from public opinion by local political institutions, such as nonpartisan ballots, off-cycle elections, and council-manager forms of government. Trump's perpetual focus on unauthorized immigrants reduces the likelihood that local officials can keep immigration off the public agenda (Hopkins 2010, 2011; Lahav 2013). In places with more Republican-leaning populations, where national Republican rhetoric surrounding immigration is resonant, Trump's immigration rhetoric is likely to increase calls for restriction, and some may result in restrictive local practices.

I have argued that when restrictive practices emerge on the local level, they often are scaled back in response to external scrutiny that casts immigrants as a protected class under civil rights law. Yet with Attorney General Jeff Sessions at the helm of the Department of Justice, the Trump administration is also systematically weakening civil rights protections. Sessions is reviewing the Department of Justice's role in investigating police misconduct, and in the case of violations he prefers settlements rather than consent decrees, which require policy change and monitoring (Huseman and Waldman 2017). Appointees to the Civil Rights Division and to other agencies' civil rights branches include attorneys who have defended civil rights violators in earlier cases and who believe the federal government should curtail civil rights enforcement (Bazelon 2017; Eilperin, Brown, and Fears 2017). The advocacy organizations and antidiscriminatory norms that have developed in response to civil rights regulations remain robust for the time being. However, external scrutiny from the media and advocacy institutions may be less influential in reining in restrictive immigration practices if local officials see that civil rights regulations will not be enforced by federal regulators.

Amid the substantial changes of Trump's first six months in office, municipal accommodation of immigrants has for the most part proved resilient. Local government officials continue to face federal requirements to serve immigrants in schools and through language access. They continue to support immigrants to bolster economic development. But local government accommodation may become more vulnerable under Trump, particularly if accommodating cities are penalized by their states, if immigration becomes politicized locally in ways that generate calls for restriction, or if the Trump administration succeeds in dismantling civil rights protections.

Regardless of what the future holds, President Trump's rhetoric and policies raise crucial questions about the future of immigrant incorporation both at the local level and beyond. In particular, the evolution of local immigrant-serving practices in recent years raises questions about how national politics influences local governments, as well as how citizens' partisan preferences influence local policies. Likewise, the evolution of local immigrant-serving practices calls into question the relative importance of accommodating, inactive, and restrictive policies for immigrant political incorporation.

The Relation between Local and National Immigration Politics

Municipal responses to immigrants provide an example of a larger trend in which federal political polarization pushes national partisan debates to the local level. In turn, local responses may shape eventual federal policymaking. On the national level, partisanship is the leading explanation for policy preferences. There is some debate, however, over whether national partisan preferences influence local government policies (Trounstine 2010; Gerber and Hopkins 2011). Some argue that partisanship will not entirely shape local politics given localities' structural and economic constraints, including federal mandates and limited options for generating revenue (Ferreira and Gyourko 2009; Gerber and Hopkins 2011). Indeed, I find that local officials accommodate immigrants in part because federal policies constrain them to do so and in part because they believe that hospitality will enhance local economic development. In accommodating immigrants, local officials are often following their own legal and economic incentives rather than attending to partisan demands.

But recent findings suggest that the partisan or ideological preferences of the electorate do meaningfully influence local policy (Hajnal and Trounstine 2010; Kraus 2013; Tausanovitch and Warshaw 2014; Einstein and Kogan 2016). How much public preferences shape local politics may depend on local discretion in a given realm. For instance, some scholars find that partisanship shapes spending patterns for public safety—an area in which localities have broad autonomy—but not other policy areas (Gerber and Hopkins 2011).

Immigration presents an interesting test of these patterns, which deserves further attention in future work. On one hand, localities are sharply constrained with respect to immigration policy, unable to control flows of immigrants to their jurisdiction and obligated to provide the foreign-born with certain services. On the other hand, localities have broader discretion on immigrant integration, an area in which the federal government has been largely silent and has provided little funding. Given this discretion, national partisan debates over immigration do appear to influence local politics, substantially with respect to officials' views on serving immigrants and somewhat with respect to actual practices, as detailed in chapters 4 and 5.

As the national partisan politics of immigration becomes increasingly polarized, cities become an attractive venue for policy change. In large cities, Democratic mayors are advancing expansionary policies by establishing immigrant affairs offices and enthusiastically welcoming Syrian refugees (Pastor, Ortiz, and de Graauw 2015; Capps 2015). National issue entrepreneurs also seek to influence local policies in response to the federal impasse. The rash of restrictive local immigration ordinances from 2006 to 2007 was in part a coordinated effort by national restrictionist issue entrepreneurs. Since prospects for federal immigration reform faded in 2012, national expansionist entrepreneurs also are pushing their agenda at the state and local levels, for instance, by promoting drivers' licenses for unauthorized immigrants (Gulasekaram and Ramakrishnan 2015).

Proactive municipal accommodation of immigrants is part of a larger trend in which local governments are pushing policies associated with Democrats while states and Congress are pushing in the opposite direction. In addition to controlling the presidency and Congress, Republicans now control nearly two-thirds of state legislative chambers and two-thirds of governorships (Bergal 2015). Cities, on the other hand, have passed progressive policies limiting fracking, banning plastic shopping bags, decriminalizing marijuana, and increasing the minimum wage and worker benefits (Bergal 2015). Similarly, Democratic mayors are taking action to address socioeconomic inequality, further evidence that "national issues and divides are manifesting in city policymaking" (Einstein and Glick 2016).

Increasingly, states are responding to this trend by preempting local efforts, often through laws distributed to states in a coordinated fashion by national conservative lobbying groups (Bergal 2015). Perhaps the most prominent example is North Carolina's now-repealed law preempting a Charlotte ordinance that allowed transgender people to use the bathrooms that correspond to their gender identities (Zezima 2016). But the trend is evident in multiple policy realms and extends to local immigration practices. Wisconsin has considered a bill that would preempt local efforts to provide municipal identification cards in Milwaukee. And North Carolina has considered a bill that would prohibit municipal agencies from accepting foreign consular cards as identification, a practice that 81 percent of police departments in my survey had already adopted, including six of nine responding cities in North Carolina. Most prominently, in 2017, thirty-three states considered laws to penalize or preempt sanctuary cities. Four states—Indiana, Louisiana, Mississippi, and Texas—have passed such measures (National Conference of State Legislators 2017).

Increasingly, state preemption laws withhold funds from localities that violate state policies and even hold elected officials legally and financially liable. Texas's antisanctuary Senate Bill 4 can remove local officials from office and punish them with jail time and fines of up to $25,000 a day (Badger 2017). Although President Trump's efforts to penalize sanctuary cities have not yet achieved their aims, some argue that Texas cities are modifying their practices in view of the steep consequences. Four of Texas's five major cities, several counties, and the tiny border town of El Cenzio have sued the state alleging that the law abridges free speech and equal protection. Yet other cities, including Laredo, which is 95 percent Latino, worry about state retaliation. Laredo mayor Pete Saenz said he hoped his colleagues on the city council would consider the risk of losing state funding when they discussed joining the suit (Mekelburg 2017).

These examples of Texas Senate Bill 4 and other Republican-sponsored legislation in mostly Republican-leaning states suggest that the national partisan politics of immigration plays out on the state level. At the local level, this book shows that partisanship influences but does not determine local responses. The case studies suggest that local officials' legal and economic incentives to accommodate immigrants dominate responses, in part because these officials are more insulated from partisan debates than are their state and national counterparts. Across the four case study cities, we see that local officials tend to accommodate unless local advocacy groups politicize immigration (as in Elgin) or candidates for elective office successfully make immigration a campaign issue (as Mayor Macdonald did in Lewiston).

The increasing percolation of national partisan issues to the local level may have crosscutting consequences for efforts to accommodate immigrants. On one hand, accommodating policies instantiated at the local level have the potential to influence the form of eventual federal reforms (Gulasekaram and Ramakrishnan 2015). If the federal government continues to stall on comprehensive immigration reform, advocacy groups may have little choice but to push their preferred policies at the state and local levels. Yet for expansionist groups, losing sight of attempts to advance federal reform would be misguided. This book shows that federal policies are a central predictor of local responses to immigrants. Federal civil rights regulations shape responses even in previously homogeneous new immigrant destinations, underscoring the influence of the federal government not only institutionally, but also normatively (Dobbin and Sutton 1998). In addition, politicizing immigration on the local level may precipitate greater constituent demand for restriction. If local officials accommodate in response to distinct incentives the public does not necessarily share, politicizing immigration by pushing a more expansionist agenda may enhance competing electoral incentives for restriction.

The Relative Importance of Municipal Restriction, Accommodation, and Inactivity

This book demonstrates that municipal accommodation efforts in new destinations do not necessarily achieve their aims. Moreover, the example of Yakima's recent advances toward political incorporation suggests that restriction and inaction may be more potent than accommodation in mobilizing immigrant participation. What do these findings say about the relative impact of restriction, inactivity, and accommodation for immigrant incorporation?

Previous findings show that restriction both causes immigrants to withdraw (Jones-Correa and Fennelly 2009; Furuseth and Smith 2010; Menjivar and Abrego 2012) and bolsters public antipathy (Flores 2014). If individuals base their views on beliefs about immigrants' effect on the nation (Hainmueller and Hopkins 2014), restrictive government policies will underscore threatening images of immigrants. In some cases, though, restriction also spurs immigrants to mobilize. To the extent that restriction encourages naturalization and voting, as occurred in the wake of California's restrictive Proposition 187 in 1994, it may augment immigrants' influence (Pantoja, Ramirez, and Segura 2001; Pantoja and Segura 2003a). Yet the widespread immigrant protests of proposed federal restrictive policies in 2006 may have had more mixed effects. These protest movements are credited with catalyzing today's influential movement of unauthorized youths known as DREAMers (Seif 2011) and increasing immigrant efficacy and support for immigrant-friendly policies (Wallace, Zepeda-Millán, and Jones-Correa 2014; Branton et al. 2015; Silber Mohamed 2017). Others argue that the protests generated public backlash against immigrants (Voss and Bloemraad 2011).

Evidence from the four cases suggests that restrictive episodes—the mayor's letter in Lewiston, the partner schools controversy in Wausau, and the housing discrimination suits in Elgin—can bring prejudices to light and spur communities to become more inclusive in response. What matters here is how the community responds to restrictive episodes. Yakima officials' silence in response to less prominent restrictive episodes perpetuated a situation in which Latinos felt they had few avenues for cooperating with local authorities. With the help of external advocacy organizations, Latinos ultimately mobilized to achieve greater political representation. Yet these advances came at a great short-term cost for Yakima. The city's insistence on fighting the ACLU Voting Rights lawsuit saddled it with nearly $3 million in legal fees. Besides, it remains unclear whether Latinos' sudden emergence as elected leaders in Yakima will foster public acceptance or further resentment. Restriction may sometimes mobilize immigrants more rapidly, but it is hardly a strategy most would embrace, given its potential to harm immigrants, bolster public antipathy, and generate costs.

As Yakima's example further demonstrates, inaction in response to growing immigrant populations can effectively amount to restriction. Inaction transforms into restriction when local governments fail to honor federal mandates requiring services for linguistically and culturally distinct newcomers. A substantial portion of local governments remain relatively inactive toward immigrants. Just under a quarter of towns responding to the MRIS have no formal interpretation mechanisms in place. Beyond these cities, some are compliant with federal mandates but otherwise entirely inactive in addressing immigrant populations. Overall, 13 percent of towns have implemented none of the independent accommodating and restrictive practices, and more than a third have adopted none of the more strenuous practices that require some degree of collective action. Is this inactivity a form of benign neglect, or does it have consequences for immigrant incorporation?

Immigrant incorporation inherently takes time. Immigrants may need years or even generations to learn English and come to understand and participate in the host society. Likewise, for established residents, adjusting to immigrants' presence can take many years. Over time, communities may mobilize resources to provide linguistically and culturally adapted services. Individuals may learn to navigate and perhaps come to appreciate differences in cultural traditions.

On the national level, the United States' approach to immigrant integration largely has been to give it time. Immigrants have access to K-12 education and some other services as well as a sophisticated civil rights infrastructure. In contrast to other advanced democracies, however, the United States has few formal programs aimed at enabling adult immigrants to adapt. Should communities leave immigrants alone to incorporate over time, or should they actively attempt to advance their incorporation?

Some would argue that evidence of immigrants' increasing linguistic and socioeconomic similarity to Americans over time shows that benign neglect is a functional strategy that lets immigrants choose the ways they adapt rather than forcing them to meet benchmarks defined by the host society. Yet immigrant incorporation in the United States continues to be marked by racial inequities (Waters and Pineau 2015), suggesting that time alone may not be enough. Moreover, incorporation is a two-way street. While immigrants are advancing, Americans remain ambivalent about their presence. President Trump's victory and widespread wariness about Syrian refugees provide ample evidence that a laissez-faire approach may fail to improve public attitudes toward immigrants.

Across the four cases, the length of immigrants' residence in the cities is not the crucial determinant of either their success or their societal acceptance. Somalis in Lewiston have made rapid progress despite their recent arrival in 2001. Latinos in Elgin still have relatively little electoral clout and faced anti-immigrant mobilization despite their large-scale presence in the city for more than twenty years. Over time, increasing familiarity does seem to enhance established residents' support for the newcomers. As a locally grown second generation emerges, immigrants occupy a greater variety of local roles and have more opportunities to shape decision making. Nonetheless, other factors are more decisive than time alone in shaping incorporation outcomes. Time may improve perceptions of immigrants, but even places with long-term immigrant populations are sensitive to external forces such as federal policies and national politics that shift definitions of immigrants.

On its face, it seems accommodation would produce the most salutary effects for immigrant incorporation. Refugees—the only American immigrant group awarded substantial federal assistance in incorporation—have better educational and labor market outcomes (Portes and Rumbaut 2006) and are more civically and politically engaged (Bloemraad 2006). With respect to societal acceptance, accommodating responses could frame immigrants as valued community members (Bloemraad 2006). Yet there is some evidence that accommodation could have a dampening effect on immigrant mobilization (Ebert and Okamoto 2013), incorporating immigrants as passive clients rather than active citizens. Accommodation could channel activists' energies away from mobilization and toward the priorities of the state (Piven and Cloward 1979).

Evidence from the MRIS suggests that, at the very least, the relation between accommodation and immigrants' perceived involvement is positive. Officials in cities that more actively accommodate immigrants were also more likely to interact with newcomers and see them as civically engaged, even holding constant the size of the immigrant population and other factors. Accommodation does not necessarily improve impressions of immigrants' civic presence, but evidence from the cases suggests it can enable collaboration between immigrants and local authorities and might provide avenues for other immigrants to become engaged.

That said, the cases raise two additional concerns about municipal efforts at accommodation. First, municipal officials incorporate immigrants in ways that strengthen immigrant elites but do not necessarily foster broader advancement of immigrants. Second, given officials' distinct understandings of immigrants, which the broader public does not fully share, accommodation may promote nativist backlash against immigrants and the officials who support them.

While these concerns are real, they are not damning to the enterprise of municipal accommodation. Rather, they show that efforts at accommodation—at least in these new destinations—may not always be effectively designed. Undoubtedly we need further research to better understand which municipal efforts best support both immigrants' advancement and their societal acceptance. Do immigrants make more substantial progress after the implementation of certain municipal accommodation programs? Do public views change in response to varying accommodation efforts? Can municipal accommodation alone advance incorporation, or must efforts involve other sectors, including political parties?[4] While additional investigation remains necessary, this book offers two key findings for local governments seeking to accommodate immigrants more effectively.

First, relying on individual intermediaries for learning about immigrants and communicating with them has clear drawbacks, both for local officials and for established residents. It is all but impossible for an individual intermediary to effectively speak for a large, diverse immigrant population. For the most part officials lack the experience necessary to identify intermediaries connected with and accountable to immigrants. If intermediaries are disconnected or are ill-suited to their role, they are in effect a bridge to nowhere, compromising intergroup relations and perhaps undermining immigrants' trust in local government. That said, intermediaries are often essential to daily functioning in immigrant destinations. Failing to identify intermediaries lessens the chances for collaborative relations between immigrants and local authorities.

Thus local governments should strive to support the development of broad-based organizations for serving immigrants, as officials did in Wausau. Ideally, supporting immigrant organizations creates a parallel process through which immigrants select their own intermediaries, who are more credible and accountable. If local governments must rely on individual intermediaries in order to respond to urgent communication needs, they should endeavor to select multiple intermediaries embodying different facets of the immigrant community rather than relying on the select few whom officials happen to feel most comfortable with. Intermediaries who speak the best English or put officials at ease may not be the same people who connect most effectively with immigrant communities.

Second, evidence from across the cases indicates that municipal efforts to foster meaningful intergroup contact between immigrants and established residents may cultivate societal acceptance by making positive understandings of immigrants more accessible and resonant. Rhetorical efforts to make the case for immigration are not effective, but gathering immigrants and established residents to participate in shared projects yields greater dividends. Rather than promoting diversity-specific programming, local governments should use their authority to promote collaborative interethnic tasks in public schools, children's play groups, adult education centers, and municipal committees. Such efforts need not be costly, as Lewiston's deployment of VISTA volunteers demonstrated.

Although my findings about how carefully constructed intergroup contact can enhance public receptivity are corroborated elsewhere (Jones-Correa 2011), they depart somewhat from the traditional model of symbolic politics, which emphasizes the role of frames in shaping public opinion. Often scholars of public opinion argue that people do not change their larger views about society based on personal interactions (Mutz 1992; Sears 1993; Kinder 1998). In this view, interacting with an immigrant would not necessarily change a person's assessment of how immigrants affect the nation as a whole. In contrast, findings in new destinations demonstrate that meaningful contact is important in shaping at least local receptivity to immigrants, a topic that needs to be examined further in future work (see, for instance, Hopkins 2010, 2011). In recognizing the influence of symbolic politics (shaped largely by external influence), we cannot overlook the importance of contact in shaping views (internal influence). Local experiences may anchor views on immigrants, perhaps lessening the influence of national political rhetoric that frames immigrants as outsiders and lawbreakers.

Since carefully constructed accommodation practices can support immigrant incorporation, should the federal government provide funds to encourage this enterprise? This book demonstrates that federal policies promoting incorporation will encourage local officials to follow suit. For towns experiencing rapid immigrant population growth, such funds could allow for a smoother transition. Lewiston officials are particularly vocal in their view that the federal government should fund towns facing substantial immigrant growth, arguing that towns cannot control immigrant flows yet bear the initial costs. There is precedent for providing what some call "impact aid" to localities. The 1986 Immigration Reform and Control Act, the last major program regularizing the status of unauthorized immigrants, offered aid to states to help defray costs of serving the newly legalized immigrant population (Garvey 2007).

Evidence from the cases suggests that while funding could ease local officials' initial challenges, any impact aid program would have to be carefully designed to avoid the impression that it offers immigrants preferential treatment. Distributing aid to help defray towns' costs rather than specifically to assist immigrants might lessen local concerns. To the extent that such funding could be channeled more directly to addressing immigrant incorporation, two promising avenues are bolstering immigrants' civic participation and funding programs that promote interethnic contact. In the MRIS, more than a third of local officials believed immigrants would prefer to keep to themselves rather than participate. Efforts to involve immigrants in voluntarism could provide evidence of their engagement. Former president Obama's Taskforce on New Americans worked with the Corporation for National and Community Service to create opportunities for immigrant youth to participate in national service (White House Task Force on New Americans 2015), and such efforts may be worth expanding when they are politically viable. Finally, if meaningful intergroup contact enhances public receptivity toward immigrants, federal, state, or local funds could productively be devoted to youth sports leagues, adult education programs, and other community-based efforts that gather diverse participants. These efforts may have the added benefit of simultaneously addressing declining social connectedness.

Examining the effects of Canadian multicultural policies and US refugee resettlement policies, Bloemraad (2006, 241) argues that national government intervention is uniquely able to "equalize the playing field" of immigrant political incorporation by reaching beyond immigrant elites to increase foreign-born participation more broadly. Evidence from across the four nontraditional destinations suggests that local governments' accommodation strategies do not consistently have this broader reach to the immigrant population as a whole. Given sharply constrained resources on the local level, many of the strategies local governments adopt—appointing immigrants, convening stakeholders, touting a commitment to diversity—are low-cost responses that involve marshaling volunteer energies rather than making substantial fiscal outlays. While these efforts do not appear to substantially dampen the potential for mobilizing immigrants, they do not consistently have the broader effects Bloemraad describes. Thus, advocates who seek progress toward incorporation only on the local level must be cognizant that the effects of municipal accommodation will likely be limited in scope.

Obstacles to Immigrant Incorporation

Finally, the book suggests that municipal advocates who seek to promote immigrant incorporation face two major obstacles: the unresolved status of unauthorized immigrants and the increasing socioeconomic gaps between Americans and their leaders. Turning first to unauthorized status, this book demonstrates that when immigrants are framed as a group worthy of protection from discrimination, localities rein in restriction. Federal civil rights regulations have contributed to an infrastructure of civil rights organizations that propagate antidiscriminatory norms.

Civil rights regulations and associated norms are therefore effective in reining in restriction except when advocates successfully foreground competing definitions of immigrants as "illegal aliens." In the 1990s a California organization promoting Proposition 187 distributed signs to protesters reading, "Calling me a racist won't get you amnesty." The signs asserted that emphasizing immigrants' racial identity would not mute the condemnation of unauthorized immigrants as lawbreakers.

Foregrounding immigrant illegality in this way is particularly successful in stirring hostility toward the foreign-born, because a majority of Americans believe that most recent immigrants are not in the country legally (National Public Radio 2004). In reality, unauthorized immigrants represent only 28 percent of the foreign-born, and their numbers have not grown in recent years (Krogstad and Passel 2015). Given misconceptions about the scale of the unauthorized population, Americans' concerns about the unauthorized are highly correlated with concerns about immigrants in general and Latinos more broadly (Abrajano and Hajnal 2015). Until federal reform resolves the status of unauthorized immigrants, restrictionist advocates can emphasize defining immigrants as lawbreakers, effectively undermining efforts to frame them as worthy of inclusion.

An additional barrier to municipal efforts to promote immigrant integration is the United States' increasing socioeconomic inequality. In his classic account of immigrant incorporation in New Haven, Connecticut, Robert Dahl wrote, "In the United States, the political stratum does not constitute a homogeneous class with well-defined class interests" (Dahl 1961, 91). Increasingly, however, the political stratum does represent a distinct class, both descriptively and substantively. The wealthy are vastly overrepresented among state and national legislators in ways that affect representatives' legislative activity and voting (Carnes 2013). Indeed, the policy preferences of the affluent increasingly shape policymaking, resulting in significant gaps between public preferences and policies on many topics (Gilens 2012).

The consequences of these gaps between citizens and their leaders were clear during the 2016 presidential election, when elites in both parties were befuddled by the unexpected preferences of their bases. Democratic elites, who had all but anointed Hillary Clinton as the nominee, were taken aback by Bernie Sanders's ascendency in the primaries. Republican elites were even more horrified by Donald Trump's capturing the nomination. To the elites, Bernie Sanders and Donald Trump were not viable candidates—so much so that establishment candidates initially did not bother to campaign against them.

While gaps between residents and local government officials are nowhere near as extreme, a parallel process is evident on the local level with respect to immigration. Local officials, through their socioeconomic standing and position, have clear legal and economic incentives to accommodate immigrants that lead them to see immigrants as clients, contributors, and worthy of protection. Their constituents often do not share these favorable impressions. Moreover, gaps between officials and residents mean that officials' attempts to make the case for immigration can be met with skepticism or hostility. Public resentment toward immigrants and the officials who support them can undermine support for redistributive policies, since residents think that officials fail to use resources effectively (Cramer 2016). Successfully promoting immigrant incorporation therefore involves attending to socioeconomic divisions between citizens and their leaders.

Without question, immigrant political incorporation occurs over time, as immigrants adapt to their host country and native-born residents adjust to the newcomers' presence. The mere passage of time, however, is inadequate to ensure increasing incorporation. As Jennifer Hochschild (2010) has written, "the key is an effective use of time." Along these lines, this book suggests that municipal accommodation can advance immigrant incorporation when effectively designed. To promote broad-based immigrant advancement, municipal officials should support immigrant organizations rather than relying on individual intermediaries. To promote societal acceptance, they should structure opportunities for meaningful interethnic contact rather than vaguely applauding diversity. Where restrictive episodes arise, advocates may scale back restriction by highlighting violations of antidiscriminatory norms.

These efforts can advance immigrant incorporation, but municipalities rarely possess adequate independent resources to substantially enhance immigrants' capacity. Even where resources are available, advocates of accommodation must be cautious about providing services that will politicize immigration on the local level and may intensify residents' calls for restriction. While municipal accommodation is important, advocates of incorporation would be far better off with comprehensive federal reform, given the federal government's resources and far-reaching influence in framing immigrants and shaping local responses. Ultimately, promoting immigrant incorporation at any level will remain challenging until the United States addresses the status of unauthorized immigrants as well as broader issues surrounding socioeconomic inequality.

Appendixes

Appendix A: Case Study Methods and Interview Guide

To select informants, I conducted both purposive and snowball sampling. In each site, I drew on contacts in local academic institutions and community foundations to develop as diverse as possible a range of primary contacts, so that my informants reached beyond a limited network.[1] At the close of each interview, I asked informants for the names of several other community leaders or residents who could help me learn more. In addition to this snowball sample, I conducted purposive sampling by ensuring that I spoke with at least these individuals across the sites: the mayor, a law enforcement officer, a public school leader, a hospital administrator, a social service provider, and representatives of the Chamber of Commerce, major local civic institutions, and immigrant or minority rights organizations.

Additionally, I worked with native Spanish speakers in 2004 and 2008 to conduct Spanish-language interviews in Elgin and Yakima. In these interviews we aimed to speak with average Latino residents rather than community leaders. For this reason we approached potential informants in markets and laundromats and conducted shorter interviews.[2] Throughout my fieldwork I closely tracked the composition of my informants to ensure that I interviewed a roughly representative group in terms of gender, race/ethnicity, age, and longevity in the community. I also tracked my informants' professional fields to ensure that I was speaking with a balanced array of individuals in all crucial sectors in each city.

Overall, I spent two and a half weeks each over two research trips to Elgin and Wausau and more than a month each over four visits to Yakima and five visits to Lewiston. Ranging from twenty minutes to more than two hours (and averaging roughly an hour), interviews were semistructured, building from a short list of questions to draw on informants' particular experiences. Where the informant agreed, I recorded interviews and also took notes. I coded transcriptions using Atlas.ti in order to identify themes.

Since immigration is a controversial topic for some, I introduced my project in general terms as an examination of changing social relations in cities across the United States. Presenting the project in this general manner allowed me to secure interviews without alienating informants or biasing their responses. In each interview I asked informants to begin with an account of how they came to be in the city and what they did (professionally or more generally) in town. Building on the information the informants offered, I asked follow-up questions that related their comments to my interest in local immigration. When this avenue ceased to be fruitful, I would ask informants to tell me about the biggest changes in their city in the past decade, which enabled me to transition to discussing local responses to immigration.

Besides interviews, when time allowed I observed community events such as a gang prevention meeting in Elgin, a sister city meeting in Yakima, an adult education class in Lewiston, and a farmers market in Wausau. When I returned from the field, I verified facts using local newspapers and other documents such as city council minutes and grant proposals. I conducted ongoing "digital observation" by reading local websites and blogs and joining local organizations' e-mail lists and online social networking groups.

Because I promised informants I would disguise their identities in citing their words and ideas, I refer to their cities of residence and their ethnicity without revealing their names or titles. Where possible while still preserving informants' anonymity, I provide additional detail on their gender, profession, and other relevant characteristics. Since these four new destinations are small cities with relatively few immigrant ethnic leaders, the descriptions attached to quotations will at times be vague in order to disguise the speakers.

Interview Guide

Although the questions below were generally asked of all informants, the semistructured format of the interviews allowed me to build on the information the informants provided to probe local responses to immigrants and their consequences for social and political incorporation.

OPENING QUESTIONS
- To start with, I'm interested to hear about your story. How did you find yourself in [TOWN] and in this position *(where relevant)*?
- *For community leaders:* Can you tell me a bit about [professional field of respondent] in [TOWN]?
- *For residents:* Can you tell me a bit about what you do here in [TOWN]?
- What would you say are the biggest changes in [TOWN] in about the past decade?

If the informant has not mentioned the growing immigrant population in the preceding discussion, I prompt with questions specific to the migration, such as the ones below.

FOR LONG-TERM RESIDENTS
- When did you first begin to notice the growth of the [IMMIGRANT GROUP] population here in [TOWN]?
- *For community leaders:* How did [YOUR ORGANIZATION] respond to the arrival of the [IMMIGRANT GROUP]?

FOR IMMIGRANTS
- Tell me about your experience when you first arrived here in [TOWN].
- Can you tell me about an experience where you have felt welcome/unwelcome here in [TOWN]?
- How did you come to be involved in [CIVIC/POLITICAL ACTIVITY]?

FOR BOTH GROUPS
- What kind of opportunities are there for interaction between the [IMMIGRANT GROUP] and longer-term residents?

QUESTIONS SPECIFIC TO LOCAL GOVERNMENT RESPONSES
- What would you say the local government has done well or poorly in responding to the growth of the [IMMIGRANT GROUP] population?
- What about the state and federal government—what have they done well or poorly?

CLOSING QUESTIONS
- We've talked a lot about the growth of the [IMMIGRANT GROUP] population in [TOWN]. Are there other major changes in [TOWN] in recent years that I should be aware of?
- Can you recommend anyone I should speak with to learn more about these issues? Could I use your name in contacting them?
- *Where appropriate*: Would you be willing to let me sit in on a meeting/event of your organization?

Appendix B: Municipal Responses to Immigrants Survey Questionnaire

1. Which factors contribute to the presence of immigrants in your community? *(Check all that apply)*

    ☐ Attractiveness of quality of life
    ☐ Attractiveness of services provided
    ☐ Demand for low-wage workers
    ☐ Proximity to major cities
    ☐ Affordable housing
    ☐ Opportunity to reunite with local family members
    ☐ Lack of effective federal government enforcement
    ☐ Other *(please describe)*

    ☐ Not sure

2. How would you characterize the conversation on immigration in your community?

    Immigration is discussed . . .
    ○ . . . frequently.
    ○ . . . occasionally.
    ○ . . . rarely.
    ○ Other *(please describe).*

3. How controversial would you say that local immigration is in your community?

- ○ Very controversial
- ○ Somewhat controversial
- ○ Not at all controversial
- ○ Other *(please describe)*

4. In the past decade, how would you characterize the growth of the immigrant population in your community?

- ○ No noticeable growth
- ○ Slow to moderate growth
- ○ Rapid growth
- ○ Not sure

5. Does your community experience a seasonal influx and departure of immigrants who are migrant workers?

- ○ Yes
- ○ No
- ○ Not sure

6. Which statement best describes the size of your community's refugee population? *(Refugees are immigrants who have escaped danger in their home country and been granted legal residence by the US government.)*

- ○ No refugees
- ○ A few refugees
- ○ A small but visible refugee population
- ○ Refugees are a substantial portion of our foreign-born population
- ○ Refugees are our dominant foreign-born group
- ○ Not sure

Your Municipality's Responses to Immigration

7. Does your [community's municipal center (city hall or equivalent)/department] provide informational materials such as brochures, fliers, and the like?

- ○ Yes
- ○ No *Go to 8*

7a. *(If yes)* How often are these informational materials translated into non-English languages?

○ Often
○ Sometimes
○ Only upon request
○ Almost never
○ Never
○ Not sure

8. What typically happens if a [municipal staff member/officer] is approached by a non-English-speaking resident and the [staff member/officer] does not speak the resident's native language?

The [staff member/officer] . . .
○ . . . calls on a translator employed by your municipality or the county.
○ . . . uses a translation service your municipality contracts with for this purpose.
○ . . . asks the resident's family member, neighbor, etc., to translate.
○ . . . refuses service to the resident.
○ Other *(please describe).*

○ Not sure.
○ Does not apply to our municipality.

9. Has your municipality adopted an "English-only" or "official English" policy for local government documents and proceedings?

○ Yes
○ No
○ Not sure

10. Does your [municipality/department] use any of the following techniques in its human resources management?

	Yes	No	Not sure
We design hiring practices to attract bilingual candidates.	O	O	O
Bilingual candidates receive extra points in the hiring process for some positions.	O	O	O
Bilingual employees in some positions receive a pay differential or additional compensation.	O	O	O

10a. *(If yes to any)* In your [municipality/department], how easy or difficult is it to attract and retain bilingual employees?

- O   Somewhat difficult
- O   Neutral
- O   Somewhat easy
- O   Easy

11. Does your [municipality/department] have a designated employee who serves as a liaison with immigrant communities?

- O   Yes
- O   No *Go to 12*
- O   Not sure *Go to 12*

11a. *(If yes)* What is the title of the employee who serves as a liaison with immigrant communities?

_____

12. Do any local government agencies/Does your department] accept consular identification cards (such as the *matricula consular*) or other foreign IDs as forms of identification?

- O   Yes
- O   No
- O   Not sure

13. *[City hall only]* In the past five years, has your municipality implemented
     any of the following measures:

	Yes	No	Not sure
Hired immigrants or members of the immigrant ethnic group as municipal employees	O	O	O
Provided funding for immigrant organizations or activities	O	O	O
Provided in-kind support for immigrant organizations or activities, such as allowing organizations to use public facilities	O	O	O
Hosted diversity event(s) to celebrate or promote immigrant contributions to the community	O	O	O
Hosted intercultural event(s) to facilitate interaction between immigrants and nonimmigrant residents	O	O	O
Issued proclamations or resolutions in support of immigrants or their organizations or events	O	O	O
Educated the public about local immigrants	O	O	O
Developed social service programs for immigrants	O	O	O
Restructured existing social service programs to better serve immigrants	O	O	O
Established or maintained a local office for immigrant services	O	O	O
Established or maintained an immigrant advisory council to advise officials on immigration-related issues	O	O	O

Local Issues and Immigration

14. *[City hall only]* Do you agree or disagree that the following statements ap-
     ply to your community?

	Strongly disagree	Disagree	Neutral	Agree	Strongly agree
Residential overcrowding is a major problem.	O	O	O	O	O
Residents often complain about code violations, such as homes or lawns that are not maintained.	O	O	O	O	O
Overcrowding and housing code violations are a problem mainly in the parts of town where many immigrants live.	O	O	O	O	O

14a. *(If agree/strongly agree to any)* In response to immigration, our municipal-
      ity has considered or passed housing or zoning ordinances.

     O   Passed
     O   Formally considered, not passed
     O   Neither considered nor passed
     O   Not sure

14b. *(If agree/strongly agree to any)* In response to immigration, our municipality has hired additional housing inspectors.

○ Yes
○ No
○ Not sure

15. In your community, have day laborers ever gathered in one or more locations looking for work?

○ Yes
○ No *Go to 16*
○ Not sure *Go to 16*

15a. Has your municipality taken any of the following steps to address day laborer gatherings? *(Please check all that apply.)*

☐ Designated an area or building at which day labor activity is allowed
☐ Provided funding to support a hiring center for day laborers (either locally or elsewhere in the region)
☐ Enforced a policy that forbids day laborers to congregate outdoors
☐ We have not instituted a policy in response to day laborers
☐ Other *(Please describe.)*

16. Which of the following statements best describes your municipality's current position on illegal immigration? *(Illegal immigrants, also called undocumented, are those who have entered the country without permission or overstayed visas.)*

Our local government . . .
○ . . . has no official policy on illegal immigrants.
○ . . . has openly declared this a "sanctuary" community for illegal immigrants who are not engaged in criminal activities.
○ . . . supports an informal policy of "don't ask, don't tell" regarding illegal immigrants, unless they are involved in serious crime.
○ . . . has developed, or is developing, policies to encourage local law enforcement to cooperate with federal authorities in enforcing immigration laws.
○ Other *(please describe).*

○ Not sure.

17. Has your municipality formally considered or passed any ordinances or laws to deter illegal immigrants from settling in your community?

  ○ Yes
  ○ No *Go to 18*
  ○ Not sure *Go to 18*

17a. *(If yes)* Please indicate which of the following measures your municipality's elected governing body has passed or formally considered.

	Passed	Considered, not passed	Neither
Impose fines on landlords who rent to illegal immigrants	○	○	○
Deny business licenses to companies that employ illegal immigrants	○	○	○
Require municipal employees to check immigration status before providing some local services	○	○	○
Require municipal employees to submit information on illegal immigrants to Immigration and Customs Enforcement (ICE)	○	○	○

17b. *(If any passed)* Could you please describe the current status of the ordinance or ordinances passed in order to deter illegal immigration? Are they currently enforced? Why or why not?

18. *[City hall only]* Our community has experienced an incident or implemented a policy related to its immigrant population that has generated attention from the media and advocacy groups outside our community.

  ○ Yes
  ○ No *Go to 19*
  ○ Not sure *Go to 19*

18a. *(If yes)* Following this incident our community experienced attention and/ or intervention from the following parties: *(Check all that apply.)*

  ☐ State officials and/or agencies
  ☐ Federal officials and/or agencies
  ☐ External media outlets

☐ External organizations that advocate for immigrant rights
☐ External organizations that advocate for restricting immigration
☐ Other *(please specify)*

18b. *(If any checked)* In what way did external attention to local relations with immigrants affect your community's policies and practices?

On the whole, our community . . .

○ . . . made greater efforts to *accommodate* immigrants.
○ . . . maintained essentially the same policies.
○ . . . made greater efforts to *restrict* immigrant access to services.
○ Other *(please describe)*.

[P16]. *[Police only]* Does your department have a written policy or procedural directives regarding when officers should verify immigration status?

○ Yes
○ No *Go to 17*
○ Not sure *Go to 17*

[P16a.] Which statement(s) describe(s) your department's written policy or procedural directives? *(Check all that apply.)*

Immigration status . . .

○ . . . is never verified.
○ . . . is verified whenever the officer has any lawful contact with a person and the officer has a reasonable suspicion that the person is an alien who is unlawfully present in the United States.
○ . . . is verified only once someone has been arrested and booked into jail.
○ Other *(please describe)*.

19. Does [the police department serving your municipality/your department] operate one or more jails?

○ Yes
○ No *Go to 20*
○ Not sure *Go to 20*

19a. Please indicate which of the following best represents your local stance with respect to Secure Communities.

○   We have a policy that encourages active participation in Secure Communities.

○   We comply with Secure Communities.

○   We have a policy that restricts compliance with Secure Communities, such as an antidetainer ordinance.

○   Other *(please specify)*.

○   Not sure.

20. Please indicate the extent to which you agree or disagree with each of the statements below.

	Strongly disagree	Disagree	Neutral	Agree	Strongly agree
There is a clear distinction in the local contributions of legal versus illegal immigrants.	○	○	○	○	○
Immigrants are a net drain on local resources.	○	○	○	○	○
Overall, immigrants have contributed to the vitality of the local economy.	○	○	○	○	○
Immigrants have caused an increase in crime in the community.	○	○	○	○	○
Gaining the trust of immigrants in our community is a high priority.	○	○	○	○	○

21. *[City hall only]* Has your municipality implemented any other policies or practices intended to respond to immigrants that have not yet been mentioned here? If so, please describe these efforts below.

Local Interaction with Immigrants

22. In your view, how well are the following groups currently represented on your municipality's boards and commissions?

	Well represented	Somewhat represented	Marginal to no representation
Hispanics/Latinos	○	○	○
African Americans/Blacks	○	○	○
Asians/Pacific Islanders	○	○	○

23. *[City hall only]* In the past five years, have local officials attempted to recruit immigrants or members of immigrant ethnic groups to serve on municipal boards or commissions?

○ Yes
○ No
○ Not sure

24. *[City hall only]* Please indicate the extent to which you agree or disagree with the following statements about immigrants' participation in local government affairs.

Immigrants and members of immigrant ethnic groups . . .

	Strongly disagree	Disagree	Neutral	Agree	Strongly agree
. . . are too busy to participate.	○	○	○	○	○
. . . do not have the language or skills necessary to participate.	○	○	○	○	○
. . . are vocal and well organized in local civic matters.	○	○	○	○	○
. . . would prefer to keep to themselves and not participate.	○	○	○	○	○

25. *[City hall only]* Have local officials ever appointed an immigrant or a member of an immigrant ethnic group to a vacant elected position, such as a city council or school board vacancy?

○ Yes
○ No
○ Not sure

26. When seeking information on local immigrant groups, which resources do you use? (*Please rank the top 5 sources of information you use. Label the most used source of information as 1 and the least used as 5.*)

⬭ Municipal departments
⬭ Local school district
⬭ State government agencies
⬭ Federal government agencies, including the Census
⬭ Immigrant/ethnic nonprofit organizations
⬭ Individual contacts within the immigrant community

⬭ Social service nonprofit organizations
⬭ Churches, faith-based organizations
⬭ Local newspapers
⬭ Professional associations
⬭ Other (*please specify*)

27. If there was an issue or a government program that you thought local immigrant residents should be aware of, which groups or individuals would you turn to in order to reach immigrant residents? (*Please list these organizations or individuals, keeping in mind that your responses will be confidential.*)

```

```

[P22]. *[Police only]* Has your department investigated a hate crime in the past five years?

- O   Yes
- O   No *Go to 23*
- O   Not sure *Go to 23*

[P22a]. Roughly how often have immigrants been the target of any alleged hate crimes in the previous decade?

- O   No times
- O   One time
- O   2–5 times
- O   6–10 times
- O   More than 10 times

28. Thinking of the average nonimmigrant resident of your community, how often would he or she interact with immigrants, for instance, having conversations or participating in activities together?

- O   Never or almost never
- O   Less than once a month
- O   1–3 times a month
- O   At least once a week
- O   Every day

29. Please describe your own level of contact with immigrants in your day-to-day life *outside the office.*

    How frequently do you . . .

	Never or almost never	Less than once a month	1–3 times a month	At least once a week	Every day
. . . see immigrants in your community?	O	O	O	O	O
. . . have conversations with immigrants in your community?	O	O	O	O	O
. . . hear other residents speaking a foreign language?	O	O	O	O	O

Local Governance and Immigration

30. What role should local governments play in immigration enforcement? *(Please check all that apply.)*

Local governments . . .

☐ . . . should set their own policies and control which immigrants settle in their jurisdictions.

☐ . . . should be empowered to enforce federal immigration laws.

☐ . . . should participate in immigration enforcement only at federal authorities' request.

☐ . . . should *not* be involved in immigration enforcement.

☐ . . . should protect immigrant residents from federal enforcement.

☐ Other *(please describe)*

☐ Not sure.

31. What role should local governments play in responding to immigrant residents? *(Please check all that apply.)*

Local governments should . . .

☐ . . . create programs and policies that help immigrants adjust to their new home.

☐ . . . provide immigrants with access to existing programs available to all residents.

☐ . . . restrict *illegal immigrant* access to programs.

☐ . . . restrict *all immigrant* access to programs, preserving benefits for native-born residents.

☐ Not sure.

32. What role should the federal government play in responding to localities with substantial immigrant populations? *(Please check all that apply.)*

The federal government should . . .

☐ . . . provide guidance and technical assistance on how to respond to immigrants.

☐ . . . provide funds to localities with large immigrant populations.

☐ . . . not be involved in local responses to immigrants.

☐ Not sure.

33. To what extent does the federal government provide funding and guidance to support your community's efforts to address immigration? *(Please check all that apply.)*

Our community . . .

☐ . . . receives no reimbursement from the federal government for providing educational, law enforcement, and/or health services to immigrants.

☐ . . . receives some reimbursement from the federal government, which does not defray the full costs associated with serving immigrants.

☐ . . . receives reimbursement from the federal government that fully defrays costs associated with serving immigrants.

☐ . . . has received guidance and/or technical assistance from federal agencies in implementing policies related to immigration.

☐ Not sure.

34. Please indicate the extent to which you agree or disagree with each of the following statements.

O Serving immigrants is . . .

	Strongly disagree	Disagree	Neutral	Agree	Strongly agree
. . . important to maintaining the local workforce.	O	O	O	O	O
. . . important to local economic development.	O	O	O	O	O
. . . important to maintaining compliance with federal regulations and funding.	O	O	O	O	O
. . . part of my professional duty.	O	O	O	O	O
. . . an important way to demonstrate that our community welcomes diversity.	O	O	O	O	O

Finally, a few basic questions about you.

35. What is the highest degree or level of school you have completed? If currently enrolled, mark the previous grade or highest degree received.
    ○ Less than high school
    ○ Some high school, no diploma
    ○ High school diploma or equivalent
    ○ Some college credit, but no degree
    ○ Associate's degree
    ○ Bachelor's degree
    ○ Master's degree (for example, MA, MS, MPA)
    ○ Professional degree (for example, JD, MD)
    ○ Doctoral degree
    ○ Prefer not to answer

36. In what year were you born? (YYYY)

37. Were you born in the United States?

    ○ Yes
    ○ No, born outside the United States to *US citizen parents.*
    ○ No, born outside the United States to *noncitizen parents.*
    ○ Prefer not to answer.

38. Is the local government position that you hold elected or appointed?

    ○ Elected
    ○ Appointed
    ○ Other *(please describe)*

39. About how many *years* have you worked in [local government/law enforcement?

40. About how many *years* have you worked in your current municipality?

41. Please specify your sex.

- ○ Male
- ○ Female
- ○ Prefer not to answer

42. Please specify your race/ethnicity. *(Check all that apply.)*

- ☐ American Indian or Alaska Native
- ☐ Asian
- ☐ Black or African American
- ☐ Hispanic or Latino
- ☐ Native Hawaiian or other Pacific Islander
- ☐ White
- ☐ Other
- ☐ Prefer not to answer

43. How would you describe the majority political ideology of your community's elected governing body?

- ○ Extremely liberal
- ○ Liberal
- ○ Slightly liberal
- ○ Moderate, middle of the road
- ○ Slightly conservative
- ○ Conservative
- ○ Extremely conservative
- ○ Prefer not to answer

44. How would you describe your own political ideology?

- ○ Extremely liberal
- ○ Liberal
- ○ Slightly liberal
- ○ Moderate, middle of the road
- ○ Slightly conservative
- ○ Conservative
- ○ Extremely conservative
- ○ Prefer not to answer

45. In politics today, do you consider yourself a Republican, a Democrat, or an Independent?

   ○ Independent
   ○ Democrat
   ○ Republican
   ○ Other
   ○ Prefer not to answer

[P41]. *[Police only]* Please enter the number of full-time paid department employees as of January 1, 2015.

   ( )

[P42]. *[Police only]* Please enter the number of employees who are certified bilingual.

   ( )

[P43]. *[Police only]* Please enter the number of sworn officers in your department.

   ( )

[P44]. *[Police only]* Please enter the number of sworn officers in your department who are:

	Number
African American/Black	
Hispanic/Latino	
Asian/Pacific Islander	

Appendix C: Municipal Responses to
Immigrants Survey Methodology

From a total sample frame of 4,069 places, the MRIS surveyed 503 immigrant destinations of 5,000 to 200,000 in population that were at least 5 percent foreign-born. In order to focus on centers of population, I stratified by region and population size. Having determined what percentage of the population lives in each stratum, I randomly selected the proportional number of cities from each. Without stratification, the sample would consist largely of the many small towns and cities that make up a relatively small portion of the overall population (Varsanyi et al. 2017).

Research assistants collected contact information for the four local officials in each town using town websites. Initial notification letters were sent to respondents in July 2014, followed by an invitation e-mail with a link to a web survey, a reminder postcard, and three e-mail reminders. Nonrespondents then received a mail version of the survey.

From July 2014 to March 2015, I received responses from 598 leaders across 373 towns in forty-six states.[1] As table AC1 indicates, I received at least one response from 74 percent of towns and two or more responses from 33 percent (167 towns). In total, 30 percent of officials surveyed responded, with 78 percent responding via the Internet and the rest responding by mail (table AC2). Response rates compare favorably with those from other recent surveys of organizational executives.[2] Although some officials and some towns did not respond to the survey, nonresponse appears to be largely randomly distributed rather than related to demographic, geographic, or ideological characteristics of the towns, as table AC3 details.

As column (a) in table AC3 demonstrates, the sample intentionally varies demographically from the frame, since the sampling technique prioritized centers of population (results from two-sided t-tests). As a result, the sample consists of larger, more racially diverse, and somewhat less affluent cities, with a greater proportion in Mexican border states. As column (b) of table AC3 indicates, there are no systematic demographic differences between the cities sampled and the cities that responded. Similarly, column (c) indicates few differences between nonresponding towns and responding towns, though nonresponding towns are more affluent. It also appears that nonresponding towns report less growth in the foreign-born population and in overall population, though this difference is not statistically significant because of high levels of underlying variation in population growth across towns. The surprisingly high averages of foreign-born population growth result from some towns that went from almost no foreign-born residents to thousands over this period. In addition, Midwestern towns were somewhat more likely to respond, while towns with populations of 50,000 to 80,000 were somewhat less likely to respond than smaller and larger towns. On the whole, responding towns effectively mirrored the sample as a whole.

TABLE AC1. **Responses per town**

Number of responses	Number of towns	Percent of towns
None	130	26
One	206	41
Two	115	23
Three	46	9
Four	6	1
Total towns	503	
Towns responding	373	74

TABLE AC2. **Response rates by local officials' roles**

	Responses	Sampled	Response rate
Mayor	120	503	24%
City councilor	128	503	25%
City manager	154	503	31%
Police chief	196	503	39%
Total	598	2,012	30%

TABLE AC3. **Demographic characteristics of sample and responding towns**

	Nation	Frame	Sample	(a)	Responding	(b)	Nonresponding	(c)
Percent foreign-born 2012	13	16	17		16		18	
Percent foreign-born population growth 1990–2012	101	706	603		704		313	
Population size 2012		26,759	58,793	***	57,586		62,283	
Population growth 1990–2012	24	67	88		96		65	
Percent poverty 2012	15	13	15	***	15		14	
Percent unemployed 2012	9	9	9		10		9	
Percent BA 2012	29	32	32		32		33	
Percent non-Hispanic white 2010	64	61	59	**	59		56	
Percent non-Hispanic black 2010	12	10	11		11		10	
Percent Hispanic 2010	16	20	22		21		23	
Percent non-Hispanic Asian 2010	5	6	6		5		7	
Median home value 2012	$181,400	$276,136	$260,819		$250,026		$292,026	**
Percent change in median home value 1990–2012[a]	33	28	26		26		24	
Median household income 2012	$53,046	$65,214	$60,445	***	$59,126		$64,256	**
Percent change in median household income 1990–2012[a]	−8	−5	−6		−6		−6	
Percent voting Romney 2012	47	46	46		46		45	
Percent Canadian border state towns		24	21		22		18	
Percent Mexican border state towns		25	35	***	33		40	
N		4,069	502		373		129	

Source: American Community Survey 2008–12.
Note: Column (a) presents the significance levels from two-sided tests comparing the demographics of the sample and the frame. Column (b) presents the significance levels from two-sided tests comparing the demographics of respondent cities with the sample. Column (c) presents the significance levels from two-sided tests comparing responding cities with nonresponding cities.
[a] In 2010 dollars.
* $p < .05$
** $p < .01$
*** $p < .001$

Appendix D: Regression Tables

TABLE AD1. **Chapter 4 regression table: Factors predicting local government response**

	Proportion accommodating practices OLS			Proportion restrictive practices OLS			Enforcement practices scale OLS			Inactive (no accommodating or restrictive practices) Probit		
	Coefficient	Standard error	p-value	Coefficient	Standard error	p-value	Coefficient	Standard error	p-value	Coefficient	Standard error	p-value
Percent change foreign-born 1900–2012	0.000	0.003		-0.005	0.003		-0.014	0.010		-0.006	0.068	
Percent foreign-born Hispanic	0.044	0.061		0.016	0.038		-0.231	0.140		-0.984	0.504	*
Percent foreign-born in poverty	0.253	0.123	**	-0.016	0.083		0.125	0.298		-1.523	1.243	
Violent crime rate per 1,000 residents	-0.004	0.003		0.003	0.003		-0.009	0.014		-0.027	0.031	
Percent homeownership	-0.091	0.071		0.080	0.063		0.289	0.217		-0.663	0.745	
Population 2012 (natural log)	0.047	0.009	****	-0.001	0.008		0.039	0.030		-0.276	0.108	**
Percent with BA degree	0.081	0.084		-0.069	0.057		-0.483	0.247	*	-0.768	0.778	
Percent change in median household income 2000–2012	0.093	0.087		0.053	0.038		-0.333	0.257		0.006	0.576	
Percent foreign-born	0.336	0.097	***	0.156	0.081	*	0.503	0.209	**	-1.475	0.910	
Refugee presence (=1)	0.111	0.026	****	0.007	0.014		-0.176	0.065	**			
State-level immigrant policy score	0.000	0.000	**	0.000	0.000		0.000	0.000		-0.001	0.001	

	Model 1		Model 2		Model 3		Model 4	
	Coef.	SE	Coef.	SE	Coef.	SE	Coef.	SE
Within 100 miles of Mexican border (=1)	−0.036*	0.018	0.089***	0.027	0.057	0.124	−0.465	0.292
Within 100 miles of Canadian border (=1)	0.009	0.025	0.083***	0.022	0.147	0.085	0.007	0.008
Percent voting Romney 2012 (county)	−0.001*	0.001	0.001	0.001	0.005***	0.002		
Latino elected official (=1)	0.018	0.025	−0.012	0.019	−0.210***	0.073	−0.264	0.358
2006 protest (=1)	0.053	0.038	−0.003	0.021	−0.318**	0.144	1.471**	2.486
Immigrant-related organizations per 1,000	0.242	0.302	−0.262	0.163	−2.300**	0.927		
Percent agricultural employment	0.239	0.250	−0.162	0.114	−0.306***	0.193	0.586	1.997
Council-manager form of government (=1)	−0.006	0.017	−0.040***	0.011	−0.051	0.063	−0.055	0.199
Police-only response	0.071**	0.029	0.004	0.019	0.037	0.076	0.717	0.219
City hall-only response	−0.026	0.020	0.018	0.012	0.149**	0.057	0.547	0.178
Constant term	−0.308****	0.108	−0.039****	0.129	2.404****	0.448	2.642****	1.700
F-test	956.21		1,199.11		624.20		62.89	
R-squared	0.326		0.115		0.224		0.136	
N =	372		372		332		372	

*p < .1
**p < .05
***p < .01
****p < .001

TABLE AD2.A. **Chapter 5 regression table: Officials' attitudes toward serving immigrants**

	Serving immigrants my professional duty			Gaining immigrants' trust important			Welcoming diversity important			Economic development			Maintaining workforce important		
	Probit			Probit			Probit			Probit			Probit		
	Coef.	S.E.	p-value	Coef.	S.E.	p-value	Coef.	S.E.	p-value	Coef.	S.E.	p-value	Coef.	S.E.	p-value
Police chief	0.326	0.174	*	0.876	0.154	****	-0.246	0.184		-0.331	0.201	*	-0.327	0.163	**
City councilor	-0.688	0.151	****	0.074	0.194		-0.596	0.168	****	-0.172	0.155		-0.303	0.173	*
Mayor	-0.579	0.200	***	0.120	0.228		-0.290	0.146	**	-0.061	0.178		-0.078	0.179	
Official's age	0.002	0.006		0.004	0.008		0.002	0.006		0.010	0.005	**	0.011	0.005	**
Official's education	0.095	0.052	*	0.139	0.059	**	0.060	0.045		0.013	0.055		0.111	0.046	**
Official is female	-0.233	0.188		-0.248	0.156		-0.187	0.137		-0.150	0.150		-0.233	0.151	
Official is non-white	0.026	0.202		0.006	0.149		-0.154	0.165		0.318	0.196		0.014	0.155	
Official is conservative	-0.280	0.169	*	-0.270	0.120	**	-0.610	0.113	****	-0.610	0.122	****	-0.633	0.096	****
Town percent foreign-born	1.315	0.796	*	3.280	0.668	****	0.192	0.864		-0.524	1.056		0.445	1.233	
Town percent change foreign-born 2000–2012	-0.057	0.050		0.003	0.041		-0.029	0.050		-0.006	0.026		-0.064	0.031	**
Town percent foreign-born in poverty	2.017	0.955	**	2.447	0.786	***	1.159	1.385		-1.106	1.146		1.025	1.209	
Town percent foreign-born Hispanic	-0.224	0.320		0.179	0.273		-0.738	0.384	*	0.118	0.261		-0.236	0.351	
Town population (natural log)	0.052	0.088		0.086	0.061		0.056	0.082		0.066	0.087		0.007	0.059	
Town percent agricultural employment	-1.290	0.878		0.030	1.056		1.247	1.193		3.523	1.580	**	0.103	1.342	
Town percent with BA degree	0.226	0.554		0.756	0.683		-0.636	0.644		0.165	0.684		-0.406	0.661	
Town percent change in median household in-	-0.295	0.605		1.032	0.744		-0.738	0.725		-0.768	0.617		0.392	0.622	

	(1)		(2)		(3)		(4)		(5)	
Town percent homeownership	−0.175	0.449	−0.311	0.679	−1.115	1.116	−1.193	0.639	−0.495	0.776
Town violent crime per 1,000 residents	0.029	0.032	0.012	0.030	0.015	0.036	0.045	0.030	−0.032	0.034
County percent voting Romney 2012	−0.003	0.007	−0.008	0.007	−0.010	0.005 *	−0.010	0.008	−0.002	0.007
State-level immigrant policy score	−0.001	0.001	0.000	0.001	0.000	0.000	0.001	0.000	0.000	0.000
Within 100 miles of Mexican border (=1)	−0.559	0.237 **	−0.701	0.536	−0.487	0.361	0.040	0.185	−0.219	0.209
Within 100 miles of Canadian border (=1)	−0.056	0.217	0.067	0.198	0.481	0.254 *	0.220	0.231	−0.144	0.222
Refugee presence (=1)	0.013	0.144	0.234	0.166	0.053	0.163	0.494	0.148 ***	0.299	0.147 **
Council-manager form of government (=1)	−0.226	0.200	−0.183	0.145	−0.271	0.152 *	−0.029	0.144	0.035	0.129
Latino elected official (=1)	0.039	0.190	0.075	0.167	0.071	0.156	0.085	0.141	0.283	0.146 **
2006 protest (=1)	0.420	0.448	−0.315	0.363	−0.238	0.250	−0.407	0.241 *	0.214	0.186
Immigrant-related organizations per 1,000	0.750	2.263	3.918	2.086 *	1.304	2.017	−0.355	2.366	0.400	2.082
Constant term / Cut 1	−0.282	1.290	−3.245	1.233 ***	1.985	1.857	0.474	1.316	−0.419	1.157
F-test	159.670	****	498.930	****	312.270	****	332.080	****	327.290	****
R-squared	0.157		0.189		0.135		0.124		0.112	
N =	453		460		460		458		459	

*p < .1
**p < .05
***p < .01
****p < .001

TABLE AD2.B. **Chapter 5 regression table: Officials' attitudes toward serving immigrants (continued)**

| | No local immigration enforcement | | | Local government service to immigrants scale | | | Immigration attitudes index | | |
| | Probit | | | Ordered probit | | | OLS | | |
	Coefficient	Standard error	p-value	Coefficient	Standard error	p-value	Coefficient.	Standard error	p-value
Police chief	−0.378	0.180	**	0.428	0.212	**	2.331	0.652	***
City councilor	−0.524	0.212	**	0.431	0.252	*	0.917	0.837	
Mayor	−0.315	0.229		0.316	0.226		0.556	0.812	
Official's age	0.003	0.008		−0.007	0.007		0.018	0.032	
Official's education	0.049	0.048		0.009	0.045		−0.436	0.189	**
Official is female	−0.178	0.260		0.135	0.146		−0.097	0.650	
Official is nonwhite	−0.150	0.161		0.100	0.202		0.584	0.822	
Official is conservative	−0.877	0.175	****	0.488	0.160	***	3.726	0.603	****
Town percent foreign-born	−0.710	0.731		−0.685	0.566		−0.697	3.020	
Town percent change foreign-born 2000–2012	0.053	0.018	***	0.004	0.019		0.302	0.152	*
Town percent foreign-born in poverty	−2.010	0.918	**	−0.762	0.828		−3.562	4.109	
Town percent foreign-born Hispanic	1.288	0.378	***	0.363	0.337		2.398	1.431	
Town population (natural log)	−0.031	0.074		−0.119	0.074		−0.722	0.347	**
Town percent agricultural employment	6.223	2.228	***	−1.871	0.869	**	−10.674	3.891	***
Town percent with BA degree	1.655	0.547	***	−0.148	0.394		−2.261	2.760	
Town percent change in median household income 2000–2012	−0.398	0.622		0.292	0.531		0.244	3.031	

	Model 1			Model 2			Model 3		
	Coef.	SE		Coef.	SE		Coef.	SE	
Town percent homeownership	−0.844	0.542		0.323	0.445		−2.870	2.577	
Town violent crime per 1,000 residents	0.025	0.030		−0.005	0.024		−0.096	0.121	
County percent voting Romney 2012	−0.015	0.006	***	0.013	0.005	**	0.007	0.026	
State-level immigrant policy score	−0.001	0.001	*	−0.001	0.000		0.001	0.003	
Within 100 miles of Mexican border (= 1)	1.012	0.344	***	0.291	0.301		−0.815	1.109	
Within 100 miles of Canadian border (= 1)	0.739	0.254	***	−0.020	0.216		−1.750	0.817	**
Refugee presence (= 1)	0.247	0.166		−0.215	0.148		0.208	0.668	
Council-manager form of government (= 1)	0.118	0.149		−0.046	0.139		−0.018	0.663	
Latino elected official (= 1)	0.033	0.219		−0.025	0.230		−0.835	0.704	
2006 protest (= 1)	−0.050	0.205		0.083	0.214		0.069	0.832	
Immigrant-related organizations per 1,000	−1.680	3.218		−1.434	2.452		−9.898	8.517	
Constant term / Cut 1	0.919	1.182	****	−0.853	0.936		28.787	3.493	****
Cut 2				0.348	0.924				
Cut 3				0.695	0.908				
Cut 4				1.626	0.955				
F-test	259.040		****	213.400		****	658.930		****
R-squared	0.170			0.079			0.285		
N =	396			414			328		

TABLE AD3.A. **Chapter 5 regression table: Comparing officials' attitudes with public attitudes**

	Immigration should be reduced (GSS-MRIS) Probit			Immigration should be reduced (GSS-MRIS) Probit			Immigration should be reduced (GSS-MRIS) Probit			Immigration should be reduced (TESS-MRIS) Probit			Immigration should be reduced (TESS-MRIS) Probit			Immigration should be reduced (TESS-MRIS) Probit		
	Coefficient	Standard error	p-value	Coefficient	Standard error	p-value	Coefficient	Standard error	p-value	Coefficient	Standard error	p-value	Coefficient	Standard error	p-value	Coefficient	Standard error	p-value
National survey respondent	0.321	0.092	***							0.264	0.123	**						
Police chief				−0.218	0.145		−0.269	0.132	**				−0.161	0.165		−0.207	0.154	
Mayor				−0.299	0.185		−0.388	0.183	**				−0.241	0.202		−0.343	0.197	*
City manager				−0.388	0.174	**	−0.465	0.159	***				−0.323	0.195	*	−0.433	0.179	**
City councilor				−0.428	0.171	**	−0.463	0.166	***				−0.380	0.190	**	−0.424	0.183	**
Republican	0.187	0.067	***	0.184	0.067	***	0.320	0.057	****	0.216	0.092	**	0.209	0.093	**	0.173	0.096	*
Conservative	0.244	0.065	****	0.245	0.065	****				0.211	0.098	**	0.209	0.099	**			
Education	−0.118	0.020	****	−0.117	0.020	****	−0.113	0.019	****	−0.129	0.030	****	−0.128	0.030	****	−0.121	0.030	****
Age	0.001	0.002		0.001	0.002		0.001	0.002		−0.001	0.003		−0.001	0.003		−0.002	0.003	
Female	0.116	0.056	**	0.120	0.056	**	0.108	0.055	*	0.184	0.096	*	0.196	0.097	**	0.182	0.095	*
Nonwhite	−0.433	0.064	****	−0.434	0.064	****	−0.468	0.062	****	−0.274	0.114	**	−0.277	0.114	**	−0.313	0.111	****
Constant term	−0.118	0.166		0.198	0.130		0.248	0.128	*	0.148	0.282		0.400	0.224	*	0.536	0.217	**
R-squared	0.050			0.050			0.050			0.060			0.060			0.060		
N =	2,291			2,291			2,338			845			845			892		

*p < .1
**p < .05
***p < .01
****p < .001

TABLE AD3.B. **Chapter 5 regression table: Comparing officials' attitudes with public attitudes (continued)**

	"Immigrants take jobs" (TESS-MRIS) Probit			"Immigrants take jobs" (TESS-MRIS) Probit			"Immigrants threaten American way of life" (TESS-MRIS) Probit			"Immigrants threaten American way of life" (TESS-MRIS) Probit		
	Coefficient	Standard error	p-value	Coefficient	Standard error	p-value	Coefficient	Standard error	p-value	Coefficient	Standard error	p-value
National survey respondent	0.729	0.136	****				0.457	0.124	****			
Police chief				-0.470	0.175	***				-0.308	0.166	*
Mayor				-1.050	0.203	****				-0.442	0.193	**
City manager				-0.931	0.193	****				-0.718	0.187	****
City councilor				-0.602	0.194	***				-0.468	0.184	**
Republican	0.142	0.111		0.113	0.112		0.426	0.099	****	0.400	0.100	****
Conservative	0.194	0.115	*	0.166	0.116		0.229	0.104	**	0.210	0.104	**
Education	-0.125	0.037	***	-0.122	0.037	***	-0.190	0.033	****	-0.186	0.033	****
Age	-0.002	0.004		-0.001	0.004		0.006	0.004	*	0.006	0.004	*
Female	0.040	0.117		0.064	0.117		0.042	0.103		0.063	0.104	
Nonwhite	-0.179	0.130	***	-0.183	0.131	****	-0.187	0.117	*	-0.197	0.116	*
Constant term	1.072	0.335		1.744	0.276		0.538	0.300		0.971	0.243	****
R-squared	0.130			0.140			0.130			0.130		
N =	848			848			844			844		

*p < .1
**p < .05
***p < .01
****p < .001

TABLE AD4. **Chapter 6 regression table: Effect of external scrutiny on maintaining a restrictive ordinance**

Dependent variable: Ordinance remains in effect (= 1)

	Model 1			Model 2			Model 3			Model 4			Model 5		
	Coefficient	Standard error	p-value	Coefficient	Standard error	p-value	Coefficient	Standard error	p-value	Coefficient	Standard error	p-value	Coefficient	Standard error	p-value
Number of media mentions	−0.069	0.029	**							−0.054	0.021	***			
Number of expansionist advocacy organizations				−0.496	0.281	*				−0.332	0.227				
Number of restrictionist advocacy organizations							−0.358	0.216	*						
External Scrutiny Scale													−0.337	0.202	*
Percent foreign-born	−8.179	3.804	**	−9.398	3.447	**	−9.953	3.113	***	−7.602	3.871	*	−7.961	4.311	*
Percent change foreign-born 2000–2012	0.000	0.000		0.000	0.000		0.000	0.000	**	0.000	0.000		0.000	0.000	**
Percent foreign-born in poverty	−14.063	4.740	***	−12.232	3.541	***	−13.230	3.226	***	−14.881	4.776	***	−12.053	3.849	***
Percent foreign-born Hispanic	3.198	1.316	**	2.792	1.328	**	3.019	1.267	**	2.785	1.333	**	2.636	1.356	*
Percent with BA degree	2.818	2.594		1.208	1.677		0.904	1.648		2.360	2.174		0.290	1.849	
Population 2012 (natural log)	0.075	0.216		0.132	0.224		0.180	0.191		0.050	0.226		0.060	0.250	

	Model 1		Model 2		Model 3		Model 4		Model 5	
Percent home-ownership	-6.343	5.277	-7.202	4.650	-6.168	4.515	-8.160	4.692	-6.236	4.461
Percent change in median household income 2000–2012	2.204	2.283	0.818	1.766	1.606	1.808	0.733	1.890	0.950	1.890
Council-manager form of government (= 1)	-0.079	0.717	-0.058	0.598	-0.200	0.780	-0.175	0.650	-0.051	0.590
Percent voting Romney 2012 (county)	0.045	0.039	0.039	0.032	0.034	0.040	0.043	0.036	0.045	0.032
State-level immigrant policy score	0.001	0.001	0.000	0.001	0.001	0.001	0.001	0.001	0.001	0.001
Constant term	2.089		2.949		1.943		4.629		3.615	
F-test	133.60****		92.91****		70.520****		401.63****		227.77****	
R-squared	0.511		0.471		0.437		0.528		0.459	
N =	51		51		51		51		51	

*p < .1
**p < .05
***p < .01
****p < .001

TABLE AD5.A. **Chapter 7 regression results: Factors explaining perceptions of immigrant civic presence**

	Immigrants vocal and organized in civic life			Immigrants too busy to participate			Immigrants lack skills to participate			Immigrants prefer to keep to themselves		
	OLS			OLS			OLS			OLS		
	Coefficient	Standard error	p-value	Coefficient	Standard error	p-value	Coefficient	Standard error	p-value	Coefficient	Standard error	p-value
Accommodating index	0.714	0.247	***	0.327	0.251		-0.788	0.330	**	-0.507	0.253	**
Restrictive index	0.301	0.328		0.323	0.273		0.388	0.281		0.313	0.345	
Percent foreign-born	-1.221	0.971		-1.344	0.673	*	-0.962	0.562	*	0.508	0.945	
Percent change foreign-born 2000–2012	-0.034	0.023		-0.001	0.014		0.007	0.021		0.021	0.026	
Percent Hispanic 2012	0.726	0.430	*	0.042	0.329		0.757	0.342	**	0.248	0.555	
Percent black 2012	-0.104	0.358		0.074	0.453		0.576	0.486		0.401	0.439	
Percent Asian 2012	1.383	0.883		-0.503	0.743		0.251	0.805		-0.058	1.379	
Percent foreign-born in poverty	-0.869	0.611		0.236	0.728		0.324	0.781		1.281	0.772	
Refugee presence (=1)	0.174	0.141		-0.300	0.095	***	0.168	0.141		-0.131	0.133	
Population 2012 (natural log)	0.060	0.069		0.098	0.052	*	-0.003	0.055		-0.040	0.063	
Percent agricultural employment	-0.243	1.018	*	0.512	1.027		-1.577	1.020		-1.041	1.756	
Percent with BA degree	0.135	0.409		0.113	0.347		-0.611	0.314	*	-0.283	0.537	
Percent change in median house-	0.516	0.286	*	-0.271	0.236		-0.018	0.348		-0.611	0.530	

	Model 1		Model 2		Model 3		Model 4	
Percent home-ownership	0.092	0.645	0.256	0.246	0.338	0.454	0.659	0.606
Violent crime rate per 1,000 residents	0.026	0.027	−0.006	0.009	−0.013	0.025	−0.021	0.018
Council-manager form of government (= 1)	−0.038	0.120	0.182*	0.102	−0.105	0.111	0.075	0.143
Percent voting Romney 2012 (county)	−0.003	0.004	−0.004	0.003	−0.005	0.003	0.004	0.004
State-level immigrant policy score	0.000	0.000	0.000	0.000	0.000	0.000	0.000	0.000
Within 100 miles of Mexican border (= 1)	−0.252	0.351	−0.210	0.132	−0.682****	0.079	−0.480***	0.128
Within 100 miles of Canadian border (= 1)	−0.197	0.131	−0.086	0.177	−0.002	0.217	−0.091	0.279
Latino elected official (=1)	0.443***	0.141	0.190*	0.111	0.075*	0.100	−0.213	0.159
2006 protest (=1)	−0.084	0.171	−0.056	0.179	0.582***	0.167	0.182	0.168
Immigrant-related organizations per 1,000	−0.959	2.098	0.254	1.251	−4.227**	1.581	−3.177	3.376
Constant term	1.690****	1.182	1.861****	0.627	3.142****	0.722	3.018***	0.885
F-test	339.96		182.24		485.84		221.18****	
R-squared	0.202		0.104		0.166		0.130	
N =	282		280		282		281	

* p < .1
** p < .05
*** p < .01
**** p < .001

TABLE AD5.B. **Chapter 7 regression results: Factors explaining perceptions of immigrant civic presence**

| | Average Resident Interaction with Immigrants | | | Officials' Interaction with Immigrants Outside Office | | | Local Hispanic Representation | | | Local African American Representation | | | Local Asian Representation | | |
| | OLS | | | OLS | | | OLS | | | OLS | | | OLS | | |
	Co-efficient	Standard error	p-value	Co-efficient	Standard error	p-value	Co-efficient	Standard error	p-value	Co-efficient	Standard error	p-value	Co-efficient	Standard error	p-value
Police-only response	-0.095	0.135		-0.290	0.433										
City Hall-only response	-0.235	0.076	***	-0.627	0.248	**									
Accommodating Index	0.977	0.370	**	3.025	0.796	****	0.529	0.189	***	0.482	0.190	**	0.188	0.225	
Restrictive Index	0.235	0.397		-0.130	1.273		-0.145	0.310		-0.100	0.295		0.588	0.364	
Percent foreign-born	2.520	0.951	**	10.239	1.772	****	-0.343	0.450		-0.405	0.404		-0.389	0.522	
Percent change FB 00–12	0.055	0.029	*	0.102	0.092		0.008	0.027		-0.006	0.025		0.039	0.024	
Percent Hispanic 2012	1.354	0.454	***	0.425	1.343		1.580	0.367	****	0.481	0.342		-0.045	0.284	
Percent Black 2012	-0.169	0.351		-1.146	1.372		-0.140	0.262		3.242	0.382	****	-0.248	0.212	
Percent Asian 2012	1.106	1.246		-0.566	1.421		1.333	0.706	*	2.200	0.966	**	3.415	0.715	****
Percent FB in poverty	0.635	0.661		1.974	1.687		-0.751	0.533		0.186	0.574		-0.821	0.469	*

Refugee presence (=1)	-0.148	0.115	0.447	0.318	-0.077	0.103	0.055	0.100	-0.051	0.083
Population 2012 (natural log)	-0.009	0.057	-0.042	0.172	0.100***	0.032	0.149****	0.034	0.091**	0.042
Percent agricultural employment	-0.988	1.962	0.594	2.623	0.022	0.628	-2.114***	0.756	1.066**	0.441
Percent BA degree	0.163	0.424	-1.433	1.839	-0.652**	0.322	-0.276	0.275	-0.097	0.235
Percent change median HH income 00–12	0.036	0.339	0.202	1.590	0.072	0.270	-0.056	0.220	-0.201	0.195
Percent home ownership	-0.188	0.579	-0.735	1.303	-0.026	0.408	0.766***	0.238	-0.392	0.238
Violent crime rate per 1,000 residents	0.041	0.031	0.005	0.073	0.008	0.013	0.017	0.013	0.001	0.012
Council-manager form of govt. (=1)	0.055	0.155	0.128	0.426	-0.001	0.055	-0.056	0.077	-0.024	0.061
Percent voting Romney 2012 (county)	0.003	0.004	0.034***	0.012	0.000	0.003	0.009***	0.003	-0.002	0.003
State-level immigrant policy score	0.000	0.000	0.001	0.001	-0.001**	0.000	0.000	0.000	0.000	0.000
W/in 100 miles of Mexican border (=1)	0.194	0.167	0.155	0.646	0.138	0.093	0.186	0.118	0.045	0.124

(continued)

TABLE AD5.B. (continued)

	Average Resident Interaction with Immigrants			Officials' Interaction with Immigrants Outside Office			Local Hispanic Representation			Local African American Representation			Local Asian Representation		
	OLS			OLS			OLS			OLS			OLS		
	Co-efficient	Standard error	p-value	Co-efficient	Standard error	p-value	Co-efficient	Standard error	p-value	Co-efficient	Standard error	p-value	Co-efficient	Standard error	p-value
W/in 100 miles of Canadian border (=1)	0.009	0.364		-0.279	0.759		-0.218	0.069	***	-0.012	0.176		0.049	0.124	
Latino elected official (=1)	-0.159	0.138		-0.479	0.390		0.361	0.094	****	-0.027	0.098		0.128	0.120	
2006 protest (=1)	0.014	0.139	*	0.561	0.335		-0.081	0.147		0.044	0.144	*	-0.086	0.147	
Immigrant-related organizations per 1,000	-3.042	1.734		5.682	5.370		-1.681	1.162		-2.33	1.240		-0.657	0.947	
Constant term	1.774	0.934	*	7.746	2.517	***	0.531	0.537		-1.172	0.389	***	0.783	0.502	
F-test	1791.05		****	928.06		****	4523.25		****	952.90		****	1374.23		****
R-squared	0.278			0.285			0.419			0.433			0.243		
N =	354			360			283			282			281		

TABLE AD6. **Chapter 8 regression results: Factors explaining local controversy over immigration**

| | Discuss immigration frequently | | | Immigration somewhat or more controversial | | |
| | Probit | | | Probit | | |
	Coefficient	Standard error	p-value	Coefficient	Standard error	p-value
Police-only response	−0.067	0.211		0.064	0.174	
City hall-only response	−0.004	0.188		−0.024	0.237	
Accommodating index	1.507	0.471	***	0.683	0.464	
Restrictive index	1.268	0.591	**	1.567	0.537	***
Percent foreign-born	−0.220	0.887		−0.530	0.742	
Percent change foreign-born 2000–2012	0.011	0.043		0.047	0.052	
Percent foreign-born in poverty	0.203	1.011		1.205	0.956	
Percent foreign-born Hispanic	0.292	0.377		1.524	0.468	***
Refugee presence (= 1)	0.515	0.198	***	0.512	0.302	*
Population 2012 (natural log)	0.058	0.101		0.103	0.093	
Percent agricultural employment	1.232	1.313		−0.199	1.850	
Percent with BA degree	−1.969	0.879	**	−0.771	0.631	
Percent change in median household income 2000–2012	1.135	0.574	***	−0.530	0.437	
Percent homeownership	0.294	0.709		0.041	0.505	
Violent crime rate per 1,000 residents	−0.099	0.033	***	−0.069	0.031	**
Council-manager form of government (= 1)	−0.223	0.146	**	−0.188	0.195	
Percent voting Romney 2012 (county)	−0.005	0.006		0.001	0.009	
State-level immigrant policy score	−0.002	0.000	***	0.000	0.001	
Within 100 miles of Mexican border (= 1)	0.209	0.212		0.392	0.208	*
Within 100 miles of Canadian border (= 1)	0.190	0.484		−1.250	0.372	***
Latino elected official (= 1)	−0.005	0.258		−0.524	0.186	***
2006 protest (= 1)	0.417	0.225	*	0.592	0.230	***
Immigrant-related organizations per 1,000	3.189	2.248		−3.629	2.114	
Constant term	−1.354	1.280		−1.496	1.187	
F-test	523.920		****	318.23		****
R-squared	0.161			0.190		
N =	364			356		

*p < .1
**p < .05
***p < .01
****p < .001

Notes

Chapter One

1. Under a 2001 Supreme Court ruling, individuals may sue agencies only for intentional discrimination (*Alexander v. Sandoval*, 2001). Federal agencies, however, have the right to take administrative action against fund recipients for failing to comply with language access guidelines, even where the recipient's actions do not constitute intentional discrimination.

2. Since 2001, annual deportations of unauthorized immigrants have more than doubled, reaching a height of 438,421 immigrants deported in fiscal year 2013 before receding in the later years of the Obama administration (Gonzalez-Barrera and Lopez 2016). Deportation numbers have held steady in Trump's early months in office, though immigration arrests are up 33 percent (Law 2017).

3. I use the terms integration and incorporation interchangeably throughout the book.

4. Republican opponents tend to use "amnesty," while Democrats use "pathway to citizenship," in referring to proposals for regularizing unauthorized immigrant status. While the terms could connote fundamentally different policies, they are often used by the different sides to refer to the same proposals for earned legalization (e.g., Barrett, Bash, and Walsh 2013).

5. Donald Trump's June 16, 2015, presidential campaign announcement: "When Mexico sends its people, they're not sending their best. They're not sending you. They're not sending you. They're sending people that have lots of problems, and they're bringing those problems with us. They're bringing drugs. They're bringing crime. They're rapists. And some, I assume, are good people" (see full text at "Full Text" 2015).

6. Some argue that the association between education and greater support for immigrants is driven by self-interest rather than by fundamental differences in understanding of the foreign-born. Educated Americans may be more supportive of immigration because low-skilled immigrants present less of a perceived

threat to these Americans' livelihood (Scheve and Slaughter 2001; Mayda 2006). Other scholars dispute this interpretation, demonstrating that educated Americans are more supportive of both low- and high-skilled immigrants, even though the latter group would ostensibly compete for their jobs (Hainmueller and Hiscox 2010). Regardless of whether educated Americans' support for immigration is driven by self-interest or alternative symbolic understandings of immigrants, the gap between them and others on this issue contributes to the distinction between local officials' views and those of the general public.

7. Counties, in contrast, have tended to be somewhat more restrictive because sheriffs are typically elected, rather than appointed like most police chiefs (Farris and Holman 2017).

8. Because Wausau and Lewiston were previously homogeneous white, Wausau's Asian population is overwhelmingly Hmong and Lewiston's black population overwhelmingly comprises recent African immigrants, primarily Somalis. I report race rather than ancestry, since race data are more comprehensive and reliable.

9. Note that figure 1.1 indicates a dip in Lewiston's black population from 2010 to 2015, but local reports do not corroborate this decline. While the 2010 Census is a full population count, the American Community Survey produces estimates by sampling a portion of the population. Since the Somalis' arrival in Lewiston in 2001, the American Community Survey has consistently undercounted their presence. The population remains undercounted owing to Somalis' limited English proficiency and higher mobility within Lewiston.

10. During the Vietnam War, US forces were not supposed to enter Laos, so US secret operatives recruited Hmong soldiers to battle Communist forces in Laos (Hein 1994). Although many Hmong fighters report that US operatives promised them protection and future benefits, the Hmong role in the Vietnam War was not officially recognized by the US government until 1997 (Vang 2010). The United States did, however, accept 90 percent of Hmong refugees in the Thai camps (Yau 2005).

11. In 2003 Karthick Ramakrishnan and Paul Lewis (2005) surveyed mayors, city councilors, police chiefs, and planning directors in California cities that were at least 15 percent foreign-born. In 2007 and 2010 Lewis and his colleagues conducted two surveys of law enforcement officials in immigrant destination cities nationwide (Lewis et al. 2013). Nadia Rubaii-Barrett surveyed US members of the International City and County Managers Association about their responses to immigrants, but the sample does not represent a random cross section of cities (Rubaii-Barrett 2008). Linda Williams (2015) conducted a nationwide survey of police officials and library directors and created a scale of "welcomeness" based on her survey of police officials.

12. Where there was no city manager or equivalent position, I surveyed the municipal clerk. In twenty-two cities, a police chief could not be identified be-

cause these municipalities contract for public safety with the county or an adjacent town. In these cases I surveyed the official charged with overseeing public safety, whether a director of public safety or a county law enforcement officer assigned to liaise with the town.

13. In addition to original questions, the survey gives priority to previously validated survey questions from the earlier surveys of local government officials (Ramakrishnan and Lewis 2005; Rubaii-Barrett 2008; Lewis et al. 2013; Williams 2013).

14. The frame excludes places with less than 5,000 residents because they are unlikely to have officials in each of the roles surveyed. It excludes places with more than 200,000 (only 109 cities in the United States), since similar surveys have found higher rates of nonresponse in large cities (Varsanyi et al. 2017).

15. The MRIS16 uses cities and towns as its unit of analysis rather than counties, owing to substantial differences in the role of counties across states. Connecticut and Rhode Island, for instance, have no county-level government, and Hawaii's municipal government operates primarily at the county level. In contrast, cities generally serve similar functions across states, allowing for a more uniform unit of comparison. In a few states, however, particularly Hawaii, Maryland, and Virginia, counties are a more dominant form of local government and fewer cities are incorporated. As a result, these states are somewhat underrepresented in the sample. Nonetheless, sampling at the city level remains appropriate to ensure comparability, since cities fulfill similar functions across states, whereas the role of counties varies greatly.

16. Marschall (2017) employs this definition of new immigrant destination.

Chapter Two

1. When comparing localities within a state, state requirements for serving immigrants can be factored into the municipal compliance point, again allowing for differentiation of compliance and independent response. Including state requirements could, in effect, expand the brackets of compliance. For instance, in a state like Arizona that requires local police involvement in enforcement, the brackets of compliance would expand to include practices considered restrictive on the national scale. In contrast, a state like California that limits localities' restriction of day laborers expands the brackets of compliance toward accommodation.

2. Other scholars have used "welcoming" to refer to similar efforts (Williams 2015). I prefer the term accommodating, since it recognizes that localities can undertake actions that provide a more hospitable environment even if they are not enthusiastic about immigrants' presence.

3. In addition to the housing enforcement controversy, School District U-46,

which includes Elgin and neighboring towns, was the defendant in a long-running school segregation suit filed after a 2004 redistricting. Though Elgin is subject to the school board's restrictive redistricting, the impetus for the redistricting came largely from outside Elgin and has been publicly challenged by the city. The city council passed a resolution urging the school board to delay the vote on the redistricting plan to allow further consideration of community concerns (Malone 2004), and several city councilors and other local leaders disapproved of the restrictive redistricting. Ultimately, in 2014 a judge ruled in the district's favor on the redistricting plan, though it ruled against the district on its treatment of gifted Spanish-speaking students ("District U-46 Settles" 2014).

4. The city challenged the court's remedy on the basis that the new districts are equal in population but lopsided in terms of citizens of voting age. In other words, the city maintained that voters in districts with more noncitizen immigrants are, in effect, overrepresented compared with voters in districts with more citizens and fewer immigrants. A Texas case raising similar claims was recently decided before the Supreme Court. Yakima filed an amicus brief in support of the Texas citizens who argued that the state's redistricting means their votes are less influential (US Supreme Court 2015). In April 2016 the Supreme Court ruled unanimously in *Evenwel v. Abbot* that states and localities may draw districts based on total population, effectively rejecting the claims from Texas and Yakima.

Chapter Three

1. For ordinal variables, the townwide response represents the average of the officials' responses within that town. For dichotomous variables, the townwide response also represents an average; however, I have omitted from consideration towns in which only two officials responded and gave opposite answers, since in this case I cannot identify the town's general tendency (Ramakrishnan and Lewis 2005). On average, only 5 percent of towns offer such conflicting responses across twenty-six dichotomous variables, suggesting that officials within towns tend to present their local responses similarly.

2. The findings remain similar, though inaction is more common since smaller towns are less likely to have implemented practices in response to immigrants. In subsequent chapters I present unweighted results, since in those cases I am more interested in relations between variables than in describing frequencies. The MRIS intentionally employs stratified random sampling to oversample larger cities within the sample frame where a greater proportion of immigrants and other Americans live. Therefore, as table AC3 in the appendix displays, the average responding town intentionally is more than twice the size of the average town in the sample frame. If I weight the results back to the frame, I am over-

weighting the small places that I intentionally undersampled. For the most part I do not weight back to the frame, since I am interested in demonstrating responses to immigrants across a range of towns, with a focus on the larger towns within this population range where most immigrants and Americans live.

3. While responses to this question indicate that roughly half of these immigrant destination towns have in-house interpretation capabilities, qualitative comments suggest that responses to non-English-speaking residents may be more variable. Eight percent of officials volunteered that responses would vary with the situation. Also, it is unclear whether towns that turn to employee interpreters have dedicated interpreters or rely on multilingual staff members in other roles, such as an assistant from another department. The latter is likely in many towns, with twenty-three respondents volunteering that they use multilingual employees in other roles to interpret.

4. The survey asked whether towns designed hiring practices to attract bilingual candidates, as well as whether bilingual candidates received "extra points in the hiring process" or whether bilingual staff in some positions received "a pay differential or additional compensation" (Williams 2013). Overall, 46 percent of towns report designing hiring to attract bilingual candidates; 19 percent report offering extra points in the hiring process, and 34 percent report providing additional pay to bilingual staff. Police officials are more likely to report providing incentive pay to attract bilingual staff.

5. The survey asked about Secure Communities since it predated the initiation of the Priority Enforcement Program, which President Obama announced in November 2014 and enacted in July 2015. President Trump reinstated Secure Communities in his January 2017 executive order on Enhancing Public Safety in the Interior of the United States.

6. In the survey I used "illegal immigrants" to refer to immigrants who entered the country without permission or overstayed visas. The terms undocumented or unauthorized are more common in academic circles, with many finding "illegal immigrants," offensive since it applies the "illegal" descriptor to a group of people rather than to their actions (Haughney 2013). On the other hand, outside academic circles, some find "undocumented" to be an inappropriate euphemism. Indeed, more restrictive voices insist that the legal term illegal alien should be used (Minuteman Project 2013). To moderate between these poles, a number of mainstream journalistic outlets continue to use "illegal immigrant" in discussing the issue, though some, such as the Associated Press and the *Los Angeles Times*, have shifted away from it (Guskin 2013). I erred on the side of using "illegal immigrant" in the survey, in an attempt to demonstrate neutrality to respondents in a context in which academics are typically assumed to be left-leaning.

7. Performing one symbolic incorporation practice is correlated with performing other symbolic practices (Pearson's $r = 0.38$–0.47).

8. Performing one material incorporation practices is correlated with performing the four others, with the Pearson's correlation ranging from a low of 0.23 to a high of 0.75.

9. Questions on Secure Communities are excluded from both the restrictive and accommodating indexes, since elected officials' responses on this question appear unreliable, given their high degree of uncertainty and their lack of knowledge about whether their towns had a jail. Excluding Secure Communities from the restrictive and accommodating index does not substantively change the results presented here, since very few towns report active engagement in or resistance to Secure Communities, with most reporting simple compliance.

10. Accepting consular identification such as the *matricula consular* is omitted from the indexes because city hall officials expressed high levels of uncertainty on this question. I report the responses from police chiefs above.

11. Cronbach's alpha for the constrained accommodating index is 0.75, indicating that the index has an acceptable level of internal consistency. Cronbach's alpha for the restrictive index, however, is only 0.49, suggesting a low level of internal consistency. This low internal consistency results from the overall low levels of restriction across the towns. Very few towns implement any restrictive practices, and of these few implement more than one, resulting in low intercorrelation among the restrictive practices. While the aggregate measure is imperfect, it is yet another signal of the dearth of restriction across the cases, which it remains worthwhile to illustrate.

12. For this reason, questions regarding Secure Communities and the specifics of bilingual hiring practices (additional points in hiring or additional compensation) were excluded from the aggregate indexes.

13. These results weight the responding towns back to the sample frame with respect to population stratum, racial demographics, percentage foreign-born, percentage with a bachelor's degree, and median household income in 2012.

Chapter Four

1. Similarly, in observing local government responses to immigrants across European and Israeli cities, Michael Alexander (2003, 2007) found that officials' perceptions of immigrants as a permanent versus temporary presence strongly shaped local responses. In his typology, cities with an expectation that immigrants are transient adopt a "non-policy," ignoring the newcomers' presence and responding only to crises. On the other hand, cities that view immigrants as permanent were more likely to adopt policies aimed at integration.

2. Differences in analytical technique may account for the conflicting outcomes of these studies. Hopkins (2010) operationalizes local partisanship using 1988 presidential elections in order to capture local party affiliation before local

demographic change. Others operationalize partisanship based on more recent elections. While Hopkins (2010) and Walker and Leitner (2011) operationalize demographic change in terms of foreign-born growth, Ramakrishnan and Wong (2010) measure Hispanic growth. Steil and Vasi (2014) control for both foreign-born and Hispanic growth, finding only the latter influential in shaping restrictive responses.

3. In chapter 3, where my aim was to gauge relative levels of accommodating and restrictive activity, I introduced a constrained index of accommodation that included only eleven accommodating responses that required deliberation and collective decision making equivalent to the restrictive responses. Here I focus on the full index of eighteen responses in order to gauge the prevalence of all types of formal and informal accommodating activity.

4. Cronbach's alpha for the full accommodating index is 0.88, indicating a high level of internal consistency. Cronbach's alpha for the restrictive index is low (0.49) because very few towns implement more than one restrictive measure.

5. Some scholars argue that while foreign-born growth does not produce threatened responses, Hispanic growth does, owing to associations between Latino immigrants and unauthorized status (Steil and Vasi 2014). Controlling for both percentage change foreign-born and percentage change Hispanic does not change the results presented here, with one small exception. If I control for both, percentage foreign-born becomes a statistically significant predictor of reduced inactivity. I choose to control for only percentage change foreign-born, since these measures are highly correlated ($r = 0.75$). In alternative specifications, I also control for the Hispanic, non-Hispanic Asian, and non-Hispanic black proportion of the population (omitting the Hispanic proportion of the foreign-born population) as well as for the square of the Hispanic population, since some argue that the effects of the size of this group are curvilinear. That is, responses become more restrictive until the population reaches a threshold of local political influence, and then responses become less restrictive and more accommodating (Abrajano and Hajnal 2015). A larger Asian population predicts less inactivity and less restrictive responses, while a larger black population also predicts less restrictive responses. The Hispanic proportion of the population and its square do not predict local responses. Including or excluding these variables does not otherwise change the main effects presented here, so I choose to omit them so my analysis most closely replicates previous analyses examining the factors that predict local responses to immigrants.

6. In including both change in median household income and percentage with a bachelor's degree, I attempt to capture both socioeconomic context and change in socioeconomic context while most closely replicating earlier studies of municipal responses, including Steil and Vasi (2014).

7. Note that percentage foreign-born and percentage Hispanic foreign-born are not collinear (Pearson's $r = 0.20$). That is, places in which there is a larger

foreign-born population are not necessarily places where the foreign-born population is more Hispanic-dominant.

8. The survey question employed a five-point scale from "no refugees" to "refugees are our dominant foreign-born group." I include it as a dichotomous measure for ease of interpretation, as well as because across the towns, 24 percent
were uncertain whether they had resident refugees. Since the variable aimed to
measure the presence of a noticeable population of refugees, I grouped towns
that were uncertain among those with no or few refugees. Nonetheless, if I rerun
analyses using the full scale of refugee presence rather than the dichotomous
variable, the findings presented in chapter 4 do not change in any meaningful
way (minor changes in the statistical significance of only five variables among
the eighty-four examined across the four models).

9. The ICI score analyzes all state laws related to immigration passed from
2005 to 2011, with the exception of resolutions. Laws are then classified as restrictive or accommodating and assigned a point value ranging from ±1 to ±4,
with accommodating laws receiving a positive score and restrictive laws a negative score. Laws assigned a higher absolute value are those that have an important effect on all aspects of immigrants' lives, such as immigration enforcement
practices. In addition to measuring state policy, the ICI score takes into account
municipal and county-level restrictive ordinances, drawing on lists of ordinances
maintained by advocacy organizations. Municipal and county ordinances are assigned a point value, and then that point value is weighted by the proportion of
the state that lives in the jurisdiction the law applies to. Therefore the ICI score
provides a holistic measure of immigration policy activism at the local, county,
and state levels. Although state responses to immigration have on the whole become more accommodating toward immigrants since 2011 (Gulasekaram and
Ramakrishnan 2015), the ICI remains an effective measure of state immigration
policy climate. A research assistant examined state immigration-related legislation from 2012 to 2014 from the National Council of State Legislatures (NCSL)
database using the methods employed by Pham and Pham (2012) and found that
while state scores change somewhat from 2011 to 2014, the Pham and Pham
scores continue to accurately approximate where states fall with respect to one
another on the statewide immigrant policies.

10. The US Border Patrol is now the United States' largest police force, with
nearly 21,000 officers, 87 percent of them stationed along the Mexican border
(US Customs and Border Patrol 2015).

11. Einstein and Kogan (2015) have generated town-level presidential partisanship in 2008 for most states, but no data are available for the states of Georgia and Oregon. Overall, town-level partisanship data are missing for forty-six
towns that responded to the MRIS, so I chose to use county-level partisanship as
a consistent metric across places.

12. Measuring immigrant organizations based on 990 forms provides an

undercount in that religious nonprofits and those with less than $25,000 in revenue are not required to submit these tax forms. While we cannot know what proportion of immigrant organizations are missing from IRS filings, Gleeson and Bloemraad (2012) find that IRS forms include 62 percent of the immigrant organizations they identified independently through fieldwork in Silicon Valley. Although the undercount is substantial, we have no better proxy for the prevalence of immigrant organizations across cities.

13. Some studies have hypothesized that proximity to major metropolitan immigrant gateways might either strengthen (Mollenkopf and Pastor 2016) or weaken (de Graauw, Gleeson, and Bloemraad 2013) capacity to respond to immigrants. In one robustness check I included a variable that measured a given town's distance to an immigrant gateway (defined as the twelve largest cities with immigrant populations of at least 20 percent: New York, Los Angeles, Chicago, Houston, Phoenix, San Diego, Dallas, San Jose, San Francisco, Austin, Boston, and El Paso). This variable did not influence local responses, though it is possible that findings would differ if metro-area influence were defined differently.

14. Where the 2011 ICMA lacked this information, we collected it from town websites or contacted city clerks to verify form of government.

15. I employ multivariate ordinary least squares (OLS) regression to analyze the continuous indexes of accommodation, restriction, and enforcement practices. I use probit to analyze the factors predicting inaction. In all analyses I employ clustered standard errors to acknowledge that towns are clustered within states. An alternative method of addressing the hierarchical structure of the data is multilevel modeling. Results are essentially the same, but likelihood ratio tests indicate that multilevel models do not provide a better fit, and therefore for ease of interpretation I present nonhierarchical models.

16. Note that I use OLS in analyzing this variable because responses are averaged across respondents from a given town, resulting in a variable that is continuous rather than ordinal.

Chapter Five

1. Although restrictive local ordinances did not arise organically at the local level, many accommodating practices did, supporting my argument about the local tendency toward accommodation. Whereas restrictionist issue entrepreneurs began pursuing a subfederal strategy in the early 2000s, issue entrepreneurs supporting immigrants' rights turned to subfederal efforts only in late 2012 (Gulasekaram and Ramakrishnan 2015). Therefore national issue entrepreneurs did not provide the inspiration for earlier accommodating practices such as the informal ones I see across the four cases much earlier than 2012.

2. Studies suggest that education affects attitudes toward immigrants through

variations in ethnocentrism and political correctness rather than self-interest (see note 6 in chapter 1). Regardless whether the variation stems from these factors or from self-interest, more highly educated people are more receptive toward immigrants, affecting local government officials' responses.

3. Spouses of American citizens may apply for naturalization after three years of legal permanent residence. Those who have served in the armed forces may also apply for naturalization before five years of continuous legal permanent residence (US Citizenship and Immigration Services 2016).

4. Since cities differ in their form of government and institutional arrangements, not all have officials in each of these positions. All cities had an elected governing body similar to a city council, though not all had an elected executive such as a mayor. In the seven cases where no mayor was present, I surveyed the city council president. In twenty-two cities no police chief could be identified, often because the municipality contracted with the county or an adjacent town for public safety. In these cases I surveyed the official charged with overseeing public safety in the town, whether a director of public safety or a county law enforcement officer assigned to liaise with the town. Finally, for the most part cities had a city manager or a similar chief appointed position. In seventeen cities where no city manager or chief appointed position could be identified, I surveyed the city clerk. (In some places city clerks are elected, including three of these seventeen places.) While these substitutions do introduce some variation within local roles, I have run the analyses presented here both including and excluding these substituted officials, and the findings do not substantively differ.

5. Demographically, the local government officials responding to the MRIS are similar to the universe of local government officials found in other national surveys. For comparison, the International City/County Management Association 2011 Municipal Form of Government survey reports that 24 percent of city councilors are women and 90 percent are white. The 2012 ICMA State of the Profession survey reports that 20 percent of city managers are women, 70 percent have a graduate degree, more than 80 percent are non-Hispanic white, and the average local government experience is twenty-one years (International City/County Managers Association 2012). The Bureau of Justice Statistics 2013 Local Police Department survey found that 3 percent of police chiefs nationwide were women, though female chiefs were more common in larger cities (Reaves 2015, 18).

6. Cronbach's alpha for the index is 0.85, indicating its reliability.

7. I control for ideology in lieu of partisanship because nonresponse is lower for ideology. I will discuss a robustness check using Republican partisanship rather than conservative ideology below.

8. I employ models appropriate to the dependent variables' forms, employing OLS for continuous variables, probit for binary variables, and ordered probit for ordinal variables. Since I am controlling for variables at the individual and con-

textual levels, hierarchical linear modeling is an appropriate technique to account for the nested structure of the data. Running multilevel models taking into account clustering at the town and state levels, however, does not make a substantive difference in the results about official role and partisanship. For ease of interpretation, I therefore present the results of OLS, probit, and ordered probit models, with clustered standard errors at the state level.

9. Living in a county with more Republican voters is associated with more restrictive responses among officials, though by a significant margin on only three of eight variables. Interestingly, working in a town within a hundred miles of the Canadian border is associated with more accommodating responses on three of eight variables. While the analysis in chapter 4 found that border proximity was associated with greater restriction and, in the case of the Canadian border, more restrictive enforcement practices, in this analysis of individual officials' attitudes, proximity to both the Mexican and Canadian borders is associated with a greater likelihood of saying local governments should *not* be involved with immigration enforcement. Perhaps these towns cooperate in federal enforcement efforts because of their location, but officials do not do so enthusiastically. Last, as the example of Yakima suggests, officials in towns with larger agricultural industries and therefore greater need for immigrant labor are more likely to support accommodating immigrants, by a statistically significant margin on four of eight variables.

10. The analysis employs the statistical software Clarify, and other variables are held at their means. The predicted values for county-level partisanship are one standard deviation below and above the mean, corresponding to 33 percent as opposed to 62 percent of the county voting for Romney in 2012.

11. GSS: "Do you think the number of immigrants to America nowadays should be . . . increased a lot, increased a little, remain the same, reduced a little, reduced a lot?" Gallup: "In your view, should immigration be kept at its present level, increased or decreased? . . . present level, increased, decreased." MRIS: "Do you think the number of immigrants from foreign countries who are permitted to come to the United States to live should be . . . decreased a lot, decreased a little, left the same, increased a little, increased a lot?"

12. *New York Times*: "Would you support or oppose local police taking an active role in identifying undocumented or illegal immigrants? . . . Support, Oppose." MRIS: "What role should local governments play in immigration enforcement? (Please check all that apply.) Local governments . . . should set their own policies and control which immigrants settle in their jurisdictions; . . . should be empowered to enforce federal immigration laws; . . . should participate in immigration enforcement only at federal authorities' request; . . . should not be involved in immigration enforcement; . . . should protect immigrant residents from federal enforcement."

Chapter Six

1. The 2001 Supreme Court ruling *Alexander v. Sandoval* places limits on some civil rights suits, in that parties must demonstrate intentional discrimination rather than discriminatory outcomes.

2. As Nadeau's comment suggests, the external scrutiny generated by Mayor Raymond's letter also spurred the state of Maine to action. Although Lewiston began actively engaging the state on immigration issues in May 2002, the governor did not form his Immigrant and Refugee Task Force, aimed to develop statewide policy on serving immigrants and refugees, until November 2002, after Mayor Raymond's October letter. The state also approved funding for the immigrant and refugee programs manager in October 2002, soon after the letter's release. In December 2002, state agencies involved in serving immigrants formed the New Residents Committee to identify additional resources to serve immigrants. Although these efforts were related to the ongoing growth of the Somali population, analysis by insiders suggests that in large part they were spurred by the external scrutiny generated by the mayor's letter (Nadeau 2003b).

3. I am grateful to Justin Steil for sharing his data with me.

4. As in chapter 4, these models employ clustered standard errors to account for my controlling for variables at the town and state levels. I do not control for proximity to the borders here, since only five of the restrictive cities are within a hundred miles of the Mexican border and none are in similar proximity to Canada. Including or excluding proximity to the Mexican border does not change the results presented here.

5. Here I use the standard deviation and mean of media attention with the high outlier of Hazleton, Pennsylvania, removed in order to display a more realistic range of media attention. Media attention remains a statistically significant predictor of whether ordinances remain in effect even when Hazleton is removed from the analysis. Indeed, the relation is more statistically significant, through the coefficient is smaller.

Chapter Seven

1. I use pseudonyms for the other intermediaries to disguise their identities, but I give Councilor Figueroa's real name because he is a public figure and the nature of his position makes it impossible to disguise his identity.

2. Prema Kurien has also looked at issues of intermediary legitimacy on the national level in the United States, asking how certain national ethnic advocacy groups "come to be recognized as the authentic voices of an ethnic community by U.S. policymakers" (Kurien 2007, 760).

3. Author's analysis. See chapter 4 for a detailed explanation.

4. These findings cannot be attributed to ordering effects, in which the more popularly chosen items were listed more prominently. On the web survey, which 78 percent of respondents completed, the order of the information sources was randomly presented. On the mail survey, immigrant and ethnic NGOs were listed above "individual contacts."

5. As elsewhere in the book, new immigrant destinations are defined as those that were less than 5 percent foreign-born in 1990, were more than 5 percent foreign-born by 2012, and experienced greater than 100 percent growth in their foreign-born population over this period (following Marschall 2017).

6. Pearson's r coefficient equals 0.43 for Latinos, 0.57 for African Americans, and 0.43 for Asians.

7. The three measures have an average interitem correlation of 0.70 and a reliability scale of 0.80.

8. I ran additional analyses that controlled for the local count of efforts to include immigrants in municipal affairs rather than the full accommodating index. This count includes hiring and appointing immigrants, recruiting them to serve on boards and commissions, hiring an immigrant liaison, appointing an immigrant or coethnic to a vacant elected position, and maintaining an immigrant advisory council. Results are essentially the same when controlling for this more specific measure of accommodation, though the count of inclusionary efforts falls below conventional thresholds of significance in predicting whether officials are more likely to see immigrants as well organized in civic life ($p = 0.21$), as well as whether they are less likely to see them as preferring to "keep to themselves" ($p = 0.17$). The count of inclusionary efforts remains a significant predictor of perceptions of greater ethnic minority representation, more interaction with immigrants, and a lesser likelihood of saying immigrants lack skills necessary to participate.

9. As elsewhere, I employ ordinary least squares regression with clustered standard errors to account for controlling for factors at both local and state levels (regression results in appendix table AD5). Dependent variables are continuous and not ordinal, since they represent averages across officials that respond within a given town.

10. This range of accommodation is roughly equivalent to varying accommodation from one standard deviation below the mean to one standard deviation above the mean.

11. On the other hand, officials were not less likely to see immigrants as too busy to participate in places that actively accommodated them. Although the relation between the two variables is not statistically significant, the coefficient is actually positive, suggesting that, if anything, places that are more accommodating are also more likely to perceive immigrants as too busy to take part. As

I will describe below, in new destinations immigrant intermediaries are often overtasked with civic responsibilities, potentially explaining this nonsignificant inverse relation.

12. The results are nearly identical if I instead analyze only the variable measuring officials' conversations with immigrants rather than this summative scale.

13. Puerto Rican leaders have also been embraced as prominent supporters of Mexicans in Chicago (Dominguez 2016, 79).

Chapter Eight

1. As I discuss below, it is possible that local controversies prompted the implementation of practices rather than the accommodating practices causing controversies. At the very least, however, implementing these policies has not assuaged local concerns.

2. While evidence for the constrict theory is mixed, recent reviews suggest that validating studies exceed confuting studies by a statistically significant margin. Merlin Schaeffer's (2014) quantitative analysis of 172 studies concludes that 60 percent confirm the negative relation, and confirmation is more likely in the United States than elsewhere. In a less expansive review, van der Meer and Tolsma (2014) find nearly equal numbers of confirmatory and confuting studies (twenty-six and twenty-five, respectively), along with thirty-nine "mixed" studies in which some findings were confirmatory while others were not.

3. Reviews of literature testing the constrict hypothesis find that diversity's effect on social cohesion is more robust with respect to trust than to participation (Schaeffer 2014; van der Meer and Tolsma 2014). Likewise, prevailing findings suggest that diversity has a more consistent effect on in-group trust than on out-group trust (van der Meer and Tolsma 2014). Thus, any mechanism attempting to explain the constrict relationship should describe the way the presence of ethnic diversity results directly in declining in-group trust. Previously proposed mechanisms fail to do so, but this alternative mechanism, which I refer to as the divergent in-group preferences mechanism, indicates how diversity can directly contribute to declining in-group trust by revealing cleavages within ethnic groups over how to respond (Williamson 2015).

4. Although I have focused here on tensions among long-term residents amid new diversity, immigrant ethnic groups also experience intragroup mistrust arising from disagreements over how to relate to the out-group. In each of the four destinations, immigrant ethnic groups experienced conflict over differing views on balancing cultural preservation and integration, which I describe more fully elsewhere (Williamson 2015).

5. Since both dependent variables are dichotomous, I employ probit models, with clustered standard errors at the state level.

6. See Mollenkopf and Pastor (2016, 275–79) for additional examples of these efforts.

Chapter Nine

1. The list of sanctuary cities (excluding sanctuary counties) includes those that self-identified as sanctuary cities in the 2014 or 2016 wave of the MRIS, those identified by President Trump's Department of Homeland Security in a report mandated by his executive order (US Immigration and Customs Enforcement 2017), those identified by the Catholic Legal Immigration Network (2014), and those identified by an Ohio anti-immigration organization, Ohio Jobs and Justice PAC (OJJPAC) (Ohio Jobs and Justice PAC, n.d.) that tracks mentions of local officials who espouse policies friendly to unauthorized immigrants. To determine the character and status of sanctuary policies in each city, research assistants conducted systematic searches using Google, LexisNexis, and municipal websites. Using a codebook, multiple coders reviewed each city to ensure comprehensive coverage and intercoder reliability.

2. Of these cities, all but four were from the OJJPAC list (see previous note), which has an expansive definition of sanctuary cities that includes even those that have no explicit sanctuary policy but whose officials make statements favorable to unauthorized immigrants. The remaining four self-identified as sanctuary cities on my survey but may have informal sanctuary practices, because we could find no public evidence of such a policy.

3. Research assistants created a comprehensive list drawing on current and archived ICE reports and cross-referenced it with a 2011 Migration Policy Institute report (US Immigration and Customs Enforcement, n.d.a, n.d.b; Capps et al. 2011). We compared archived lists with current lists to determine which agreements were inactive, renewed, and new.

4. Dobbs (2017) suggests that municipal efforts to involve immigrants politically are circumscribed unless political parties are interested in involving the newcomers.

Appendixes

1. Community foundations provide a particularly useful entrée to a community in that they often work across sectors, interacting with donors in the private sector and grantees in the public and nonprofit sectors. I benefited from the con-

tacts that the Saguaro Seminar for Civic Engagement in America had made in conducting the year 2000 Social Capital Community Survey, which was stratified by geographic area and funded by a coalition of national and local community foundations. In Lewiston, the Maine Community Foundation and its academic partners from Lewiston-Auburn College provided an initial list of contacts. In Elgin, the Evanston Community Foundation directed me to the Grand Victoria Foundation, which provided an initial list of contacts. In Wausau, the Community Foundation of North Central Wisconsin provided initial contacts. In Yakima, academics at the University of Washington provided initial contacts in the Yakima nonprofit sector who in turn directed me to others.

2. In 2004 I worked with Dr. María Chávez to conduct interviews in Yakima. In January 2008 my translators were from Bridges Language, Training, and Staffing in Elgin and Alba Enterprises in Yakima.

3. Owing to their demographic or administrative characteristics, no towns from Alaska, Hawaii, Nebraska, and Montana were sampled.

4. Analyzing 231 surveys of organizational executives published in top management journals from 1992 to 2003, Cycyota and Harrison (2006) found average response rates of 32 percent, with response rates declining over time. Analyzing 117 studies across seventeen highly ranked management and behavioral science journals, Baruch and Holtom (2008) find average response rates of 36 percent, though not all of these surveys addressed executives like the local government officials in question here. Looking specifically at surveys of local government officials' responses to immigrants, Ramakrishnan and Lewis's (2005) 2003 California survey received responses from 86 percent of cities, though they interviewed more than four officials in each city. They received response rates of 62 percent among police chiefs and 30 percent among elected officials. My response rate of 25 percent for elected officials is only slightly lower. It also exceeds the 20 percent response rate from a 2012 survey of elected municipal officials (Butler and Dynes 2016). More recent response rates for police chiefs have ranged from 19 percent (Williams 2015) to 52 percent (Lewis et al. 2013), placing my police response rate toward the top of that range and well above the averages reported in the broader meta-analyses.

References

Abbs, Donald B. 2007. "AFLA Trying to Offer Local Solutions to Illegals Problem." *Elgin Courier News*, December 12.

Abrajano, Marisa, and Zoltan Hajnal. 2015. *White Backlash: Immigration, Race, and American Politics*. Princeton, NJ: Princeton University Press.

Agusti-Panareda, Jordi. 2006. "Cross-cultural Brokering in the Legal, Institutional and Normative Domains: Intercultural Mediators Managing Immigration in Catalonia." *Social and Legal Studies* 15 (3): 409–33.

Ahler, Douglas, and David E. Broockman, n.d. "The Delegate Paradox: Why Polarized Politicians Can Represent Citizens Best." *Journal of Politics*, forthcoming.

Alesina, A., and E. La Ferrara. 2000. "Participation in Heterogeneous Communities." *Quarterly Journal of Economics* 115:847–904.

———. 2002. "Who Trusts Others?" *Journal of Public Economics* 85:207–34.

Alexander, Michael. 2003. "Local Policies toward Migrants as an Expression of Host–Stranger Relations: A Proposed Typology." *Journal of Ethnic and Migration Studies* 29 (3): 411–30.

———. 2007. *Cities and Labour Immigration: Comparing Policy Responses in Amsterdam, Paris, Rome and Tel Aviv*. Surrey, UK: Ashgate.

Alft, E. C. 2000. *Elgin: An American History*. Elgin, IL: ElginHistory.com.

Allport, Gordon W. 1954. *The Nature of Prejudice*. Reading, MA: Addison-Wesley.

Ammons, David N., and Charldean Newell. 1989. *City Executives: Leadership Roles, Work Characteristics, and Time Management*. Albany: State University of New York Press.

Anderson, Kristi. 2008. "Parties, Organizations, and Political Incorporation: Immigrants in Six U.S. Cities." In *Civic Hopes and Political Realities: Immigrants, Community Organizations, and Political Engagement*, edited by Karthick S. Ramakrishnan and Irene Bloemraad. New York: Russell Sage Foundation.

Anderson, Kristi, and Elizabeth F. Cohen. 2005. "Political Institutions and Incorporation of Immigrants." In *The Politics of Democratic Inclusion*, edited
by Rodney E. Hero and Christina Wolbrecht, 186–205. Philadelphia: Temple
University Press.

"Arizona Demonstrates the Lunacy of Mass Deportations." 2011. *Washington
Post*, March 28.

Bada, X., J. Fox, E. Zazueta, and I. Garcia. 2006. "Immigrant Marches Database." *Mexico Institute: Mexican Migrant Civic and Political Participation,
Woodrow Wilson International Center for Scholars*, August 1. Accessed August, 2013, at http://www.wilsoncenter.org/publication/2006-immigration
-marches-database.

Badger, Emily. 2017. "Blue Cities Want to Make Their Own Rules. Red States
Won't Let Them." *New York Times*, July 6.

Bailey, Mike. 1999. "And the City Council Winner Will Be." *Elgin Courier
News*, May 9.

Bain, Kaitlin. 2017. "Yakima City Council Declines to Move Forward on Formalizing Immigration Policy." *Yakima Herald Republic*, July 12.

Baker, Bryan, and Nancy Rytina. 2014. *Estimates of the Lawful Permanent Resident Population in the United States: January 2013*. Washington, DC: US
Department of Homeland Security, Office of Immigration Statistics. https://
www.dhs.gov/sites/default/files/publications/ois_lpr_pe_2013_0.pdf.

Banting, Keith, and Will Kymlicka. 2013. "Is There Really a Retreat from Multiculturalism Policies? New Evidence from the Multiculturalism Policy Index."
Comparative European Politics 11 (5): 577–98.

Barreto, Matt A. 2007. "¡Si Se Puede! Latino Candidates and the Mobilization
of Latino Voters." *American Political Science Review* 101 (3): 425–41.

Barrett, Ted, Dana Bash, and Deirdre Walsh. 2013. "Immigration Q&A: Amnesty or Path to Citizenship?" *CNN*, January 29. Accessed June 1, 2016, at
http://www.cnn.com/2013/
01/28/politics/immigration-qa/.

Baruch, Yehuda, and Brooks C. Holtom. 2008. "Survey Response Rate Levels
and Trends in Organizational Research." *Human Relations* 61 (8): 1139–60.

Bazelon, Emily. 2017. "Department of Justification." *New York Times*, February 28.

Beck, Roy. 1994. "The Ordeal of Immigration in Wausau." *Atlantic Monthly* 273
(4): 84–97.

Belson, Ken, and Jill P. Capuzoo. 2007. "Towns Rethink Laws against Illegal
Immigrants." *New York Times*, September 26.

Benjamin-Alvarado, Jonathan, Louis DeSipio, and Celeste Montoya. 2009. "Latino Mobilization in New Immigrant Destinations: The Anti-H.R. 4437 Protest in Nebraska's Cities." *Urban Affairs Review* 44 (5): 718–35.

Bergal, Jenni. 2015. "Cities Forge Policy apart from States." *Pew Charitable Trusts*, January 15. Accessed May 5, 2016, at http://www.pewtrusts.org/en/research-and-analysis/blogs/stateline/2015/1/15/cities-forge-policy-apart-from-states.

Bernal, Rafael. 2017. "Trump Administration Will No Longer Treat Miami as 'Sanctuary City.'" *Hill*, August 7. Accessed August 9, 2017, at http://thehill.com/latino/345660-trump-administration-will-no-longer-treat-miami-as-sanctuary-city.

Besteman, Catherine. 2016. *Making Refuge: Somali Bantu Refugees and Lewiston, Maine*. Chapel Hill, NC: Duke University Press.

Besteman, Catherine, and Ismail Ahmed. 2010. "Refugee Economic Impact Study, Lewiston, Maine." Accessed February 4, 2016, at http://www.scribd.com/doc/75938418/Refugee-Economic-Impact-Study-Lewiston-Maine.

Blalock, Hubert M., Jr. 1967. *Toward a Theory of Minority-Group Relations*. New York: John Wiley.

Bledsoe, Timothy. 1993. *Careers in City Politics: The Case for Democracy*. Pittsburgh: University of Pittsburgh Press.

Bleich, Erik. 2002. "Integrating Ideas into Policy-Making Analysis: Frames and Race Policies in Britain and France." *Comparative Political Studies* 35 (9): 1054–76.

Bloemraad, Irene. 2006. *Becoming a Citizen: Incorporating Immigrants and Refugees in the United States and Canada*. Berkeley: University of California Press.

Bloemraad, Irene, and Els de Graauw. 2012. "Immigrant Integration and Policy in the United States: A Loosely Stitched Patchwork." In *International Perspectives: Integration and Inclusion*, edited by James Frideres and John Biles, 205–32. Montreal: McGill-Queen's University Press.

Bonacich, Edna. 1973. "A Theory of Middlemen Minorities." *American Sociological Review* 38:583–94.

Bouffard, Kevin, and Aurora Rodriguez. 2006. "Who's Welcome, Who's Not? Many Business People Say Proposed Ordinance Would Cut Sales Dramatically." *Ledger*, July 23.

Brader, Ted, Nicholas A. Valentino, and Elizabeth Suhay. 2008. "What Triggers Public Opposition to Immigration? Anxiety, Group Cues, and Immigration Threat." *American Journal of Political Science* 52 (4): 959–78.

Branton, Regina, Valerie Martinez-Ebers, Tony E. Carey, and Tetsuya Matsubayashi. 2015. "Social Protest and Policy Attitudes: The Case of the 2006 Immigrant Rallies." *American Journal of Political Science* 59 (2): 390–402.

Brettell, Caroline B. 2008. "'Big D': Incorporating New Immigrants in a Sunbelt Suburban Metropolis." In *Twenty-First Century Gateways: Immigrant Integration in Suburban America*, edited by A. Singer, S. W. Hardwick, and C. B. Brettell, 53–86. Washington, DC: Brookings Institution Press.

Briggs, Xavier de Souza. 2003. *Working the Middle: Roles and Challenges of Intermediaries*. Cambridge, MA: Art and Science of Community Problem-Solving Project at Harvard University.

Bristol, Chris. 2008. "Demise of Citizens Advisory Group for Police Frustrates Members." *Yakima Herald-Republic*, February 17.

———. 2009. "Conservatives Say Election Was Not Race-Based." *Yakima Herald-Republic*, November 5.

Brooks, Nicole, and Steven Ross Johnson. 2007. "Is Language the Answer?" *Elgin Courier News*, December 9.

Browning, Rufus P., Dale Rogers Marshall, and David H. Tabb. 1984. *Protest Is Not Enough*. Berkeley: University of California Press.

———, eds. 2003. *Racial Politics in American Cities*. 3rd ed. New York: Addison-Wesley Education Publishers.

Brunner, Jim. 2011. "In Yakima, Other Areas, Growing Latino Population Invisible Politically." *Seattle Times*, July 2.

Brunschon, Dennis. 2007. "Worried about Popularity with Spanish Citizens." *Elgin Courier News*, December 21.

Bumiller, Kristin. 1992. *The Civil Rights Society: The Social Construction of Victims*. Baltimore: Johns Hopkins University Press.

Burt, R. 1992. *Structural Holes: The Social Structure of Competition*. Cambridge, MA: Harvard University Press.

Butler, Daniel M., and Adam M. Dynes. 2016. "How Politicians Discount the Opinions of Constituents with Whom They Disagree." *American Journal of Political Science* 60 (4): 975–89.

Calandriello, Erin. 2008. "U46 Chooses Its New Superintendent." *Chicago Daily Herald*, May 6.

Campbell, Andrea Louise. 2005. *How Policies Make Citizens: Senior Political Activism and the American Welfare State*. Princeton, NJ: Princeton University Press.

Canfield, Clark. 2012. "Maine Mayor: Somalis Should Leave Culture at Door." *Associated Press*, October 4.

Capps, Kriston. 2015. "Governors Don't Want Syrian Refugees. Mayors Are Asking for Even More." *Atlantic Monthly–CityLab*, November 19. Accessed July 12, 2016, at http://www.citylab.com/politics/2015/11/governors-who-dont -want-syrian-refugees-versus-mayors-who-are-asking-to-take-more/416718/.

Capps, Randy, Michael Fix, Julie Murray, Jason Ost, Jeffrey S. Passel, and Shinta Herwantoro. 2005. *The New Demography of America's Schools: Immigration and the No Child Left Behind Act*. Washington, DC: Urban Institute.

Capps, Randy, Marc R. Rosenblum, Cristina Rodriguez, and Muzaffar Chishti. 2011. *Delegation and Divergence: A Study of 287(g) State and Local Immigration Enforcement*. Washington, DC: Migration Policy Institute.

Carnes, Nicholas. 2013. *White-Collar Government: The Hidden Role of Class in Economic Policy Making*. Chicago: University of Chicago Press.

Casas, Gloria. 2015. "Centro Continues Meeting Needs in Hispanic Community." *Elgin Courier News*, May 6.

Catholic Legal Immigration Network (CLINIC). 2014. "States and Localities That Limit Compliance with ICE Detainer Requests." Accessed July 27, 2017, at https://cliniclegal.org/sites/default/files/anti-detainer_policies_11_21 _14.pdf.

CBS News Transcripts. 1994. "Enough: Wausau Tries to Deal with Improving the Living Standards of Its Increasing Immigrant Influx While Keeping the Standard of Living up for Its Original Inhabitants." *CBS News*, October 16.

Chambers, Stefanie. 2017. *Somalis in the Twin Cities and Columbus: Immigrant Incorporation in New Destinations*. Philadelphia: Temple University Press.

Chambers, Stefanie, Diana Evans, Anthony Messina, and Abigail Fisher Williamson. 2017. *The Politics of New Immigrant Destinations: Transatlantic Perspectives*. Philadelphia: Temple University Press.

Chavez, Leo. 2013. *The Latino Threat Narrative: Constructing Immigrants, Citizens, and the Nation*. Palo Alto, CA: Stanford University Press.

"Chicago Matters: Beyond Borders; Live Forum from Elgin." 2007. WTTW, October 2.

Chong, Dennis, and James N. Druckman. 2007. "Framing Theory." *Annual Review of Political Science* 10:103–26.

City Council of Hazleton, Pennsylvania. 2006. *Illegal Immigration Relief Act Ordinance*. Accessed May 31, 2016, at https://www.aclu.org/hazleton-pa -ordinance-no-2006-18.

City of Lewiston. 2008. "City Council Minutes." January 7. Accessed June 7, 2016, at http://www.lewistonmaine.gov/ArchiveCenter/ViewFile/Item/432.

———. 2017. "Legacy Lewiston: City of Lewiston Draft Comprehensive Plan." Accessed December 1, 2017, at http://www.lewistonmaine.gov/Document Center/View/7101.

City of Wausau. n.d. *Minority Affairs Office*. Brochure.

City of Yakima. n.d. "About Yakima." Accessed June 7, 2016, at https://www .yakimawa.gov/visit/about/.

Cohen, Cathy. 1999. *The Boundaries of Blackness: AIDS and the Breakdown of Black Politics*. Chicago: University of Chicago Press.

Constable, Pamela. 2008. "Bill on Migrants Splits a Town with Few; What Some Called a Preventive Measure Seemed to Others an Effort to Fan Biases." *Washington Post*, January 15.

Cook, James. 2016. "President-Elect Trump Insults Maine Residents, but Is He Right?" *Central Maine*, December 13. Accessed August 8, 2017, at http://www .centralmaine.com/2016/12/13/president-elect-trump-insults-maine-residents

-but-is-he-right-examining-crime-data-in-maine-and-beyond-shows-that
-evidence-fails-to-support-donald-trumps-denigration-of-refugees-in-maine
-james-co/.

Costa, Dora, and Matthew Kahn. 2003. "Civic Engagement and Community Heterogeneity, An Economist's Perspective." *Perspectives on Politics*. 1:103–11.

Cox, Ted. 2010. "28 Arrested in ICE Sweep." *Daily Herald*, April 29.

Cramer, Katherine J. 2016. *The Politics of Resentment: Rural Consciousness in Wisconsin and the Rise of Scott Walker*. Chicago: University of Chicago Press.

Cullen, Andrew. 2011. "A Decade Later: The City, Somalis and Spending." *Lewiston Sun Journal*, December 18.

Cycyota, C. S., and D. A. Harrison. 2006. "What (Not) to Expect When Surveying Executives." *Organizational Research Methods* 9:133–60.

Dahl, Robert. 1961. *Who Governs? Democracy and Power in an American City*. New Haven, CT: Yale University Press.

Dally, Chad. 2010. "Diversity Effort's Future Uncertain in Wausau, Marathon County." *Wausau Daily Herald*, November 20.

Davis, Sarah. 2012. "'Welcoming Maine' Seeks to Integrate New and Native Mainers." *Twin City Times*, September 13.

de Graauw, Els. 2013. "Immigrants and Political Incorporation in the United States." In *Immigrants in American History: Arrival, Adaptation, and Integration*, edited by Elliott Robert Barkan, 4:1875–92. Santa Barbara: ABC-CLIO Books.

———. 2014. "Municipal ID Cards for Undocumented Immigrants: Local Bureaucratic Membership in a Federal System." *Politics and Society* 42 (3): 309–30.

———. 2015. "Polyglot Bureaucracies: Nonprofit Advocacy to Create Inclusive City Governments." *Journal of Immigrant and Refugee Studies* 13 (2): 156–78.

———. 2016. *Making Immigrant Rights Real*. Ithaca, NY: Cornell University Press.

de Graauw, Els, Shannon Gleeson, and Irene Bloemraad. 2013. "Funding Immigrant Organizations: Suburban Free Riding and Local Civic Presence." *American Journal of Sociology* 119 (1): 75–130.

Derthick, Martha. 1979. *Policymaking for Social Security*. Washington, DC: Brookings Institution.

DeSipio, Louis. 2001. "Building America, One Person at a Time: Naturalization and Political Behavior of the Naturalized in Contemporary American Politics." In *E Pluribus Unum: Contemporary and Historical Perspectives on Immigrant Political Incorporation*, edited by Gary Gerstle and John Mollenkopf, 67–106. New York: Russell Sage Foundation.

Deufel, Benjamin J. 2006. "Trial Membership: Responses to Immigrants in American Communities." PhD diss., Harvard University.

Dewees, Sarah, Linda Lobao, and Louis E. Swanson. 2003. "Local Economic Development in an Age of Devolution: The Question of Rural Localities." *Rural Sociology* 68 (2): 182–206.

Diaz, Fernando. 2009. "Driving While Latino." *Chicago Reporter*, March 1.

Dillman, Don A., Jolene D. Smyth, and Leah Melani Christian. 2008. *Internet, Mail, and Mixed-Mode Surveys: The Tailored Design Method.* New York: John Wiley.

DiStefano, John. 2007. "'Elm City Resident Card' Helps All Residents Access City Services–and More in New Haven." *U.S. Conference of Mayors*, August 13. Accessed May 31, 2016, at http://www.usmayors.org/uscm/us_mayor _newspaper/documents/08_13_07/pg3_new_haven.asp. Discontinued.

"District U-46 Settles Discrimination Case for $2.5 Million." 2014. *Daily Herald*, February 25.

Dobbin, Frank, and John R. Sutton. 1998. "The Strength of a Weak State: The Rights Revolution and the Rise of Human Resources Management Divisions." *American Journal of Sociology* 104 (2): 441–76.

Dobbs, Erica. 2017. "Bureaucrats and the Ballot Box: State-Led Political Incorporation in Ireland." In *The Politics of New Immigrant Destinations: Transatlantic Perspectives*, edited by Stefanie Chambers, Diana Evans, Anthony Messina, and Abigail Fisher Williamson, 41–60. Philadelphia: Temple University Press.

Dolan, Julie, and David H. Rosenbloom. 2003. *Representative Bureaucracy: Classic Readings and Continuing Controversies.* Armonk, NY: M. E. Sharpe.

Dominguez, Jaime. 2016. "Machine Matters: The Politics of Immigrant Integration in the Chicago Metro Area." In *Unsettled Americans: Metropolitan Context and Civic Leadership for Immigrant Integration*, edited by John Mollenkopf and Manuel Pastor, 77–101. Ithaca, NY: Cornell University Press.

Donato, Katharine M., and Leslie Ann Rodríguez. 2014. "Police Arrests in a Time of Uncertainty: The Impact of 287(g) on Arrests in a New Immigrant Gateway." *American Behavioral Scientist* 58 (13): 1696–722.

Dovi, Suzanne. 2007. *The Good Representative.* Malden, MA: Blackwell.

Downing, Suzanne. 2017. "Homer City Council Members Certify Their Own Election." *Must Read Alaska*, July 1. Accessed August 9, 2017, at http://mustreadalaska.com/homer-city-council-certify-own-election/.

Dritschilo, Gordon. 2016. "Migration to Maine: A Look into How Lewiston Embraced Somalis." *Barre-Montpelier Times-Argus*, July 10.

Duffy, John. 2007. *Writing from These Roots: Literacy in a Hmong-American Community.* Honolulu: University of Hawaii Press.

Ebert, Kim, and Dina G. Okamoto. 2013. "Social Citizenship, Integration and

Collective Action: Immigrant Civic Engagement in the United States." *Social Forces* 91 (4): 1267–92.

Eilperin, Juliet, Emma Brown, and Darryl Fears. 2017. "Trump Administration Plans to Minimize Civil Rights Efforts in Agencies." *Washington Post*, May 29.

Einstein, Katherine Levine, and David M. Glick. 2016. "Mayors, Partisanship, and Redistribution: Evidence Directly from U.S. Mayors." *Urban Affairs Review*, November 28.

Einstein, Katherine Levine, and Vladimir Kogan. 2016. "Pushing the City Limits: Policy Responsiveness in Municipal Governance." *Urban Affairs Review* 52 (1): 3–32.

"Elgin, Illinois, Will Revamp Enforcement of Occupancy Code to Settle Complaints by Hispanic Families of Housing Discrimination." 1999. *PR Newswire*, October 8.

Ellison, Jesse. 2009. "Lewiston, Maine, Revived by Somali Immigrants." *Newsweek*, January 16.

Enos, Ryan D. 2014. "Causal Effect of Intergroup Contact on Exclusionary Attitudes." *Proceedings of the National Academy of Sciences* 111 (10): 3699–704.

Epp, Charles R. 2009. *Making Rights Real: Activists, Bureaucrats, and the Creation of the Legalistic State*. Chicago: University of Chicago Press.

Epp, Charles R., Steven Maynard-Moody, and Donald P. Haider-Markel. 2014. *Pulled Over: How Police Stops Define Race and Citizenship*. Chicago: University of Chicago Press.

Ersanilli, Evelyn, and Ruud Koopmans. 2011. "Do Immigrant Integration Policies Matter? A Three-Country Comparison among Turkish Immigrants." *West European Politics* 34 (2): 208–34.

Evans, Thayer. 2007. "English Proposal Still Pursued in Friendswood." *Houston Chronicle*, January 29.

Fahim, Kareem. 2007. "Presidential Candidate Blames Killings on Newark Sanctuary Policy." *New York Times*, August 21.

Fair Immigration Reform Movement (FIRM). 2007. "Database of Recent Local Ordinances on Immigration." Accessed September 25, 2015, at observatoriocolef.org/_admin/ . . . /FIRM-LocalLegislationDatabase.doc. Discontinued.

Fandetti, D. V., and J. Goldmeier. 1988. "Social Workers as Culture Mediators in Health Care Settings." *Health and Social Work* 13 (3): 171–79.

Farris, Emily M., and Mirya R. Holman. 2017. "All Politics Is Local? County Sheriffs and Localized Policies of Immigration Enforcement." *Political Research Quarterly* 70 (1): 142–54.

Faulk, Mike. 2011. "Yakima Council Accepts Mexican Hero's Bust." *Yakima Herald Republic*, April 20.

———, 2015. "Voting Rights: Despite Pleas, Yakima Council Stands By Appeal of ACLU Case." *Yakima Herald Republic*, June 16.

———. 2016. "Yakima City Council Abandons Appeal of ACLU Voting Rights Suit." *Yakima Herald Republic*, April 8.

Fazio, Russell, and Laura Hilden. 2001. "Emotional Reactions to a Seemingly Prejudiced Response." *Personality and Social Psychology* 27 (5): 538–49.

Ferrarin, Elena. 2014. "New Elgin Council Member Appointed." *Daily Herald*, May 28.

———. 2017. "Elgin Police Not Changing Stance on Immigration." *Daily Herald*. February 27.

Ferreira, Fernando, and Joseph Gyourko. 2009. "Do Political Parties Matter? Evidence from U.S. Cities." *Quarterly Journal of Economics* 124 (1): 349–97.

Filindra, Alexandra, and Shanna Pearson-Merkowitz. 2013. "Research Note: Stopping the Enforcement 'Tide': Descriptive Representation, Latino Institutional Empowerment, and State-Level Immigration Policy." *Politics and Policy* 41 (6): 814–32.

Fletcher, Michael A. 2000. "Latinos See Bias in Elgin's Fight against Blight." *Washington Post*, May 29.

Flores, René D. 2014. "Living in the Eye of the Storm: How Did Hazleton's Restrictive Immigration Ordinance Affect Local Interethnic Relations?" *American Behavioral Scientist* 58 (13): 1743–63.

Florida, Richard. 2002. *The Rise of the Creative Class: And How It's Transforming Work, Leisure, Community and Everyday Life.* New York: Basic Books.

Frasure, Lorrie A., and Michael Jones-Correa. 2010. "The Logic of Institutional Interdependency: The Case of Day Laborer Policy in Suburbia." *Urban Affairs Review* 45 (4): 451–82.

Frasure-Yokley, Lorrie. 2015. *Racial and Ethnic Politics in American Suburbs.* New York: Cambridge University Press.

Freeman, G. 1995. "Modes of Immigration Policies in Liberal Democratic States." *International Migration Review* 29 (4): 881–902.

French, P. Edward. 2005. "Policy, Management, and Political Activities: A Current Evaluation of the Time Allocations of Mayors and Managers in Small Cities and Towns." *Social Science Journal* 42 (4): 499–510.

French, P. Edward, and David H. Folz. 2004. "Executive Behavior and Decision Making in Small U.S. Cities." *American Review of Public Administration* 34 (1): 52–66.

Froberg, Vincent A. 2007. "Other Questions for the Mayor, City Council." *Elgin Courier News*, December 21.

"Full Text: Donald Trump Announces a Presidential Bid." 2015. *Washington Post*, June 16. Accessed August 10, 2017, at https://www.washingtonpost.com/news/post-politics/wp/2015/06/16/full-text-donald-trump-announces-a-presidential-bid/?utm_term=.dfce057872c3#annotations:7468752.

Furuseth, Owen, and Heather Smith. 2010. "Localized Immigration Policy: The View from Charlotte, North Carolina, a New Immigrant Gateway." In *Taking Local Control: Immigration Policy Activism in U.S. Cities and States*, edited by Monica W. Varsanyi, 173–92. Palo Alto, CA: Stanford University Press.

Galofaro, Claire. 2017. "How a Community Changed by Refugees Came to Embrace Trump." *Associated Press*, April 19. Accessed August 8, 2017, at https://apnews.com/7f2b534b80674596875980b9b6e701c9.

Gamson, William A., and Andre Modigliani. 1987. "The Changing Culture of Affirmative Action." In *Research in Political Sociology*, edited by Richard D. Braungart, 3:137–77. Greenwich, CT: JAI Press.

García Bedolla, Lisa. 2005. *Fluid Borders: Latino Power, Identity, and Politics in Los Angeles*. Berkeley: University of California Press.

Garvey, Deborah L. 2007. "Designing an Impact Aid Program for Immigrant Settlement." In *Securing the Future: U.S. Immigrant Integration Policy*, edited by Michael Fix, 153–64. Washington, DC: Migration Policy Institute.

Gathman, Dave. 2015. "Chicago Candidate 'Chuy' Garcia Wishes Trump Could See Elgin-area Latinos." *Elgin Courier News*, September 12.

Gelatt, Julia, and Michael Fix. 2007. "Federal Spending on Immigrant Families' Integration." In *Securing the Future: US Immigrant Integration Policy*, edited by Michael Fix, 61–80. Washington, DC: Migration Policy Institute.

Gerber, Elisabeth R., and Daniel J. Hopkins. 2011. "When Mayors Matter: Estimating the Impact of Mayoral Partisanship on City Policy." *American Journal of Political Science* 55 (2): 326–39.

Gerstle, Gary, and John H. Mollenkopf. 2001. *E Pluribus Unum? Contemporary and Historical Perspectives on Immigrant Political Incorporation*. New York: Russell Sage Foundation.

Gilbert, Larry. 2011. "Mayor's Corner: Recent Mass Immigration Isn't So Recent; It's 10 Years Old." *Twin City Times*, September 22.

Gilbert, Lauren. 2009. "Citizenship, Civic Virtue, and Immigrant Integration: The Enduring Power of Community-Based Norms." *Yale Law and Policy Review* 27:335–89.

Gilens, Martin. 2012. *Affluence and Influence: Economic Inequality and Political Power in America*. Princeton, NJ: Princeton University Press.

Gilens, Martin, Paul Sniderman, and James Kuklinski. 1998. "Affirmative Action and the Politics of Realignment." *British Journal of Political Science* 28 (1): 159–83.

Glaser, James. 2003. "Social Context and Inter-group Political Attitudes: Experiments in Group Conflict Theory." *British Journal of Political Science* 33 (4): 607–20.

Gleeson, Shannon, and Irene Bloemraad. 2013. "Assessing the Scope of Immigrant Organizations Official Undercounts and Actual Underrepresentation." *Nonprofit and Voluntary Sector Quarterly* 42 (2): 346–70.

Gonzalez-Barrera, Ana, and Jens Manuel Krogstad. 2014. "U.S. Deportations of Immigrants Reach Record High in 2013." *Pew Research Center*, October 2. Accessed April 10, 2016, at http://www.pewresearch.org/fact-tank/2014/10/02/u-s-deportations-of-immigrants-reach-record-high-in-2013/.

Gonzalez-Barrera, Ana, and Mark Hugo Lopez. 2016. "U.S. Immigrant Deportations Fall to Lowest Level since 2007." *Pew Research Center*, December 16. http://www.pewresearch.org/fact-tank/2016/12/16/u-s-immigrant-deportations-fall-to-lowest-level-since-2007/.

Gozdziak, Elzbieta M., and Susan F. Martin, eds. 2005. *Beyond the Gateway: Immigrants in a Changing America*. Lanham, MD: Lexington Books.

Graham, Hugh Davis. 2001. "Affirmative Action for Immigrants? The Unintended Consequences of Reform." In *Color Lines: Affirmative Action, Immigration, and Civil Rights Options for America*, edited by John David Skrentny, 53–70. Chicago: University of Chicago Press.

Gregory, John. 2013. "Mayors Want Immigration Reform." *WBGZ Radio*, October 25.

Griswold, Eliza. 2016. "Why Is It So Difficult for Syrian Refugees to Get into the U.S.?" *New York Times Magazine*, January 20.

Gulasekaram, Prattheepan, and S. Karthick Ramakrishnan. 2015. *The New Immigration Federalism*. New York: Cambridge University Press.

Gundel, Joakim. 2003. "The Migration-Development Nexus: Somalia Case Study." In *The Migration Development Nexus*, edited by Nicholas Van Hear and Ninna Nyberg Sorenson, 233–58. Geneva: International Organization for Migration.

Guskin, Emily. 2013. "'Illegal,' 'Undocumented,' 'Unauthorized': News Media Shift Language on Immigration." *Pew Research Center*, June 17. Accessed September 25, 2015, at http://www.pewresearch.org/fact-tank/2013/06/17/illegal-undocumented-unauthorized-news-media-shift-language-on-immigration/.

Guzman, Daniel Eduardo. 2010. "There Be No Shelter Here: Anti-immigrant Housing Ordinances and Comprehensive Reform." *Cornell Journal of Law and Public Policy* 20 (2): 399–439.

Hainmueller, Jens, and Michael Hiscox. 2010. "Attitudes toward Highly Skilled and Low-Skilled Immigration: Evidence from a Survey Experiment." *American Political Science Review* 104 (1): 61–84.

Hainmueller, Jens, and Daniel Hopkins. 2014. "Public Attitudes toward Immigration." *Annual Review of Political Science* 17:225–49.

———. 2015. "The Hidden American Immigration Consensus: A Conjoint Analysis of Attitudes toward Immigrants." *American Journal of Political Science* 59 (3): 529–48.

Hajnal, Zoltan. 2014. "Why the Democratic Party–Not Just the GOP–Has an Immigration Problem." *Scholars Strategy Network Basic Facts*, December. Accessed April 12, 2016, at http://www.scholarsstrategynetwork.org/brief/why-democratic-party-%E2%80%93-not-just-gop-%E2%80%93-has-immigration-problem.

Hajnal, Zoltan L., and Jessica Trounstine. 2010. "Who or What Governs? The Effects of Economics, Politics, Institutions, and Needs on Local Spending." *American Politics Research* 38 (6): 1130–63.

Hantschel, Allison. 1999a. "Former Outreach Worker Applies for Council Seat." *Elgin Courier News*, May 11.

———. 1999b. "Elgin Councilman Organizing 'Housing Fair.'" *Elgin Courier News*, August 29.

Harris, Bernard. 2007. "Council to Back 'Earned Amnesty' Legislation." *Lancaster Online*, January 23. Accessed January 27, 2016, at http://lancasteronline.com/news/council-to-back-earned-amnesty-legislation/article_585aaf19-148d-5406-871a-3986b805c93d.html.

Haughney, Christine. 2013. "The Times Shifts on 'Illegal Immigrant,' but Doesn't Ban the Use." *New York Times*, April 23.

Hawes, Daniel P., and Rene R. Rocha. 2011. "Social Capital, Racial Diversity, and Equity: Evaluating the Determinants of Equity in the United States." *Political Research Quarterly* 64 (4): 924–37.

Hays, Michael. 2007. "Council OKs Law to Ensure Legal Employment, City Gives Final Stamp on Immigration Ordinance." *Havasu News*, March 14.

Hein, Jeremy. 1994. "From Migrant to Minority: Hmong Refugees and the Social Construction of Identity in the United States." *Sociological Inquiry* 64 (3): 281–306.

Hernández-León, Rubén, and Victor Zúñiga. 2005. "Appalachia Meets Aztlán: Mexican Immigration and Inter-group Relations in Dalton, Georgia." In *New Destinations: Mexican Immigration to the United States*, edited by V. Zúñiga and R. Hernández-León, 244–73. New York: Russell Sage Foundation.

Hero, Rodney. 2007. *Racial Diversity and Social Capital: Equality and Community in America*. Cambridge: Cambridge University Press.

Hertel, Nora. 2015a. "Hmong Memorial Donor Will Match up to $100K." *Wausau Daily Herald*, June 12.

———. 2015b. "Hmong Memorial Organizers Ready for Fundraising Push to Bring Sculpture to Marathon County." *Wausau Daily Herald*, June 13.

Higham, John. 1983. *Strangers in the Land: Patterns of American Nativism, 1860–1925*. New Brunswick, NJ: Rutgers University Press.

Hinckley, Story. 2017. "In One Town, How Mainers and New Immigrants Learned to Coexist–until Trump." *Christian Science Monitor*, March 6. Accessed August 8, 2017, at https://www.csmonitor.com/USA/Society/2017/0306/In-one-town-how-Mainers-and-new-immigrants-learned-to-coexist-until-Trump.

Hitzeman, Harry. 2008a. "'It's a Better Elgin Now' and City Wants It to Continue." *Daily Herald*, October 12.

——. 2008b. "Elgin to Pursue Illegals in City New Screening, Job Checks Eyed." *Daily Herald*, January 23.

——. 2009a. "Did Immigration Group Affect Elgin City Council Race?" *Daily Herald*, April 9.

——. 2009b. "Elgin to Audit More for Illegal City Workers." *Daily Herald*, September 20.

——. 2010. "Elgin Police Chief: Illegal Immigration Is a Federal Issue." *Daily Herald*, February 25.

Hochschild, Jennifer L. 2010. "International Migration at a Crossroads: Will Demography Change Politics before Politics Impedes Demographic Change?" Paper prepared for conference on Citizenship in a Globalized World: Perspectives from the Immigrant Democracies, University of New South Wales, Australia, July 13–15.

Hochschild, Jennifer, Jacqueline Chattopadhay, Claudine Gay, and Michael Jones-Correa. 2013. *Outsiders No More? Models of Immigrant Political Incorporation*. Oxford: Oxford University Press.

Hodgkin, Doug. 2001. "Historic Lewiston: A Self-Guided Tour of Our History, Architecture, and Culture." Historic Preservation Review Board, City of Lewiston, Maine. http://www.ci.lewiston.me.us/DocumentCenter/Home/View/1141.

Hopkins, Daniel J. 2010. "Politicized Places: Explaining Where and When Immigrants Provoke Local Opposition." *American Political Science Review* 104 (1): 40–60.

——. 2011. "National Debates, Local Responses: The Origins of Local Concern about Immigration in Britain and the United States." *British Journal of Political Science* 41 (3): 499–524.

Hopkins, Daniel J., Van C. Tran, and Abigail Fisher Williamson. 2014. "See No Spanish: Language, Local Context, and Attitudes toward Immigration." *Politics, Groups, and Identities* 2 (1): 35–51.

Horton, Sarah. 2004. "Different Subjects: The Health Care System's Participation in the Differential Construction of the Cultural Citizenship of Cuban Refugees and Mexican Immigrants." *Medical Anthropology Quarterly* 18 (4): 472–89.

Huber, Gregory A., and John S. Lapinski. 2006. "The Race Card Revisited: Assessing Racial Priming in Policy Contests." *American Journal of Political Science* 50 (2): 421–40.

Huckfeldt, Robert, and Paul Allen Beck. 1994. "Contexts, Intermediaries, and Political Behavior." In *The Dynamics of American Politics: Approaches and Interpretations*, edited by Lawrence C. Dodd and Calvin Jillson, 252–76. Boulder, CO: Westview Press.

"HUD Report Details Possible Housing Discrimination against Hispanic Families in Elgin, IL." 2000. *PR Newswire*, August 1.

Huntington, Samuel. 2004. *Who Are We? The Challenges to America's National Identity*. New York: Simon and Schuster.

Huseman, Jessica, and Annie Waldman. 2017. "Trump Administration Quietly Rolls Back Civil Rights Efforts across Federal Government." *ProPublica*, June 15. Accessed August 9, 2017, at https://www.propublica.org/article/trump-administration-rolls-back-civil-rights-efforts-federal-government.

Hutchings, Vincent L., Hanes Walton Jr., and Andrea Benjamin. 2010. "The Impact of Explicit Racial Cues on Gender Differences in Support for Confederate Symbols and Partisanship." *Journal of Politics* 72 (4): 1175–88.

"Immigrant Phobia." 1997. *USA Today*, August 11.

International City/County Managers Association. 2012. "ICMA State of the Profession 2012 Survey Results." Accessed June 7, 2016, at http://icma.org/en/icma/knowledge_network/documents/kn/Document/305096/ICMA_2012_State_of_the_Profession_Survey_Results.

Itzigsohn, José. 2009. *Encountering American Faultlines: Race, Class, and the Dominican Experience in Providence*. New York: Russell Sage Foundation.

Jaworsky, Bernadette Nadya, Peggy Levitt, Wendy Cadge, Jessica Hejtmanek, and Sara R. Curran. 2012. "New Perspectives on Immigrant Contexts of Reception: The Cultural Armature of Cities." *Nordic Journal of Migration Research* 2 (1): 78–88.

Johnson, Jenna, and David Weigel. 2015. "Donald Trump Calls for 'Total' Ban on Muslims Entering United States." *Washington Post*, December 8.

Jones-Correa, Michael. 2005. "Bringing Outsiders In: Questions of Immigrant Incorporation." In *The Politics of Democratic Inclusion*, edited by Rodney E. Hero and Christina Wolbrecht, 75–101. Philadelphia: Temple University Press.

———. 2008. "Race to the Top? The Politics of Immigrant Education in Suburbia." In *New Faces in New Places: The Changing Geography of American Immigration*, edited by Douglas S. Massey, 308–40. New York: Russell Sage Foundation.

———. 2011. "All Immigration Is Local: Receiving Communities and Their Role in Successful Immigrant Integration." *Center for American Progress*, September. Accessed September 25, 2015, at https://cdn.americanprogress.org/wp-content/uploads/issues/2011/09/pdf/rci.pdf.

———. 2016. "The Kindness of Strangers: Ambivalent Reception in Charlotte, North Carolina." In *Unsettled Americans: Metropolitan Context and Civic Leadership for Immigrant Integration*, edited by John Mollenkopf and Manuel Pastor, 163–88. Ithaca, NY: Cornell University Press.

Jones-Correa, Michael, and Els de Graauw. 2013. "Looking Back to See Ahead: Unanticipated Changes in Immigration from 1986 to the Present and Their

Implications for American Politics Today." *Annual Review of Political Science* 16 (1): 209–30.

Jones-Correa, Michael, and Katherine Fennelly. 2009. "Immigration Enforcement and Its Effects on Latino Lives in Two Rural North Carolina Communities." Paper presented at conference on Undocumented Hispanic Migration: On the Margins of a Dream, Connecticut College, New London, Connecticut. Accessed December 1, 2017, at https://s3.amazonaws.com/academia.edu.documents/42901681/Immigration_Enforcement_and_Its_Effects_20160221-18753-2u5dg4.pdf?AWSAccessKeyId=AKIAIWOWYYGZ2Y53UL3A&Expires=1512185492&Signature=G5PIR%2Fr43P93i7mRh7EuzqHHh8I%3D&response-content-disposition=inline%3B%20filename%3DImmigration_Enforcement_and_Its_Effects.pdf.

Karczweski, Adam. 2007. "Coming to America: How States and Municipalities Deal with Undocumented Immigrants." *New Jersey Lawyer*, November 26.

Kasinitz, P., J. H. Mollenkopf, M. C. Waters, and J. Holdaway. 2008. *Inheriting the City: The Children of Immigrants Come of Age.* New York: Russell Sage Foundation.

Kenning, Chris, and Joseph Ax. 2017. "Chicago to Sue Trump Administration over Sanctuary City Funding Threat." *Reuters.com*, August 6. Accessed August 9, 2017, at https://www.reuters.com/article/us-usa-immigration-sanctuary-idUSKBN1AM0Q5.

Kerr, Juliana, Paul McDaniel, and Melissa Guinan. 2014. *Reimagining the Midwest: Immigration Initiatives and the Capacity of Local Leadership.* Chicago: Chicago Council on Global Affairs and American Immigration Council.

Key, V. O. 1949. *Southern Politics in State and Nation.* New York: Knopf.

Kinder, Donald R. 1998. "Communication and Opinion." *Annual Review of Political Science* 1:167–97.

Klinkner, Philip. 2017. "Yes, Trump's Hard-Line Immigration Stance Helped Him Win the Election—but It Could Be His Undoing." *Los Angeles Times*, April 17. Accessed July 27, 2017, at http://www.latimes.com/opinion/op-ed/la-oe-klinker-immigration-election-20170417-story.html.

Klinkner, Philip A., and Rogers M. Smith. 2016. "Trump's Election Is Actually a Return to Normal Racial Politics. Here's Why." *Washington Post*, November 17, sec. Monkey Cage. https://www.washingtonpost.com/news/monkey-cage/wp/2016/11/17/trumps-election-is-a-return-to-normal-at-least-in-u-s-attitudes-on-race/.

Koltyk, Jo Ann. 1998. *New Pioneers in the Heartland: Hmong Life in Wisconsin.* Boston: Allyn and Bacon.

Kraus, Neil. 2013. *Majoritarian Cities: Policy Making and Inequality in Urban Politics.* Ann Arbor: University of Michigan Press.

Kraus, Scott. 2007. "City Brings Back Immigration Issue." *Morning Call*, February 8.

Krogstad, Jens Manuel, and Jeffrey Passel. 2015. "Five Facts about Illegal Immigration in the U.S." *Pew Research Center*, November 19. Accessed April 10, 2016, at http://www.pewresearch.org/fact-tank/2015/11/19/5-facts-about -illegal-immigration-in-the-u-s/.

Kurien, Prema. 2007. "Who Speaks for Indian Americans? Religion, Ethnicity, and Political Formation." *American Quarterly* 59 (3): 759–83.

Kusow, Abdi M. 2006. "Migration and Racial Formations among Somali Immigrants in North America." *Journal of Ethnic and Migration Studies* 32 (3): 533–51.

Ladd, Helen F., and John Yinger. 1989. *America's Ailing Cities: Fiscal Health and the Design of Urban Policy*. Baltimore: Johns Hopkins University Press.

LaFlamme, Mark. 2004. "Lewiston Official Charged." *Lewiston Sun Journal*, August 19.

La Ganga, Maria. 2014. "Yakima Valley Latinos Getting a Voice, with Court's Help." *Los Angeles Times*, September 24.

Lahav, Gallya. 2013. "Threat and Immigration Attitudes in Liberal Democracies: The Role of Framing in Structuring Public Opinion." In *Immigration and Public Opinion in Liberal Democracies*, edited by Gary P. Freeman, Randall Hansen, and David L. Leal, 232–53. London: Routledge.

Law, Anna O. 2017. "This Is How Trump's Deportations Differ from Obama's." *Washington Post*, May 3. https://www.washingtonpost.com/news/monkey -cage/wp/2017/05/03/this-is-how-trumps-deportations-differ-from-obamas/.

Lawder, Melanie. 2015. "New Sports Bar to Open on Wausau's West Side." *Wausau Daily Herald*, June 19.

Lawless, Jennifer L. 2012. *Becoming a Candidate: Political Ambition and the Decision to Run for Office*. New York: Cambridge University Press.

Lay, J. Celeste. 2012. *A Midwestern Mosaic: Immigration and Political Socialization in Rural America*. Philadelphia: Temple University Press.

Leal, David L., Valerie Martinez-Ebers, and Kenneth J. Meier. 2004. "The Politics of Latino Education: The Biases of At-Large Elections." *Journal of Politics* 66 (4): 1224–44.

Lee, Larry. 2015. "American Legion Post 10 Donates towards Hmong Memorial." *Wsau.com*, August 1.

Levesque, Leon. 2002. "Impact of Somali Migration on Lewiston School System." In "Report to Governor Angus King: New Somali Arrivals and Other Issues Relative to Refugee/Secondary Migrants/Immigrants and Cultural Diversity in the City of Lewiston." City of Lewiston, May 9.

Lewis, David, and David Mosse. 2006. *Development Brokers and Translators*. Bloomfield, CT: Kumarian Press.

Lewis, Ethan, and Giovanni Peri. 2015. "Immigration and the Economy of Cities and Regions." In *Handbook of Regional and Urban Economics*, edited by

Gilles Duranton, J. Vernon Henderson, and William C. Strange, 625–85. Oxford: North-Holland.

Lewis, Paul G., Doris Marie Provine, Monica W. Varsanyi, and Scott H. Decker. 2013. "Why Do (Some) City Police Departments Enforce Federal Immigration Law? Political, Demographic, and Organizational Influences on Local Choices." *Journal of Public Administration Research and Theory* 23 (1): 1–25.

Lewis, Paul G., and S. Karthick Ramakrishnan. 2007. "Police Practices in Immigrant-Destination Cities: Political Control or Bureaucratic Professionalism?" *Urban Affairs Review* 42 (6): 874–900.

Lewiston Auburn Economic Growth Council. 2015. "LA Forward: An Economic Growth Strategy for Lewiston-Auburn Maine." Accessed April 1, 2016, at http://www.lewistonmaine.gov/ArchiveCenter/ViewFile/Item/2859.

Light, Ivan. 1984. "Immigrant and Ethnic Enterprise in North America." *Ethnic and Racial Studies* 7 (2): 195–216.

Lucio, Joanna D. 2013. "Public Administrators and Noncitizens." *Administration and Society*, November 11.

Macdonald, Robert. 2012a. "Enough Is Enough: LHS Graduation Marred by Teens' Rude Behavior." *Twin City Times*, June 9.

———. 2012b. "Enough Is Enough: Extremist Liberals Widen the Divide with Somalis." *Twin City Times*, September 6.

———. 2014. "Enough Is Enough: There Are Now Two Visions of the American Dream." *Twin City Times*, July 9.

MacQuarrie, Brian, and Vivian Wang. 2016. "Mainers Defend Somali Neighbors against Trump." *Boston Globe*, August 5.

Malcolm, Wade, and Andrea Turano. 2006. "Immigration Bill Delayed by Judge." *Republican Herald*, November 2.

Malone, Tara. 2004. "U-46 Tangle Coming to a Vote: Boundary Controversy May or May Not End." *Chicago Daily Herald*, March 14.

Malone, Tara, and Naomi Dillon. 2004. "Great Silent Minority: Culture, Language Barriers Keep Latinos Quiet." *Chicago Daily Herald*, February 15.

Mansbridge, Jane. 1999. "Should Blacks Represent Blacks and Women Represent Women? A Contingent 'Yes.'" *Journal of Politics* 61 (3): 628–57.

Marrow, Helen B. 2005. "New Destinations and Immigrant Incorporation." *Perspectives on Politics* 3 (4): 781–99.

———. 2009. "Immigrant Bureaucratic Incorporation: The Dual Roles of Professional Missions and Government Policies." *American Sociological Review* 74 (5): 756–76.

———. 2011. *New Destination Dreaming*. Palo Alto, CA: Stanford University Press.

Marschall, Melissa J. 2005. "Minority Incorporation and Local School Boards."

In *Besieged: School Boards and the Future of American Politics*, edited by William G. Howell, 173–98. Washington, DC: Brookings Institution.

———. 2017. "Immigrant Incorporation in Local Schools: School Policy and Practices in New vs. Established Destinations." In *The Politics of New Immigrant Destinations: Transatlantic Perspectives*, edited by Stefanie Chambers, Diana Evans, Anthony Messina, and Abigail Fisher Williamson, 248–76. Philadelphia: Temple University Press.

Marschall, Melissa J., Elizabeth Rigby, and Jasmine Jenkins. 2011. "Do State Policies Constrain Local Actors? The Impact of English Only Laws on Language Instruction in Public Schools." *Publius: The Journal of Federalism* 41 (4): 586–609.

Martinez, Gebe. 2011. "Unconstitutional and Costly: The High Price of Local Immigration Enforcement." *Center for American Progress*, January 24.

Martinez-Cosio, Maria, and Rosario Martinez Iannacone. 2007. "The Tenuous Role of Institutional Agents-Parent Liaisons as Cultural Brokers." *Education and Urban Society* 39 (3): 349–69.

Marwell, Nicole. 2007. *Bargaining for Brooklyn: Community Organizations in the Entrepreneurial City*. Chicago: University of Chicago Press.

Massey, Douglas S. 2008. *New Faces in New Places: The Changing Geography of American Immigration*. New York: Russell Sage Foundation.

Massey, Douglas S., Jorge Durand, and Nolan J. Malone. 2002. *Beyond Smoke and Mirrors: Mexican Immigration in an Era of Economic Integration*. New York: Russell Sage Foundation.

Mathewson, Tara Garcia. 2011. "Illegal Immigration Hot Issue at Elgin Mayoral Forum." *Elgin Daily Herald*, March 16.

Mayda, Anna Maria. 2006. "Who Is against Immigration? A Cross-Country Investigation of Individual Attitudes toward Immigrants." *Review of Economics and Statistics* 88 (3): 510–30.

Mayhew, David. 1974. *Congress: The Electoral Connection*. New Haven, CT: Yale University Press.

McGreevy, Patrick. 2016. "California Effort Is Underway to Allow Immigrants in U.S. Illegally to Buy Healthcare Coverage." *Los Angeles Times*, April 14.

Meier, Kenneth J. 1993. "Latinos and Representative Bureaucracy Testing the Thompson and Henderson Hypotheses." *Journal of Public Administration Research and Theory* 3 (4): 393–414.

Meier, Kenneth J., and Laurence J. O'Toole. 2006. "Political Control versus Bureaucratic Values: Reframing the Debate." *Public Administration Review* 66 (2): 177–92.

Meier, Kenneth J., and Joseph Stewart. 1992. "The Impact of Representative Bureaucracies: Educational Systems and Public Policies." *American Review of Public Administration* 22 (3): 157–71.

Meier, Kenneth J., Robert D. Wrinkle, and J. L. Polinard. 1999. "Representative Bureaucracy and Distributional Equity: Addressing the Hard Question." *Journal of Politics* 61 (4): 1025–39.

Mekelburg, Madlin. 2017. "Local Officials Fear State Retaliation over 'Sanctuary Cities' Lawsuits." *USA Today*, July 6.

Melnick, Shep R. 2014a. "Courts and Agencies in the American Civil Rights State." In *The Politics of Major Policy Reform in Postwar America*, edited by Jeffrey A. Jenkins and Sidney M. Milkis, 77–102. New York: Cambridge University Press.

——. 2014b. "The Odd Evolution of the Civil Rights State." *Harvard Journal of Law and Public Policy* 37 (1): 113–34.

Mendelberg, Tali. 2001. *The Race Card: Campaign Strategy, Implicit Messages, and the Norm of Equality*. Princeton, NJ: Princeton University Press.

Mendoza, Jessica. 2016. "As US Braces for Refugees, One Maine Town Offers Lesson of Inclusion." *Christian Science Monitor*, February 8.

Menjívar, Cecelia, and Leisy Abrego. 2012. "Legal Violence: Immigration Law and the Lives of Central American Immigrants." *American Journal of Sociology* 117 (5): 1380–1421.

Messina, Anthony. 1983. *Race and Party Competition in Britain*. New York: Oxford University Press.

Messina, Anthony, and Abigail Fisher Williamson. 2017. "Introduction: Dimensions of Variation in Newly Diverse Transatlantic Destinations." In *The Politics of New Immigrant Destinations: Transatlantic Perspectives*, edited by Stefanie Chambers, Diana Evans, Anthony Messina, and Abigail Fisher Williamson, 1–37. Philadelphia: Temple University Press.

Mettler, Suzanne. 2002. "Bringing the State Back in to Civic Engagement: Policy Feedback Effects of the G.I. Bill for World War II Veterans." *American Political Science Review* 96 (2): 351–65.

Mettler, Suzanne, and Joe Soss. 2004. "The Consequences of Public Policy for Democratic Citizenship: Bridging Policy Studies and Mass Politics." *Perspectives on Politics* 2 (1): 55–73.

Migration Policy Index. 2015. "Anti-discrimination." Accessed April 10, 2016, at http://www.mipex.eu/anti-discrimination.

Minkowsky, James. 2002. "Lewiston Police Department Observations." In *Report to Governor Angus King: New Somali Arrivals and Other Issues relative to Refugee/Secondary Migrants/Immigrants and Cultural Diversity in the City of Lewiston*, edited by Phil Nadeau, 1–24. Lewiston, ME: City of Lewiston.

Minuteman Project. 2013. "Legal Publication Rejects Use of Term Illegal Alien, Suggests Undocumented Immigrant Instead." Accessed September 25, 2015, at https://minutemanproject.com/legal-publication-rejects-use-of-term-illegal-alien-suggests-undocumented-immigrant-instead/. Discontinued.

Mocarsky, Steve. 2007. "Local Municipalities Mulling Law, Not Acting." *Wilkes Barre Times Leader*, April 2.

Mollenkopf, John, and Manuel Pastor. 2016. *Unsettled Americans: Metropolitan Context and Civic Leadership for Immigrant Integration*. Ithaca, NY: Cornell University Press.

Morales, Laura, and Katia Pilati. 2014. "The Political Transnationalism of Ecuadorians in Barcelona, Madrid and Milan: The Role of Individual Resources, Organizational Engagement and the Political Context." *Global Networks* 14 (1): 80–102.

Morse, Janice M. 2003. "Principles of Mixed Methods and Multimethod Research Design." In *Handbook of Mixed Methods in Social and Behavioral Research*, edited by Abbas Tashakkori and Charles Teddlie, 189–208. Thousand Oaks, CA: SAGE.

Motel, Seth, and Eileen Patten. 2012. "The 10 Largest Hispanic Origin Groups: Characteristics, Rankings, Top Counties." *Pew Hispanic Center*, June 27. Accessed April 27, 2016, at http://www.pewhispanic.org/2012/06/27/the-10 -largest-hispanic-origin-groups-characteristics-rankings-top-counties/.

Moyer, Christine S. 2006. "A March into History Books: Waves of Support on Elgin Streets." *Elgin Courier News*, May 2.

Mutz, Diana C. 1992. "Mass Media and the Depoliticization of Personal Experience." *American Journal of Political Science* 32 (3): 483–508.

Nadeau, Phil. 2002a. *Report to Governor Angus King: New Somali Arrivals and Other Issues relative to Refugee/Secondary Migrants/Immigrants and Cultural Diversity in the City of Lewiston*. Lewiston, ME: City of Lewiston.

———. 2002b. "Weekly Update-Somali Secondary Migrant and General Multicultural Activity." City of Lewiston, ME, September 19.

———. 2003a. "Lewiston Leads: Community Dialogue for Change." Community Building Planning Committee Report to the Mayor and City Council.

———. 2003b. "The Somalis of Lewiston: Community Impacts of Rapid Immigrant Movement into a Small, Homogeneous Maine City." *Edmund S. Muskie School of Public Service Capstone Report*, January.

Nalbandian, John. 1999. "Facilitating Community, Enabling Democracy: New Roles for Local Government Managers." *Public Administration Review* 59 (3): 187–97.

National Conference of State Legislators. 2017. "Report on 2017 State Immigration Laws, January-June." Accessed August 8, 2017, at http://www.ncsl.org/ research/immigration/report-on-2017-state-immigration-laws-january-june .aspx#table.

National Public Radio/Kaiser Family Foundation/Kennedy School of Government. 2004. "Immigration in America Poll." Accessed July 13, 2016, at http:// www.npr.org/news/specials/polls/2004/immigration/questionnaire.pdf.

Nelson, Kimberly, and James Svara. 2014. "The Roles of Local Government

Managers in Theory and Practice: A Centennial Perspective." *Public Administration Review* 75 (1): 49–61.

Nelson, Thomas E., and Donald R. Kinder. 1996. "Issue Frames and Group-Centrism in American Public Opinion." *Journal of Politics* 58 (4): 1055–78.

Nelson, Wes. 2000. "Fired Yakima Policeman Fights Back." *Yakima Herald-Republic*, August 18.

———. 2002a. "Police Profiling Proposal Is Back." *Yakima Herald-Republic*, September 24.

———. 2002b. "Yakima Rejects Empowered Citizen Panel." *Yakima Herald-Republic*, October 17.

Newton, Lina. 2005. "It Is Not a Question of Being Anti-immigration: Categories of Deservedness in Immigration Policy Making." In *Deserving and Entitled: Social Constructions and Public Policy*, edited by Anne Larason Schneider and Helen Ingram, 139–72. Albany: State University of New York Press.

Nivola, Pietro. 2002. *Tense Commandments: Federal Prescriptions and City Problems*. Washington, DC: Brookings Institution Press.

Oberfield, Zachery. W. 2010. "Rule Following and Discretion at Government's Frontlines: Continuity and Change during Organization Socialization." *Journal of Public Administration Research and Theory* 20 (4): 735–55.

Odem, Mary. 2008. "Unsettled in the Suburbs: Latino Immigration and Ethnic Diversity in Metro Atlanta." In *Twenty-First Century Gateways: Immigrant Integration in Suburban America*, edited by A. Singer, S. W. Hardwick, and C. B. Brettell, 105–36. Washington, DC: Brookings Institution Press.

Office of Refugee Resettlement. 2001. *Annual Report to Congress*. Washington, DC: US Department of Health and Human Services.

Ohio Jobs and Justice PAC. n.d. "The Original list of Sanctuary Cities, USA." Accessed August 9, 2017, at http://www.ojjpac.org/sanctuary.asp.

Okamoto, Dina, and Kim Ebert. 2010. "Beyond the Ballot: Immigrant Collective Action in Gateways and New Destinations in the United States." *Social Problems* 57 (4): 529–58.

O'Konowitz, Tom. 2003. "Elgin Mayor, Challenger Talk Diversity." *Daily Herald*, March 18.

Pantoja, Adrian, Ricardo Ramirez, and Gary M. Segura. 2001. "Citizens by Choice, Voters by Necessity: Patterns in Political Mobilization in Naturalized Latinos." *Political Research Quarterly* 54 (4): 729–50.

Pantoja, Adrian D., and Gary M. Segura. 2003a. "Does Ethnicity Matter? Descriptive Representation in Legislatures and Political Alienation among Latinos." *Social Science Quarterly* 84 (2): 441–60.

———. 2003b. "Fear and Loathing in California: Contextual Threat and Political Sophistication among Latino Voters." *Political Behavior* 25 (3): 265–86.

Parker, Christopher S., and Matt A. Barreto. 2014. *Change They Can't Believe*

In: The Tea Party and Reactionary Politics in America. Princeton, NJ: Princeton University Press.

Partnership for a New American Economy. n.d. "About." Accessed June 7, 2016, at http://www.renewoureconomy.org/about/.

Pastor, Manuel, Rhonda Ortiz, and Els de Graauw. 2015. "Opening Minds, Opening Doors, Opening Communities: Cities Leading for Immigrant Integration." Report to the Americas Society/Council of the Americas and University of Southern California Center for the Study of Immigrant Integration, December 15.

Pedraza-Bailey, Silvia. 1985. "Cuba's Exiles: Portrait of a Refugee Migration." *International Migration Review* 19 (1): 4–34.

Peffley, Mark, and Jon Hurwitz. 2007. "Persuasion and Resistance: Race and the Death Penalty in America." *American Journal of Political Science* 51 (4): 996–1012.

Peterson, Paul E. 1981. *City Limits.* Chicago: University of Chicago Press.

———. 1995. *The Price of Federalism.* Washington, DC: Brookings Institution Press.

Pettigrew, Thomas F., and Linda R. Tropp. 2006. "A Meta-analytic Test of Intergroup Contact Theory." *Journal of Personality and Social Psychology* 90 (5): 751–83.

Pham, Huyen, and Van H. Pham. 2012. "Measuring the Climate for Immigrants: A State-by-State Analysis." In *The Role of States in Immigration Enforcement and Policy,* edited by Gabriel Jack Chin and Carissa Hessick, 21–39. Rochester: New York University Press.

Phillips, Anne. 1991. *Engendering Democracy.* College Station: Penn State University Press.

Phillips, Rob. 2007. "Happy Birthday, Centro. Elgin Advocacy Group Marks Fruitful 35 Years." *Chicago Daily Herald,* March 2.

Pierson, Paul. 1993. "When Effect Becomes Cause: Policy Feedback and Political Change." Edited by Gosta Esping-Andersen, Peter Hall, Douglass C. North, and Theda Skocpol. *World Politics* 45 (4): 595–628.

———. 2000. "Increasing Returns, Path Dependence, and the Study of Politics." *American Political Science Review* 94 (2): 251–67.

Pitkin, Hannah. 1967. *The Concept of Representation.* Berkeley: University of California Press.

Piven, Frances Fox, and Richard Cloward. 1979. *Poor People's Movements: Why They Succeed, How They Fail.* New York: Vintage.

Polansek, Tom. 2006. "Rights Rally Slated Locally." *Elgin Courier News,* April 28.

Portes, Alejandro, and Rubén G. Rumbaut. 2006. *Immigrant America: A Portrait.* 3rd ed. Berkeley: University of California Press.

Pound, William T., Larry Naake, Dan Sprague, and Donald J. Borut. 2007. "Joint Letter to Senate Party Leaders from the National Conference of State

Legislatures, Council of State Governments, National Association of Counties, National League of Cities," March 7.

Prewitt, Kenneth. 1970. *The Recruitment of Political Leaders: A Study of Citizen-Politicians.* New York: Bobbs-Merrill.

Price, Marie, and Audrey Singer. 2008. "Edge Gateways: Immigrants, Suburbs, and the Politics of Reception in Metropolitan Washington" In *Twenty-First Century Gateways: Immigrant Incorporation in Suburban America*, edited by Audrey Singer, Susan B. Hardwick, and Caroline B. Brettell, 137–70. Washington, DC: Brookings Institution Press.

Provine, Doris Marie, Monica Varsanyi, Paul Lewis, and Scott Decker. 2016. *Policing Immigrants: Law Enforcement on the Front Lines.* Chicago: University of Chicago Press.

Putnam, Robert D. 1993. *Making Democracy Work.* Princeton, NJ: Princeton University Press.

———. 2000. *Bowling Alone: The Collapse and Revival of American Community.* New York: Simon and Schuster.

———. 2007. "E Pluribus Unum: Diversity and Community in the Twenty-First Century: The 2006 Johan Skytte Prize Lecture." *Scandinavian Political Studies* 30 (2): 137–74.

Ramakrishnan, Karthick. 2005. *Democracy in Immigrant America: Changing Demographics and Political Participation.* Stanford, CA: Stanford University Press.

Ramakrishnan, S. Karthick, and Irene Bloemraad. 2008. *Civic Hopes and Political Realities: Immigrants, Community Organizations, and Political Engagement.* New York: Russell Sage Foundation.

Ramakrishnan, S. Karthick, and Paul G. Lewis. 2005. *Immigrants and Local Governance: The View from City Hall.* San Francisco: Public Policy Institute of California.

Ramakrishnan, S. Karthick, and Tom Wong. 2010. "Immigration Policies Go Local: The Varying Responses of Local Governments to Low-Skilled and Undocumented Immigration." In *Taking Local Control: Immigration Policy Activism in U.S. Cities and States*, edited by Monica W. Varsanyi, 73–93. Palo Alto, CA: Stanford University Press.

Raymond, Larry. 2002. "Text of Letter to the Somali Community." Accessed January 2004 at http://www.sunjournal.com/story.asp?slg=100402letter. Discontinued.

"Readers Sound Off on Mexico Project." 1995. *Yakima Herald Republic*, March 4.

Reaves, Brian. 2015. "Local Police Departments, 2013: Personnel, Policies, and Practices." *Bureau of Justice Statistics, U.S. Department of Justice*, May. Accessed June 7, 2016, at http://www.bjs.gov/content/pub/pdf/lpd13ppp.pdf.

Reed, Brian. 2017. "Fear and Loathing in Homer and Rockville." *This American Life.* WBEZ (Chicago). July 21.

Rich, Michael J. 2003. "The Intergovernmental Environment." In *Cities, Politics, and Policies: A Comparative Analysis*, edited by John Pelissero, 35–67. Washington, DC: Congressional Quarterly Press.

Rocha, Rene R., and Daniel P. Hawes. 2009. "Racial Diversity, Representative Bureaucracy, and Equity in Multiracial School Districts." *Social Science Quarterly* 90 (2): 326–44.

Rocha, Rene R., Caroline J. Tolbert, Daniel C. Bowen, and Christopher J. Clark. 2010. "Race and Turnout: Does Descriptive Representation in State Legislatures Increase Minority Voting?" *Political Research Quarterly* 63 (4): 890–907.

Rodriguez, Cristina M. 2008. "The Significance of the Local in Immigration Regulation." *Michigan Law Review* 106:567–642.

Rosenstone, Steven J., and John Mark Hansen. 1993. *Mobilization, Participation, and Democracy in America*. New York: Macmillan.

Rozek, Dan. 2000. "Elgin Denies Housing Bias against Hispanics." *Daily Herald*, October 3.

Rubaii-Barrett, Nadia. 2008. "Immigration Reform: An Intergovernmental Imperative." *International City/County Management Association,* 2008. https://icma.org/sites/default/files/100065_Immigration_Reform_An_Inter governmental_Imperative.pdf.

Russel, Eric. 2012. "Is Lewiston Mayor Thwarting Progress?" *Portland Press Herald*, October 7.

Ryan, Camille L., and Julie Siebens. 2012. *Educational Attainment in the United States*. Current Population Report. Washington, DC: US Census Bureau.

Scales-Trent, Judy. 1999. "African Women in France: Immigration, Family and Work." *Brooklyn Journal of International Law* 24 (3): 705–38.

Schaeffer, Merlin. 2014. *Ethnic Diversity and Social Cohesion: Immigration, Ethnic Fractionalization and Potentials for Civic Action*. London: Ashgate.

Scheve, Kenneth, and Michael Slaughter. 2001. "Labor Market Competition and Individual Preferences over Immigration Policy." *Review of Economics and Statistics* 83:133–45.

Schier, Steven. 2000. *By Invitation Only: The Rise of Exclusive Politics in the United States*. Pittsburgh: University of Pittsburgh Press.

Schildkraut, Deborah. 2005. *Press One for English: Language Policy, Public Opinion, and American Identity*. Princeton, NJ: Princeton University Press.

———. 2011. *Americanism in the Twentieth Century: Public Opinion in the Age of Immigration*. New York: Cambridge University Press.

Schmidt, Ron, Sr. 2000. *Language Policy and Identity Politics in the United States*. Philadelphia: Temple University Press.

———. 2007. "Comparing Federal Government Immigrant Settlement Policies in Canada and the United States." *American Review of Canadian Studies* 37 (1): 103–22.

Schneider, Anne, and Helen Ingram. 1993. "Social Construction of Target Populations: Implications for Politics and Policy." *American Political Science Review* 87 (2): 334–47.

———. 1997. *Policy Design for Democracy*. Lawrence: University Press of Kansas.

———, eds. 2005. *Deserving and Entitled: Social Constructions and Public Policy*. SUNY Series in Public Policy. Albany: State University of New York Press.

Schulte, Laura, and Peter Wasson. 2016. "County Board Upholds Brad Karger Suspension." *Wausau Daily Herald*, August 18.

Scott, Victoria A. 2003. "Immigrant and Refugee/Multicultural Activity Report." City of Lewiston, February 26.

Sears, David O. 1993. "Symbolic Politics: A Socio-psychological Theory." In *Explorations in Political Psychology*, edited by Shanto Iyengar, Williams McGuire, and William James, 113–49. Duke Studies in Political Psychology. Durham, NC: Duke University Press.

Seelye, Katherine Q. 2015. "Mayoral Race in Maine Could Help Define City's Future amid Demographic Shift." *New York Times*, December 6.

Seif, Hilda. 2011. "'Unapologetic and Unafraid': Immigrant Youth Come out from the Shadows." *Youth Civic Development: Work at the Cutting Edge. New Directions for Child and Adolescent Development* 134:59–75.

Shah, Paru. 2009. "Motivating Participation: The Symbolic Effects of Latino Representation on Parent School Involvement." *Social Science Quarterly* 90 (1): 212–30.

Shepherd, Michael. 2015. "Macdonald Easily Beats Chin in Lewiston Mayor's Race." *Bangor Daily News*, December 8.

Sides, John. 2017. "Race, Religion, and Immigration in 2016." Democracy Fund Voter Study Group, June. Accessed July 27, 2017, at https://www.voterstudygroup.org/reports/2016-elections/race-religion-immigration-2016.

Silber Mohamed, Heather. 2017. *The New Americans? Immigration, Protest, and the Politics of Latino Identity*. Lawrence: University Press of Kansas.

Singer, Audrey. 2004. *The Rise of New Immigrant Gateways*. Living Cities Census Series, February 2004. Washington, DC: Brookings Institution. https://www.brookings.edu/wp-content/uploads/2016/06/20040301_gateways.pdf.

———. 2008. "Twenty-First-Century Gateways: An Introduction," In *Twenty-First Century Gateways: Immigrant Incorporation in Suburban America*, edited by Audrey Singer, Susan B. Hardwick, and Caroline B. Brettell, 11–29. Washington, DC: Brookings Institution Press.

Singer, Audrey, Jill H. Wilson, and Brooke DeRenzis. 2009. *Immigrants, Politics, and Local Response in Suburban Washington*. Washington, DC: Brookings Institution.

Skocpol, Theda. 2003. *Diminished Democracy: From Membership to Management in American Civic Life*. Norman: University of Oklahoma Press.

Skocpol, Theda, and Vanessa Williamson. 2012. *The Tea Party and the Remaking of Republican Conservatism.* Oxford: Oxford University Press.

Skrentny, John David, ed. 2001. *Color Lines: Affirmative Action, Immigration, and Civil Rights Options for America.* Chicago: University of Chicago Press.

"Suburbs Becoming More Ethnically Diverse." 2001. ABC News, *World News Tonight*, June 25.

Small, Mario Luis. 2011. "How to Conduct a Mixed Methods Study: Recent Trends in a Rapidly Growing Literature." *Annual Review of Sociology* 37 (1): 57–86.

Smith, James P., and Barry Edmonston. 1997. *The New Americans: Economic, Demographic and Fiscal Effects of Immigration.* Washington, DC: National Academy Press.

Soss, Joe. 1999. "Lessons of Welfare: Policy Design, Political Learning, and Political Action." *American Political Science Review* 93 (2): 363–80.

Soss, Joe, and Vesla Weaver. 2017. "Police Are Our Government: Politics, Political Science, and the Policing of Race–Class Subjugated Communities." *Annual Review of Political Science* 20:565–91.

Sowers, Bennie. 2007. "Real Issue Is Burdens Illegals Place on Citizens." *Elgin Courier News*, December 20.

Spak, Kara. 2002a. "Overcrowded Houses Still Plague Towns in Fox Valley." *Chicago Daily Herald*, May 17.

———. 2002b. "Elgin Agrees to Settlement in Housing Bias Cases: City Will Distribute $500,000 among Varied Parties, Alter Inspection Practices." *Chicago Daily Herald.* August 20.

Steil, Justin Peter, and Ion Bogdan Vasi. 2014. "The New Immigration Contestation: Social Movements and Local Immigration Policy Making in the United States, 2000–2011." *American Journal of Sociology* 119 (4): 1104–55.

Steinhauer, Jennifer. 2008. "Judge Rejects Bid to Let Police Check Immigration Status." *New York Times*, June 26.

Stone, Clarence. 1989. *Regime Politics.* Lawrence: University Press of Kansas.

Tajfel, H., and J. C. Turner. 1986. "The Social Identity Theory of Intergroup Behavior." In *Psychology of Intergroup Relations*, edited by S. Worchel and W. G. Austin, 7–24. Chicago: Nelson-Hall.

Tarrow, Sidney. 2004. "Bridging the Qualitative-Quantitative Divide." In *Rethinking Social Inquiry: Diverse Tools, Shared Standards*, edited by Henry E. Brady and David Collier, 171–80. Lanham, MD: Rowman and Littlefield.

Tausanovitch, Chris, and Christopher Warshaw. 2014. "Representation in Municipal Government." *American Political Science Review* 108 (3): 605–41.

Taylor, Scott. 2008. "Coming to America." *Lewiston Sun Journal,* April 18.

———. 2012. "Mayor Macdonald Talks with Somali Elders." *Lewiston Sun Journal*, December 10.

Temple, Elena. 2017. "The U.S. Conference of Mayors Registers Strong Sup-

port for Refugees and Immigrants." Accessed July 26, 2017, at https://www
.usmayors.org/2017/01/31/the-u-s-conference-of-mayors-registers-strong
-support-for-refugees-and-immigrants/.

Tichenor, Daniel J. 2002. *Dividing Lines: The Politics of Immigration Control in
America*. Princeton, NJ: Princeton University Press.

———. 2013. "The Congressional Dynamics of Immigration Reform." James
A. Baker III Institute of Public Policy, Rice University, April 2013.
https://www.bakerinstitute.org/media/files/Research/2a9bc2e6/LAI-pub
-TichenorCongressionalDynamicsImmigration-040813.pdf.

Tiebout, Charles. 1956. "A Pure Theory of Local Expenditures." *Journal of Political Economy* 64 (5): 416–24.

Tomz, Michael, Jason Wittenberg, and Gary King. 2003. "CLARIFY: Software for Interpreting and Presenting Statistical Results." *Journal of Statistical Software*, January 5. https://web.stanford.edu/~tomz/software/clarify.pdf.

Trounstine, Jessica. 2010. "Representation and Accountability in Cities." *Annual Review of Political Science* 13:407–23.

US Citizenship and Immigration Services. 2016. "A Guide to Naturalization."
Last modified June 20, 2017. https://www.uscis.gov/us-citizenship/citizenship
-through-naturalization/guide-naturalization.

US Congress, Congressional Budget Office. 2007. *The Impact of Unauthorized
Immigrants on the Budgets of State and Local Governments*. https://www.cbo
.gov/sites/default/files/110th-congress-2007-2008/reports/12-6-immigration
.pdf.

US Court of Appeals. 2013. *Lozano v. City of Hazleton*. Third Circuit Court.
http://www2.ca3.uscourts.gov/opinarch/073531p.pdf.

US Customs and Border Patrol. 2015. "United States Border Patrol Sector Profile." Accessed January 12, 2016, at http://www.cbp.gov/sites/default/files/
documents/USBP%20Stats%20FY2014%20sector%20profile.pdf.

———. 2016. "Southwest Border Unaccompanied Alien Children Statistics FY
2016." Accessed January 13, 2016, at http://www.cbp.gov/newsroom/stats/
southwest-border-unaccompanied-children/fy-2016.

US Department of Homeland Security. 2009. "Delegation of Immigration Authority, Section 287(g), Immigration and Nationality Act–Fact Sheet,"
May 19. Accessed July 25, 2017, at http://bento.cdn.pbs.org/hostedbento
-prod/filer_public/productions/ndn/pdf/Section287_g.pdf.

———. 2010. "The Performance of 287(g) Agreements. Office of the Inspector
General." Accessed December 1, 2017, at https://www.oig.dhs.gov/assets/
Mgmt/OIG_10-63_Mar10.pdf.

US Department of Justice. 2004. "Justice Department Settles Voting Rights
Lawsuit with Yakima County, Washington." Accessed June 7, 2016, at http://
www.justice.gov/opa/pr/2004/July/04_crt_467.htm.

US Department of Justice, Civil Rights Division. 2013a. "Civil Rights Division Accomplishments, 2009–2012." Last modified November 20, 2015. https://www.justice.gov/crt/us-department-justice-civil-rights-division -accomplishments-2009-2012.

———. 2013b. *Selected Accomplishments, 2013.* https://www.justice.gov/sites/ default/files/crt/legacy/2014/05/12/accomp2013.pdf.

US Immigration and Customs Enforcement. 2017. "Weekly Declined Detainer Outcome Report," January 28–February 3.

———. n.d.a. "287(g)-Memorandums of Agreement/Understanding (Archive)." ICE. Accessed July 25, 2017, at https://www.ice.gov/287g-archive.

———. n.d.b. "Delegation of Immigration Authority Section 287(g) Immigration and Nationality Act." Accessed July 25, 2017, at https://www.ice.gov/ factsheets/287g.

———. n.d.c. "Priority Enforcement Program." Accessed September 23, 2015, at http://www.ice.gov/pep.

———. n.d.d. "Updated Facts on ICE's 287(g) Program." Accessed September 23, 2015, at http://www.ice.gov/factsheets/287g-reform.

US Supreme Court. 2015. *Brief of the City* of Yakima as Amicus Curiae. Accessed March 14, 2016, at http://www.scotusblog.com/wp-content/uploads/ 2015/08/14-940-tsac-Yakima-WA.pdf.

Valencia, Milton. 2017. "Chelsea, Lawrence Challenge Trump on Sanctuary Cities." *Boston Globe*, February 8.

Valenzuela, Abel, Jr. 2003. "Day Labor Work." *Annual Review of Sociology* 29:307–33.

Van Der Meer, Tom, and Jochem Tolsma. 2014. "Ethnic Diversity and Its Effects on Social Cohesion." *Annual Review of Sociology* 40:459–78.

Vang, Chia Youyee. 2010. *Hmong America: Reconstructing Community in Diaspora.* Urbana: University of Illinois Press.

Varsanyi, Monica. 2007. "Documenting Undocumented Migrants: The Matrículas Consulares as Neoliberal Local Membership." *Geopolitics* 12 (2): 299–319.

———. 2008. "Immigration Policing through the Backdoor: City Ordinances, the 'Right to the City,' and the Exclusion of Undocumented Day Laborers." *Urban Geography* 29 (1): 29–52.

———. 2010a. *Taking Local Control: Immigration Policy Activism in U.S. Cities and States.* Palo Alto, CA: Stanford University Press.

———. 2010b. "City Ordinances as 'Immigration Policing by Proxy': Local Governments and the Regulation of Undocumented Day Laborers." In *Taking Local Control: Immigration Policy Activism in U.S. Cities and States*, edited by Monica Varsanyi, 135–56. Stanford, CA: Stanford University Press.

Varsanyi, Monica W., Paul G. Lewis, Doris Marie Provine, and Scott Decker. 2012. "A Multilayered Jurisdictional Patchwork: Immigration Federalism in the United States." *Law and Policy* 34 (2): 138–58.

———. 2017. "Immigration and Policing Practices in New Destinations." In *The*

Politics of New Immigrant Destinations: Transatlantic Perspectives, edited by Stefanie Chambers, Diana Evans, Anthony Messina, and Abigail Fisher Williamson, 225–47. Philadelphia: Temple University Press.

Vertovec, Steven, and Susanne Wessendorf. 2010. *The Multiculturalism Backlash: European Discourses, Policies, and Practices.* London: Routledge.

Voss, Kim, and Irene Bloemraad. 2011. *Rallying for Immigrant Rights: The Fight for Inclusion in 21st Century America.* Berkeley: University of California Press.

Voyer, Andrea. 2013. *Strangers and Neighbors: Multiculturalism, Conflict, and Community in America.* New York: Cambridge University Press.

Walker, Kyle. 2010. "Local Policy Responses to Immigration in the United States." *CURA Reporter* 40 (3–4): 27–34.

Walker, Kyle E., and Helga Leitner. 2011. "The Variegated Landscape of Local Immigration Policies in the United States." *Urban Geography* 32 (2): 156–78.

Wallace, Sophia J., Chris Zepeda-Millán, and Michael Jones-Correa. 2014. "Spatial and Temporal Proximity: Examining the Effects of Protests on Political Attitudes." *American Journal of Political Science* 58 (2): 433–48.

Ward, Leah. 2006. "'Sleeping Giant' Awakes." *Yakima Herald-Republic*, May 2.

Washuk, Bonnie. 2013. "Mohamed Seeking School Committee Seat as Write-in." *Lewiston Sun Journal*, October 29.

Waters, Mary C., and Tomas R. Jiménez. 2005. "Assessing Immigrant Assimilation: New Empirical and Theoretical Challenges." *Annual Review of Sociology* 31:105–25.

Waters, Mary, and Marisa Gerstein Pineau, eds. 2015. *The Integration of Immigrants into American Society.* Washington, DC: National Academies Press.

Waugh, Danielle. 2016. "Somali Community Receives Support from Mayor in Lewiston, Maine." *New England Cable News (NECN)*. November 16. Accessed August 8, 2017, at http://www.necn.com/news/new-england/Somali-Community-Receives-Support-From-Mayor-in-Lewiston-Maine-401577886.html.

Wausau Area Community Foundation. 1989. *Gannett Foundation CPP Final Report.*

"Wausau Area Hmong Mutual Association Changes Name." 2014. *Wausau Daily Herald*, August 21.

Weaver, Vesla M., and Amy E. Lerman. 2010. "Political Consequences of the Carceral State." *American Political Science Review* 104 (4): 817–33.

Welcoming America. 2013. "Stronger Together: Making the Case for Shared Prosperity through Welcoming Immigrants in Our Communities." *Welcoming Refugees, 2013.* https://www.welcomingamerica.org/sites/default/files/Stronger%20Together%20Toolkit.pdf.

White, Ismail K. 2007. "When Race Matters and When It Doesn't: Racial Group

Differences in Response to Racial Cues." *American Political Science Review* 101 (2):339–54.

White House Task Force on New Americans. 2015. "One-Year Progress Report." Accessed December 1, 2017, at https://obamawhitehouse.archives.gov/sites/default/files/image/tfna_progress_report_final_12_15_15.pdf.

Williams, Linda M. 2013. "Welcoming the Outsider: Local Construction of the Law towards Immigrants." PhD diss., University of Kansas.

———. 2015. "Beyond Enforcement: Welcomeness, Local Law Enforcement, and Immigrants." *Public Administration Review* 75 (3): 433–42.

Williamson, Abigail Fisher. 2011. "Beyond the Passage of Time: Local Government Response in New Immigrant Destinations." PhD diss., Harvard University.

———. 2015. "Mechanisms of Declining Intra-ethnic Trust in New Immigrant Destinations." *Journal of Ethnic and Migration Studies* 41 (11): 1725–45.

Wolbrecht, Christina, and Rodney E. Hero, eds. 2005. *The Politics of Democratic Inclusion*. Philadelphia: Temple University Press.

Wong, Cara. 2010. *Boundaries of Obligation in American Politics*. Cambridge: Cambridge University Press.

Wong, Janelle. 2006. *Democracy's Promise: Immigrants and American Civic Institutions*. Ann Arbor: University of Michigan Press.

Xaykaothao, Doualy. 2016. "To Be both Midwestern and Hmong." *Atlantic*, June 3. Accessed June 7, 2016, at http://www.theatlantic.com/politics/archive/2016/06/wausau-wisconsin-southeast-asia-hmong/485291/.

Yang, Kaifeng, and Kathe Callahan. 2007. "Citizen Involvement Efforts and Bureaucratic Responsiveness: Participatory Values, Stakeholder Pressures, and Administrative Practicality." *Public Administration Review* 67 (2): 249–64.

Yau, Jennifer. 2005. "The Foreign-Born Hmong in the United States." *Migration Policy Institute*, January 1. Accessed June 19, 2016, at http://www.migrationpolicy.org/article/foreign-born-hmong-united-states.

Yee, Vivian. 2017. "Judge Blocks Trump Effort to Withhold Money from Sanctuary Cities." *New York Times*, April 25.

Zezima, Katie. 2016. "Charlotte Set Off the Fight over the 'Bathroom Law.' Now It's Dealing with the Fallout." *Washington Post*, May 10.

Zimmerman, Wendy, and Karen C. Tumlin. 1999. "Patchwork Policies: State Assistance for Immigrants under Welfare Reform." *Urban Institute*, April 1. Accessed June 1, 2016, at http://research.urban.org/PDF/occ24.pdf.

Zúñiga, Victor, and Rubén Hernández-León, eds. 2005. *New Destinations: Mexican Immigration to the United States*. New York: Russell Sage Foundation.

Index

"DiverCity" campaign, Elgin, 45, 171, 255
diversification, ethnic, 17–20, *17*, 185, 199
diversity: in backlash, 238, 265, 273; benefits of, 133–34, 255–56; and competition, 237–38; in Elgin, 29, 47; in group
relations theories, 237, 238; in immigrant destinations, 22–23; in intergroup
relations, 265, 344n3; and intermediaries, 199, 221, 227–28; in officials' attitudes, 138, 140–41, 144–45, 152–53, 159;
and social connectedness, 235; training in, 257
Diversity Affairs Department, Wausau,
41–42
"don't ask, don't tell" policies, 62, 75–76,
160, 269
Dovi, Suzanne, *The Good Representative*, 197
DREAMers, 282

economic contributions of immigrants, 5,
85, 97–98, 130–34, 273
economic development, 131–34, 138, 140–
41, 154, 162, 243, 261, 272
economics, local, 97–98, 126, 240–41
Edler, Dave, 50–51
education: in federal regulations, 6–7; in
interethnic contact, 258–61, 263–64; in
municipal responses, 57, 59; in officials'
incentives, 126, 130–31, 339–40n2; in
predicting enforcement practices, 113,
119; of the public, 35–37, 41–43, 253–
56; in public opinion, 14, 331–32n6. *See
also* public schools
elected officials: anti-immigration stance
of, 125; attitudes of, 136–59, *142–43*;
immigrants and coethnics as, 48, 115,
214–15, 232, 268–69; incentives of, 24,
130–36, 159; intermediaries as, 197–
98, 226–27; legitimacy of, 9–10, 166–67,
232; partisanship of, 15, 127–30, 273;
roles of, 56–57; in the Trump era, 276.
See also officials, local; sheriffs, county
(elected)
electorate, 3–4, 135–36, 199–200, 272,
278–79
Elgin, IL: anti-immigration sentiment in,
45–47, 125, 244–45; backlash in, 243,
244–45, 246; case study of, 16–20, 43–
47; descriptive representation in, 199–

200; electoral influence of immigrants
in, 135; federal policy in, 91, 92–93, 119;
framing of immigrants in, 86; housing discrimination in, 45, 170–71; intermediaries in, 198–99, 216–18, 220,
222–24, 227, 231–32; Latinos in, 43–47,
95–96, 223–24; local government inclusion in, 262–63; national rhetoric in, 98;
partisanship in, 94; public messaging
in, 253–54; responses in, 29, 43–47, 52–
53, 268; schools and interethnic contact
in, 258–59; scrutiny of responses in,
170–72; symbolic support in, 255–56;
trend toward accommodation in, 80
Elgin Hispanic Network, 44
elites: benefits of accommodation for, 25; in
framing, 12, 14–15; in grassroots incorporation, 233; in group relations theories, 238; immigrant, 15, 220–21, 232–
33, 284; as intermediaries, 200, 220–21,
232–33; intermediaries as, 227–28; and
intermediary organizations, 230–31;
tensions of with residents, 238, 241–47,
264, 273; in Wausau, 39–40
ELLs (English-language learners), 6, 34–
35, 93–94, 164
"Elm City Resident Card" (New Haven,
CT), 4
enforcement of immigration regulations,
165–66; in Elgin, 45–47; and framing,
24, 119, 271; local police in, 7–8, 14, 46–
47, 62–63, 100; municipal responses on,
57, 60–63; officials' attitudes on, 138–
39, 140–41, 146, 152–54, 160–61; predicting, 99–100, 111–15, *114*, 119; pub-
lic/official attitudes on, 157–58; in the
Trump era, 275–76. *See also* ICE (Immigration and Customs Enforcement)
English-only ordinances, 59, 171, 175–76,
179–80
Enhancing Elgin committee, 29, 45
entrepreneurs: expansionist, 279; framing
of immigrants as, 272; intermediaries
as, 195–96; restrictionist, 129–30, 279,
339n1; Somali, 38–39
ethnic change patterns, 17–20, *17*, 185, 199
ethnicity: in ethnic threat, 122–23; in federal requirements, 49; in tensions over
intermediaries, 222–24; in visibility,
118–19